IN THE FULLNESS OF TIME

Richard Bauckham

IN THE FULLNESS OF TIME

Essays on Christology, Creation, and Eschatology
in Honor of
RICHARD BAUCKHAM

Edited by

Daniel M. Gurtner
Grant Macaskill
Jonathan T. Pennington

WILLIAM B. EERDMANS PUBLISHING COMPANY
GRAND RAPIDS, MICHIGAN

Wm. B. Eerdmans Publishing Co.
4035 Park East Court SE, Grand Rapids, MI 49546
www.eerdmans.com

© 2016 Daniel M. Gurtner, Grant Macaskill, and Jonathan T. Pennington
All rights reserved

Hardcover edition 2016
Paperback edition 2021

ISBN 978-0-8028-7998-1

Library of Congress Cataloging-in-Publication Data

A Cataloging-in-Publication record is on file with the Library of Congress

Contents

Richard Bauckham: Christian Historian   vii
    Jonathan T. Pennington

Witness   xi
    Micheal O'Siadhail

Introduction   1

Part 1: Thematic Studies

The Birth of God and the Resurrection of Life   17
    Jürgen Moltmann

Time and Eternity: Richard Bauckham and the Fifth Evangelist   29
    Jeremy S. Begbie

Parmenides, Particularity, and *Parousia*: Identifying the One
Who Will Come to Judge the Living and the Dead   49
    Trevor Hart

The Bible and Wider Culture: Animals as a Test Case   65
    David Brown

Worship and Divine Identity: Richard Bauckham's
Christological Pilgrimage   82
    Larry W. Hurtado

"The Agent of the King Is Treated as the King Himself":
Does the Worship of Jesus Imply His Divinity?   97
   Philip Alexander

Christianity without Paul   115
   James D. G. Dunn

Part 2: Textual Studies

God Put Jesus Forth: Reflections on Romans 3:24–26   135
   N. T. Wright

Jesus the Baptist: The First Temptation of Christ   162
   Sean M. McDonough

Giving the Kingdom to an *Ethnos* That Will Bear Its Fruit:
Ethnic and Christ-Movement Identities in Matthew   177
   Philip F. Esler

Mark's Gospel for the Second Church of the Late First Century   197
   Bruce W. Longenecker

The Book of Revelation and the Hekhalot Literature   215
   James R. Davila

Bibliography   229
   Publications by Richard Bauckham   229
   General Bibliography   249

Contributors   261

Index of Authors   263

Index of Scripture and Other Ancient Texts   266

Richard Bauckham: Christian Historian

Jonathan T. Pennington

When one tries to answer the question, "Who is the scholar Richard Bauckham?" the answer quickly becomes complicated. This is because the areas in which Professor Bauckham has produced significant scholarship and is a recognized expert are so manifold. Possible and valid answers to the question include: New Testament scholar; historical theologian; student of Second Temple Judaism and apocalyptic literature; Moltmann expert who, according to Moltmann, knows his theology better than Moltmann does himself; specialist on the Bible and ecology; expert in first-century Jewish history; systematic theologian of Christology; analyst of Old Testament pseudepigrapha; commentator on John's Gospel; investigator of the archaeology of Magdala; and Revelation scholar, to name just a few.

In our modern age of micro-specialization Richard is simultaneously a doyen in his chosen fields of study and a scholar whose breadth of knowledge and abilities makes him more than a specialist; he is one who regularly builds deep and wide tunnels between what are typically separate silos of scholarship.

One result of his wide-ranging interests and intellectual curiosity is that not once but several times over his academic career Bauckham has stepped into an existing scholarly dialogue, quickly mastered it, and then made an original contribution, breaking old paradigms by virtue of his fresh and rigorous arguments. Over the last forty years this has happened in the discussion of Jürgen Moltmann and eschatology, Second Temple Judaism and apocalyptic, Christology, Gospel studies, the interpretation of James, pseudepigraphical writings, and others. Not surprisingly, sometimes this has resulted in the chagrin of the resident experts, enlivening no small debate and disagreement. But none would deny that when Bauckham weighs in on a topic, the dialogue is affected and the interlocutors must take note.

Is there anything that drives all of this scholarly output and ties it all together? Richard's recent autobiographical reflections reveal that there is—a love for history.[1] He recounts the beginnings of his passionate drive to understand the past with an anecdote from his early adolescent years. When given the assignment to write an essay about a book he had read over the summer holiday, thirteen-year-old Richard chose to write about the ICC volume on Ezra-Nehemiah that he had spent the summer reading, resulting in his own original theory as to how this part of Israel's story fit together historically! Looking back over the subsequent fifty-seven years of his scholarship, this love for figuring out the past proves to be the lodestar that grounds and guides Bauckham's varied and adept contributions to our understanding of the world. When one reconsiders Richard's scholarly output, the golden thread of history—especially making good historical arguments and dismantling bad ones—appears throughout nearly everything he has done.

But Richard is also more than a scholarly historian. He is also a Christian. This means he has, for as long as he can recall, been a believer in the grand tradition of historical Christian orthodoxy and more personally, its risen God-Man Jesus. This fact of who Richard is has obviously guided his interests and his lifelong commitment to the church in service. Yet at the same time, this personal commitment has not driven him to do his scholarship as a sort of apologetic for the faith. Often his positions have supported traditional and evangelical understandings, resulting in his popularity among more conservative scholars. But by his own confession, this has never motivated his scholarship explicitly. Rather, he is a Christian historian, with both of those descriptions fully up and running. He is a Christian who does historical work and he is a historian who is also a Christian.

As to the more traditional biographical facts, Richard was born in London on September 22, 1946. Upon entering university he read history at Clare College in Cambridge (1966–1972) and then was a Fellow of St John's College (1972–1975). He was granted the MA and PhD degrees, writing a dissertation on a sixteenth-century apocalyptic theologian, William Fulke. During his time in Cambridge he also attended the New Testament seminars of C. F. D. Moule, to whom Richard counts much of his initial training in NT studies.

---

1. See his delightful chapter in John Byron and Joel Lohr, eds., *I (Still) Believe: Leading Bible Scholars Share Their Stories of Faith and Scholarship* (Grand Rapids: Zondervan Academic, 2015), 17–28.

Bauckham commenced his professorial career by teaching theology for one year at the University of Leeds, followed by two different fifteen-year teaching posts, providing a nice symmetry that defines his vocation. The first of these quindecim stints was as Lecturer and then Reader in the History of Christian Thought at the University of Manchester (1977–1992). His interests in eschatology and connecting theology to contemporary life deepened during this time, resulting in publication on subjects such as theology and the nuclear debate, in addition to the well-regarded *Word Biblical Commentary* on 2 Peter and Jude.

Looking back, these years prove to be the calm before the storm of Richard's massive output that corresponded with his move to the second fifteen-year post—as Professor of New Testament Studies (later Bishop Wardlaw Professor) at the University of St Andrews, Scotland (1992–2007). These years were remarkably productive for Richard, with monographs and articles spanning many subjects including Second Temple Jewish literature, Revelation, James, the Book of Acts, apocalyptic literature, Christology, and the Gospel of John. This is in addition to supervising many postgraduate students, lecturing in Bible and theology to undergrads, giving various lectures throughout the world, and serving in St Andrew's Scottish Episcopal Church in St Andrews (affectionately known as "St Andrew's, St Andrews").

In 2007 Richard retired and returned to Cambridge, living within walking distance of the University and Tyndale House. He continues to research and write and serves as a senior scholar at Ridley Hall in Cambridge and visiting professor at St Mellitus College in London. He also does some teaching for an MA course and remains involved in discussion groups with students. Richard continues to travel extensively, giving lectures and teaching both in academic and church settings. Always a mind awake, he continues to pursue new lines of academic interest, including most recently, trips to Galilee to research the ancient town of Magdala.

Richard is a Fellow of the British Academy (FBA) and Fellow of the Royal Society of Edinburgh (FRSE). He has also been a member of the Doctrine Commission of the Church of England. In addition to being the invited lecturer in many venues throughout the world, Richard's books have also won several awards, including the 2007 *Christianity Today* book award in Biblical Studies for his *Jesus and the Eyewitnesses*. For this book he also won the prestigious Michael Ramsey Prize (2009). In 2010 his volume *The Jewish World around the New Testament* won the Franz-Delitzsch Award.

In addition to his academic scholarship, Richard is a great lover of poetry and fiction and has produced much of both. He has written several poems, some for publication, in addition to many in his beloved form of Haiku.² Since his childhood he was an avid reader and collector of the cartoon world of the Moomins, created by the Finnish artist and author Tove Jansson.³ His love for Haiku, thoughtful and mysterious children's literature, and his time in Scotland conjoined in Richard's two children's novellas, *The MacBears of Bearloch*, and *The MacBears and Bishbirds*.⁴

The editors and contributors to this volume in honor of Richard Bauckham count it a great privilege to have known him as a scholar, mentor, and friend.

---

2. See the Bibliography and http://richardbauckham.co.uk/index.php?page=poetry.
3. https://www.moomin.com/en/history/.
4. These can be read at http://www.richardbauckham.co.uk/index.php?page=macbears.

Witness

(For Richard Bauckham)

How it happens still a mystery—
Two gospels say two angels, two say one,
Rolled away the stone to raise God's son,
Who in taking flesh joins history.

Do the women run to tell the men
Or bewildered do they just sing dumb,
Fearing still Christ's tomb from which they come?
So to truth not fact we say amen.

Matthew's women run to share delight;
Mark's unsure, still fear where Christ has gone.
Human Matthew, Mark and Luke and John
Catch time's sacred bird to snatch in flight

Shimmering perspectives on the past
Four believing witnesses broadcast.

Micheal O'Siadhail

Introduction

The breadth and extent of Richard Bauckham's influence in so many areas of biblical and theological scholarship renders the prospect of including all the scholars who would want to honor him an impossible task. For purposes of brevity contributions in the present volume are confined to senior scholars who had been close colleagues of Richard during his academic career, or who had been his most prominent interlocutors in the development of his own research, or through his Fellowship of the British Academy.

The result of limiting the contributors to a select few is itself a quite remarkable testimony to the significance of his work. The essays that are assembled in this volume have been contributed by some of the most eminent figures in modern biblical and theological scholarship. Some have taken elements of Richard's work and developed it further, applying it in ways or to problems that were not in view in his own writings; some have presented fresh research of their own that aligns well with Richard's own work over the years and stands fittingly alongside it; some have taken the opportunity to continue their debates with Richard, offering more critical thoughts and asking probing questions, though always with warmth and respect. Taken together, it is a fitting work of honor to a scholar whose mind has been restlessly inquisitive, and whose scholarship has seldom been limited by the usual boundaries of academic specialism. Richard has never been a scholar content to buttress and fortify his particular claims; he has always listened to critics, engaged with their arguments, and refined his own positions. Running through all such interactions has been an awareness that the various fields of research are interconnected and mutually informative and, in the end, demand something of us, as servants of Wisdom. For all its critical rigor, Richard's work is not "detached": it recognizes that the pursuit of knowledge and understanding brings with it responsibilities toward God and his world. "So to truth not fact we say amen," as Micheal O'Siadhail writes in his contribution to this volume, the poem "Witness." That beautiful line captures the recognition that Richard handles facts not as brute things to be owned and dissected, but as participants in the truth of God and his dealings with the cosmos. The essays that follow reflect such an interaction with Truth both in the broad, thematic sense (Part 1) and in the particulars of textual analysis (Part 2).

Part 1: Thematic Studies

In "The Birth of God and the Resurrection of Life," **Jürgen Moltmann**'s task is one of reflection on the relation between incarnation and resurrection, beginning (§1) by asking: why the incarnation? Girded with patristic soteriology, Moltmann finds that Jesus of Nazareth "became flesh" in order to heal flesh, to enable humans to participate in the divine life of God. It transforms all things in him, evidenced already where reconciliation has occurred through faith in the cosmic victory of the risen Christ. For Moltmann the origins of the doctrine of the incarnation (§2) cannot be explained merely by the birth, life, ministry, even crucifixion of Jesus of Nazareth. Rather, the "cognitive ground" for the view of God's incarnation is to be found in the resurrection and exaltation. In this way the incarnation presents the entirety of Jesus's life and ministry in light of his resurrection. Here Moltmann finds an "eschatological logic" in which the last—Christ's resurrection—reveals the first, his being the incarnate Son of God. The exaltation reveals Christ being the foundation of all things in creation, inaugurating the new creation in which all things receive their abiding form.

When considering what is meant by "flesh" (§3), Moltmann finds that all the meanings of the Hebrew word *basar* are present in the fundamental Christological tenet: "The Word became flesh and dwelt among us and we beheld his glory." These include the whole human being, body and soul, indeed all living things. In this sense "flesh" may find a better rendering in "life," which encompasses all components and is promised a common future in the kingdom of God's glory in both the human and natural spheres.

The pneumatological principle that God's Spirit is poured out on all flesh (§4) requires a distinction from the incarnation of Christ. The latter takes place for the benefit of many, whereas the former occurs so that the many—in the

Introduction

church and in the cosmos—may be united in the One, Christ. The "pouring out" of the Spirit uses a water metaphor that delineates the flow from the Spirit itself to the gifts it bestows, ending differences within the Spirit-imbued community. The patristic tenet of the "resurrection of the flesh" is Moltmann's starting point for the final component of the Hebrew *basar* (§5). For him, the modern rendering of "the resurrection of the dead" limits the resurrection to a personal, human sense. But Moltmann sees the resurrection of the flesh far more comprehensively—it entails everything living. The earth also awaits its new creation, not in terms of "eternal life" but as the Nicene Creed has it: "the life of the world to come." The cosmic implications are nothing less than "the resurrection of life" and "the eternal life of the world to come." This is a cosmic eschatology achieved by the coming of God into this creation.

Jeremy S. Begbie's "Time and Eternity: Richard Bauckham and the Fifth Evangelist" is a tribute to the capacity of Bauckham's writings to engage issues beyond the traditional parameters of New Testament studies. While music is a world largely left out of Bauckham's work, his biblically informed conception of time and eternity speaks to some leading musicological studies of Bach.

Begbie begins with an assessment of Karol Berger's study of perceptions of time in modernity as exemplified in Bach's music. Berger finds in the *St Matthew Passion* evidence of the suppression of linearity for the sake of a "simultaneity of the present" with little interest in the temporal ordering of musical events. Bach has achieved a "timeless eternity" in which a distinction between the present and past is neutralized. Though Berger presents this view as that of "mainstream" Christianity, Begbie finds difficulty in its conception of eternity as "radically disconnected with, and ontologically superior to, time." Instead he turns to Bauckham's probing on the biblical material on time and eternity to find a fundamentally different perspective, which recognizes the intrinsic place of time as a good dimension of God's created order. For Bauckham, God's eternity engages created time as an aspect of God's self-revelation and saving action, and the temporality of the eschatological future is not simply an extension of this world's time. Instead the new creation involves an all-encompassing recovery and transformation of created time, redeemed from transience along with the whole of creation. Bauckham's model calls for a thoroughgoing orientation toward a radically new future for this world, and is thus not a license to withdraw from this-worldly responsibilities. Finally, Bauckham is cautious about the use of circular imagery with respect to the redeemed future because it precludes novelty. For Begbie, Bauckham's conception more readily resonates with Christianity's sacred texts than does Berger's. Through careful investigation of Bach's Lutheran context, and drawing on John

Butt's analysis of directionality in Bach, he presents a forceful case that Bauckham's understanding resonates also with the composer's theological outlook. Further, Begbie finds in Bach's music evocations of a new creation that includes the possibility of novelty and change. Furthermore, he entertains the possibility of a change not from imperfect to perfect, but from one degree or form of perfection to another. If temporality is an aspect of the new creation, Begbie concludes it would have to be of a sort in which the dynamic was one of addition without loss, expansion without diminution, yet utterly consistent, never arbitrary, always resisting static completeness.

Trevor Hart's essay, "Parmenides, Particularity, and *Parousia*: Identifying the One Who Will Come to Judge the Living and the Dead," builds upon one of Bauckham's less well-known articles, a piece titled "Christology Today" that was published in the South African journal *Scriptura* in 1988. There, Bauckham asserts the soteriological significance of the human particularity of Jesus, resisting the common tendency to see this as a "scandal," a theological problem to be overcome in some way. Particularity is essential to human existence; it is, indeed, a universal of the humanity redeemed by the Son of God that we are particular and that our relations are governed by this truth. Hence, "since humanity does not exist as an abstraction but only in the form of particular human lives lived, this same Son of God embraced to the full the contingency of historical existence, becoming the particular man Jesus of whose actions, words, and suffering the gospels are concerned to tell us."

As an example of a theologian who believes such a position to be problematic, Hart notes the work of Daphne Hampson, who considers the "maleness" that is particular to the incarnation of God in Jesus of Nazareth to have generated androcentric views of divinity in western thought. In Hampson's case, this rests in turn on her sharing of the traditional theological premise that "like can only be saved by like," demonstrated by her own extended reflection on the problems generated by the maleness of Jesus for the traditional maxim that "what is not assumed is not healed." Precisely for this reason, Hampson finds the male particularity to be a scandal. In distinction to Hampson, though, Bauckham asserts that the redemptive significance of Jesus involves a constant interplay of sameness and difference, a "differential solidarity." This involves the difference between the created and the uncreated, and between the good and the bad, but also involves the complex of differences that ground relationality.

This, for Bauckham, establishes the place that the gospel narratives of Jesus's life have in the experience of salvation: there we encounter the particularity of Jesus redemptively, and our redemption requires such an encounter.

Introduction

Hart traces this further, though, into the eschatological realities of ascension and *parousia*: precisely because salvation involves the particularity of Jesus, it cannot be reduced to a universalism that does not assert the personal significance of Jesus for the one who is saved. Hart does not see this as shrinking the scope of salvation, though, and the key to understanding this is an affirmation of the continuing activity of the unique man Jesus beyond the limits of this present time and place. Once the limits of our earthly span are rightly reevaluated in the light of eternity, the scope of the saving work of Jesus can also be extended, but without losing sight of his personal and dynamic involvement, in the way that so much modern theology does.

David Brown affirms and then probes Bauckham's theology of ecology and the environment, particularly his challenge to the dominance of the "stewardship" model of ecological concern. Bauckham argues that this neglects the solidarity between humanity and all other created beings—our participation in the community of creation—and that a rounded theological account of ecology must do justice to the biblical material that depicts such solidarity, resisting the influence of Stoic thought, which considers animals simply to be there for human use, with no obligation devolved upon humans for their care.

In his contribution, "The Bible and Wider Culture: Animals as a Test Case," Brown agrees with the core of Bauckham's case, particularly as it responds to Lynn White's (in)famous claim that Christianity, in assigning a place of superiority to humanity, is responsible for the environmental crisis. White's conclusion fails to recognize that human superiority is found widely in ancient thought, in material that antedates Christian influence. Nonetheless, some pagan material (e.g., Plutarch) affirmed the value of animals in their own right. So the later position within the history of Christianity cannot be wholly blamed on a monolithic classical culture. Brown argues that "it was precisely because some elements in the biblical picture seemed so congruent with Stoic ideas that Stoicism in effect won the day." Brown's far-reaching essay moves at pace through a range of texts from the classical world, from the Bible itself, and from historical theology, as he approaches his conclusion that the partial congruence of biblical material with Stoic thought helps to explain the shape of the dominant view in the tradition, that humanity is something *apart from* and *above* the rest of the created order, including the animals.

Although not questioning the rightness of the conclusions, Brown notes two Christian theological claims that were particularly influential in the dynamic of this process. First, the abolition of animal sacrifice from Christian practice entailed a desacralization of animals; for those unaware of the necessary holiness of those things offered upon the altar, this is an important observation, particularly when one reflects on the persistence of the view that human life (by contrast) *is* sacred. Second, the doctrine of incarnation—the taking of specifically human flesh by the Son—left a sense that human life had a special significance, different from all other life. Beyond these points, though, Brown's essay presses toward a more significant point of practical difference with Bauckham: where Bauckham finds a neglected richness in the biblical material itself, Brown finds some of that material complicit with regrettable tendencies elsewhere and thus requiring to be transformed by the developing world of knowledge outside it. Whether Bauckham quite suggests the degree of scriptural self-sufficiency that Brown suggests is open to debate,[1] but for readers willing to reflect seriously on this fundamental difference of approach, Brown's essay will contribute in fascinating ways to the question of theological method that runs through so much of Richard's work.

Larry W. Hurtado's contribution, "Worship and Divine Identity: Richard Bauckham's Christological Pilgrimage," focuses on those features of Bauckham's scholarly work that have been most intertwined with his own, particularly the study of earliest reverence for Jesus. Bauckham has shown that the exalted Jesus is widely treated as the rightful co-recipient of heavenly praise and worship. For Hurtado the quick exaltation of Jesus to cultic reverence is perhaps "the key indicator of the distinctive nature of the young Jesus-movement." In this respect Jesus is revered *along with* God, not in place of him. There is no new cultus or separate deity. However, Bauckham's contention that this reflects the inclusion of the risen Jesus within "the divine identity" raises three questions for Hurtado.

First, Hurtado asks why Bauckham's "divine identity" is incompatible with the view that the concept of a "chief agent" may have provided earliest Christianity with a category by which to accommodate the unique relation of Jesus with God and his superiority to all other beings. For Hurtado, there is sufficient evidence that Second Temple Jews did often think of God as having one or another particular figure distinguished from all the rest of the divine retinue and functioning as the unique agent of his purposes.

Second, Hurtado asks whether Bauckham gives an adequate explanation for *how* and *why* Jesus was included within the "divine identity" so rapidly and

---

1. Compare, for example, the comments that he makes in his autobiographical entry in J. Byron and J. N. Lohr, eds., *I (Still) Believe: Leading Bible Scholars Share Their Stories of Faith and Scholarship* (Grand Rapids: Zondervan Academic, 2015), 22, or in *God and the Crisis of Freedom: Biblical and Contemporary Perspectives* (Louisville: Westminster John Knox, 2002), ch. 3, "Authority and Scripture."

Introduction

so early in the "post-Easter" period. For Hurtado, the answer to why certain texts were so central and distinctively interpreted lies in the powerful experiences of earliest believers that conveyed new convictions about Jesus's exalted status. These convictions prompted them to search their scriptures, finding the heavenly exaltation of Jesus in Psalm 110:1, for example. Their understanding, then, was not founded upon extant exegetical methods from antiquity, but prompted and guided by revelatory experiences of early believers in Jesus and their conviction that God had exalted Jesus to heavenly glory and now demanded that he be reverenced.

Third, Hurtado questions whether Bauckham is correct that the inclusion of Jesus as co-recipient (with God) of cultic worship is adequately understood historically as a "corollary" of Jesus's inclusion in the "divine identity." Not only is this lacking in the NT writings themselves, but it also remains unclear how Jewish believers would so readily amend their devotional practice to include Jesus. Instead, for Hurtado, the inclusion of Jesus into the devotional practice of early Jewish believers could only have emerged among Jews based on the strong and novel conviction that it was required by God himself.

Recognizing that not only is Jesus's significance defined with reference to God, but that God is also now identified with reference to Jesus, Hurtado suggests that in the New Testament the understanding and representation of "divine identity" is adjusted accordingly: the emphasis on the centrality of Jesus now renders inadequate any description of God made apart from reference to him.

Philip Alexander's essay, "'The Agent of the King Is Treated as the King Himself': Does the Worship of Jesus Imply His Divinity?," engages with the pivotal issue of Jewish monotheism, and the related question of monolatry, around which Bauckham's arguments for an early high Christology turn (and which are crucial also to Larry Hurtado's account of Christological development, reflected in his own contribution to this volume). Alexander begins by questioning whether the specifically apocalyptic trope of an angel refusing worship is necessarily evidence for widespread strict monotheism in early Judaism. Rather, he considers the trope to be something of a genre marker, a theme that gives a certain unity to particular writings, rather than one intended to radically distinguish Jewish views of true worship from those held by others. This serves as the departure point for an examination of the key texts from the Old Testament/Hebrew Bible generally brought forward in support of the view that early Judaism was stringently monotheistic, including the Shema and the creation accounts. These, in fact, bear witness to the presence in earlier Israelite circles of either non-monotheistic or more loosely monotheistic views than sometimes acknowledged, with these reflected (even negatively) in the monotheistic assertions. Alexander acknowledges the response that Bauckham and others might make, that such early Israelite views do not have material bearing on the beliefs held in a much later period by Second Temple Jews. Yet, he finds evidence that the variegation of views concerning divine uniqueness persisted into later Judaism, reflected in the complex representations of heavenly figures such as Metatron, the Second Yahweh, or agents of divine activity, such as Wisdom or the Memra. If such ideas can be found in very early and very late texts, with a measure of continuity identifiable between them, then should we not be cautious of identifying late Second Temple Judaism, specifically, as more stringently monotheistic? Running through the evaluation of the texts and their handling is a sensitivity to the questions of function and ontology and to the language used to describe them.

Alexander's critical engagement with Bauckham's arguments sits nicely alongside the contributions of Hurtado and Dunn. Taken together with Bauckham's own writings, with which they engage, they constitute a sophisticated scholarly debate about the conceptuality, language, and attested praxis found in the New Testament writings, set within their complex historical contexts. The debate will undoubtedly continue for years to come, but the present collection of essays constitutes a particularly important contribution to it, one shaped by the programmatic work of Bauckham in this area.

James D. G. Dunn's essay asks the question, "What would Christianity have looked like without Paul?" The question is not asked out of contempt for Paul, but as a thought experiment intended to highlight the extent of the apostle's influence on the fundamental character of developing Christianity. In particular, the question is focused on the development of the Jesus movement from that of a Jewish restoration community to one principally Gentile in composition, asking about the part that Paul, specifically, played in this development. Here, Dunn's question draws upon the legacy of Bauckham's work on the relationship of the New Testament writings, and within them the letters of Paul, to the Jewish world from which they emerged.

Dunn approaches the question by moving through the wider New Testament and analyzing how each author represents the Jesus movement in relation to the story of Israel and the practices/beliefs of Judaism, on one hand, and the Gentile world, on the other. He pays particular attention to the identity markers of Judaism, circumcision and the food laws, and how these are represented in the works of each writer. In Dunn's analysis, the commitment of Paul to the abolition of such markers, and his determination not to capitulate on this—explored in the final part of the essay, as Dunn turns to the Pauline

Introduction

material itself, sets him apart from the other New Testament writers. Effectively, Dunn shows how distinctive Paul is within the wider body of New Testament writings. His conclusion is a provocative one: "If we owe Christianity's universal character in such large part to Paul, do we also have to acknowledge that his universalizing mission was what in the event caused the schism between Judaism and Christianity?" It is a fascinating point of dialogue with the work of Bauckham, which has devoted such attention to the relationship of early Christian theology to its Jewish contexts.

Part 2: Textual Studies

N. T. Wright's "God Put Jesus Forth: Reflections on Romans 3:24–26" builds on some of the core observations made by Bauckham in his seminal study, *God Crucified*.[2] There, Bauckham considered the early Christian reading of Isaiah 40–55 and its role in the identification of Jesus in relation to the work of Israel's God. Where Bauckham's discussion is particularly oriented toward Christology, however, Wright's focuses on soteriology, particularly on the conceptuality of atonement. Reading this key text against a properly understood Jewish background leads to a very different understanding of atonement than that commonly taken, particularly in Protestant scholarship.

Wright's argument begins by considering some of the problems with "traditional" readings of Romans 3:24–26 (a discussion that he acknowledges to have been developed in dialogue with the recent doctoral research of Norio Yamaguchi). First, the view that the death of Jesus is represented in these verses as involving substitutionary punishment is demonstrated to be problematic: such conceptuality is incompatible with the imagery of cultic sacrifice in Judaism, in which the victim is always sacred and holy, not impure, and is never punished. Second, Wright notes the necessary distinction between being "justified by [the Messiah's] blood" and being "saved from anger (or wrath)" in Romans 5:8–10. The two are logically linked, but are not identical, and much confusion is saved by recognizing the distinction. Third, the covenant associations of *dikaiosynē* are asserted: the word here does not mean something radically different from its usage in the Old Testament, where it points to God's faithfulness to maintaining his covenant relationship with Israel. If this is acknowledged, the covenant associations of the other key terms in the text are

---

2. *God Crucified* (Carlisle, UK: Paternoster; Grand Rapids: Eerdmans, 1998). Reproduced in *Jesus and the God of Israel* (Carlisle, UK: Paternoster, 2008).

also recognized. For Wright, only an *a priori* rejection of the covenantal implications of such language by scholars can explain their refusal to admit it to the interpretation of this verse.

Having made these core observations, Wright approaches the text of Romans 3:24–26 according to the terms of his own recent major interpretation of Paul, the title of which neatly captures what he sees to be at work in this verse: *Paul and the Faithfulness of God*. That is, he understands Paul to represent the death of the messiah as an act of covenant faithfulness on God's part, bringing to fulfillment the same plan to redeem humanity from sin that involved the covenant with Israel. In particular, this reading involves a careful contextualization of the verses in question into Wright's fresh interpretation of 2:17–24 and Romans 4; these, taken together, point inward to the way in which *precisely* by remaining faithful to the covenant with Israel in the sacrifice of Jesus, God has dealt with the problem of worldwide human sin. A crucial element in this is provided by the narrative of Isaiah 40–55, and particularly by the distinctive reading of Isaiah 53 that came to be influential in early Christian theology. Here, the intersection of Wright's work with that of Bauckham is clearest: truly a conversation between giants.

In "Jesus the Baptist: The First Temptation of Christ," **Sean M. McDonough** draws upon Bauckham's contributions to the study of John's Gospel. Bauckham has resisted the tendency to see the Fourth Gospel as the product of a community, somewhat estranged from the wider church, and has instead asserted its historical value as a witness to the ministry of Jesus, intended to complement the other circulating gospels, and associated with the testimony of a disciple close to Jesus. McDonough focuses particularly on the accounts of a baptizing ministry performed by Jesus in John 3–4, tracing some of the evidence that supports the historical veracity of the accounts and then examining the theological motivations behind their inclusion in the Fourth Gospel, and their location in the narrative. Such discussions, of course, also require some reflection on why there is no report of Jesus baptizing in the Synoptic Gospels and whether, even in John, there is a cessation of this aspect of Jesus's ministry.

McDonough's careful study identifies important parallels between the eschatological locus of Jesus's baptizing ministry in John 3–4 and that of the temptation narratives of the Synoptics: both speak of the continuity between John and Jesus, while also speaking of the advance that takes place in the narrative movement from the former to the latter. To use McDonough's imagery, both accounts depict the passing of the baton from John to Jesus. The wilderness around the Jordan provides the necessary context for both accounts, laden as it is with both connotation and expectation. Here, McDonough argues, lies the reason that baptism ceases to be such a prominent part of Jesus's ministry: there is a conspicuous messianism to the practice in this context, one that is vulnerable to the pressure of wrong expectations. Jesus refuses to be the messiah his compatriots want, and insists instead on being the one that they need; in this lies a parallel between his rejection of Satan's temptation to worship, as a step to gaining total power, and his refusal to turn a successful baptizing ministry into "a messianic *tour de force*." Bauckham's work provides the impetus for such a reading of John 3–4, as a historically defensible account intended to be read alongside (and not against) the Synoptic accounts.

In "Giving the Kingdom to an *Ethnos* That Will Bear Its Fruit: Ethnic and Christ-Movement Identities in Matthew," **Philip F. Esler** raises subtle questions of identity in the Second Temple context that has been so important to Bauckham's research, particularly on early high Christology. Esler examines Matthew 21:43—"the kingdom of God will be taken away from you and given to an *ethnos* bearing its fruit"—in relation to the rest of that gospel and its themes. For Esler, "this verse goes right to the heart of the meaning Matthew intended for his original audience, especially on the critical relationship between Judeans and non-Judeans in the Christ-movement." His essay, then, sits nicely alongside that of Dunn; both works feature this important question of how the identity of those whose roots could be traced to Judea factored into the cultural and ideological development of earliest Christianity.

Crucial to this discussion is a right understanding of the significance of the word *ethnos* and its particular place within the web of elements by which personal and social identities are constituted. Distinctively, though not uniquely, Esler argues for clear distinctions to be maintained between ethnicity and "race," on one hand, and "religion," on the other. Race is a distinctively modern way of categorizing people according to "observable, inheritable, physical characteristics," and was originally wrapped up with hierarchical assumptions (e.g., of white supremacy). Ethnicity—the identification of inclusion within an ethnos—has, by contrast, a complex of features wrapped up with collective history, myth, and values and, strikingly, association with particular geographical locations. Religion may be one element within the collective associations of the ethnos, but it is a mistake to see it as the primary one and without careful definition the word itself can be dangerously misleading. What this means, for Esler, is that the term *Ioudaios* is an ethnic one and not a religious one, better rendered as "Judean" than as "Jew," a move that has significant critical implications for all talk of "Second Temple Judaism," if correct.

Esler applies this to the text of Matthew's Gospel as a whole, but with a particular focus on Matthew 21:43. Readers will doubtless debate his core claims about the relationship of ethnicity and religion and, indeed, about the meaning and value of the latter term in discussions of identity. Even so, they will find his sensitivity to the overlooked ethnic significance of a range of elements in the text of Matthew to be fascinating and will find much to reflect upon in his proposals for how this might be understood theologically. It is a fitting dialogue with Bauckham's work from a long-time colleague and friend.

Bruce W. Longenecker's essay, "Mark's Gospel for the Second Church of the Late First Century," is a fascinating, and methodologically subtle, exercise in reading the biblical text—here Mark's Gospel—in terms of a particular context of reception. The essay builds on the challenge leveled by Bauckham and others to the "community theory" of gospel authorship. Acknowledging the evidence for the wide circulation of the gospels, Longenecker asks how the Gospel of Mark would have been read by "second church." In using this term, Longenecker draws upon Ramsay MacMullen's identification of popular Christianity from 200 to 400 CE: MacMullen argues that the greatest proportion of the church (95 percent) incorporated pagan practices extensively into their Christ-devotion. This popular Christianity is the "second church," existing alongside the "first church" that is more familiar to us through the patristic writings; while it is the first church that appears to be dominant or normal, it is the second church that is truly representative of popular Christianity.

Longenecker accepts the broad credibility of MacMullen's arguments, and adds to them further evidence that the second church might have been a reality even in the earliest years of the Christian church (i.e., during the New Testament period itself). He then engages in a carefully controlled imaginative reading of Mark, as it would likely have been read by the second church in the first century. Longenecker's reading is informed by his recent argument for the presence of Jesus-devotion in Pompeii (destroyed in the eruption of Vesuvius in 79). His data suggest that Christians in Pompeii were markedly interested in the benefits of Jesus's power to enhance their lives. If this form of Jesus-devotion were widespread in the second half of the first century, the Gospel of Mark would have unqualified force in addressing it. Strikingly, the Gospel resists second-church culture in crucial ways, speaking back to it and challenging it through the imposition of the apostolic voice. In this way, the second church cannot walk away from a reading (or hearing) of Mark unscathed. Whether or not Longenecker is correct in each of his suggested interpretations, the essay invites readers to approach a familiar text in a very

Introduction

fresh way and, in doing so, to reflect on their own unwitting assumptions and assimilations—a truly evangelical task.

A significant part of Bauckham's research—as far back as his doctoral work on Tudor apocalyptic in sixteenth-century England—has been devoted to the study of Jewish and Christian apocalyptic literature. One particular strand of this has focused on the book of Revelation (the Apocalypse of John), which has contributed in important ways to his reflections on creation, eschatology, and Christology. The contribution by **James R. Davila**, "The Book of Revelation and the Hekhalot Literature," is a fitting tribute to this area of Bauckham's work. Davila's essay involves a comparative analysis of Revelation and the pre-Kabbalistic Jewish mystical texts known as the Hekhalot literature. These works may well preserve older traditions of Merkavah mysticism, broadly coeval with Revelation, but in their textual form they are significantly later. Davila's study moves point by point through some of the more striking connections and similarities between the two bodies of literature, such as the representations of the exalted Jesus and the figure of the Youth, which overlap considerably. He notes and explores some of the common textual backgrounds and exegetical practices that explain these, but does not allow the recognition of similarity to mask the deeper differences. These are works with radically different agendas: while Revelation is "an apocalypse that aims to reassure the followers of Jesus that he will soon triumph over the evil Roman persecutors," the "Hekhalot texts are instruction manuals for achieving altered states of consciousness that allow the practitioners to translate themselves into the celestial throne room." The parallels, then, are as much windows onto difference as similarity and it is here that the real value of the study lies, throwing into sharper relief the distinctive aims or beliefs of each writer.

PART 1

Thematic Studies

The Birth of God and the Resurrection of Life

Jürgen Moltmann

For more than twenty-five years Richard Bauckham has been a faithful companion on my theological paths. He introduced me to the theological world in England, and far beyond. Through his commentaries on my books he has not only walked beside me but has also not infrequently pointed me forward.

His book *Moltmann: Messianic Theology in the Making* appeared in 1987.[1] In my preface I tried to become clear for myself about my methods in my theological beginnings. For in his account of my so-called trilogy *Theology of Hope*, *The Crucified God*, and *The Church in the Power of the Spirit*,[2] Richard held up to me a profound portrait or "mirror" of what I had written. After his book I was able to understand my theological path better and became clearer about what I was trying to do.

In 1995 his second book about me appeared, *The Theology of Jürgen Moltmann*.[3] With this he also turned to the series of my "systematic contributions to theology," which began in 1980 with *The Trinity and the Kingdom of God: A Social Doctrine of the Trinity* (1980)[4] and *God in Creation: An Ecological Doctrine of Creation*, the Gifford Lectures (1985).[5]

It was typical of Richard that he should have dedicated this book "To Jürgen Moltmann from whose work I have learned rather less than I think and

[1]. Richard Bauckham, *Moltmann: Messianic Theology in the Making* (Basingstoke, UK: Marshall Pickering, 1987).
[2]. (Minneapolis: Fortress, 1993) for all three.
[3]. Richard Bauckham, *The Theology of Jürgen Moltmann* (Edinburgh: T&T Clark, 1995).
[4]. English (Minneapolis: Fortress, 1993).
[5]. English (Minneapolis: Fortress, 1993).

a lot more than I realize."[6] I gladly acknowledge that with his book I had a similar experience: I thought I knew what I had written, but in the "mirror" that Richard held up to me I perceived much more than I had been conscious of. That was due to the acute interpretations with which he accompanied his accounts. He showed me not only the potential implicit in my ideas; he gave me new ideas as well.

His third book about me was published in 1999: *God Will Be All in All: The Eschatology of Jürgen Moltmann.*[7] My Christian eschatology, *The Coming of God*, had appeared in German in 1995[8] and in English in 1996.[9] Richard Bauckham, Trevor Hart, and Timothy Gorringe had worked through and commented on the individual chapters. In June 1997 I came to St Andrews for a long weekend, in order to put forward my responses to their accounts and questions. The time we spent together was marked by deep mutual understanding and friendly criticism. We dedicated this book to Margaret Kohl, who translated all my books into English from *The Church in the Power of the Spirit* onward. We wrote in the introduction: "All English-speaking readers of Moltmann are immensely indebted to her skilful and readable translations, which are informed by her own considerable familiarity with his work and undertaken with enthusiasm for it to be widely read and appreciated. As an expression of thanks we are dedicating this book to her."

Richard Bauckham is an astonishing scholar. When I first met him he was Lecturer in the History of Christian Thought at the University of Manchester. When I worked with him, he was Professor of New Testament Studies at the University of St Andrews, with far-reaching interests in systematic theology. Today he has retired in order to concentrate on research and writing, and is senior scholar at Ridley Hall in Cambridge. But his special interest in Christian eschatology has remained. He began with his *Tudor Apocalypse: Sixteenth Century Apocalypticism, Millenarianism and the English Reformation, from John Bale to John Foxe and Thomas Brightman*[10] and, as New Testament scholar, soon after he wrote a *Theology of the Book of Revelation* (1993).[11] What I admire about him, and the link between us, is the conviction that Christian theology

---

6. Bauckham, *The Theology of Jürgen Moltmann*, v.
7. (Minneapolis: Fortress, 2001).
8. *Das Kommen Gottes: Christliche Eschatologie* (Gütersloh: Christian Kaiser Verlag, 1995).
9. (Minneapolis: Fortress, 1996).
10. Richard Bauckham, *Tudor Apocalypse: Sixteenth Century Apocalypticism, Millenarianism and the English Reformation, from John Bale to John Foxe and Thomas Brightman* (Abingdon, UK: Sutton Courtenay, 1978).
11. (Cambridge: Cambridge University Press, 1993).

The Birth of God and the Resurrection of Life

is rooted in the biblical traditions and is inspired by them, but that it must prove itself in the problems and potentialities of the present day. It can best do this if it looks beyond the present into God's future, to which the biblical promises point. It then moves beyond fundamentalist withdrawal and liberalist conformity. A good example is Richard Bauckham's new book, *Bible and Ecology: Rediscovering the Community of Creation* (2010).[12]

I am grateful for having come to know Richard Bauckham, and still expect much from him. In his honor, I am putting forward the following thoughts about the relation between incarnation and resurrection, and I greet him with Psalm 84:2: "My heart and my flesh cry out for the living God."

1. Why Did the Divine Logos "Become Flesh" in Jesus of Nazareth?

"God became human so that we human beings might become gods."

(Athanasius, *De incarnatione* 52)

In order to understand the first proposition about the incarnation we have to take note of the clause that follows. The main Christological statement is explained only by the soteriological purpose-clause.

Athanasius's thesis is a good rendering of the Christological dialectic:

Jesus Christ:
   crucified – raised
   died – risen
   humiliated – exalted
   become human – Lord of the world.

The soteriological significance of this dialectic is brought out very well by the patristic axiom: "What is not assumed cannot be healed." That can be interpreted in Athanasius's sense to mean: "God has become human so that we human beings can participate in the divine life as God's sons and daughters"; or, following Martin Luther: "God becomes human in order to turn us from being unhappy and proud gods into true human beings who accept their lowliness."[13]

---

12. (Waco, TX: Baylor University Press, 2010).
13. M. Luther, *Werke*, Weimar Ausgabe V, 128–29: "Humanitatis seu (ut Apostolus loquitur) carnis regno, quod in fide agitur, nos sibi conformes facit und crucifigit, faciens ex infoe-

God the Son humiliates himself to the point of death on the cross in order to exalt all the humiliated to God.

More, the eternal Word of creation became "flesh" in order to heal "all flesh"—that is to say, all the living.

In the double event of Christ's incarnation and resurrection we can see the tremendous divine dynamic that drives towards the transformation of all things into their true and abiding form. Nothing that *is* remains just *as* it is once it is accepted by Christ and transformed in him.

Where this dynamic of the crucified and raised Christ is present, "the old has passed away, behold, the new has come" (2 Cor. 5:17). Can we discern this transforming dynamic only in human beings who through faith "are in Christ"? According to the Epistles to the Colossians and the Ephesians, we can also perceive the cosmic Christ in all things that the exalted Christ has "reconciled" (Col. 1:20). We recognize the cosmic Christ in the cosmos that has been reconciled and made ready for transformation. Paul has unjustly been accused of anthropocentricism, but for Paul too, God was first "in Christ reconciling the cosmos with himself" before he "entrusted to us the message of reconciliation" (2 Cor. 5:19). Why? Because for Paul too Christ is the mediator of creation "through whom are all things and through whom we exist" (1 Cor. 8:6). Is that speculation, or pure mythology, as Rudolf Bultmann thought?[14] I may point to the Egyptian "desert fathers," who were in reality divinely enthused young men who withdrew into the desert, the land where it was not the gods who ruled but which was the home of demons, so that there they might experience the victory of the cosmic Christ.[15] Anthony was the most

---

licibus et superbis diis homines veros, idest miseros et peccatores. Quia enim ascendimus in Adam ad similitudinem dei, ideo descendit ille in similitudinem nostram, ut reduceret nos ad nostri cognitionem. Atque hoc agitur sacramento incarnationis. Hoc est regnum fidei, in quo Crux Christi dominatur, divinitatem perverse petitam deiiciens et humanitatem carnisque contemptam infirmitatem perverse desertam revocans." I understand this not as an antithesis but as a necessary complement to Athanasius: the becoming human of God serves the becoming human of the self-deifying human being, and hence the becoming God of the true human being. The sonship and daughterhood of God is the result of the forgiveness of sins. To put it in modern terms; when modern human beings renounce their unhappy "God complex" (as the psychoanalyst H. E. Richter called it) they become more human, and in their human vulnerability and mortality experience the nearness of the incarnate God. Cf. J. Moltmann, *Experiences in Theology*, trans. Margaret Kohl (London: SCM; Minneapolis: Fortress, 2000), 2.

14. See here now C. Landmesser, ed., *Theologie und Wirklichkeit. Diskussionen der Bultmann-Schule* (Neukirchen-Vluyn: Neukirchener, 2011)

15. H. C. Zander, *Als die Religion noch nicht langweilig war: Die Geschichte der Wüstenväter* (Gütersloh: Gütersloher Verlagshaus, 2011).

The Birth of God and the Resurrection of Life

famous of them. Pachomius built the first Christian monastery in the desert. It is true that today we no longer believe in demons, but the struggle with fears in the deserts of our world, and faith in the cosmic victory of the risen Christ, have more topical force today than ever before.

2. Christ's Resurrection and Incarnation

Before we follow up this cosmic Christology further in the linguistic contexts of the biblical words *basar* and *sarx*, we have to ask how people arrived at knowledge of the Son of God who in Jesus of Nazareth became human—knowledge of the Logos who in him became flesh. That cannot be seen from Jesus's birth and his life and ministry, let alone from his death on the Roman cross. The *cognitive ground* for the perception of God's incarnation in Jesus is to be found in his "resurrection from the dead" and his exaltation to God—"designated Son of God in power . . . by his resurrection from the dead," as Paul puts it (Rom. 1:4).[16] Without the event that the women and the disciples called "resurrection," we should know nothing about a Jesus of Nazareth. But the *true substantive ground* for his exaltation lies in his humbling of himself to the point of death on the cross, as the hymn in the Epistle to the Philippians says (Phil. 2:6-11). The presupposition for that, however, is the birth of God in the becoming-human of Christ.

The incarnation of the Son of God presents Jesus's whole life and death *sub specie eternitatis* or, to put it more exactly, sets it in the light of his resurrection. The Gospels relate "the history of a living person," as Edward Schillebeeckx said, not the story of someone dead. So the incarnation of God comprehends Jesus's whole life and death as the Christ of God. Wolfhart Pannenberg has talked about the "retrospective power" of Christ's resurrection on his life and death.[17] That is thought of chronologically. But "the resurrection of the dead" is an eschatological symbol. So I would prefer to talk about the eschatological logic: the last reveals the first.[18] Christ's resurrection from the dead reveals him as being the incarnate Son of God. His exaltation as the cosmic

---

16. H.-J. Eckstein and M. Welker, *Die Wirklichkeit der Auferstehung* (Neukirchen-Vluyn: Neukirchener, 2001); J. Moltmann, "Christ's Resurrection—the Resurrection of the Body—the Resurrection of Nature," in *Sun of Righteousness, Arise! God's Future for Humanity and the Earth*, trans. Margaret Kohl (London and Minneapolis: Fortress, 2010), 37-73.

17. W. Pannenberg, *Jesus: God and Man*, trans. L. L. Wilkins and D. A. Priebe (London: SCM, 1968).

18. Moltmann, *Sun of Righteousness*, 53-55.

Christ reveals him as being the foundation of all things in creation. The "fullness of life" which has "appeared" in the risen Christ makes the intention of his participation in our life and his assumption of our death manifest.

Because in the resurrection of the crucified Christ it is not only One ahead of the general resurrection of the dead who has appeared, and because in this One, death itself has been overcome (has been "slain," as Luther put it), Christ is also the beginning of the new creation of all things out of their transience into their abiding form which does not pass away. The resurrection of Christ has to be grasped not only in the framework of a historical eschatology, but in cosmic eschatology too. The risen Christ is not just a hope for eternal life given to mortal human beings; he is also the future of all things in "the new heaven and the new earth in which righteousness dwells" (2 Pet. 3:13).

In the perspective of this eschatology, we have to cast another glance at the incarnation of God. His "taking flesh" sets Jesus's whole person within his relationship to God. "In him the whole fullness of the Godhead dwells bodily" (Col. 2:9). So it is impossible to say that "in Christ the being of God" consisted only of his "unremittingly powerful God-consciousness," as Friedrich Schleiermacher taught in his doctrine of faith (*Glaubenslehre*).[19] The Gospels related the story of Jesus's miracles in such a way as to show that healing powers also emanated from his body (Matt. 9:18–26: the woman with an issue of blood).

A person does not only consist of body and soul, but subsists in his or her relationships as well. That is why Jesus's relationships to the sick, the poor, and the outcasts, and his relationships with women and his disciples, are important for the perspectives of the "incarnation." These perspectives also include the incarnate God's relationships to nature: "He was with the wild beasts" (Mark 1:13) and "the wind and sea obeyed him" (Mark 4:35–41).

In his encyclical *Dominion et vivificantem* of 18 May 1986, John Paul II wrote (50): "The incarnation of God's Son means not only the assumption of human nature into unity with God, but in some sense the assumption of everything that is 'flesh'—the assumption of the whole humanity, of the whole visible and material world. The incarnation therefore also has a cosmic significance and dimension."

Does this "assumption" of the cosmos into unity with God result in a

---

19. F. Schleiermacher, *Der christliche Glaube: Nach den Grundsätzen der evangelischen Kirche im Zusammenhange dargestellt*, 2nd ed. 1830/31, ed. Martin Redeker (Berlin: De Gruyter, 1960), §84: "The Redeemer is thus like to men by virtue of the identity of the human nature, but differs from all through the unremitting power of his God-consciousness, which was a particular being of God in him." §100: "The Redeemer takes believers into the power of his God-consciousness, and this is his redeeming activity."

God-cosmos instead of the God-human being? How are we then to understand the human history of Jesus from the manger to the cross?

The incarnation perspective sets not only Jesus's *person* in the light of a cosmic eschatology, but the *path* Jesus took as well. That began in a stable and ended on the gallows. It is a way taken by Christ with God through human conditions of life and death, from the endowment with God's Spirit at his baptism to God-forsakenness on the cross, so that everything might be filled with his presence. In his death, it is *his path into the world of the dead*, so that the world of the dead too might be irradiated with his gospel. It is his *descent into hell*, so that the gates of hell might be destroyed. It is his *rising from the dead*, so that the dead might be redeemed; it is his *ascent into heaven*, so that heaven too might be possessed, and his exaltation "to the right hand of God" so that the cosmos might be reconciled, and all things "in heaven, on earth and under the earth" prepared for the new creation. Why? The Orthodox Easter liturgy proclaims:

> Now everything is filled with light,
> heaven and earth
> and the realm of the dead.
> The whole creation exults in Christ's resurrection.[20]

If Christ's resurrection has such a universal, cosmic significance, then a universal and cosmic light falls on his incarnation too. But this then also raises the critical question: In what is God not incarnate?

If in Jesus God has "become flesh," then he is not incarnate in the demonic, political, and natural enemies, who withstood Jesus's gospel, were the adversaries of his life, tortured him, and brought him to death on the cross. These are the "every rule and every authority and power" that killed Christ and that the risen Christ will, for his part, "destroy" (1 Cor. 15:24). But "he must reign until he has put all his enemies under his feet. The last enemy to be destroyed is death" (15:25-26). These are the powers of chaos, the forces hostile to human beings and creation, the godless destructive forces of annihilation. In these God is not present; on the contrary, the creation of the world *ex nihilo* and the resurrection of Christ from the dead are God's protest against the deadly powers and the annihilating nothingness.

Here a far-reaching difference between Paul and the so-called Deutero-

---

20. E. Benz, ed., *Das Buch der heiligen Gesänge der Ostkirche* (Hamburg: Furche-Verlag, 1962), 103.

Pauline writers emerges. The quotation from 1 Corinthians shows that where the "principalities and powers" were concerned, Paul was an eschatological anarchist: these forces are to be "destroyed." But according to the Epistles to the Ephesians and Colossians, the cosmic Christ will merely strip them of their power, reconcile them, and put them to rights. "He has disarmed the principalities and powers and made a public example of them, triumphing over them in him" (Col. 2:15). For Christ "is the head of all" the principalities and powers (Col. 2:10). In the Epistle to the Ephesians this happening is called the *anakephalaiōsis tōn pantōn*: "to unite all things in him, things in heaven and things on earth" (Eph. 1:10). With his resurrection from the dead, Christ is set "at the right hand of God" "far above all rule and authority and power and dominion, and above every name that is named, not only in this age, but in that which is to come" (Eph. 1:21). Here Christ's dominion over the world is conceived as eschatological hierarchy. It is consequently final, not provisional as it is in Paul, for whom it antecedes the kingdom of God which will fulfill all things (1 Cor. 15:28). Here there is no "handing over of the kingdom" by the Son to the Father. The rule of Christ has no end, not even in God. *Christus pantocrator* is already the consummation of the world. It was from this that the Christian empire in Byzantium took its religious legitimation.[21] The Christian empire is the completion of world history. In this way what was originally an anarchistic eschatology turned into a conservative ideology of the state. The *imperium sanctum* became the reflection of Christ's heavenly rule; the imperator rules in the name of the *pantocrator*.

3. "The Word Became Flesh": What Is Meant by "Flesh"?

The Hebrew word *basar* can mean different things in different contexts, but all its meanings are present in the fundamental Christological tenet: "The Word became flesh and dwelt among us and we beheld his glory."

1. It means the whole human being, body and soul. For example: "O thou who hearest prayer, to thee shall all flesh come" (Ps. 65:2); "Let all flesh bless his holy name" (Ps. 145:21).

2. It means the bodily part of the human being. For example: "In my flesh I shall see God" (Job 19:26); "My flesh sings for joy to the living God" (Ps. 84:2); "They become one flesh" (Gen. 2:24).

---

21. *Fischer Weltgeschichte*, vol. 13, *Byzanz*, ed. F. G. Maier (Frankfurt: S. Fischer Verlag, 1973), 33. On political theology in Byzantium, see 21-24.

3. It means everything that lives, in its weakness, helplessness, transience, and mortality. For example: "All flesh is grass, and all its beauty is like the flower of the field. The grass withers, the flower fades" (Isa. 40:6–7).

4. It means the whole human race, in community with all the living. For example: "The Lord has an indictment against the nations; he is entering into judgment with all flesh" (Jer. 25:31); the covenant with Noah is concluded "with you and your descendants after you, and with every living creature" (Gen. 9:9–10).

Perhaps "flesh" can best be translated as "life," especially in the phrase *kol basar*, "all flesh." The human being is living in his or her totality; the human race is living in its community with everything that lives on earth. Everything living shares the fate of vulnerability, mortality, and transience. Everything living is promised a common future in the kingdom of God's glory: "The glory of the Lord shall be revealed and all flesh shall see it together" (Isa. 40:5).

Consequently the essential thing is to respect and hold fast to the community of all living things. Human beings are their "fellow creatures." It is only "together," not separately, that the glory of the Lord will be visible. The human being is not a person who stands over against the rest of the world; human beings are "part of nature," as the Earth Charter of Rio de Janeiro says (1992, 2000).[22] They are the part of nature in which nature becomes aware of itself. So it makes sense to understand human beings from the standpoint of the life of the earth, and to develop anthropology in the light of cosmology, not conversely, as is the case in modern philosophical anthropology.

"The human being is a hypostasis of the whole cosmic nature," says Dumitru Stăniloae in his *Orthodox Dogmatics*.[23] This does not mean that all forms of life are present in the human being, but it does mean the presence of all the elements of life. As genetic research shows, the human being exists in a natural affinity with all other living things. The earth is not just the habitat shared by all the living. It is also their womb. "Let the earth bring forth living creatures" (Gen. 1:24). That includes human beings: "You are dust and to dust you shall return" (Gen. 3:19).

In his incarnation God assumes not only human nature but the nature of all the living too: "The Word became flesh." The whole vulnerable, mortal

---

22. The Earth Charter, final version of 2000, Preamble: "Humanity is part of a vast evolving universe."

23. D. Stăniloae, *Orthodoxe Dogmatik* (Gütersloh: Gütersloher Verlagshaus, 1985), 1:294; J. Moltmann, *God in Creation: An Ecological Doctrine of Creation*, Gifford Lectures 1984–1985, trans. Margaret Kohl (London and San Francisco: SCM, 1985): "Before we interpret [the human being] as *imago Dei*, we shall see him as *imago mundi*" (186).

nature is assumed by God in his becoming human, in order that it may be healed, reconciled, and glorified. The Old Testament's account of creation begins with "heaven and earth" and ends with the creation of human beings; the New Testament's account of the new creation of all things begins with the incarnation of God and ends with the creation of a new heaven and a new earth in which God dwells.

4. "Poured Out on All Flesh"

All the meanings of "flesh" we have listed are present in the pneumatological principle: "God's Spirit is poured out on all flesh."[24] This outpouring of the divine Spirit has to be distinguished from the incarnation of God's Son. The incarnation takes place in the one—Jesus Christ—for many; the outpouring of the Spirit takes place in many so that they may be united with the one head, Christ. That comes about both in the church and in the cosmos, for the human being receives "the breath of life" from God's Spirit (Gen. 2:7) just as do all living things and the earth itself: "When thou sendest forth thy Spirit they are created; and thou renewest the face of the ground" (Ps. 104:30). In the New Testament everything serves the *recapitulatio omnia in Christo*.

The Spirit does not become human, nor does it become flesh; it is "poured out." This "water" metaphor delineates the transitions from the Spirit itself to the gifts of the Spirit, from the *charis* to the *charismata*, as flowing emanations. The powers of the Spirit are God's creative energies and stand between the uncreated energies and the created ones. Like the Old Testament Shekinah, the divine Spirit indwells all the living, so as to fill everything with primal livingness. It is the Spirit of God that makes hoping human beings yearn for the redemption of the body from the fate of death, and the oppressed nonhuman creation sigh for redemption from transience.

According to Joel 2 (quoted in Acts 2), in the human world the fruitful outpouring of the Spirit has a revolutionary effect. Sons and daughters will prophesy, the old and the young will see visions, servants and maidservants will be seized by the Spirit. In the Spirit-imbued community, the differences between the sexes, the differences between the generations, and the social differences will be ended. During the Reformation period the Anabaptist

---

24. J. Moltmann, *The Spirit of Life: A Universal Affirmation*, trans. Margaret Kohl (London: SCM, 1992), 157-60; M. Welker, *God the Spirit*, trans. J. F. Hoffmeyer (Minneapolis: Fortress, 1994), 214-58.

movements acted in just this revolutionary way. Today Pentecostal movements should take Joel 2 to heart. The fruitful outpouring of the Spirit extends not only to the human world but to nature as well:

> When the Spirit is poured upon us from on high, the wilderness will become a fruitful field, and the fruitful field will be deemed a forest. Then justice will dwell in the wilderness, and righteousness abide in the fruitful field. (Isa. 32:15–16)

5. The Resurrection of the Flesh

Finally, all the Hebrew meanings of *basar* are also present in the eschatological tenet: "I believe in the resurrection of the flesh and the life eternal."

The patristic church introduced this realistic phrase *resurrectio carnis* into the Apostles' Creed, running counter to the general Gnostic spiritualizing tendencies prevalent in the culture of the late ancient world. In his famous treatise *De Resurrectione Mortuorum* (212), Tertullian developed this idea further:

> *Resurgit igitur caro,*
> *et quidem omnis,*
> *el quidem ipsa,*
> *et quidem integra.*

He undoubtedly understood *caro* to mean the human body: the body will be raised, everything about the body, the same body, the whole body. In addition he declared the body to be "the key to redemption"—"*caro salutis est cardo*"[25]— because it is in our lived lives that we encounter the living God. But that does not have to be restricted to human bodies.

About forty years ago the Protestant and Roman Catholic churches replaced "the resurrection of the body" with "the resurrection of the dead," in order to avoid modern misunderstandings. Does this mean the same thing? No, the resurrection of the dead is related to human beings, and is meant in a

---

25. Tertullian, *De Resurrectione Mortuorum* (CCL 2; 1954), VIII.2; LXII.1, with comment by G. Greshake (p. 191): "Celsus had already grasped that if God himself descends to human beings and becomes 'flesh,' he brings about a 'revolution' in the world, since in this way the whole self-contained natural order is overthrown. Cf. Origen, *C. Cels.* IV.5."

personal sense. But the resurrection of the flesh is meant ecologically, and is related to everything living. Human beings will be redeemed together with the whole groaning creation. The earth, too, is waiting for its new creation in justice and righteousness. That is why the Nicene Creed does not talk just about "eternal life" but about "the life of the world to come."[26] I would propose replacing "the resurrection of the dead" with "the resurrection of life," and adding "the eternal life of the world to come."

If cosmic eschatology is a constitutive part of Christian faith, then we shall also be able to talk about a "deification of the cosmos" in the coming of God into this creation.[27] This certainly cuts across all cosmological trend analyses. It also cuts across the evolution of life on this planet through birth and death. But it is the most important thing we can say theologically about the future of the cosmos and the future of life. Everything else is generally merely a reiteration of what the sciences themselves already say about the cosmos and the evolution of life, and there is no need for it to be said again by theologians. Dialogues about truth develop out of contradictions.

---

26. Compared with Vatican II's Pastoral Constitution *Gaudium et Spes*, Benedict XVI's hope encyclical *Salvi Spes* of 2007 is a reduction of "the life of the world to come" to the "eternal life" of human beings, and is hence a restriction of cosmic Christian eschatology to individual eschatology.

27. J. Moltmann, *The Coming of God: Christian Eschatology*, trans. Margaret Kohl (London: SCM; Minneapolis: Fortress, 1996).

Time and Eternity: Richard Bauckham and the Fifth Evangelist

Jeremy S. Begbie

One of the most impressive features of Richard Bauckham's work is his capacity to engage with issues that lie far beyond the traditional boundaries of New Testament studies. Ecology, painting, literature, poetry, politics, philosophy—these are just some of the fields he traverses with skill and flair. However, the world of music is one that he has left largely to one side. This essay is an attempt to bring a major segment of his work—his writing on time and eternity—into engagement with some recent treatments of the music of J. S. Bach. Given that Bauckham is an eminent scholar of the Gospels, and that Bach has sometimes been dubbed "the fifth evangelist," it is perhaps especially fitting that we should bring these two together.

In academic music circles over the last two decades we can discern a fresh willingness to engage the theological dimensions of Bach's work seriously,

---

I am immensely grateful to Professor Daniel Chua and his colleagues in the Music Department of the University of Hong Kong for their invitation to deliver an early version of this paper, and for the stimulating discussion which followed. My grateful thanks also go to Professor Stephen Crist of Emory University, Atlanta, for his detailed and incisive comments on a later draft. Large parts of this chapter appeared in pp. 41–72 of *Music, Modernity, and God: Essays in Listening*, by Jeremy Begbie, 2014, and are used here by permission of Oxford University Press, https://global.oup.com/academic/product/music-modernity-and-god-9780199292448?cc=us&lang=en&#.UXouTZXCE1E. Parts of the chapter were published in Jeremy S. Begbie, "Pressing at the Boundaries of Modernity: A Review Essay on *Bach's Dialogue with Modernity: Perspectives on the Passions* by John Butt (CUP, 2010)," *Christian Scholar's Review* 40, no. 4 (Summer 2011): 453–65.

something greatly to be welcomed.[1] However, I shall argue that when it comes to his approach to the interrelation of time and eternity, insofar as an "approach" can be discerned, at least some leading musicological studies of Bach in recent years could benefit from being far more sensitive to the shape and depth of biblically informed, classic teaching in this area, and it is in this respect that Bauckham's work can be of considerable assistance.

Bach's Cycle?

As a primary focus, we will consider a relatively recent book, *Bach's Cycle, Mozart's Arrow*, by Karol Berger, Osgood Hooker Professor of Fine Arts at Stanford University.[2] This substantial and highly acclaimed monograph is in effect a study of different perceptions of time in modernity, as exemplified in music. Bach and Mozart provide the two main centers of interest; we shall concentrate here on Berger's treatment of Bach.

Undaunted by postmodern qualms about metanarratives, Berger boldly claims: "[T]he main job of art before it became fully modern in the late eighteenth century was to give sensuous embodiment to the eternal—cosmic or divine—order and truth. Since that time, by contrast, the tendency has been to use art to proclaim human autonomy; for the moderns, for us, art is mainly a tool of self-affirmation" (42). Within this giant story, he delineates a more localized trajectory, running from J. S. Bach (1685-1750) to Mozart (1756-1791). Berger detects a telling shift between these two, from a preference for "circular" to "linear" time, consonant with a metaphysical and theological shift from a perspective in which the world's time is understood to be held within God's all-embracing eternity to one in which time effectively excludes, even abolishes any "higher" or primary eternity. Berger reads Bach as a "late representative of

---

1. See, e.g., John Butt, "Bach's Metaphysics of Music," in *The Cambridge Companion to Bach*, ed. John Butt (Cambridge: Cambridge University Press, 1997), 46-71; Peter Smaill, "Bach Among the Heretics: Inferences from the Cantata Texts," *Understanding Bach* 4 (2009): 101-18; Wilfrid H. Mellers, *Bach and the Dance of God* (Oxford: Oxford University Press, 1981); Michael Marissen, "The Theological Character of J. S. Bach's *Musical Offering*," in *Bach Studies 2*, ed. Daniel R. Melamed (Cambridge: Cambridge University Press, 1995), 85-106; Eric T. Chafe, *Tonal Allegory in the Vocal Music of J. S. Bach* (Berkeley: University of California Press, 1991); Eric T. Chafe, *Analyzing Bach Cantatas* (Oxford: Oxford University Press, 2000).

2. Karol Berger, *Bach's Cycle, Mozart's Arrow: An Essay on the Origins of Musical Modernity* (Berkeley: University of California Press, 2007). Throughout this section, page references given in parentheses in the text refer to this work.

the premodern ways of shaping musical time," and Mozart as an early representative of a "fully developed modern approach to musical temporality" (10).

As far as Bach is concerned, Berger's thesis is supported by, among other things, a close reading of the opening chorus of his *St Matthew Passion*. This vast work, written for a Good Friday Vespers service in 1727, opens with a giant movement, described by Christoph Wolff as "a funeral march for the multitude of believers who ascend to Mount Zion and the holy city of Jerusalem."[3] One choir sings the part of the Daughter Zion, the other the words of the Faithful. The Daughter Zion calls out to the Faithful to witness the sacrifice of Christ; the Faithful respond with short and puzzled questions. A third choir of sopranists, the choir of the heavenly Jerusalem, sings a chorale, a metrical paraphrase of the "Agnus Dei" which concludes the Good Friday afternoon service.

Structurally, Berger sees the chorus as a "varied da capo" form, in which a return of the opening text with its music is adapted so as to enable a return to the tonic (or home key). But this particular varied *da capo* has a highly unusual ending: what would normally be extended in a series of phrases Bach condenses into a single phrase, creating a "synthesizing culmination" (59). There is "no sense of imbalance, no sense that the end does not match the expansive beginning, no sense of something missing" (59). Berger takes this as evidence of Bach's efforts to neutralize or circularize time, "to abolish the succession of past, present, and future" in favor of the "simultaneity of the present" (59). Indeed, Berger contends that in both his instrumental and vocal music, Bach shows relatively little interest in "linear time," the temporal ordering of musical events.[4]

Bach's Privileging of Eternity

Berger proceeds to give this a strongly theological interpretation. In the case of the *Passion*'s opening chorus, the temporal circularity is designed to facilitate a particular stance or attentive attitude on the part of the listener. The two

---

3. Christoph Wolff, *Johann Sebastian Bach: The Learned Musician* (New York: W. W. Norton, 2000), 302.

4. Not surprisingly, Berger cites Laurence Dreyfus's important work on Bach's instrumental music which demonstrates that the ordering in time of events is normally far less important to Bach than the need to show the multiple possibilities that open up through transforming often very simple musical material. Laurence Dreyfus, *Bach and the Patterns of Invention* (Cambridge, MA: Harvard University Press, 1996).

choirs, he stresses, are not active protagonists in the events, but reflective observers or "contemplators." As such, they occupy a distinct temporal level. In fact, considered as a whole, the *St Matthew Passion* exhibits three such levels—there is the time narrated by the Evangelist (the time of the narrated events themselves), the time of the Evangelist's narrating, and the time of those who contemplate the narration, whose "time" is in effect a neutralizing of time. Berger wants us to see the fundamental determinative temporality as that of contemplation. For him, this provides the perceptual grid of the work. Certainly, the narrated story must be present (this is obviously the center of the listener's attention), and so must the time of the narrator, but "[s]tructurally, ontologically . . . the frame is more important." The two temporalities of story and storytelling are "nested" within the temporality of contemplation, which is to say, within "timeless eternity" (107).

Berger goes on to observe that the story's personages and the contemplators, although undoubtedly distinct, nevertheless both belong to the "world" being represented by the *Passion*. In most (if not all) of the *St Matthew Passion*, those who play the role of contemplators *"want to feel what it was like to be there.* The temporal distance between them and the personages of the story cannot be obliterated, but in imagination they can bridge it" (117, my emphasis). This seems to be the only way of explaining chorales such as no. 17, where Peter and the disciples assure Jesus they will not deny him: "I will stand here with you"; or Aria no. 20 in the context of Gethsemane—"I want to keep watch beside my Jesus."

"Zion and the rest," then—the contemplators—"are there to tell us what to do, feel, and think" (110). Through them, we today are being summoned to identify with the personages of the story ("we were there") in order that the story's truth may be internalized in the present. Important research has shown that Picander, Bach's librettist, was strongly influenced by the Lutheran sermon tradition which laid considerable stress on the goal of inward change, the transformation of the individual's heart.[5] We recall that not only was this setting of the *Passion* part of a preaching service (Vespers), with a sermon coming between each half, but was *itself* regarded as a form of preaching, through which the Gospel could take root in the hearer. These events have happened *propter nos* and *pro nobis*.[6] The listeners are thus being enjoined "to do the

---

5. Elke Axmacher, *"Aus Liebe will mein Heyland sterben": Untersuchungen zum Wandel des Passionsverständnisses im frühen 18. Jahrhundert* (Neuhausen-Stuttgart: Hänssler-Verlag, 1984).

6. On this, see Robin A. Leaver, *J. S. Bach as Preacher: His Passions and Music in Worship* (St. Louis: Concordia, 1984).

Time and Eternity

impossible and enter the world of the story as participants" (114). Hence Bach's "thwarting of time"; according to Berger, Bach must make it possible for the audience, by virtue of an imaginative act, to close the distance between the past and our present: "time has to be rendered impotent, its flow either stopped or bent into a circle" (117).

Berger's theological construal of the *Passion* is widened to assimilate a further perspective. Bach, he claims, is attempting to neutralize time because of the way in which Christ is conceived in the theological tradition. The life of Jesus as a historical figure is understood by the New Testament writers as enclosed within eternity—he is the enfleshment of the eternal Logos. Classical orthodoxy invites us to see the history of humanity as displaying a similar structure—human history's linear temporality is bounded by a beginning and end, "beyond" which lies "God's infinite time"—eternity. Bach, like his contemporaries, is acutely aware of the ravages of irreversible time running toward death, time devouring all that we value, robbing us of all that is good. "In man's time all is vanity because sooner or later everything passes into oblivion. Our only hope of permanence is the promise that we may be translated into God's time" (120).

The vista is thus one in which this world's irreversible time is embedded, enfolded in what Berger calls "the hierarchically more fundamental eternity of God" (119). In this connection, Berger cites the opening declaration of Cantata 106: "Gottes Zeit ist die allerbeste Zeit" ("God's time is the very best time"). It is this preference for "God's time," i.e. eternity, that more than anything else accounts for Bach's fondness for cyclic structures and his relative indifference (in many of his pieces at least) to the temporal disposition of musical events. It also stands behind Bach's privileging of harmony: "music's sounding harmony reflects the intelligible harmony of God's creation" (127). The cosmically embedded principles of harmony are permanent and unchanging (even if they are played out in time): "the exploration of musical harmony is one way to contemplate what truly endures" (127).

Bach's musical articulation of time and eternity, thus understood, is regarded by Berger as emblematic of an essentially "Christian" view of reality. Indeed, critical to his thesis is his belief that just as Bach characterizes the premodern, Christian outlook ("the traditional Christian worldview" [176]), so Mozart represents the modern. The Salzburg genius exhibits a musical world where temporal linearity is "emancipated" from eternity and assumes the leading role; in music, temporal order and succession becomes critically important. Mozart's is the age in which a profound belief in human autonomy comes into its own. Freed from the obligations of eternal divine law, human beings begin to regard themselves as masters of their own destiny, and the future lies open to the potentially limitless capacities of human achievement and progress. It is quintessentially modern conceptions such as these, Berger believes, that can be discerned in the temporality of Mozart's works.

Berger on Time and Eternity

It is when Berger contrasts "Christian" with "modern" outlooks that his assumptions about the outlines of purportedly standard Christian teaching on time and eternity are thrown into relief. Sample quotations from this and related sections will have to suffice here. Christians, we are told, "take the existence of the supernatural realm for granted" (158); "humanity's participation in two different orders of reality, natural and supernatural, is precisely what the Christian worldview proclaims" (143). "In thinking about their individual existence, Christians above all desire salvation in the afterlife, and in the meantime they wish to do good in this life" (158). The Christian God determines "the bliss each individual saved soul will enjoy in heaven" (163); "the desired end is eternal rest and peace in God's heaven" (166). "Of course, a Christian [like the modern] wants to be happy . . . but he most desires eternal bliss hereafter" (159). Speaking of Immanuel Kant, Berger writes that "unlike the otherworldly goal of Augustine, [Kant's goal] neither postulates the eventual escape from time into eternity nor privileges rest over change. . . . The end of history is not the state of passive, atemporal contemplation of divine perfection but rather a state of active, open-ended development" (170). Consistent with such claims, Berger writes that "Christianity's greatest contribution to politics was the recognition that politics did not matter all that much. . . . Jesus . . . advised leaving politics to Caesar, since politics do not affect human salvation" (160). The following compresses the assumed overarching metaphysics *in nuce*:

> Like the universe of Plato, the universe of Christians is split into two—the temporal, mutable here and now, this world in which humans are born, dwell, and die, and the atemporal, immutable, transcendent beyond of God. But these two realms do not simply exist side by side. Rather, this world is enveloped in the transcendent one, is dependent on it, and owes its existence to it. (118)

We are, it seems, being presented with a characterization of mainstream Christian thought in which "supernature" is distinguished from "nature," eternity conceived as radically disconnected with, and ontologically superior to, time, and the Christian life portrayed as heading toward a release from time into the otherworldly "beyond of God" (rendering politics in this life irrelevant), the ultimate goal being the soul's blissful, "passive, atemporal contemplation of divine perfection."

Although there have of course been currents in the Christian tradition that exhibit elements of the vision Berger ascribes to the church (not least in much contemporary popular Christianity), it is a vision that turns on markedly different axes from, say, Nicene trinitarian orthodoxy, and it is unquestionably divergent in critical respects from the testimony of the New Testament.[7] This is so even if many will want to endorse Berger's account of broad changes in the development of modernity with regard to perceptions of time and history: the intense privileging of time over eternity, the way in which "modernity emancipates human time from the enveloping divine eternity" (167), modernity's secularization of Christianity's grand narrative, and so forth.

Bauckham on Time and Eternity

We can fruitfully turn to Richard Bauckham's work to help us probe, clarify, and reorient us more fully to the biblical material pertinent to our concerns. Bauckham is especially instructive here, not only because of his conceptual lucidity, but also because as a biblical theologian he presses us to sense the prevailing logic and pressures of scriptural texts, and is not afraid to risk metaphysical claims in fields where many in the textual-critical guild fear to tread.[8]

---

7. Part of the trouble here may be Berger's adoption of Augustine as his central, representative Christian theologian. Assuming for the moment that he interprets Augustine aright (and that itself is open to debate), many would argue that even though Augustine may be said to represent mainstream Christian thought on many matters, when it comes to his treatment of the nature and character of time and eternity, for all his astonishing perception and insight, questions still need to be asked about whether his reflections are sufficiently rooted in the Christologically shaped ontology mandated by the biblical texts. See Jeremy S. Begbie, *Theology, Music and Time* (Cambridge: Cambridge University Press, 2000), 75-85.

8. Here I draw mainly on his lengthy essay "Time and Eternity," in *God Will Be All in All: The Eschatology of Jürgen Moltmann*, ed. Richard Bauckham (Edinburgh: T&T Clark, 1999), 155-226; Richard Bauckham, *The Theology of the Book of Revelation* (Cambridge: Cambridge University Press, 1993); Richard Bauckham and Trevor A. Hart, *Hope Against Hope: Christian Eschatology at the Turn of the Millennium* (Grand Rapids: Eerdmans, 1999); and his essay written with Trevor Hart, "The Shape of Time," in *The Future as God's Gift: Explorations in Christian Eschatology*, ed. Marcel Sarot and David Fergusson (Edinburgh: T&T Clark, 2000),

I shall concentrate on matters that directly relate to Berger's discussion of time and eternity in Bach.

On many issues, Bauckham would have no quarrel with Berger, but their understandings of the contours of a distinctively Christian metaphysics of time and eternity differ quite drastically. First, implicit in Bauckham's biblically oriented work is a commitment to the primordial goodness and full reality of time, that time is a dimension intrinsic to the created order (including human life), and wholly willed by God as such. This is especially clear when he argues that Platonism's devaluation of time—in which what is truly real (eternally enduring, timeless, and immutable being) is set in radical contrast to what is temporary, time-laden, and changeable—is beset by a "failure to distinguish successiveness, in which all created things become what they are, and transience, in which all things pass away."[9] Transience is not itself evil, though we can and should grant that its negating power—the fact that because of transience, all things come to nothing—has been exploited by human evil. This distinction between temporal successiveness and transience eludes Berger entirely.

Consonant with this, second, Bauckham's is a theology in which God's self-revealing and saving action entails the direct involvement and interaction of God's eternity with created time, implicating time-embedded purposeful trajectories that lead toward the consummation of all things.[10] This is integral to Bauckham's scripturally derived conviction that the Creator is faithful to his creation and committed to its eschatological renewal,[11] a conviction that pivots crucially on what has been concretely enacted in the history of Jesus Christ. He speaks of three constant features of human experience of time: successiveness, transience, and the openness of the future to the new. "All three," he writes,

> are redeemed in Christ. In his incarnate life he becomes who he is in his human identity in the successiveness of time, which is essential to all creaturely becoming and identity. In his death, he is subject both to the transience which brings all things to nothing and to the human evil that exploits

---

41–72. (I am assuming that the last of these, although co-produced, faithfully reflects his own convictions!)

9. Bauckham and Hart, "The Shape of Time," 46.

10. See his very concise essay, "Reading Scripture as a Coherent Story," in *The Art of Reading Scripture*, ed. Ellen F. Davis and Richard B. Hays (Grand Rapids: Eerdmans, 2003), 38–53.

11. See, for example, his comments on the new creation in Bauckham, *The Theology of the Book of Revelation*, 51–53.

this negating power of time. In his resurrection, he is the promise of a new future which takes successiveness into eternity and redeems the transience from the past.[12]

A key concomitant of this account is that eternity and time are not to be understood as abstract conditions or dimensions, applicable to all entities univocally, but strictly in relation to the realities of which they are predicated. In biblical-theological terms, this means that the significance of eternity and time can in the last resort only be properly explicated with respect to the eternity of the triune God and the temporality of God's created cosmos, which in turn means only in relation to Jesus Christ, who embodies the climactic and soteriologically decisive interaction of triune eternity and creation. Berger certainly seems aware of the centrality of the incarnation for Christian faith, but fails to grasp its soteriological import, its integral place in the saving sweep of God's redeeming purposes for all temporally embedded created things, the way in which, along with the resurrection, it vindicates creation, a vindication that proleptically prefigures the final vindication of all things. To come at it from the other side, eternity is being conceived by him *a priori*, in abstraction from the incarnation and God's triune love, and is thus evacuated of its irreducibly personal, covenantal, and world-committed character.

This leads us to a third way in which Bauckham differs from Berger: his construal of the final consummation as including the taking up of time into eternity. Among other places, this appears in a lengthy exposition of Jürgen Moltmann's theology of time and eternity, a theology which in many (but not all) respects Bauckham appears to share.[13] The new creation, the eschatological fulfillment of all things, is not to be thought of as entailing the extension of this world's time but rather "the recovery and transformation of the whole diachronic extent of this world's time. All times will be gathered into eternity. . . . In this way the whole creation, in its whole diachronic extent, will be redeemed from transience."[14] In this outlook, "transient time is essential to the kind of goodness [creation] has,"[15] and its darker side, the consequent loss of all that is good, is countered in the eschaton's redemptive restoration. To share fully in

---

12. Bauckham and Hart, "The Shape of Time," 47.

13. Bauckham, "Time and Eternity." There are some other aspects of Moltmann's account he is prepared to criticize quite sharply; see, e.g., Bauckham, "Time and Eternity," 175–83.

14. Bauckham, "Time and Eternity," 183. "The end of history will happen to all history. In the resurrection all the dead of all history will rise to judgement and life in the new creation." Bauckham and Hart, *Hope Against Hope*, 39.

15. Bauckham, "Time and Eternity," 183.

redeemed temporality through Christ is to be delivered not only from the sin that takes advantage of transience, but from transience itself. Demanding as this may be to conceptualize, it is at root only the theo-logical consequence of taking creation's primordial temporality—as part of its inherent goodness—seriously: the cosmos was made not *in tempore* but *cum tempore*.

In this outlook, clearly, belief in God's promised future cannot (*pace* Berger) be used to justify a withdrawal from our responsibilities vis-à-vis worldly power and its potential victims. Quite the opposite. With Trevor Hart, Bauckham urges:

> Knowing that all generations have a future in God's new creation, we practise solidarity with their sufferings, their achievements and their hopes, telling their stories as still relevant parts of the grand narrative of God's love for the world. . . . Not only the dead, but the living for whom there can be no more hope in this world, who can neither assist nor benefit from the onward march of progress—the desperately and incurably sick, the dying, the wretched of the earth—must not be left behind, but cherished with the special care God has for the most hopeless, since the future we cannot give them is promised them by God.[16]

Further, for Bauckham, the promised future is eschatologically new, in the sense that it cannot be generated or arise from within the immanent potentialities of this temporal world. It is a "radically new future that takes the temporal beyond time . . . the radically new future which can only be the gift of the transcendent God."[17] The same circle of ideas appears in Bauckham's exposition of the book of Revelation:

> Creation is not confined for ever to its own immanent possibilities. It is open to the fresh creative possibilities of the Creator. . . . [The Creator] can give *new* life—eschatologically new life raised for ever beyond the threat of death. Whereas mortal life, cut off from its source, ends in death, God can give new life which is so united to his own eternal life that it can share his own eternity.[18]

---

16. Bauckham and Hart, *Hope Against Hope*, 40.
17. Bauckham and Hart, "The Shape of Time," 47.
18. Bauckham, *The Theology of the Book of Revelation*, 48–49. He goes on to explain that this applies not just to humans but to the entire created order: creation is given "a quite new form of existence, taken beyond all threat of evil and destruction, indwelt by his own glory, participating in his own eternity" (49). For further reflections on the "novel" logic of the

Berger is unable to accommodate such a possibility, for his ontology of eternity is essentially inert, precluding the possibility of a fresh form of temporality being generated *by* eternity *out of* created temporality.

Fourth, it is worth noting that Bauckham hesitates when Moltmann recommends the use of circular imagery in speaking of the redeemed future, "the cyclical movements of life's eternal joy in the unceasing praise of the omnipresent God."[19] The drawback of this, says Bauckham, is that it seems to preclude novelty, implying nothing new is possible.[20] Bauckham himself keeps an open mind about whether a Christian eschatology *requires* the inclusion of novelty in the eschaton, but he is clearly not content with excluding the possibility of change, and this presumably because of his unwavering commitment to a belief in the "taking up" of time into God's eternity.[21]

In any case, by now it will be evident that the disparity between Berger's worldview and Bauckham's more biblically founded ontology is acute and far-reaching. Some, doubtless, will object that we are being unnecessarily heavy-handed on Berger. He is, after all, writing as a musicologist, not a theologian. Though the point is not without force, we should remember that Berger, armed with what he takes to be the lineaments of mainstream Christian belief, is advancing a remarkably bold thesis about a shift from premodern to modern casts of mind, in which premodern is aligned with "Christian," and "Christian" is assimilated to a grand and all-encompassing theology of time and eternity with a quite definite profile. It is hardly unreasonable to ask whether this theology accords with one that takes its chief bearings from Christianity's foundational texts.

A rather more telling objection to our comments would be that Berger's focused interest (at least in the first part of his book) is in Bach, and that the decisive issue is not about truthfulness to biblical texts or even the mainline

---

resurrection, see Richard Bauckham, "God Who Raises the Dead: The Resurrection of Jesus in Relation to Early Christian Faith in God," in *The Resurrection of Jesus Christ*, ed. Paul D. L. Avis (London: Darton, Longman & Todd, 1993), 136–54.

19. Bauckham, "Time and Eternity," 184.

20. Bauckham, "Time and Eternity," 184.

21. Bernard Williams famously wrote an article in which he argued, inter alia, that immortality would be intolerable because of the lack of change. He cites Karel Capek's play "The Makropolous Case," in which Elina Makropolous, having consumed an elixir of life, has been permanently aged forty-two for three hundred years: "Her unending life has come to a state of boredom, indifference, and coldness. Everything is joyless: 'In the end it is the same,' she says, 'singing and silence.' She refuses to take the elixir again; she dies." Bernard Williams, "The Makropolous Case: Reflections on the Tedium of Immortality," in *Problems of the Self*, ed. Bernard Williams (Cambridge: Cambridge University Press, 1976), 82.

dogmatic tradition but about whether or not Berger has identified the theological shape of Bach's musical world correctly. This, then, provokes us to ask: To what extent is Berger's interpretive "frame" with respect to time and eternity anachronistic with respect to Bach? The question can be asked (a) with attention to Bach's own "theological world"—taking into account the textual evidence of his ecclesiastical and liturgical milieu, and even of his own beliefs inasmuch as they can be determined; and (b) with attention to the musical techniques and strategies that might be considered relevant to the evocation of time and eternity, especially as they appear in his settings of sacred texts.

Bach's Theological World

Detailed conclusions about the conceptions of time and eternity that would have informed Bach's creative mind are hard to draw. His was, after all, an age of rapid change and intense debate. Nonetheless, some things can fairly safely be assumed. It is generally agreed that Bach's theological outlook was shaped more than anything else by the Lutheranism of his day, and in his case, a Lutheranism that was consonant with Nicene orthodoxy, neither strictly Pietist (though Pietist sentiments are undoubtedly present in Bach's output) nor driven by the particular polemics of the stricter seventeenth- and eighteenth-century Lutheran theologians.[22] Bach himself appears to have been devout (although not exceptionally so for his time and place), and a serious student of the Bible.[23]

As far as eschatology is concerned, it is unlikely that Bach and his librettists would have envisaged a return of Christ within their own lifetime, but their milieu was one in which a sense of the brevity of life, coupled with a belief in the judgment of each person after death, and the importance of living with that judgment ever in mind, was widely presumed. Many have noted a marked tendency to allow this to narrow the theological significance of the span of history between the present and the end of history, so that the faith and repentance of the individual in the present becomes paramount above all else. In

---

22. For discussions, see, e.g., Eric T. Chafe, *Analyzing Bach Cantatas* (Oxford: Oxford University Press, 2000), ch. 1; Robin A. Leaver, *Music as Preaching: Bach, Passions and Music in Worship* (Oxford: Latimer House, 1983); Michael Marissen, *Lutheranism, Anti-Judaism, and Bach's St. John Passion* (New York: Oxford University Press, 1998); Jaroslav J. Pelikan, *Bach among the Theologians* (Philadelphia: Fortress, 1986).

23. For a summary of discussions of Bach's own theological commitments, see Jeremy S. Begbie, *Resounding Truth: Christian Wisdom in the World of Music* (Grand Rapids: Baker, 2007), 121-22.

many of the cantatas, for example, we find a pronounced sense of the transience of our lives, the fleetingness of this world's pleasures, and the foolishness of putting one's trust in them. There is evident a certain internalization of eschatology, very much part of the Pietist ethos, in which biblical end-times metaphors are "bent backwards" to confront us now with the need for a change of heart.[24] The eternal beckons us at every moment, the crisis of faith is ever-present. There is something to be said, then, for the view that Bach displays what Frank Kermode regards as a modern refiguring of the ancient expectation of an end-times crisis into a sense of a repeated judgment in the present moment, an "eternal transition, perpetual crisis."[25] At the same time, for the Christian, death can also be welcomed—since it will mark the end of sufferings and tribulations, and the beginning of a new life; it is a deliverance "out of the Egypt of this world" (Cantata 70). Bach can set texts which are somewhat startling in the way they address death warmly as a friend—"With joy I anticipate my death: / Ah! If only it had taken place already!" (Cantata 82).

All this might suggest an outlook that leans strongly in the Berger direction: a devaluing of time, this world, and the significance of our earthly lives in favor of a radically atemporal and infinitely more excellent future life. However, there are countervailing considerations. And they all turn on Christology.

With respect to the believer's final joyful destiny, in Bach's texts we find a persistent stress on the centrality of Christ and the believer's faith-union with him.[26] "Eternity" cannot be detached from eschatological encounter and communion with Christ, for it is with him supremely that we are given access to the eternity of God. The focus is on a person, not a state. The final chorale from Cantata 70 encapsulates the sentiment well:

> Not for the world, not for heaven
> Does my soul desire and yearn;
> I desire Jesus and his light,
> He who has reconciled me with God,
> Who frees me from judgement;
> I will not let my Jesus go.

---

24. See, e.g., Cantatas 20 and 60. For discussion, see John Butt, *Bach's Dialogue with Modernity: Perspectives on the Passions* (Cambridge: Cambridge University Press, 2010), 114–18.

25. As in Butt, *Bach's Dialogue with Modernity*, 117.

26. Robin A. Leaver, "Eschatology, Theology and Music: Death and Beyond in Bach's Vocal Music," in *Bach Studies from Dublin*, ed. Anne Leahy and Yo Tomita (Dublin: Four Courts, 2004), 145–46.

Eternal life is essentially the life that Christ imparts, God's own abundant life mediated in and through him. And, it should be added, eternal life through Christ can be known now: "Yes, yes, I hold Jesus firmly, / Then I also enter into heaven, / Where God and his Lamb's guests / Are in crowns at the Wedding. / There I shall not part from you, my salvation" (Cantata 157). In Cantata 60, Jesus responds to the believer's fear with the words "Blessed are the dead who die in the Lord, from now on [*von nun an*]." "Fear" later responds: "Well, then! / If I am to be blessed from henceforth: / Then appear again, O Hope! / My body may rest in sleep without fear, / My spirit can catch a glimpse of the joy hereafter." As Eric Chafe puts it, "[T]he final words of Jesus' promise, 'von nun an,' enable the believer to live in the hope of eternal life and even to experience a vision of that life in the present through the Spirit."[27]

Bearing this Christological perspective in mind—in which eternity is known in Christ and through faith in him, now and in the future—a number of comments are in order. First, it would be anachronistic to suppose that these and similar texts (or Bach) are presuming a radical discontinuity of value between this life and the next. There is no question that the life of the world to come is thought to be superior in quality to life here and now. But there is little to suggest that we should read into this any diminishment of the intrinsic value of the concrete realities of this time-bound life. While acknowledging a proneness in the texts Bach sets to downplay the theological import of the time-span between the present and the end in the interests of an ever-pressing final judgment, this needs to be qualified by recognizing the themes of discipleship that pervade, for instance, many of the cantatas.[28] Further, although we find an irrepressible assurance that a believer's physical distress will cease, this does not presuppose a devaluing of the body *per se*, either in this life or in the life to come. Belief in the bodily resurrection of Christ was, after all, basic to the Bachian *credo*.

In this connection it is worth noting that we should not be caught out by the phrase that opens Cantata 106—"Gottes Zeit ist die allerbeste Zeit" ("God's time is the very best time"). Berger takes this as demonstrating Bach's prefer-

---

27. Chafe, *Analyzing Bach Cantatas*, 223. In fact, Chafe misunderstands those last words of "Fear," rendering them "*the Spirit* can take a glance into that joyful state." The context makes clear that *Der Geist* is not a reference to the Holy Spirit but the believer's "spirit," here contrasted with the body. Fortunately, it is a theologically felicitous mistake, for it was certainly held in Bach's time that it is by the Spirit that an eschatological foretaste is made possible now.

28. See, e.g., Cantatas 39, 77; and the discussion in Calvin Stapert, *My Only Comfort: Death, Deliverance, and Discipleship in the Music of Bach* (Grand Rapids: Eerdmans, 2000), Part III.

ence for eternity over time. He writes that "God's time" (eternity) "is not just ontologically more important—prior in some sense, one without which there would be no time of the created world—but it is also better, 'the very best,' even."[29] But this is almost certainly a misreading of the phrase. As the context makes clear, "God's time" refers not to eternity, but to God's timing—his perfect will for things happening at the right time.[30]

Second, bound up with this, we should not be misled by descriptions of the future life we find in, say, the cantatas, that could suggest a somewhat motionless (and individualized) state of affairs. While Bach would have subscribed to the believer's immediate post-mortem future as involving "rest," this would have been regarded as occurring prior to the New Creation. Constrained by the liturgical requirements of the church's year, Bach is obliged to set texts that deal directly and unambiguously with the dynamic (and corporate) dimensions of Scripture's portrayal of the eschaton, which themselves, emerging out of the logic of the bodily resurrection of Christ, do little to encourage a sense of the abandonment or erasure of all time and motion. Cantata 140 is perhaps the most conspicuous example, which picks up biblical wedding feast imagery—the bridegroom, Christ, coming to receive his bride, the church (alluding to Matthew 25)—and closes with a richly worded chorale evoking the joyful, doxological city of unceasing worship portrayed in Revelation 21 and 22.[31]

Third, with respect to Bach's approach to death, we should be careful not to read quasi-Platonic sensibilities too quickly into his Lutheranism. Some of Bach's texts (especially nonbiblical ones) do appear to be compliant, perhaps even at times sentimental, in the face of death, embracing it as a longed-for friend. Others, however, exhibit a shuddering fear that seems almost pathological. The key to understanding this is Christological. Alfred Dürr helpfully sees the Bachian outlook on death in terms of Luther's *simul iustus et peccator*—death is at one and the same time to be feared (sin brings the possibility of damnation after death) and welcomed (through Christ our righteousness, death is the gateway to glory).[32] Christ has borne the ultimate consequence of

---

29. Berger, *Bach's Cycle, Mozart's Arrow*, 119–20.

30. The text continues: "'In him we live, move, and have our being,' as long as he wills. / In him we die at the right time, when he wills."

31. For further examples of expressions of the fullness of life in the eschaton, see, e.g., the texts of Cantata 70, with the significant line "You shall flourish in Eden / To serve God for ever."

32. Alfred Dürr, "'Ich freue mich auf meinen Tod': Sterben und Tod in Bachs Kantaten aus musikwissenschaftlicher Sicht," in *Jahrbuch des Staatlichen Instituts fur Musikforschung*

sin—death, and his victory over sin is confirmed on the third day. Death is not to be trivialized. But nor is it ever to be treated without hope: those belonging to the risen Christ have nothing to fear, for they will themselves be raised with him to everlasting life.[33]

Fourth, if we favor Bauckham's biblical ontology over Berger's, arguably, a rather different reading of the *St Matthew Passion* begins to emerge. We recall that for Berger, the "contemplators" in the opening chorus who are witnessing Christ's sacrifice stand in the same represented world as the personages in the events portrayed; there is a bridging of temporal distance between the world of the story and the contemplators' world. Likewise, for contemporary listeners, Bach wants to "neutralize" the time between present and past, so that the truth of what is portrayed may be internalized deep within each of us. We, like them, are to consider ourselves *there*. Bach therefore deploys a variety of techniques to ensure that time is thwarted, rendered unimportant, "insignificant in its relentless flow from past to future," the aim being to frame and "embed the time of the story within the timelessness of contemplation."[34]

Berger's point about listeners considering themselves as "being there" is surely very much to the point, as is his stress on the goal of rendering Christ present "here" in the heart of the believer. But what Berger gives with one hand he takes away with another. In his keenness to evacuate time of any ultimate theological significance, in true idealist fashion he seems to assume the significance of the Passion story can be extracted from its embeddedness in concrete happenings in time, which *as such* constitute a promise for a comprehensive New Creation. This privileges a contemplative posture rather than one in which the believer participates in the temporally extended redemption of created reality, enacted and embodied in Christ.

Suppose we refuse these assumptions, however, and adopt a theology of time and eternity more in tune with Bauckham's? In that case, instead of pre-

---

Preussischer Kulturbesitz (1996): 41–51. It is worth recalling that Bach himself knew death at close quarters, not least in his own family: both his parents died when he was nine, his first wife died when he was thirty-five, and he outlived eleven of his own children. (I owe this reminder to Dr Stephen Crist.)

33. See, e.g., Cantatas 8, 27, 60, 72, 82, 95, 125, 156, 157, 161. On Bach and death, see Richard J. Plantinga, "The Integration of Music and Theology in the Vocal Compositions of J. S. Bach," in *Resonant Witness: Conversations between Music and Theology*, ed. Jeremy S. Begbie and Steven R. Guthrie (Grand Rapids: Eerdmans, 2011), 215–39. Leaver, "Eschatology, Theology and Music." For a detailed examination of Cantata 60, "O eternity, you word of thunder," see Chafe, *Analyzing Bach Cantatas*, ch. 9; Robert E. A. Lee, "Bach's Living Music of Death," *Dialog: A Journal of Theology* 24, no. 2 (1985): 102–6.

34. Berger, *Bach's Cycle, Mozart's Arrow*, 117.

suming that in the "contemplative" sections of the *St Matthew Passion* we are being offered a "timeless" perspective on the Passion story, geared toward our eventual removal from temporality, we might rather presume we are being called to see ourselves "there," and to be inwardly transformed now, in order that we might view these events from the perspective of God's historically embedded purposes for humankind into which we are being invited, and which will reach their ultimate fulfillment in the new creation. In this scenario, God, in and through Jesus Christ, grants us a glimpse *from within time* of his intentions for the entirety of creation's time-span, intentions into which he longs to draw us, temporally and concretely. Or, to put it differently, we are indeed enabled to participate in eternity, through Christ the Son of the Father who lives in us by and through his Spirit, but *only as creatures*, which is to say, never in a way that removes us from our temporality.[35] We cannot of course prove this was the way Bach was conceiving things, but there is nothing to preclude the possibility, and much to support it.

Music's Own Witness

We have been concentrating on texts. What can we say about the way in which Bach's music might, or might not, participate in these theological dynamics? Space forbids a detailed case—a few pointers will have to suffice.

A useful starting point is John Butt's gentle distancing of himself from Berger in his recent and closely argued book *Bach's Dialogue with Modernity*.[36] We have seen how Berger interprets Bach's musical procedures as tending heavily toward the cyclic, in contrast with what he sees as the directional and linear inclinations of modernity's temporality. Butt concedes that in the course of the late eighteenth and nineteenth centuries, the temporal order of

---

35. John Butt takes issue with Berger on the place of the contemplators in the *St Matthew Passion*. He wants to see them belonging "very much to our world," not as part of the world represented by the Passion setting. Butt, *Bach's Dialogue with Modernity*, 38. Butt stresses that from the Lutheran perspective, the function of the Passion is to help generate an experience *in the present* of Christ in our hearts. "To see the two worlds [of personages in the story and contemplators] merely as one *representation* . . . would suggest that the listener is necessarily separate from the performance and thus, to some degree, passive." Butt thus prefers to see the contemplators standing primarily in *our* time, with us and not as part of the one representation of the story. Butt, *Bach's Dialogue with Modernity*, 38n7.

36. Butt, *Bach's Dialogue with Modernity*, 109–11. Hereafter, page references from this work are given in parentheses in the text.

musical events became far more crucial than it ever was for Bach. Nonetheless, he wants to see Bach as standing "on the cusp of musical modernity" (109), combining repetitive, symmetrical components with directionality (albeit to different degrees in different pieces), thus mingling premodern and modern sensibilities. With regard to the *St Matthew Passion*, while acknowledging its symmetries, Butt claims that the sense of "linear, passing time" (106) is in fact vivid and pronounced here, much more so than in the *St John Passion*. There is an "overwhelming sense of change" (107) and a recognition of the uniqueness of its critical narrative events, many of which are portrayed as effecting subsequent change. Butt underlines the opening movement's heterogeny and discontinuities, and argues that its ritornello is strikingly open-ended both harmonically and melodically (66-67, 101-2). Indeed the entire *Passion* is "lacking tonal closure . . . the work somehow craves completion beyond its own span" (100). Even in the more symmetry-laden *St John Passion*, Bach balances "repetitively ordered (or symmetrical) elements with a sense of musical direction" (109). And speaking of sections of the *Mass in B Minor*, Butt comments:

> Bach has given us a sense of symmetrical circular time simultaneously with a linear or progressive quality. The Bachian sense of time demands progress within stability, a dynamic approach to cyclic time that evokes something of the energy of a spiral. (110)[37]

These specifically musical observations suggest a far subtler and more interesting theological scenario than that suggested by Berger, and with respect to time and eternity, one that can be read in many respects as far more suggestive of Bauckham. If Butt is along the right lines, Bach's musical treatment of the *St Matthew Passion* narrative, with its directionality infused with repetition (or repetition infused with directionality), is highly congruent with viewing these happenings as the expression of a purposeful, time-implicated interaction of God's eternity with human history. The features that Butt highlights—consistency interlaced with directionality, unique interruptions that issue in fruitful change, an irreducible open-endedness that resists tidy closure—are hardly unfamiliar to an informed scholar of the Passion narratives, and not foreign to a vision of human history as being drawn toward its fulfill-

---

37. Of the *Goldberg Variations* Butt notes the presence of "a sense of recurrence that could go on *ad infinitum*, but it is one in which things are somehow different at each recurrence" (109).

ment by a God of faithfulness, the God of Jesus Christ crucified and risen, a fulfillment that this world cannot of itself generate.

Could this music's "open-endedness" provoke us to go further? If what has been embodied in the history of Jesus Christ, and our participation in him, is itself an anticipation of the eschaton, would it be out of place to ask if we might hear some characteristics of Bach's music as evocations of the new creation? Great care is needed here lest we fall into undisciplined hyperbole. But the question is at least worth asking. We can cite our earlier comments on novelty and change. Envisaging the taking up of created time into God's eternity may well indeed stretch the human imagination to breaking point, but, as we noted in connection with Bauckham's work, it is not clear that we are required to exclude the possibility of change in the eschaton altogether. Tentatively, we could speak not of change from imperfect to perfect but from one degree or form of perfection to another. So David Bentley Hart can write: "Christian eschatology promises only more and greater harmony, whose developments, embellishments, and movement never end and never 'return' to a state more original than music."[38] Or, in Anthony Thiselton's words, "To pass *from glory to glory* would not be an eternal *fortissimo*, but a crescendo of wonder and praise."[39] It is intriguing that both these writers resort to musical metaphors. If we are hesitantly and reverently to speak of temporality in the new creation, it would have to be of a sort in which the dynamic was one of addition without loss, expansion without diminution, yet utterly consistent, never arbitrary, always resisting static completeness; and it is just this which scholars such as Butt have drawn attention to in much of Bach's music.[40] In the *Mass in B Minor*, when Bach evokes the life of the world to come ("Et expecto resurrectionem mortuorum"), he does so by throwing us into an irrepressible dance—the corrupt body is liberated at last. Furthermore, contrary to images of the new creation that would portray it as a place of dull singularity,

---

38. David Bentley Hart, *The Beauty of the Infinite: The Aesthetics of Christian Truth* (Grand Rapids: Eerdmans, 2003), 284.

39. Anthony C. Thiselton, *The Hermeneutics of Doctrine* (Grand Rapids: Eerdmans, 2007), 578.

40. In addition to the Butt citations above, see Peter F. Williams, *Bach: The Goldberg Variations* (Cambridge: Cambridge University Press, 2001), 45–46. The dynamic includes constraint and contingency in contrast, interplay and mutual enhancement. Indeed, much of Bach's music sounds improvised. This was one of the things about Bach which so intrigued the nineteenth-century composer and virtuoso Franz Liszt (1811–1886)—who himself transcribed and arranged many of Bach's works—and which captivates many jazz musicians. (It is no accident that Bach was a superb improviser.)

when Bach concludes the vast *Mass* with "Dona Nobis Pacem," we are offered a peace indeed, but one of abundant musical lines, multiply superimposed and overlapping, tumbling over each other as the counterpoint expands, a spatially and temporally structured space, certainly, but one that is yet strangely uncontainable—the multidimensional and ever-widening *shalom* toward which all things are being directed by God's eternity. Needless to say, such a differentiated vision makes considerably more sense if we are prepared to forgo a nameless, bland, unitarian eternity and allow differentiation to characterize the divine life: only a trinitarian eternity makes sense of Bach.

Conclusion

My argument is certainly not that Bach's work reflects something akin to a perfectly rounded comprehensive theology of time and eternity (whatever that might be). Indeed, some will find his particular tradition of Lutheranism wanting in a number of respects.[41] Our argument has been more modest, namely that once we are freed from certain common but questionable assumptions about time and eternity in the Christian tradition (questionable, that is, if this tradition wishes to look to scriptural texts as normative), and begin to adopt the kind of Christologically shaped and biblically grounded perspective clarified by Bauckham and others, we will discover rather more in Bach's output than we might have first supposed was there, a greater richness in both text and music, and indeed, extraordinary resources for exploring and explicating such a vision in our own day.

A wider implication is worth noting. Despite the extreme suspicion of Christian faith that pervades some academic circles, in certain fields of cultural study, especially where Christian themes are overt and unavoidable (such as the study of Bach), it is obviously imperative that the scholar's grasp of the Christian tradition is commensurate with the subtlety and depth of the material being handled. Some treatments of Bach are exemplary in this respect, some are not. Richard Bauckham's work represents a type of scholarship—all too rare—that can prove invaluable in the attempt to achieve just this subtlety and depth, as I hope we have amply demonstrated.

---

41. One might have wished for a clearer recognition of the inherent goodness of time, a greater stress on God's purposes for creation as a whole. Some will also point to an undue stress on the dynamics of the individual soul and an underdeveloped theology of the Spirit.

Parmenides, Particularity, and *Parousia*: Identifying the One Who Will Come to Judge the Living and the Dead

Trevor Hart

In this essay I hope to accomplish at least two things: first, to bring together some of the theological concerns identifiable in Richard Bauckham's work over the years, and, in doing so, to draw renewed attention to a short article ("Christology Today") published in the South African journal *Scriptura* in 1988.[1] Though it is relatively little known, I have always found this article particularly helpful and suggestive, and have both recommended it to students and returned to it myself on numerous occasions over the years. Some of the themes and ideas explored in it, such as the centrality to its argument of the categories of identity, identification with, and identification as, have duly been taken up and taken further in later publications such as *God Crucified* and *Jesus and the God of Israel*.[2] Others remain as yet to be worked out at comparable length,

---

1. Richard Bauckham, "Christology Today," *Scriptura* 27 (1988): 20–28.
2. The careful use of the category of "identity" in discussions of Christology in preference both to the classical language of "substance" and "persons" and to the long-established distinction typically drawn between "ontological" and "functional" Christologies by New Testament scholars is one of the distinctives of Bauckham's work over the past twenty years. It has successfully recast the terms in which Christological questions may helpfully be asked and answered, and opened up new possibilities for serious conversation between biblical and systematic theology, not least by contradicting the assumption that "high" dogmatic Christology was something that only eventually emerged (legitimately or otherwise) from a "low" biblical starting point. While the immediate concerns of the earlier piece are different ones ("to bring together constructively . . . a concern about the meaning of the doctrine of the incarnation . . . and a concern to put the praxis of the historical Jesus back at the centre of Christology"), the categorical precursor to such use is already to be found in its central thesis that, in Jesus's identification of himself with the Father's will and his concrete identification with the plight

hopefully in the years of productivity still to be looked forward to. At the heart of the piece lies a characteristic upending of the assumptions in terms of which a familiar philosophical and theological problem is typically cast; namely, the relationship (typically construed as a dialectic) between the universal and the particular, especially as that plays out in Christology and soteriology in one form or another of the so-called "scandal" of particularity. It is with this cluster of issues, albeit approached for the moment from a slightly different angle, that I begin.

1. Between Parmenides and Plurality— Pursuing a Community of the Different

In his 1992 Bampton Lectures Colin Gunton observes that the question of the one and the many, the universal and the particular, "takes us to the very beginnings of philosophy and theology" and unites the concerns of ancient human wisdom with those of the modern and postmodern condition.[3] These concerns themselves, Gunton suggests (with his tongue only lightly lodged in his cheek), are thus at least recurrent if not universal in the history of human thought, though, irritatingly, of course they arise in a host of different particular forms. Among the recurrent features seemingly essential to the debate is a tendency to view universality on the one hand and particularity on the other as opposing principles in an unstable dialectic constantly threatening to resolve itself unhelpfully so as to privilege one term (by bestowing upon it logical and ontological priority) to the inevitable detriment of the other. Gunton adopts the pre-Socratic monism of Parmenides (for whom "what is" is timeless, uniform, necessary, and unchanging) as a convenient figure representing philosophies tending finally toward a "homogenizing abolition of particularity" (a tendency Gunton finds prevalent in much post-Enlightenment modern thought),[4] while Parmenides's contemporary Heraclitus, taking his stand resolutely in the flowing waters and slippery banks of plurality and flux, serves as the champion (if not the essence, since that would be self-referentially incoherent) of the radically plural and the particular, and thus the patron saint

---

of other people, God "identifies himself in identifying with us." Bauckham, "Christology Today," 20, 25.

3. Colin E. Gunton, *The One, the Three and the Many: God, Creation and the Culture of Modernity* (Cambridge: Cambridge University Press, 1993), 17.

4. Gunton, *The One, the Three and the Many*, 46.

of postmodernity. The seemingly ethereal questions of ontology and theology from which discussions about such things take their bearings and to which they finally return are, nonetheless, Gunton notes, bound up with very down-to-earth and practical considerations, such as the quest for rationality and meaning, and the desire to negotiate the peaceful ordering of human relationships.[5]

If we turn to Christian theology in particular, then here too we find that questions about universality and particularity, sameness and difference, what is shared and what sets things and people apart from one another, arise and solicit answers from us at almost every turn. They are to be found, for instance, at the heart of the doctrine of creation, which both posits a vital relationship between God and the world while yet, through the asymmetry of that relationship, setting God equally clearly apart from the world as its uncreated source, and thus radically and uniquely "other." Such questions are fundamental, too, of course, to the grammar of Christology, and its attempts to parse the claim that in Jesus of Nazareth the eternal Word or Son has taken flesh and become a man. In the Christologies of the Nicene and Chalcedonian formularies just as surely as in the *prima facie* blasphemous biblical conjunction of a particular human life with the identity, presence, authority, and action of the Holy One of Israel, it is precisely questions about sameness and difference, unity and distinction, universality and particularity, the one and the many, that are at stake. And here, too, questions of such enormous metaphysical import are finally inseparable from questions of praxis, and thus of a distinctly Christian way of modelling human community (i.e., one earthed in, growing naturally out of, and reflecting the answers we give to such questions about reality's ultimate provenance, nature, and destiny in the hands of the God we know as the Father of Jesus Christ).

For the sake of argument, one might summarize the character of authentic Christian community—modelled in the church not just *ad intra* but *ad extra* too in its ways of *being* the church in the midst of the world for the sake of which it exists—as one marked by an unconditional respect and love for the other as other, by becoming what Jürgen Moltmann calls a "community of the different."[6] Of course, difference obtains at various levels of personal existence—between individuals, between social and economic groups, between

---

5. Gunton, *The One, the Three and the Many*, 21.
6. See "The Knowing of the Other and the Community of the Different" in Jürgen Moltmann, *God for a Secular Society: The Public Relevance of Theology* (Minneapolis: Fortress, 1999), 135–52. Bauckham's engagement with Moltmann's work over several decades makes the latter a particularly appropriate resource to draw upon at this point.

nations, between ethnic groups, between religions, between civilizations, and so on. It all depends where we choose to draw the relevant boundaries.[7] And we must avoid reifying or absolutizing difference in unhealthy or dangerous ways. The idea of that which is "other" is susceptible to all manner of abuse socially and politically. As a social construct, "otherness" has much to answer for in the long history of man's inhumanity to man, being grist to the mill of every form of tribalism.[8] So, for a Christian, acknowledgment of the genuine and significant differences that do exist must always take place within the context of a countervailing recognition of what is held in common (even when this cannot always easily be specified), and the recognition of the "other" first and foremost as a fellow human being made in the image and likeness of God and heir to the covenant promises of God. Yet the danger exists, too, of failing to respect the particularity of others, of a "homogenizing abolition of particularity" that either seeks to marginalize the things others hold dear in the interests of a peaceful coexistence, or else demands that they abandon them and become like us as the condition of their acceptance. This, too, Moltmann argues, is an error Christians must avoid.

In his essay "The Knowing of the Other and the Community of the Different," Moltmann identifies both of these errors as products of the ancient epistemic principle that "like is only truly known by like," which he traces back to Aristotle's *Metaphysics* (II, 4, 1000b) and dubs the "principle of analogy." In this case, he observes, what is genuinely other cannot be known at all, and our acquisition of knowledge about the world, the other person, or God himself amounts only to "the continually reiterated self-endorsement of what is already

---

7. As Paul Ricoeur observes in his 1991 Gifford Lectures, the phenomenology of everyday experience suggests that each of us actually encounters "otherness" *within ourselves* too, a point drawn attention to by habits of speech in which, without any apparent sense of risk, we straddle ourselves awkwardly in syntax between grammatical subject and object—in such phrases as "I look after myself," "She caught herself staring at him," and so on. French, Ricoeur reminds us, admits this internal opposition more consistently through its widespread use of pronominal verbs (conjugated by prefixing the reflexive pronoun *se* to the infinitive form—*Elle se promène, Tu te baigne, Nous nous habillons*, etc.). Paul Ricoeur, *Oneself as Another* (Chicago: University of Chicago Press, 1992). Ricoeur's discussion of the nature of personal identity in this work, his development of the distinction between *idem-* and *ipse-* identity, and of categories as "identification as" and "identification with" seems likely to have fed constructively into Bauckham's own distinctive appropriation and development of the terms in his writings since the 1996 Didsbury Lectures, duly published as *God Crucified* in 1998.

8. For a discussion of the nature of identity and the origins of contemporary concern with it, see helpfully Zygmunt Bauman, *Identity: Conversations with Benedetto Vecchi* (Cambridge: Polity Press, 2004).

known."⁹ As regards knowledge of God, Moltmann observes, this principle necessarily supposes that the human self is in some sense already "divine," otherwise it could not recognize that divine reality which transcends it.¹⁰ It is thus constantly prone either to the deification of the human knower or the reduction of God to a projection of the creaturely imagination. In personal, social, and political terms, the conviction that "like is only known by like" tends to be either indifferent toward or anxious about that which is different (and thus forever alien) in the other, rather than curious about or fascinated by it. It typically seeks to neutralize and domesticate otherness, either by force (some version of exclusion, colonialism, or globalization), or by the more humane but equally disrespectful mechanisms of a "dialogue" intended to establish a shared denominator of human experience and outlook as "what really matters," and to secure homogeneous cultural expressions of the same, thus marginalizing and belittling the very things that grant particular identities their value and color.¹¹

The second principle Moltmann identifies is that according to which "other is only truly known by other" (the "principle of dialectic"), a model he also credits to Greek philosophy (Euripides, Anaxagoras), but for which he finds significant theological grounds in the dialectical relationship that occurs in communion between ourselves and the God who is Wholly Other. We might add—though Moltmann does not in this context—the distinctly Christian conviction that in God himself there is eternal communion between three persons constituted as much by their differences from one another as by their sharing of a single nature. Triunity, in other words, is at one level an exemplification of communion evinced and constituted in genuine diversity, albeit one only analogously related to the creaturely circumstance. Where creatures (and fallen creatures at that) are concerned, Moltmann notes, our initial experience of that which is different, strange, or new is one of resistance to the self and attendant pain or suffering caused. Genuine otherness is discerned by way of contradiction and contrast rather than correspondence, and we quickly sense "the claim of the new" and our need to accommodate it or adjust ourselves

---

9. Moltmann, *God for a Secular Society*, 139.
10. Moltmann, *God for a Secular Society*, 140.
11. It might also be noted that such putative "shared" perspectives frequently end up looking very much like an assemblage of fundamental and particular convictions held by the dominant party or power group within the plural exchange, and thus amount in reality to a form of colonialism by stealth. Genuinely shared territories of meaning can only be established or identified when all the differences that divide are taken fully into consideration and allowed full play, and not despite these.

accordingly.¹² The point here, of course, is precisely that knowledge of difference and knowledge of self/same arise together and dialectically. Knowing ourselves, we are able readily to identify that which differs from and resists ourselves, and become curious and wonder about the contours of its otherness. "I can only understand (what is other)," Moltmann writes, "by changing myself, and adjusting myself to it. In my perception of others I subject myself to the pains and joys of my own alteration, not in order to adapt myself to the other, but in order to enter into it."¹³ It is by way of such willing subjection and the imaginative transcendence of the established boundaries of "self" alone that genuine community rather than artificial homogeneity can be established and sustained. Thus, universal and particular, sameness and difference, arise here not in a self-destructive tension but in a mutually defining and mutually enriching, albeit costly, interplay.¹⁴

2. Scandalous Particularity—Jesus and the Self-Identification of God

In "Christology Today" Bauckham traces parallels and resonances with all this not in the doctrine of God as such, but in Christology and its wrestling with the question of how the historical Jesus can be identifiable as the One who made and sustains all things in heaven and earth, and how the accidents of his particular life and death and resurrection can be of universal redemptive significance. On the one hand, in "taking flesh" and sharing creatureliness with us, the Son of God held in common with us all that is shared in our human "nature" and existence, thus identifying himself with us. Yet, since humanity does not exist as an abstraction but only in the form of particular human lives lived, this same Son of God embraced to the full the contingency of historical existence, becoming the particular man Jesus of whose actions, words, and suffering the gospels are concerned to tell us.

It is precisely in this latter acknowledgment or insistence, though, that various strands of modern Christology have identified a problem for soteriology, generating different versions of a scandal of particularity. One prominent strand of this presupposes something very like what Moltmann identifies as the Aristotelian "principle of analogy," insisting now that "like can only

12. Moltmann, *God for a Secular Society*, 144.
13. Moltmann, *God for a Secular Society*, 145.
14. For a more developed consideration of the issues treated in this section see Trevor Hart, "Conversation after Pentecost? Theological Musings on the Hermeneutic Motion," in *Literature and Theology* 28, no. 2 (June 2014): 164–78.

Parmenides, Particularity, and Parousia

be *saved* by like." A forthright and persuasive statement of the case that particularity (or "difference") is corrosive of Jesus's universal redemptive significance in this way is found, for instance, in its (post-Christian) feminist version in the writings of Daphne Hampson.[15] For Hampson, unsurprisingly, it is Jesus's maleness—the fact that the incarnation necessarily entails gender specificity—that is the problem. The claim that God has entered the stream of human history as a man, she argues, is by definition at odds with the other claim Christians typically make, namely, that in his redemptive significance Christ is inclusive of all humans.[16] On the contrary, Hampson insists, a God who, in becoming flesh uniquely, actually becomes *male* flesh, entails the unique symbolizing of God in a manner suggesting that maleness is identifiable with God in a way that femaleness is not, thereby preventing women from ever finding themselves in God in the way that men now can and might be encouraged to. Hampson traces to this singular fact the whole history of western religious thought (and much of western culture in its wake) as "ideologically loaded against women."[17] Considered on its own terms, Hampson's case is robust and well made; though, as Bauckham points out, maleness is only one significant marker of difference among humans, and there is no reason why, in our plural and postmodern context, parallel cases might not be made by others on the grounds of race/culture, marital status, age and breadth of life experience, economic status, the fact that (so far as we know) Jesus had to endure no physical or mental disability, and so on.[18] In each case it might be argued by some that, precisely because Jesus was "different" to them in one way or another he could have no ultimate religious significance for them.[19] Indeed, since no human life is ever wholly like another, the logical *reductio ad absurdum* of the case would be the denial that a genuine human life (i.e., one lived in all the unique particularity that in reality marks *every* human life out as different from any other) could ever be redemptively significant for any other, let alone for all.

What makes Hampson's case persuasive (though not immune from sus-

---

15. For what follows see especially Daphne Hampson, *Theology and Feminism* (Oxford: Blackwell, 1990), 50–80.

16. Strictly speaking, therefore, it is specificity rather than maleness here that is the problem for Hampson. Though she does not say so, the drift and terms of her argument would have to apply equally had God become a woman.

17. Hampson, *Theology and Feminism*, 51.

18. Bauckham, "Christology Today," 22–23.

19. N.B., Hampson acknowledges that, for example, a similar case might be made by Gentiles on the basis of Jesus's Jewishness. See Hampson, *Theology and Feminism*, 55.

ceptibility to the *reductio* alluded to above) is the extent to which she engages directly with Christian attempts to address this perceived problem. In particular, she attends closely and carefully to the development of patristic Christologies which attempt to do precisely this, and finally finds them wanting for reasons Bauckham himself in part shares.[20] The patristic theologians, Hampson notes, recognized that human difference in the context of an incarnational Christology was intrinsically problematic for soteriology, and sought to address it. Precisely because (in the familiar terms coined by the Cappadocians) "What is not assumed is not healed," theologians from Irenaeus onward sought to maximize and to draw attention to the levels of *likeness* between the incarnate Son and those he came to save. This led most notably to their insistence that what mattered soteriologically (and, by association, Christologically) was the fact that in Christ God took upon himself our common human "flesh" (the "human nature" in which, regardless of our gender, we all share) and redeemed it. Thus, considerations of a more particular sort can be set aside (deliberately or tacitly) as Christologically and soteriologically *adiaphora*. Jesus's Jewishness, his masculinity, his having lived for only thirty or so and not eighty years, his lack of experience of married life or of being a parent, or of being demon-possessed, and so on—all of this can be safely acknowledged, leaving his salvific significance "for all" essentially unscathed.[21] Because what he did "for all" was done precisely at the level of what the "all" in question have in common—viz., our shared "human nature" in which he suffered and died and rose again.[22]

20. Hampson, *Theology and Feminism*, 53–58.

21. It is clear, though, that Irenaeus continues to feel the force of the sort of problem Hampson poses; thus his rather awkward insistence that, in order to sanctify all people regardless of their age, the Son of God became an infant in order to sanctify infants, a child for children, a youth for youths, and "an old man for old men" (*Against Heresies*, 2.22.4). Why particularity of age should be reckoned significant and other dimensions of human particularity (gender, race, etc.) not so is an avenue that Irenaeus (perhaps wisely) leaves unexplored.

22. Although Hampson does not draw attention to the fact, most of the fathers place due weight on the events of Jesus's passion and resurrection which, they insist, he endured and experienced "in our nature" and thus "for us." Some, following Irenaeus (and the New Testament), also place considerable weight on the importance of Jesus's obedience to the Father as displacing our disobedience in fashioning a "new humanity." These, though, tend to be addressed precisely as qualities of a shared human condition, empirical and promised. Other events in Jesus's history—particular things he did, conversations he had with others, ways in which he was treated by his friends and his enemies, his responses to those who encountered him, and so on (i.e., the very things of which, notwithstanding the weight afforded to the passion narratives, the canonical gospels largely consist)—tend to fall into the background of consideration for soteriological and Christological purposes.

Parmenides, Particularity, and Parousia

Having reckoned fully with this attempt to redress the scandal of particularity, Hampson finally rejects it. Her reasons for doing so are, chiefly, its alleged reliance on a Platonic philosophical notion of "universals" which modern (and postmodern) humans can no longer take seriously.[23] In doing so it plays down the importance of particularity and specificity in a manner that is no longer tolerable. Bauckham, too, demurs from the emphasis of much patristic Christology on relatively abstract notions of humanity, but his reasons for doing so are more solidly theological. Whatever their merits, he insists, there can be little warrant in theological terms for stripping Christology of so much of what the New Testament is concerned to tell us about Jesus, in effect overlooking the particularity of the Jesus whose ministry is related in the gospels, and moving quickly to a much more abstract theological principle concerned with "natures" and the mode of their hypostatic union.

The reason that Hampson can spend so long sympathetically entertaining the Christological views of the church fathers, it seems, is that she shares with them the same basic soteriological premise: viz., that in the final instance "like can only be saved by like," and that human particularity is therefore a significant stumbling block rather than a positive consideration in the attempt to develop an account of the universal relevance of the incarnation. Yet it is precisely this premise that Bauckham is concerned to reject. If we abandon the tenuous supposition that the redemptive significance of Jesus for each of us consists only (or even primarily) in whatever we happen to hold in common with him and he with us, he argues, then a wholly new Christological and soteriological vista opens up for our consideration and exploration.

Instead, Bauckham maintains, it is by virtue of a complex *interplay* of sameness and otherness that Jesus's redemptive being and action is realized, his "universal" saving significance being bound up just as thoroughly with the particular and peculiar things he is reported to have said and done and suffered as it is with his assumption of "humanity" and sharing of "the human condition." Thus it is precisely the shape of Jesus's character and personhood (whether encountered in first-century Palestine in the flesh or through the narration of his story in the church today) which, as it interacts with others,

---

23. Significantly, suffering and death are, among those experiences available to humanity, some of those most resistant to postmodern skepticism about a "shared human condition." As Terry Eagleton notes, we all die. "It is, to be sure," he writes, "a consoling thought for pluralists that we meet our end in such a richly diverse series of ways, that our modes of exiting from existence are so splendidly heterogeneous, that there is no drearily essentialist 'death' but a diffuse range of cultural styles of expiring. . . . But we die anyway." Terry Eagleton, *Sweet Violence: The Idea of the Tragic* (Oxford: Blackwell, 2003), xiii.

transforms them redemptively; and the form of his identification with some (the poor and the downtrodden) will differ significantly from his identification with others (the Pharisees and teachers of the law), because their particularity is respected rather than marginalized, and demands a wholly different response and relationship from the particular person Jesus himself is. In Jesus, Bauckham insists, the universal Lord identifies himself with humankind not in some homogenous or abstract manner that robs both him and us of the very particulars that make us each who we are, but in the particular form of Jesus of Nazareth whose story intersects and interferes with our particular stories in a plethora of different possible ways and combinations, each redemptive, but each equally distinctive. Thus God's solidarity with us is not that of a symbolic Everyperson, but precisely a "differential solidarity," global in its reach, but infinitely variegated in its precise configurations, a solidarity "with people not only in the common human condition" as Christology is sometimes prone to suggest, "but with people in all the varieties of the human condition." Again, sameness and difference, universality and particularity, are here not locked in mortal combat with one another, their respective concerns to be secured only despite one another, but instead belong together in a fruitful if at times complex and costly give-and-take.

Notice that, here, the concerns of two distinct strands of contemporary Christological reflection are held together and seen properly to belong together rather than pulling in different directions. On the one hand, a concern to reclaim and make sense of the heritage of creedal profession of the incarnation of God's eternal Son, and on the other an insistence that we do justice to the specifics of Jesus's particular history as narrated in the gospel traditions. So, Christologies "from above" and "from below" as they have often been dubbed prove not to be feasible as opposites at all, but only as emphases that require and complete one another within a more unified scheme of things. The one who comes to us from above is never known or knowable to us as a *logos asarkos*, but only as one clothed in the contingencies of a particular historical existence, while the story of the man Jesus has universal redemptive significance (or for that matter *any* significance for us other than as a historical curio) precisely and only because it is held to be the concrete form of God's own self-identification in the world. Matters of epistemology and soteriology stand and fall together here, since it is precisely the particular form of God's self-identifying that cuts across our existence with redemptive effect, banishing the idols that religious imagination so readily sets up, and, by showing us the Father's heart of holy love, drawing us back from our alienated state to receive our adoption as forgiven sons and daughters.

Parmenides, Particularity, and Parousia

Of course, the incarnation does not reduce God to this particular form; God remains mysterious and beyond the grasp of our thought and speech even in the midst of his self-identifying; but here, God also "comes out of his mystery and gives himself a particular this-worldly identity by which we may identify him,"[24] thus meeting the fundamental religious need to specify who God is, and to form a concrete image of him. This insistence provides a helpful corrective to crypto-Hegelian suspicion of the economy of the image as such in Christology, such as T. F. Torrance's insistence that all images must properly give way in theology to an "imageless" relation secured by the superior mediation of our knowing by "pure concepts."[25] Visibility of sorts is, whether we like it or not, one of the characteristics of the flesh and of our embeddedness as creatures in the world of the senses, and we cannot strip it away to the point where it ceases to be noticed (becoming, as it were, not just transparent and translucent as a mediator of the divine reality, but in effect *invisible*) without removing it altogether, thereby effectively reversing the direction and the accomplishment of the incarnation and God's accommodation to our epistemic condition. Again, God is not reduced to the form of Jesus's humanity; but if our knowing of God is always about more than the human Jesus alone, it is never about anything less, and the extent to which it drifts free of its moorings there is the extent to which it is in danger of either agnosticism or the sort of sheer imaginative construction that was Feuerbach's diagnosis of the whole religious and theological enterprise.[26] The doctrines of the resurrection and the ascension are our theological warrant for insisting that the humanity of Jesus remains theologically basic rather than a fleeting flirtation with the flesh to be transcended both by Christ and by us as we ascend instead to some fleshless and timeless sphere of forms. That, surely, is one of the most basic differences between a Christian account of reality and any one of those derived variously from the philosophy of Plato. And, to reiterate the point, the humanity of Jesus we are talking about is no bloodless abstraction, but the historically particular flesh-and-blood individual who lived and died and rose from the

24. Bauckham, "Christology Today," 24.
25. See, e.g., Thomas F. Torrance, *Theology in Reconstruction* (London: SCM, 1965), 20; Thomas F. Torrance, *Theological Science* (London: Oxford University Press, 1969), 20; Thomas F. Torrance, *God and Rationality* (London: Oxford University Press, 1971), 23. For a full development of the point (and a more measured account of Torrance's case than is possible here) see Trevor Hart, *Between the Image and the Word: Theological Engagements with Imagination, Language and Literature* (Farnham, UK: Ashgate, 2013), 13–42.
26. Ludwig Feuerbach, *The Essence of Christianity* (*Das Wesen des Christentums*, 3rd ed., 1849), trans. George Eliot (London: Kegan Paul, Trench, Trübner & Co., 1893).

tomb somewhere around 33 CE in Palestine. Whatever sense we make of this, it is precisely *this* that we must make sense of, and not something else.

It should not be supposed, though, that Bauckham dismisses the importance of Christological and soteriological claims directed toward what is shared among human beings, and thus between Christ and those for whom he is held to be salvifically significant. Indeed, Bauckham takes the apostle Paul's concentration on Jesus's death on the cross as "the ancestor of all those atonement doctrines which find Jesus's universality in his relevance to the human condition as such" (i.e., our shared subjection to sin and condemnation, and our need of forgiveness and reconciliation to God).[27] But while this may be important, it is not the whole truth with which soteriology must grapple. Put bluntly, "we are all sinners in different ways,"[28] and an adequate soteriology must get to grips too with the particularities of *our* lives, and the ways in which Christ is religiously significant for those. And it is precisely here, Bauckham argues, that the particularities of Jesus's humanity as transmitted to us in the gospel accounts can and must be brought fully into play. Appealing again to the categories of narrative as a way of speaking both about Jesus's particular identity (and of God's self-identification in him) and of our identities, he thus insists that there are both points at which "Jesus' story intersects every other human story in the same way" and others (an infinitely varied number) where his story and ours intersect uniquely, being the interplay of one unsubstitutable human identity with another.[29] Jesus's "identification with" us, in other words, involves both an engagement of like with like *and* an equally vital play of difference with difference. And within this salvific play of difference, Bauckham observes suggestively, it is both the radical particularity of the Jesus of the gospels that cuts across ours redemptively (uttering words of judgment, or encouragement, or healing, or forgiveness, or whatever the particular manifestation of sin in our lives might demand) and his identification and solidarity with those who are very different to ourselves. Thus, "[w]hen American black theologians began to claim that 'Jesus is black'— which I have suggested can be understood as 'black by identification'—they did not, if I have understood them, mean only that Jesus is black for blacks. Jesus is also black for whites—just as, for the Pharisees, Jesus was identified with tax-collectors and sinners. They could, as it were, only know his solidarity with themselves via his solidarity with the people they excluded."[30]

27. Bauckham, "Christology Today," 26.
28. Bauckham, "Christology Today," 26.
29. Bauckham, "Christology Today," 25.
30. Bauckham, "Christology Today," 28.

3. Ascension, *Parousia*, and Eschatological Imagination

Insofar as our salvation is contingent upon an encounter with the particularity of Jesus, of course, it quickly presents yet another version of the scandal of particularity. Bauckham insists that "Jesus is God's loving identification with all humanity" which is, as such, "in principle unlimited and potentially universalizable."[31] If, though, this loving identification is mediated uniquely through the particular history of Jesus, if Jesus is, as Bauckham puts it, "God's own particular, this worldly identity, and so . . . the form in which God can be encountered and known,"[32] then a question quickly arises about the *de facto* rather than the *de jure* scope of such redemptive encounter. *Prima facie*, as Bauckham himself notes, such encounter is in one sense limited to the circle of Jesus's empirical human acquaintance, i.e., "the actual men and women Jesus encountered in his earthly life."[33] Bauckham's appeal at this point to a version of narrative theology (Jesus's particular identity, which is the form of God's self-identification with us and for us, is subsequently narrated in Scripture and thence in the teaching, preaching, and other proclamation of the church[34]) certainly widens the scope of the circle considerably, but does not yet universalize it. It continues to exclude all those (doubtless increasingly few today, but across the history of humankind as a whole surely the vast majority?) who have never heard the story. It was this problem of "epistemic particularism" and its apparent soteriological implications that motivated John Hick and others in the 1970s gradually to abandon the doctrine of the incarnation, conveniently discovering its origins as a "myth" separable from the redemptive significance of Jesus, and identifying the latter in generic and universalizable religious considerations that could be abstracted from the body of Jesus's recorded teachings and example just as surely as the notion of "human nature" had earlier been abstracted from the more complex contours of biblical Christology as a whole.[35] More theologically orthodox responses to the circumstance have also tended to move quickly from the complexities and contin-

---

31. Bauckham, "Christology Today," 21–22.
32. Bauckham, "Christology Today," 24.
33. Bauckham, "Christology Today," 21.
34. It is, of course, through an encounter with the Risen Christ that this occurs, but it occurs nonetheless through our engagement with the particulars of his human story, and not otherwise. See Bauckham, "Christology Today," 25.
35. See, e.g., John Hick, *God and the Universe of Faiths: Essays in the Philosophy of Religion* (London: Macmillan, 1973), ch. 9; John Hick, ed., *The Myth of God Incarnate* (London: SCM, 1977), ch. 9.

gencies of Jesus's life and ours to embrace a drama seemingly conducted at a higher level and, in practice, over our heads. So, for instance, Vernon White argues boldly for an atonement conducted by the incarnate Son objectively "for us," our inclusion in which does not demand any knowledge on our part of the drama having occurred, let alone of the details of Jesus's life and ministry.[36] No matter how helpful and rich many of the things White's argument affirms may be as versions of a Christian understanding of the person and work of Christ, Bauckham's steadfast resistance to the abolition of particularity in Christology and soteriology seems bound to preclude him accepting it as an adequate response to religious pluralism of the sort Hick espouses. Again, both positions (i.e., White's and Hick's) are premised on the flawed notion that Jesus's universal significance can only be had (and may in fact be had) at the expense of a full-blooded reckoning with and insistence upon the historically particular shape and substance of his humanity.

We return, though, to the historically non-gainsayable point that many, and probably the greater bulk of particular human souls who have ever lived, have never enjoyed the opportunity for the sort of meaningful encounter with the particular identity of God manifest in Jesus to which Bauckham refers us. If, as he maintains, this sort of encounter is important for a full understanding of Jesus's religious and redemptive significance, rather than readily elided or substitutable with encounters of other sorts, then to make sense of the claim that what is in principle *universalizable* here may finally become *universal* in its actual salvific reach we must begin to reckon with questions lying solidly in the domain of another of Bauckham's major theological concerns, namely, eschatology. More broadly, indeed, since few believers will suppose that their redemptive encounter with the Jesus revealed in the gospels is likely to be wrapped up satisfactorily by the point of their death, some continuation of that same encounter beyond death must meaningfully be imagined. Readers who baulk at the use of the term "redemptive" in the context of anything occurring post-mortem should feel free to coin some alternative vocabulary. The point remains one to be grappled with. Thus P. T. Forsyth once averred that the Protestant church, in its abandonment of the medieval doctrine of a purgatorial state, had thrown the baby out with the bathwater, and that—shorn of its association with spiritually toxic notions of post-mortem atonement for personal debts laid up in this life—the idea of a continuing relationship with Jesus in which we are changed ever more fully into his likeness (albeit by an

---

36. See Vernon White, *Atonement and Incarnation: An Essay in Universalism and Particularity* (Cambridge: Cambridge University Press, 1991).

encounter precisely with his *difference* from us) was a perfectly cogent and warranted one. More recently Jürgen Moltmann has suggested something similar in his sustained wrestling with eschatological questions.[37] Whether we choose to entertain and explore such eschatological scenarios or not, though, Bauckham's insistence that it is in, and not apart from, the particular identity of Jesus that God identifies himself as "God for us" has profound eschatological implications; for it entails the further claim that it will only be through a continuing encounter with Jesus (and not some "fleshless" eternal Son) that our knowing of God in eternity will be enjoyed. In other words, the knowledge of God "face to face" may well transcend the knowledge we have now "through a glass, darkly," but it will still in some identifiable sense be an encounter with the face of Jesus. Again, the theological force of the Christological doctrines of resurrection and ascension provide vital ballast for such a claim. The incarnation is no mere temporary theophany, but a permanent tabernacling of God in the enhistoricized "flesh" of our humanity, through encounter with which alone—now and "forever"—we may properly apprehend and commune with God's glory.

Bauckham's insistence on the self-identification of God in history in the story of Jesus provides, in fact, a vital clue to help us grapple with the wider problem of eschatological imagining—the problem, in other words, of thinking beyond the thresholds not just of human history but of the present space-time reality itself, and thus beyond the warranted range of human language and conceptuality as such.[38] Just as Israel's protological saga is identifiably bathed in the light of her historical relation with *Adonai*, creation itself being presented as an act of grace consonant with the character of the One who delivered her from slavery and called her into covenant fellowship, so, too, for Christians the constant that straddles the logical gap between historical present and post-historical future is precisely the *character* of the God of the promise, who himself transcends all creaturely reality, but who has identified himself concretely and definitively in the contingencies of the historical Jesus. To repeat: God cannot be reduced or limited to the form of Jesus's humanity; but if this is the form in which God particularizes himself for us, then we can never set it aside or skirt around it in our knowing of God, even in eternity.

If so, then in the meanwhile this same concrete form must shape our own

37. See, e.g., Jürgen Moltmann, *The Coming of God: Christian Eschatology* (London: SCM, 1996), 116–18.

38. For discussion of the issues see Richard Bauckham and Trevor Hart, *Hope Against Hope: Christian Eschatology at the Turn of the Millennium* (London: Darton, Longman & Todd, 1999; Grand Rapids: Eerdmans, 1999), ch. 4.

imaginative trespass beyond what can meaningfully be known or understood about the eschatological future, providing the vital template and compass for our thinking about the substance of the divine promise. In particular, in closing, it would seem that one vital theological function of the doctrine of the *parousia* or second coming of Christ is precisely to insist that the eschatological judgment of the quick and the dead (a scenario more prone than most, perhaps, to flights of imaginative fancy and projection as the history of western visual art bears eloquent witness) lies securely in the hands of the one who characterizes himself most fully in having borne the place of judgment for us, making it his own, and thus robbing us of any right to the leasehold. The one who comes to judge us is not just some abstract "Risen Lord," but the selfsame Jesus whose character we know from the gospel accounts, and who bore our sins to the cross in his body. Whatever account of final judgment we have to offer, therefore, it cannot and must not be one developed without constant reference to the judgment already borne for us on Calvary, or the character of the judge who allowed himself to be judged in our place and "descended to the dead." Unable to hold him—the one who is like us in all things, and yet (thank God) so very different—the gates of that death have been broken wide open by his rude departure from it, once and for all. No more theologically basic or ultimate characterization of God must be permitted to haunt our eschatological imagination; for anything that seeks to go behind the back of Jesus in this way resorts, in effect, to the fashioning of idols again, albeit ones crafted with the flotsam and jetsam of scattered biblical texts and fired by exegetical enthusiasm.

The Bible and Wider Culture: Animals as a Test Case

David Brown

Bauckham is that rare breed of scholar, equally competent and learned in writing about the history of the church as in biblical studies. He has a remarkable facility to integrate the two, not least in throwing light on the history of scriptural exegesis. Although he has always displayed an interest in the nonhuman creation, in recent years articles and books on the subject have taken a more prominent form, among them *The Bible and Ecology: Rediscovering the Community of Creation* from 2010 and *Living with Other Creatures* from 2012. It is on this latter work that I will focus here.[1] In the course of demolishing Lynn White's familiar thesis that the Bible in giving humanity a dominant place is responsible for the present ecological crisis, Bauckham offers numerous insights into how a very different picture is in fact presented, one in which human beings do not even have a day of creation to themselves[2] nor any special superiority in praising God; instead the nonhuman creation is, in its very fact of being, seen as offering praise.[3] Again, over four chapters Bauckham successfully demonstrates how closely Jesus's teaching and ideas are bound up with the natural world, and possibly also in the theme of the temptations in the wilderness.[4]

---

1. *Bible and Ecology* (London: Darton, Longman & Todd, 2010); *Living with Other Creatures* (Milton Keynes, UK: Paternoster, 2012).
2. *Living with Other Creatures*, 4.
3. *Living with Other Creatures*, 12, 147–84; Islam expresses this nicely as "each creature knows its prayer and psalm" (Qur'an 24.41).
4. *Living with Other Creatures*, 63–146, esp. 111–32. I say "possibly" because the fact that a key role is given to the beasts only in Mark and not in the other Synoptics makes one wonder

While all this seems exactly right in terms of where the primary general thrust of the biblical witness really lies, I am less happy with Bauckham's account of why historical Christianity moved in a rather different direction. He consistently places the blame on entirely external influences, and in particular Stoic ethics with its twofold insistence: first, that the rest of the animal creation is there to serve humanity's needs;[5] and, second, that this brings with it no reciprocal obligations on our part since animals lack the essential element that generates such obligations, the rational thinking that generates moral responsibility.[6] There seem to me at least two problematic aspects to such an account. The first is that it presupposes too simplistic a view of the wider classical world in which the early church was set. Certainly, all human beings find it very hard to stand outside cultural perspectives that dominate the particular society in which they find themselves, and so, had this Stoic position totally dominated the classical world, then the likelihood of early Christians succumbing to such ideas would seem highly plausible. But what I would like to suggest in what follows is that this was very far from being the case. The classical tradition in fact already contained ideas of the kind that Bauckham finds in Scripture, and which could therefore have been used to enhance the dominant biblical position. So the puzzle of why preference was given to Stoicism remains, and that brings me therefore to the second aspect of what I would propose in what follows: that it was precisely because some elements in the biblical picture seemed so congruent with Stoic ideas that Stoicism in effect won the day.

That in turn will lead toward my conclusion, which is that Bauckham unnecessarily simplifies divine action in the world. In his desire to maintain the relevance of Scripture to Christian life today, he attempts to assign it too large a place that fails to take sufficient account of the complexities of history that, if rightly understood, would have called him back to his earlier engagement with the history of the church. That is to say, Bauckham is right that the Bible has a distinctive contribution to make but wrong that this stands complete in itself. Indeed, its truths as well as its falsehoods, as I shall indicate, actually contributed toward leading the church astray, and it needed the force of the discovery of evolution to set it once more on the right track. Provocatively, I shall end by suggesting wider ramifications for the approach adopted here.

---

whether an eschatological focus was in fact Mark's primary purpose or simply the wilderness seen as threatening.

5. For the sake of a simpler English style, "the rest of the animal creation" will hereafter be abbreviated to just "animals."

6. First mentioned in *Living with Other Creatures*, 20.

Variety of Positions in the Classical World

There can be no doubt that it was the Stoic position that eventually prevailed in later antiquity; no doubt too that Stoic arguments are the ones most frequently used to bolster what became the dominant Christian position. Indeed, given that the writings of major figures in the Stoic tradition such as Cleanthes, Chrysippus, and Posidonius have for the most part perished, in ascertaining what those arguments were, Christian writers such as Origen and Augustine (or Philo from the Jewish world) are usually our easiest points of access, perhaps apart from Cicero and Seneca. Although the Stoic position denied rationality to animals, with their existence seen wholly for human benefit and without any corresponding obligations toward them, this emphatically did not entail that Stoics happily endorsed the legitimacy of inflicting gratuitous pain, but it did mean that the reasons for its exclusion were seen in resultant effects on human character rather than on the animals themselves.[7] So certainly one way of seeing how attitudes developed in the ancient world is to tell a progressive account that begins with Aristotle's rejection of animal rationality and culminates in Christian adoption of what had by then become orthodoxy on the matter.[8]

Nonetheless, it just will not do to suggest that the Stoic victory was inevitable, as though the Stoic view was the only seriously canvassed position in the ancient world. Writing in the sixth century BCE, the historian Herodotus is quite clear that animals are not exclusively for the benefit of humans.[9] Instead, providence is concerned for the flourishing of all species alike, making, for example, the more vulnerable like hares more productive in offspring by way of compensation. Again, if Plato is right in his account of Protagoras's position, most animals were created better fit to survive than humans, and it was only divine afterthought that ensured additional resources for humanity in fire and the arts.[10]

---

7. Seen, e.g., in the way Seneca argues against arena blood sports: *Epistulae Morales* 7.2–4.

8. Aristotle, *Nicomachean Ethics* 1097b33–1098a4; *Politics* 1332b3–8. "A single decision in Aristotle, the denial to animals of reason and belief, led in Aristotle and the Stoics to a massive re-analysis of psychological capacities": R. Sorabji, *Animal Minds and Human Morals: The Origin of the Western Debate* (London: Duckworth, 1993), 103.

9. Herodotus, *Histories* 3.99–108. Also relevant is *Histories* 1.23–24 where the story is told of Arion being saved by a dolphin. Pliny the Elder in his *Natural History* relates so many close connections with humanity that he talks of dolphins as capable of being a "friend" to human beings (*homini . . . amicum animal*: 9.24).

10. Plato, *Protagoras*, 320C–322D.

But it is Plato himself who can be credited, if somewhat hesitantly,[11] in directing the whole tradition that stems from him in a quite different direction from the Stoics. Brief expositions of Plato often put such emphasis on his belief in the immortality of the human soul that the wider context of this belief is often forgotten, and in particular his acceptance, ultimately from Pythagoras, of the transmigration of souls. However, the implication is clear in the mythical account of creation that he offers in his dialogue *Timaeus*. There no significant distinction is drawn between human and animal souls. It is merely that animals (and women for that matter) fail to realize their full potential, perhaps because of restrictions their bodies impose upon them.[12]

But it is really only with the later Platonic tradition that we discover significant arguments on the other side that make no use of Plato's own controversial metaphysical assumptions. Ironically, two of the most important authors in this respect coincide with the rise of Christianity. Philo (c. 20 BCE–50 CE) in the end sides with the Stoics but not before giving the Platonic position a fair and lengthy exposition, in words attributed to his nephew, Alexander. Considerably more than half the text in *On Whether Dumb Animals Possess Reason* is assigned to what could conceivably have been the historical Alexander's own views. Innate reason, he suggests, is displayed in numerous planned activities while acquired reason is demonstrated in what can be taught to them by humans. Not only that, moral judgment and virtue (or its reverse) are observable as courage in defense of their young and sexual restraint in social relations. So justice is required in our relations with them. The surprising element, though, is that in taking the contrary position Philo relies entirely on Stoic arguments. The Bible is never mentioned. The reason may be because Alexander was apparently an apostate from Judaism. Certainly, humanity's God-given rule over animals is appealed to elsewhere.[13]

It is, therefore, to another Platonist of the time that we must turn for such arguments not only considered but fully endorsed and developed. Plutarch (c. 46–120 CE) provides us with two short treatises that consider the issue. In his *De sollertia animalium* ("On the Cleverness of Animals") he argues that on any criteria the Stoics offer, animals would also have to be accorded rationality, there only being a difference in degree from human beings, not one of kind. In one nice touch, he turns the argument against hunters by suggesting that

11. *Symposium* 207a–c and *Republic* 440e–441b could be read as encouraging a different direction of thought.

12. *Timaeus* 40–42; see also C. Osborne, *Dumb Beasts and Dead Philosophers* (Oxford: Oxford University Press, 2007), 54–57.

13. E.g., in *Exposition of the Laws of Moses* (see on Gen. 1:26–28).

the only reason they value their expertise (as against catching fish, for example) is that the pursued animals show no less skill in avoiding their predations.[14] But in any case reason is in part a matter of training and so humans differ in the degree to which they possess it no less than animals, just as degree of virtue or vice varies to the same extent for both animal and human being.[15] Cooperative or social virtue is also illustrated by the way in which a herd of elephants will help one of their number by constructing a means of escaping a human trap.[16] In view of current philosophical debates about the rationality of the emotions, it is also interesting to observe Plutarch insisting that sentience of itself must bring rationality, and so distinguishing the useful and the harmful is not simply instinctual but also rational.

Particularly interesting is his short work on the subject known as *Gryllus* or *Beasts Are Rational*, in which the lead speaking role is given to a pig. Written in a lively, engaging style, it portrays an arrogant human (Odysseus) encountering a former human who has been turned into a "pig" (*gryllus*) and claims that his new identity is preferable to his old. The opening exchange is characteristic. *Gryllus* contrasts the unequivocal bravery of the animal world with the "tricks" and "frauds" that have been the recurring pattern of Odysseus's so-called bravery.[17] None of this is to deny that even among opponents of the Stoics much of the discussion of the treatment of animals is given a primary human emphasis, with for example, vegetarianism—in contrast to modern positions—most commonly defended in terms of its benefit to humans rather than to the animals themselves.[18] Thus Plutarch spends much of his discussion of the issue noting the deleterious consequences of meat to human health. Even so, he does not hesitate also to condemn what he sees as barbaric ways of breeding animals, including the ancient equivalents of what we would now call factory farming.[19]

Another later vegetarian Platonist who writes at rather greater length on the subject is Porphyry (234–305 CE). Book 3 of his *De abstinentia* repeats

14. 965F–966C.

15. 962.

16. 972B.

17. 987C. Both works are part of Plutarch's *Moralia*, and easily available in the Loeb translation, vol. 12 (London: Heinemann, 1957).

18. For further reflections on the difference between ancient and modern attitudes, see my "Symbol, Community and Vegetarianism," in *Eating and Believing: Interdisciplinary Perspectives on Vegetarianism and Theology*, ed. Rachel Muers and David Grumett (Edinburgh: T&T Clark, 2008), 219–31.

19. *On the Eating of Flesh* 996E–997A.

almost verbatim large chunks of Plutarch's earlier discussion about the rationality of animals. That such rationality requires them to be treated justly is one recurring theme.[20] Another is that such rationality includes language, not to be discounted simply because we cannot understand it. Indeed, the seers, Tiresias and Melampous, are quoted as examples of men who were given such gifts of comprehension. Not that Platonists are the only philosophers to adopt this type of approach. Lucretius appears at one point to rebel against his master Epicurus in suggesting that animals can enter into contractual relations, while the Skeptic Sextus Empiricus also endorses rationality in animals.[21]

But perhaps it will be objected that in quoting mainly philosophical texts I have wrongly discounted where the real pressure came from toward endorsing the Stoic view, and that was the general indifference to the animal world in ancient society. Certainly, the numbers slaughtered in the arena were on a vast scale, no less than eleven thousand, for example, in just over one hundred days in 108–109 CE to celebrate a triumph of Trajan.[22] But on the other side needs to be set Seneca's already-noted objections, as well as Cicero's report that at least on one occasion the sympathy of the crowd went with the tortured animals (elephants in this case) and against the conqueror (Pompey).[23] Moreover, despite common assertions to the contrary,[24] it is clear that some Romans at least did have pets in a relation analogous to the modern one. There is too much evidence from funereal monuments and epigrams for it to be plausible to maintain otherwise.[25] The poet Martial is among those who sing a dog's praise in tones that could rival anything today: "[I]f she whimpers, you will think her speaking; she feels both sadness and joy; lying close to her master's neck she takes her slumbers so quietly that no sighs are heard; if overcome by bodily needs, no stain betrays the coverlet but with gentle touch of foot she rouses him."[26]

It is also true that some of the best-loved biblical passages find corre-

---

20. *De abstinentia* 3.11–12 and 18.

21. S. T. Newmyer, *Animals in Greek and Roman Thought* (London: Routledge, 2011), 29–30, 64–65.

22. Dio Cassius 68.15.1.

23. Cicero, *Epistulae ad familiares* 7.1.3; cf. Pliny, *Natural History* 8.7.20–21. In the letter Cicero actually suggests a fellowship (*societas*) between humans and animals that he had denied elsewhere, e.g., *De natura deorum* 2.154–59.

24. E.g., I. S. Gilhus, *Animals, Gods and Humans* (London: Routledge, 2006), 29.

25. See J. M. C. Toynbee, *Animals in Roman Life and Art* (London: Thames & Hudson, 1973), 87–90 (for cats); 109–24 (for dogs).

26. Martial 1.109, lines 6–12 (my trans.).

sponding parallels in the Roman poets. So the golden age envisaged by Virgil will see a day when "the herds will not fear the mighty lions" and "the timid deer come to drink beside the hounds."[27] Indeed, the related pagan image of Orpheus taming the beasts quickly became a popular theme in both Judaism and Christianity.[28] Again, long before Kenneth Grahame's famous evocation of animal worship in *The Wind in the Willows* (1908) the pagan ancient world had contemplated a similar possibility as fact. Thus it is that we find Pliny the Elder noting various ways in which elephants might be said to worship and pray.[29] So even at the popular level it would be quite false to suggest the total dominance of attitudes similar to the Stoic. In other words, there were plenty of alternative approaches to which the Judeo-Christian tradition might have appealed. So why did it not do so?

The Sources within Scripture Itself

In searching for an answer, it will be helpful to consider the most significant early text on this subject, which occurs in Origen's *Contra Celsum*. Origen responds to Celsus's critique of Origen's claim that "God made all things for man" by observing not that Celsus is wrong about Christian claims but that Christianity has excellent allies. As he puts it, "he seems to me to talk rather like the people who, because of their hostility to their enemies, accuse them of the things for which their best friends receive credit . . . so also in the same way Celsus, being muddle-headed, did not see that he is also criticizing the Stoic school of philosophers."[30] In other words, Origen is quite clear that this is the biblical position, and that the Stoic role is to provide additional philosophical support, and not to be the primary basis for such a belief. Even so, what then follows displays an overwhelming debt to Stoic arguments with only an occasional appeal to Scripture. So, whatever the formal structure of his argument, it would be easy to suppose that Stoicism is its real inspiration and not theology. But that would be to ignore what precedes the passage quoted where Origen is at pains to underline the uniqueness of human beings as alone made in the image of God, and with that the significance of the incarnation

---

27. Virgil, *Eclogues* 4.22; 8.27-28 (my trans.); cf. Horace, *Epodes* 16.33.
28. Including the synagogue at Dura-Europos: Toynbee, *Animals in Roman Life and Art*, 288-94.
29. *Natural History* 8.1.
30. *Contra Celsum* 4.74, ed. and trans. H. Chadwick (Cambridge: Cambridge University Press, 1953).

as salvation for a humanity quite different from the rest of the animal world.[31] Against such a background it would seem quite natural that Augustine should extrapolate to the view that only humans can approach God,[32] as also to the more extreme claim that animals are really there to suit human needs: "because it is not given to them to have reason in common with us, by the most just decree of the Creator both their life and death are subordinate to our use."[33]

However, that said, it is not yet quite clear why that trajectory should have been pursued that begins with humanity created in the divine image and continues with it not only restored but raised to new heights in Christ rather than some alternative, integrated or otherwise, in which serious cognizance is taken of a world without meat-eating prior to the Flood[34] as also the apparent occurrence in the Law of several strong injunctions urging compassion toward animals. Why in the latter case appearances turn out to be deceptive, I will indicate shortly. But in the meantime the meaning of Genesis 1:26–28 needs to be considered. I have already indicated my acceptance of Bauckham's arguments against Lynn White's extreme interpretation, that the passage in effect legitimated a free-for-all approach toward animals. Nonetheless, there are grounds for supposing that in the opening section of Genesis animals emerged less well off than is commonly supposed among Christians in our own day. This is because of the curse imposed on the ground because of Adam's sin (Gen. 3:17–18), which is very easy to read as purely relational—the difficulty represented something imposed on Adam, not a change in nature as such—whereas it was in fact clearly seen in antiquity as a curse imposed on nature generally (including animals), as can be deduced from Paul's interpretation in Romans 8:20: "the creation was subjected to vanity, not of its own will but by reason of him who subjected it in hope" (AV). The linguistic style may be convoluted but commentators appear virtually unanimous in agreeing that the one referred to is most naturally read as an allusion not to Adam or Satan but to God.[35] Cranfield attempts to offer a positive gloss: "We may think of the

---

31. Book 4 begins with a defense of the incarnation and then continues by expounding Genesis, including a defence of the fact that humans are next to God in rank (along with the angels) as rational beings (sect. 29)

32. *Confessions* 7.17.

33. *De civitate Dei* 1.20 (my trans.).

34. Contrast Gen. 1:29–30 and Gen. 9:2–3.

35. W. Sanday and A. C. Headlam, *Romans*, International Critical Commentary (Edinburgh: T. & T. Clark, 2nd ed., 1896), 208; C. E. B. Cranfield, *Romans*, International Critical Commentary (Edinburgh: T. & T. Clark, 1975), 413; J. Ziesler, *Paul's Letter to the Romans* (London: SCM, 1989), 219–20; J. A. Fitzmyer, *Romans*, Anchor Bible (New York: Doubleday, 1993),

whole magnificent theatre of the universe together with all its splendid properties and all the chorus of subhuman life, created to glorify God but unable to do so fully, so long as man the chief actor in the drama of God's praise fails to contribute his rational part."[36] But the truth is that God is perceived as imposing penalties on the animal creation for an entirely human fault, and with that assessment is therefore conjoined a devaluing of what the animal creation can offer on its own.

How far this goes is a moot point, as is well illustrated by a rather sharp interchange between two distinguished Durham professors on how Paul's attitude in the following verses (21–23) on creation "groaning" in expectation is to be interpreted, especially given Paul's move elsewhere toward reinterpretation in a human direction of the Law's injunction against muzzling an ox. Commenting on Deuteronomy 25:4, "You shall not muzzle an ox while it is treading out the grain," he observes: "Do you suppose God's concern is with oxen? Or is the reference clearly to ourselves? Of course, it refers to us" (1 Cor. 9:9–10 NEB). While conceding that Paul's main interest in the Romans passage is in the coming glory of believers, Cranfield declares: "to state categorically that 'Paul is not concerned with creation for its own sake,' as Barrett does in his comment on v. 19, is surely to go beyond what is warranted by the evidence—even when full weight is given to the existence of I Cor. 9.9."[37] This may possibly be true in the Romans passage. But, as the "of course" of the quoted translation indicates,[38] there seems little room for maneuver in the Corinthians context, something also amply demonstrated by Barrett.[39]

To draw different implications from the two passages would seem to make Paul inconsistent, but then many great thinkers often have been. There is, however, an alternative, and that is to find in the Corinthians passage Paul pursuing what is in any case the natural meaning rather than one forcibly attuned to his own needs. While on first hearing allowing an ox to feed while working may seem an act of charity, cool reflection suggests that it is in any

---

508. Several mention the difficulty of interpreting "subjecting in *hope*" unless God is the referent.

36. Cranfield, *Romans*, 414.

37. Cranfield, *Romans*, 415. The issue is pursued at rather greater length in C. E. B. Cranfield, "Some Observations on Romans 8.19–21," in *Reconciliation and Hope: New Testament Essays on Atonement and Eschatology*, ed. R. J. Banks (Exeter, UK: Paternoster, 1974), 224–30.

38. The Greek is *pantōs*—"wholly" or "entirely."

39. C. K. Barrett, *The First Epistle to the Corinthians*, 2nd ed. (London: A. & C. Black, 1971), 205.

case sound economic sense. Not only does the animal become less resistant to work, it also is not exhausted and physically weakened in the process. So Paul would be simply widening that underlying principle of human self-concern. The difficulty, though, with such an analysis is that it reduces the issue to one of self-interest whereas both Deuteronomy and Paul seem to assume a moral dimension. This is where an article by Jan Verbruggen is of particular interest.[40] He notes that the Hebrew speaks only of "the ox" and does not specifically indicate that it is the owner who is being addressed. So Verbruggen's suggestion is as follows: "If we read Deut. 25.4 in the context of a rented or borrowed ox, then the law makes more sense. The person who hired an ox for threshing cannot attempt to shortchange the owner of the ox by not allowing the animal to eat while it is doing the work."[41] The injunction then not only fits well with the rest of the chapter's concern with relations with neighbors but also with Paul seeing it as having moral and not just practical implications.

A similar explanation is also available for the equally puzzling demand that in stealing birds' eggs the mother should not be killed (Deut. 22:6-7). It can hardly be without significance that neither here nor in the previous case is empathy given as a reason in the way it is where human suffering is at issue.[42] Indeed, were such a requirement intended as an injunction of compassion toward the mother, it would surely have included insistence on the survival of at least some of the future chicks. The fact that all may be slaughtered suggests a more human motivation, of allowing the mother to breed once more and so provide a fresh set of eggs for a new human marauder.[43] That would seem a more plausible explanation than either compassion toward the bird itself or the general direction of subsequent Jewish exegesis which, as with Maimonides, detected either a test without explanation or a way of encouraging compassion to other human beings.[44]

None of this is to deny the presence in Scripture of a positive evaluation for the nonhuman creation in its own right, but it is to assert that it is not quite as central as Bauckham insists. Further evidence for this comes from the New Testament itself where two types of animals in particular, the pig and the dog, seem to be accorded a largely negative value. Take first the story of the Gadarene

---

40. J. L. Verbruggen, "Of Muzzles and Oxen: Deuteronomy 25:4 and I Corinthians 9:9," *Journal of the Evangelical Theological Society* 49 (2006): 699-711.

41. Verbruggen, "Of Muzzles and Oxen," 705.

42. E.g., Deut. 15:12-15; 24:17-18.

43. Either in the same year or in the following year, depending on the breed of bird.

44. For the range of Jewish exegesis, E. Segal, "Justice, Mercy and a Bird's Nest," *Journal of Jewish Studies* (1991): 176-95. For the early and late Maimonides, 186-90.

swine.⁴⁵ Bauckham pleads by way of extenuation that the ancient belief was that the devils had to go somewhere.⁴⁶ But there are at least three things wrong with this response. First, in other cases of Jesus exorcizing devils, no record of them moving elsewhere is given.⁴⁷ Second, even if the logic of the day required them to go somewhere, this did not mean that they could legitimately be turned upon some innocent bystander. So, third, that same logic would appear to suggest that there was something after all wrong with the pigs that justified their treatment. The contrast with the Platonist Plutarch could thus scarcely be more marked since, as I observed earlier, one of Plutarch's shorter treatises (the *Gryllus*) actually adopts the pig as spokesperson for the worth of animals.⁴⁸ Pigs were of course ritually unclean but so was the camel, and so this in itself cannot be the explanation. Perhaps it was simply a case of Matthew or his source sharing the common ancient, and not so ancient, prejudice against the behavior of pigs, an attitude that in fact runs right throughout Scripture.⁴⁹

In a similar way, unless we make the book of Tobit canonical, nowhere in Scripture are dogs treated positively or as of any worth. It is an attitude that continues in much of the Middle East to this day, perhaps hardly surprising given the way dogs are treated, with them roaming wild and utilizing village refuge heaps. Even in Tobit the reference is probably to what might well have been a rather fierce guard dog rather than the pet of so many later Christian paintings.⁵⁰ Given that the *kunaria* to which the Syro-Phoenician woman alludes is a diminutive, some commentators have detected an allusion to "puppies" and so to pets.⁵¹ But the sentimental overtones that the translation carries

---

45. Mark 5:1-17; Luke 8:26-39. Gadara, one of the cities of the Decapolis, is too far from the Sea of Galilee to fit the narrative. As early as Origen, Gergesa was being suggested because the land there falls steeply into the lake.

46. Mark 5:1-20; Bauckham, *Living with Other Creatures*, 97-98.

47. E.g., with Mary Magdalene, Luke 8:2 ("out of whom went seven devils").

48. In contrast to Plutarch's high evaluation, the Stoic Chrysippus claimed that Providence had made pig flesh sweet specifically for the benefit of humanity: F. H. Sandbach, *The Stoics* (London: Chatto & Windus, 1975), 80.

49. Prov. 11:22; Isa. 3:21; 65:4; 66:3, 17; Luke 15:15-16; 2 Pet. 2:22. Their wallowing in mud and roaming free in Gentile territory seems to have been the main grounds for complaint, though we now know that pigs are actually highly intelligent animals that can even be kept as indoor pets.

50. As in Verrochio's *Tobias and the Angel* (National Gallery, London) or Titian's *Archangel Raphael and Tobias* (Church of St Marziale, Venice).

51. Even as distinguished a New Testament scholar as Charles Cranfield insists that the reference is to pet dogs: *The Gospel according to St Mark* (Cambridge: Cambridge University Press, 1977), 248.

in English is almost certainly a mistake, as there is no evidence that dogs were ever treated as pets in the Palestine of the time.[52] Of course, part of the motivation for the translation is a reluctance to ascribe to Jesus such a rough dismissal of a Gentile woman as would be implied by a diminutive of contempt, but that seems to me more likely. Indeed, one might argue that the incident was preserved precisely because it marked a turning point in Jesus's attitude to Gentiles, away from the traditional Jewish attitude of seeing them as "dogs." It would thus be Jesus at his most human, shocked into a very different attitude by the effectiveness of the woman's response.[53]

The aims of this survey of the biblical material should not be misunderstood. I agree with Bauckham that Lynn White is wrong and that the Bible in fact includes various positive evaluations of animals, and nature more generally, that cannot be easily reduced to the Stoic view. Nonetheless, not only is the evidence not nearly as strong as Bauckham supposes, but there are also quite a number of passages that would help suggest an easy and natural trajectory toward the Stoic position. Even so, that trajectory might not have been realized had it not been for the higher evaluation of humanity afforded by the incarnation. As my discussion of Origen was intended to indicate, that belief generated a plausible, if regrettable, tendency to see human beings as quite distinct from the rest of the animal world. Nor was this the only area in which this proved to be the case. Another obvious instance is on the question of the immortality of the soul, which even Protestants long retained as a dogma.[54]

One factor that I had not previously considered and that may well have played a part was the abolition of animal sacrifice and its replacement by the once-and-for-all human sacrifice of Christ. This change is taken as integral to explaining wider social change in the early Christian centuries by the Norwegian scholar, Ingvild Saelid Gilhus. Animals, she suggests, were in effect desacralized because the offering of something to the gods was no longer required as part of their slaughter and consumption.[55] By contrast, human reality was given an even higher worth as the only object worthy of sacrifice. Lactan-

---

52. Mark 7:24-30, esp. 28. The list of negative references would be a long one, and three times they are juxtaposed with swine: Isa. 66:3; Matt. 7:6; 2 Pet. 2:22.

53. If it be objected that they are "under the table" and so inside the home as pets, I would observe that in hot climates not only is the door frequently left open but also eating often takes place outside.

54. Immortality of the soul was affirmed at the Fifth Lateran Council in 1513: Heinrich Denzinger and Adolf Schönmetzer, *Enchiridion Symbolorum*, 36th ed. (Freiburg: Herder, 1976), 353-54. It is also endorsed in the Calvinist Westminster Confession of 1647 (ch. 32).

55. For an outline of her thesis, *Animals, Gods and Humans*, 2-3.

tius, for example, declares that "God does not desire the sacrifice of a dumb animal, or of death and blood, but of man and life."[56] The apocryphal *Gospel of Philip* even draws the inference that those who accepted animals were not really gods since "God is a man-eater."[57] How significant such changes might have been in directing a path toward Stoicism is hard to assess. Those inclined to social accounts of change are likely to support Gilhus, but there is no reason why the intellectual changes mentioned earlier, especially the divine humanity of Christ, should not also have played an indispensable part, and almost certainly in my view the predominant role.

Conclusion

In short, then, so far from Stoicism exercising an unnatural influence on Christianity, elements explicit in, or derived from, Scripture can be seen to have been responsible for establishing an effective congruence that resulted in Christianity endorsing a role for animals that made them firmly subordinate to human concerns. Classical culture had in fact offered a wide range of options but Christian theologians chose Stoicism because not only did specific aspects of the biblical witness seem to point in that direction but also its general theological assumptions in incarnation and atonement could be taken to imply a similar trajectory. Aquinas's often-quoted declarations were thus very far from being an aberration and that no doubt helps explain why it has taken till the present papacy for them to be put firmly in the past.[58]

What of course made the difference was the discovery of evolution in the nineteenth century, which effectively challenged any very sharp distinction between humanity and the rest of the animal creation. Indeed, it is intriguing to find Darwin making very similar observations about animal rationality and emotions as I have noted earlier coming from Plutarch and others in the Platonic tradition. Indeed, in some ways he goes further since he has no hesitation

---

56. 149; Lactantius, *Divine Institutes* 6.24.

57. 150; *Gospel of Philip* 62.35–63.5.

58. For Aquinas suggesting that charity is impossible to animals, see *Summa Theologiae* II-II, 25, 3; for him interpreting the biblical injunctions in terms of improving human beings, *Summa contra Gentiles* II, 112. Contrast the second encyclical of Pope Francis's reign, *Laudato si'* (May 24, 2015). For an attempt nonetheless to build on Thomist presuppositions in a direction more friendly to animals, see J. Berkman, "Towards a Thomistic Theology of Animality," in *Creaturely Theology*, ed. C. Deane-Drummond and D. Clough (London: SCM, 2009), 21–40.

in ascribing to them a moral sense that includes altruistic inclinations, while in "the deep love of a dog for its master" he finds an analogue for religious devotion.[59] It is a trend that continued into the twentieth century and beyond. In general there is now a much higher evaluation of animal intelligence than there was in the past. This has been achieved partly by looking at last at animal behavior in its own right without any relation to human concerns. Iris Murdoch makes the point well in connection with a suddenly observed flight of a kestrel. Although it may restore our own equilibrium, that is emphatically not the most important conclusion to draw. As she observes, "more naturally, as well as more properly, we take a self-forgetful pleasure in the sheer, alien pointless independent existence of animals, birds, stones and trees."[60] A similar result has also been accomplished by disentangling such analyses from human projection onto animals of what are in fact human failings. Another philosopher, Mary Midgley, has been particularly successful in this respect, ridiculing, for example, the use of "beast" as a metaphor (found even in as great a linguistic philosopher as Wittgenstein) or an image like "wolf," almost all of whose putative characteristics are shown to be false.[61]

In an essay as brief as this it is quite impossible for me to explore what implications might follow from our changed perception of the relation between the animal and human. All I can do is note the way in which it seems to require modifications to traditional approaches to revelation. So far from Scripture being self-contained, we can now see that its meaning for the community has been significantly modified by truths discovered outside that context. In other words, evolution requires us to go back the Bible, and acknowledge not only that implications drawn from Scripture sometimes pulled us in the wrong direction but also some explicit statements in the Bible itself. Naturally biblical scholars would like to see as much of its text as relevant today as it ever was. So the temptation is to insist that, even if the opening chapters of Genesis must be pronounced nonhistorical, the myths they em-

---

59. "Some distant approach to this state of mind": C. Darwin, *The Descent of Man* (New York: Modern Library, n.d.), 470.

60. I. Murdoch, *The Sovereignty of Good* (London: Routledge & Kegan Paul, 1970), 84. It is a theme taken up by Stephen H. Webb in *On God and Dogs: A Christian Theology of Compassion for Animals* (New York: Oxford University Press, 1998): "Animals do not serve a metaphysical or moral purpose; they are just there. . . . The Christian message is that God loves that which is without reason or place . . . that which is purposeless or anarchic according to the human standards of utility and value" (121).

61. M. Midgley, *Beast and Man: The Roots of Human Nature* (Hassocks, UK: Harvester Press, 1978), for Wittgenstein, 34; for the wolf, 26.

The Bible and Wider Culture

body are still all fundamentally true. But can this really apply to every aspect of those myths? Even as distinguished a theologian as Jürgen Moltmann can sometimes talk as though death was not part of the original divine plan, nor animal suffering.[62] Yet evolution surely suggests that both are built into the very nature of the world that human and animal inhabit, and so a theology is necessary that starts from the assumption that no other alternative was ever envisaged. As Elizabeth Johnson observes, "convincing evidence exists that pain, suffering and death existed long before *homo sapiens* emerged and that such afflictions have played an irreplaceable role in the emergence of complex and beautiful life forms."[63]

But in conceding this much, equally this should not be taken to entail a total retreat from making any use at all of such theology of animals as is present in Scripture. Of continuing relevance will be many of the other passages highlighted by Bauckham, not least those that speak of the natural world in itself offering its worship to God, and the less controversial cases where human compassion and concern for animals are evident.[64] Even where I have argued that this was not the intended meaning, no harm will be done in now so reading them, provided that we do not deceive ourselves into pretending that the more complex picture that I have indicated never existed. Unwillingness to face such complexity will generate an inward-looking community that is quite likely sometimes to fail to hear God's address in the totality of the world that is the divine creation and not just from some smaller part of it, however important.

This may seem a matter of no great moment, but I believe this to be far from so. Let me, therefore, end by briefly indicating a more frequently discussed issue where I think the same question applies. This is the equality of the sexes, where Galatians 3:28 is commonly used to argue that the primitive biblical witness was already along the right lines, and that it was the later church that produced prejudice against women. The fact that Jesus chose

---

62. E.g., "The living God and death are irreconcilable opposites": *Sun of Righteousness, Arise!* (Minneapolis: Fortress, 2010), 81.

63. E. A. Johnson, *Ask the Beasts: Darwin and the God of Love* (London: Bloomsbury, 2014), 188–210, esp. 188. As she puts it a couple of pages later: "In its free working evolution brought forth the kind of life that always entails death and, in its later development, pain and suffering" (191).

64. As, for example, in Eliezer choosing a wife for Isaac on the basis of whether she would offer water for his camel as well as for himself (Gen. 24:14), the angel criticizing Balaam's harshness toward his ass (Num. 22:21–33), and Nathan's account of the poor man's pet lamb (2 Sam. 12:3).

twelve male apostles should have produced some hesitation, for it seems as though, however open he was to women in his ministry, Jesus's model for authority followed the traditional Jewish one. But, perhaps more importantly, both the wider context in Paul and the long history of the passage's exegesis should have warned New Testament scholars that such equality is not its most obvious meaning.

Certainly, read in isolation it sounds as though unequivocal endorsement is being given to equality of race, class, and gender. But comparison with what Paul says elsewhere leaves little doubt that he must have had something else in mind. Thus in Romans 11 he insists on the privileged position of the Jew; the Gentile wild olive shoot has merely been grafted on to the cultivated olive tree that is the Jew, and we Gentiles are not to boast since it is not we who support the Jewish root but the Jewish root who supports us (cf. vv. 17-18). Equally on slavery the letter to Philemon urges acceptance of the returning slave, not the immediate granting of his freedom. Moreover, if equality of the sexes really was Paul's aim, why did he omit any reference to women in parallel passages to the Galatians-style argument where Jew and Greek, slave and free nonetheless do find mention?[65] One might also add the curious omission of any mention of female witness to the resurrection in 1 Corinthians 15, as also the clearly subordinationist passages in the Pauline corpus, some of which are almost certainly traceable to the apostle himself.[66]

Turn to subsequent exegesis, and the same picture emerges. Of course, some comments can be put down to sheer prejudice, but it is the same analysis that also emerges among those most devoted to careful study of the biblical text. Luther, for example, asserts: "[I]n the world and according to the flesh there is a great difference and inequality of persons, and these must be diligently observed.... In Christ, on the other hand... there is but one body, one spirit, one hope of vocation for us all."[67] In other words, what matters is equality of regard or esteem, not equality of status.

So, as with the animal passages discussed earlier, here too it is past context and subsequent history that remain all important in determining intended meaning. So far as the New Testament as a whole is concerned, then, its value lies in generating a community in which women were more highly valued than

---

65. 1 Cor. 12:13; Col. 3:11.

66. In order of plausibility, 1 Cor. 11, 1 Cor. 14, and 1 Tim. 2.

67. My translation of his 1535 *Commentary on Galatians*, in *Luthers Werke* (Weimar edition, 1911), vol. 40.1, 542, and 544-45. For my own discussion of this issue at greater length, *Discipleship and Imagination: Christian Tradition and Truth* (Oxford: Oxford University Press, 2000), 11-31.

in the ancient world generally.[68] Even so, as with the theology of animals, though, it took another new piece of external knowledge to move the community toward belief in total equality, and that was the steep learning curve that gradually took women out of the home and into work contexts where their capacities could at last be recognized as in no way inferior to those of men. In other words, a new potential trajectory from Scripture could then be developed once these became known and their implications were accepted: Galatians 3:28 then reread in its modern sense as the direction toward which, with external help, the Bible might eventually point.

In short, while the community of faith can for the most part legitimately be proud of what is to be found in the Bible on these two issues, there remains the danger of, as it were, over-icing the cake. For the final stage, reliance was necessary on some further external factor—science (in the case of animals) and experience (in the case of women)—to produce a more rounded view. But this was no less the work of God because Christianity believes in a God who works both within the community of faith and beyond as Lord of both.

---

68. The value of the reciprocal household codes should not be underestimated, especially Eph. 5:22–29. They assert equality of value even where difference of status is acknowledged, and so continue to be of relevance nowadays wherever unequal relations necessarily must remain, for example between the great mass of humanity and those with mental disabilities.

Worship and Divine Identity: Richard Bauckham's Christological Pilgrimage

Larry W. Hurtado

I consider Richard Bauckham one of the most significant contributors to the study of the New Testament and early Christianity of our time. His body of published work reflects a wide range of interests and, still more impressively, a correspondingly wide range of competence, within standard issues in New Testament studies and beyond, including contributions to the study of extracanonical texts, modern theological issues, and other subjects. In this essay I focus on those features of his scholarly work that have been most influential on my own, and these are particularly his key contributions to the study of earliest reverence for Jesus. In referring to his "Christological pilgrimage" I perhaps ascribe an intention and an awareness of movement and a direction of development that he may not recognize. So, consider the title of this essay more reflective of my own sense of things, perhaps more poetry than prose.[1] My main purpose here is to underscore and engage two main emphases in his work on the place of Jesus in earliest Christian faith and practice: his earlier, seminal focus on the significance of the worship of Jesus, and his later proposal that Jesus was included within a "divine identity."

---

1. My title draws upon an earlier use of a similar expression: Norman Perrin, *A Modern Pilgrimage in New Testament Christology* (Philadelphia: Fortress, 1974). But I intend no particular association or linkage of Bauckham and Perrin.

The Worship of Jesus

One of the most stimulating essays I have read in some forty years of post-PhD research remains Bauckham's 1981 article, "The Worship of Jesus in Apocalyptic Christianity."[2] Beginning in the late 1970s, inspired by and also critical of Bousset's classic work, *Kyrios Christos*, I set out to attempt my own thorough study of earliest beliefs about Jesus.[3] At some point shortly after it appeared I came across Bauckham's article, as I was formulating plans for a project to be undertaken in my first research leave in the 1983–84 academic year. My recollection is that, together with a couple of other stimulating studies that I read in that period (particularly, Alan Segal's landmark analysis of "Two Powers" controversies in rabbinic texts, and key publications by Martin Hengel), Bauckham's article was important in developing my project for that research leave.[4]

My project involved exploring the Jewish context of earliest Christianity, particularly for any analogies and/or resources to help us understand historically the remarkable treatment of Jesus as worthy of worship. Bauckham's article underscored how remarkable it was for Jesus to be treated as a co-recipient of worship, particularly in texts such as Revelation, and so I sought to probe questions about how early this cultic devotion to Jesus began and what historical factors might have helped to prompt and shape it. The results of that research have appeared in my 1988 book, *One God, One Lord: Early*

---

2. Richard Bauckham, "The Worship of Jesus in Apocalyptic Christianity," *New Testament Studies* 27 (1981): 322–41.

3. Wilhelm Bousset, *Kyrios Christos: A History of the Belief in Christ from the Beginnings of Christianity to Irenaeus*, trans. J. E. Steely (Nashville: Abingdon, 1970, translated from the German fifth edition, 1921; the first edition, 1913). In a 1979 article I lodged some criticisms that demanded a fresh analysis: Larry W. Hurtado, "New Testament Christology: A Critique of Bousset's Influence," *Theological Studies* 40 (1979): 306–17. See now my introduction to the reprint of the English translation: *Kyrios Christos* (Waco, TX: Baylor University Press, 2013), v–xx; and my article, "Wilhelm Bousset's *Kyrios Christos*: An Appreciative and Critical Assessment," *Early Christianity* 6 (2015): 1–13.

4. Alan F. Segal, *Two Powers in Heaven: Early Rabbinic Reports about Christianity and Gnosticism*, Studies in Judaism in Late Antiquity 25 (Leiden: E. J. Brill, 1977; reprinted Waco, TX: Baylor University Press, 2013); Martin Hengel, "Christologie und neutestamentliche Chronologie: Zu einer Aporie in der Geschichte des Urchristentums," in *Neues Testament und Geschichte: Historisches Geschehen und Deutung im Neuen Testament, Festschrift Oscar Cullmann*, ed. H. Baltensweiler and B. Reicke (Zürich: Theologischer Verlag; Tübingen: Mohr-Siebeck, 1972), 43–67; ET, "Christology and New Testament Chronology," in *Between Jesus and Paul* (London: SCM, 1983), 30–47; idem, *The Son of God: The Origin of Christology and the History of Jewish-Hellenistic Religion* (ET, Philadelphia: Fortress, 1976; German 1975).

Christian Devotion and Ancient Jewish Monotheism.[5] From that book onward I have continued to emphasize the history-of-religion significance of the early eruption of cultic "Jesus-devotion" as perhaps the most significant development in earliest circles of the post-Easter Jesus movement, and I freely acknowledge Bauckham's article as a key contribution to my thinking at the early stage of my own work on this topic. Over the years since *One God, One Lord*, I followed up with a number of other publications on the subject of early Jesus-devotion, culminating in my large 2003 work, *Lord Jesus Christ*.[6] But *One God, One Lord* remains foundational for all of my subsequent work, and Bauckham's 1981 article was a crucial factor shaping the research that led to that book.

In that 1981 article, which focused on the remarkable reverence accorded to Jesus in Revelation (especially 5:1-14), Bauckham incisively and insightfully underscored the importance of this precisely in the context of the emphasis in Revelation on refusing worship to any recipient other than the one God. Bauckham pointed to the two striking instances where the seer's misguided attempts to offer worship to the angel-interpreter are forbidden by the angel (Rev. 19:10; 22:8-9), pointing out that this sort of prohibition was also a motif/feature of some other texts of roughly the same period (e.g., *Ascen. Isa.* 8:5; Tob. 12:18). Bauckham then cogently underscored the significance of the depiction of heavenly (ideal) worship in Revelation 5:1-14, where "the Lamb" is included as co-recipient with God ("the one seated on the throne"). In short, precisely in Revelation, with its emphatic affirmation of the cultic exclusivity that included refusing worship even to ranking members of God's own angelic retinue, it is remarkable that we see the exalted Jesus treated as the rightful co-recipient of heavenly praise and worship.

In several subsequent publications, Bauckham further emphasized the significance of Jesus's place in earliest Christian worship and prayer-practice. These include his entry on the subject in the *Anchor Bible Dictionary*, the expanded version of his 1981 journal article in his book *The Climax of Prophecy*, his discussion of the worship of Jesus in a multi-author volume on Philippians 2:6-11, his contribution to the St. Andrews conference volume, *The Roots of Christological Monotheism*, and some parts of a 2008 collection of

---

5. Larry W. Hurtado, *One God, One Lord: Early Christian Devotion and Ancient Jewish Monotheism* (Philadelphia: Fortress; London: SCM, 1988; reprint Edinburgh/London: T&T Clark, 1998). A third edition appeared in 2015 (London: Bloomsbury T&T Clark), with an extensive epilogue reviewing scholarly discussion of the key issues raised in the book since the 1998 edition.

6. Larry W. Hurtado, *Lord Jesus Christ: Devotion to Jesus in Earliest Christianity* (Grand Rapids/Cambridge: Eerdmans, 2003).

several previous publications and conference papers, *Jesus and the God of Israel*.[7] Indeed, it is not an exaggeration to say that Bauckham's emphasis on the significance of the worship of Jesus was perhaps the most influential factor that occasioned and framed the focus of that St. Andrews conference in 1998.

Moreover, the influence of Bauckham's seminal article is also reflected in Loren Stuckenbruck's 1993 PhD thesis (subsequently published), which included a programmatic study of "angelic-refusal" tradition in Jewish texts (references to angels refusing worship as in the passages in Revelation cited already), along with other data about the veneration of angels. Stuckenbruck basically confirmed Bauckham's point about the significance of the depiction of Jesus as co-recipient of heavenly worship in Revelation.[8]

In my view, the point made first by Bauckham and then confirmed by Stuckenbruck is highly important. That the exalted Jesus so quickly and readily was given cultic reverence is remarkable (more remarkable than recognized by many New Testament scholars), and is a (perhaps the) key indicator of the distinctive nature of the young Jesus movement, especially in the context of the Second Temple Jewish matrix in which it first appeared.[9] This cultic reverence

---

7. Richard Bauckham, "Jesus, Worship of," *Anchor Bible Dictionary* 3:812-19; idem, "The Worship of Jesus," in *The Climax of Prophecy: Studies on the Book of Revelation* (Edinburgh: T&T Clark, 1993), 118-49; idem, "The Worship of Jesus in Philippians 2:9-11," in *Where Christology Began: Essays on Philippians 2*, ed. Ralph P. Martin and Brian J. Dodd (Louisville: Westminster John Knox, 1998), 128-39; idem, *God Crucified: Monotheism and Christology in the New Testament* (London: Paternoster, 1998); idem, "The Throne of God and the Worship of Jesus," in *The Jewish Roots of Christological Monotheism: Papers from the St. Andrews Conference on the Historical Origins of the Worship of Jesus*, ed. Carey C. Newman, James R. Davila, and Gladys S. Lewis (Leiden: Brill, 1999), 43-69; idem, *Jesus and the God of Israel: 'God Crucified' and Other Studies on the New Testament's Christology of Divine Identity* (Milton Keynes, UK: Paternoster, 2008).

8. Loren T. Stuckenbruck, "'Do Not Worship Me, Worship God': The Problem of Angel Veneration in Early Judaism and Aspects of Angelomorphic Christology in the Apocalypse of John" (PhD diss., Princeton Theological Seminary, 1993), thereafter published: *Angel Veneration and Christology*, Wissenschaftliche Untersuchungen zum Neuen Testament 2/70 (Tübingen: Mohr Siebeck, 1995). Stuckenbruck proposed, however, that what he called "venerative language" about angels (referring to/describing angels in exalted terms) may have been a partial precedent for the full cultic veneration of Jesus in earliest Christian circles.

9. In this, I echo the judgments of earlier scholars, e.g., Johannes Weiss, *Earliest Christianity* (ET, New York: Harper Torchbooks, 1959; German orig. ed., 1917), 1:37, who described prayer and cultic reverence to the exalted Jesus as "the most significant step of all in the history of the origins of Christianity." My own contribution has included an emphasis on the constellation of the specific actions that comprised the novel "mutation" in Second Temple Jewish worship practice that took place so remarkably early in circles of Jewish believers. See, e.g., Hurtado, *One God, One Lord*, 100-114.

of Jesus did not displace or minimize the worship of God; instead, it formed a key part of what I have referred to as a "binitarian" or "dyadic" pattern of worship in early Christian circles, in which Jesus was reverenced along with God.[10]

This emphasis on cultic reverence offered to Jesus has drawn the attention of other scholars as well. Casey and Dunn, for example, queried whether it is accurate to posit that the "worship" of Jesus is reflected in Paul's epistles (though they each grant that it is reflected in later New Testament writings).[11] But it seems to me that they both fail to engage adequately the specifics of the devotional practices reflected in Paul's letters (and so fail to recognize the significance of these practices). Moreover, they also both seem to presume that for Jesus to have been given worship in any robust sense would have required him to be treated almost as a separate deity in his own right.[12] So, lacking evidence of the latter, they judge that Jesus was not worshiped. But I underscore the point that the worship of Jesus in earliest Christian circles did not comprise a new cultus to an additional or separate deity. The pattern of earliest Christian worship was not di-theistic (two deities). Instead, it amounted to a distinctive "mutation" in the ancient Jewish devotional/worship pattern, in which the ("monotheistic") worship of the one God also required reverencing Jesus, and so Jesus was reverenced as sharing the glory of the one God.[13] Consequently, the objections of Casey and Dunn seem to me misdirected and ineffective.[14] In any case, Bauckham's early em-

---

10. See, e.g., Larry W. Hurtado, "The Binitarian Shape of Early Christian Worship," in Newman, Davila, and Lewis, eds., *The Jewish Roots of Christological Monotheism*, 187-213, republished in my book, *At the Origins of Christian Worship* (Grand Rapids: Eerdmans, 1999), 63-97. More recently, I have shifted to the term "dyadic," to counter misunderstanding of my use of "binitarian," e.g., in my book *God in New Testament Theology* (Nashville: Abingdon, 2010).

11. Maurice Casey, "Monotheism, Worship and Christological Developments in the Pauline Churches," in Newman, Davila, and Lewis, eds., *The Jewish Roots of Christological Monotheism*, 214-33; James D. G. Dunn, *Did the First Christians Worship Jesus? The New Testament Evidence* (London/Louisville: SPCK/Westminster John Knox, 2010).

12. A similar critique applies to the curious line of argument by Dunn's former PhD student, James F. McGrath, *The Only True God: Early Christian Monotheism in Its Jewish Context* (Urbana: University of Illinois Press, 2009). Cf. my online review: https://larryhurtado.files.wordpress.com/2010/07/mcgrath-review-essay1.pdf.

13. In *One God, One Lord*, the chapter on earliest Christian devotion to Jesus was titled "The Early Christian Mutation" (93-124). On Jesus and the glory of God, see esp. Carey C. Newman, *Paul's Glory-Christology: Tradition and Rhetoric*, Supplements to Novum Testamentum 69 (Leiden: E. J. Brill, 1992).

14. See my online review of Dunn's book: https://larryhurtado.files.wordpress.com/2010/07/dunn-was-jesus-worshipped-review.pdf.

phasis on the significance of the worship of Jesus, an emphasis that I have echoed and tried to reinforce, has now become a more salient topic in the field of Christian Origins, and Bauckham deserves credit in helping to make this so.[15]

Divine Identity and the Worship of Jesus

I turn now to another (and subsequent) emphasis in Bauckham's work on early Christology. This is his contention that the risen Jesus was perceived in earliest Christian circles as included within what Bauckham terms "the divine identity," and that this in turn explains why Jesus was worshiped. This contention appeared somewhat later in Bauckham's work, first coming to my attention in his Didsbury Lectures, *God Crucified*, published in 1998; and he then also presented his arguments in his contribution to the St. Andrews conference volume.[16] In order to ensure engagement with his most recently available thoughts, I focus my discussion here on his 2008 book, *Jesus and the God of Israel*, in which he presents expanded and reworked versions of a number of earlier essays and develops this emphasis further.[17]

Foundational for Bauckham's case is his observation that in Second Temple Jewish tradition YHWH was distinguished from all other heavenly/divine beings and treated as *sui generis*.[18] This ancient Jewish conviction, Bauckham contends, involved both a rhetoric in which YHWH was portrayed as unique, and also a corresponding cultic practice of exclusivity, restricting worship to YHWH and refusing cult to the many other deities of the ancient world.[19] That

---

15. See, e.g., Andrew Chester, "High Christology—Whence, When and Why?" *Early Christianity* 2 (2011): 22–50, who judged that "[t]he clear (though not unanimous) scholarly consensus is that, despite all the problems it creates for our understanding of early Christianity, a Christology that portrays Christ as divine emerges very early, in distinctively Jewish terminology and within a Jewish context" (38), and that "Hurtado makes a sustained, cumulative case for there being some kind of cult of Christ in Christian circles in Palestine as well as in the Pauline communities" (39).

16. Richard Bauckham, *God Crucified: Monotheism and Christology in the New Testament* (Carlisle, UK: Paternoster, 1998); idem, "The Throne of God and the Worship of Jesus."

17. Richard Bauckham, *Jesus and the God of Israel: God Crucified and Other Studies on the New Testament's Christology of Divine Identity* (Milton Keynes, UK: Paternoster, 2008), esp. 182–232.

18. In these paragraphs I draw particularly on Bauckham's discussion in *Jesus and the God of Israel*, 182–84.

19. On the rhetoric of ancient "monotheism," see now Darina Staudt, *Der eine und einzige*

is, YHWH had a distinctive identity, not as one among a species/class of comparable beings but as distinct from all else. This included other heavenly/spirit/divine beings, not simply the deities of other nations. More specifically, Bauckham posits, the biblical God was distinguished and identified as having created everything else (including all other heavenly/spirit beings), and as the universal sovereign ruler.

Bauckham submits that, although it is not used in ancient sources, the expression "divine identity" more adequately captures the particular nature of ancient Jewish God-discourse than do terms such as divine "nature," used later in Christian doctrinal controversies. That is, in ancient Jewish thought what distinguished YHWH, what *identified* YHWH, was not speculation about his "nature" (Greek: *physis*) but these key ascriptions of unique roles and status in relationship to all other things.

Bauckham further contends that already in earliest Christian texts Jesus was included within this "divine identity," specifically by being uniquely involved in the crucial actions and attributes that comprise the notion of God's "divine identity."[20] For example, already in Paul's letters, Jesus is posited as having uniquely participated in the creation of all things, as the one "through whom all things" are (1 Cor. 8:6). Also, various New Testament texts reflect the conviction that Jesus now shares in God's rule over all things (as in 1 Cor. 15:27; Phil. 2:9-11; and John 5:22-23). In particular, Jesus is portrayed as exalted above all other heavenly beings, whether hostile or friendly to God, all of them, including angels, now made subject to him (e.g., Heb. 1:1-4). Moreover, of course, Jesus is posited in numerous New Testament texts as the unique eschatological redeemer who executes the divine purposes of salvation.

The first thing I want to say about Bauckham's proposal of "divine identity" is that I affirm it as helpful for capturing and characterizing key aspects of the ways that the biblical deity was distinguished and identified in ancient Jewish discourse. As a small initial quibble, in an essay that forms part of the *Jesus and the God of Israel* volume, Bauckham also refers to the biblical God as identifiable with reference to "his covenant relationship with Israel"; but then, curiously, in the ensuing discussion he does not seem to make much of this, focusing instead on the two other roles of universal creator and universal sovereign.[21] But I should think that this emphasis on YHWH as the protector

---

Gott: Monotheistische Formeln im Urchristentum und ihre Vorgeschichte bei Griechen und Juden, Novum Testamentum et Orbis Antiquus 80 (Göttingen: Vandenhoeck & Ruprecht, 2012).

20. Bauckham, *Jesus and the God of Israel*, 184-85.
21. Bauckham, *Jesus and the God of Israel*, 183.

and redeemer (and judge!) of the people of Israel is sufficiently important in ancient Jewish God-discourse to include it as well.[22]

Nevertheless, I do think that Bauckham's proposal that Jewish God-discourse affirmed a unique "identity" for YHWH is valid and helpful. It is a cogent attempt to capture the conceptual categories at work in ancient Jewish and earliest Christian texts, and avoid thereby the anachronism of reading these texts through the lens of later doctrinal developments. I think he is correct that the way God was distinguished in ancient Jewish discourse has more to do with what we might term "functional" categories, God defined with reference to God's attributes, actions, and purposes. But in what follows I want to offer three questions that are intended to engage Bauckham's proposals about "divine identity," with a view to promoting further constructive discussion. Then, I will offer a suggestion about possibly developing the discussion of "divine identity" further.

My first question is why Bauckham seems to regard his emphasis on "divine identity" as incompatible with the proposal that several scholars (including myself) have made that in Second Temple Jewish tradition we have various expressions of what can be called a "chief-agent" idea, and that this may have provided earliest (Jewish) Christian circles with a basic and initial category by which to accommodate Jesus conceptually in a unique relationship with God and as superior to all other beings. Granted, Bauckham rejects this proposal because, he contends, this chief-agent category was not really as much a part of ancient Jewish tradition as its proponents (myself prominently) have claimed.[23] I do not have the time here to make the case, and I will simply point to the extended analysis of the evidence that I offered in my 1988 book, *One God, One Lord*. In spite of Bauckham's contention otherwise, I remain persuaded that the varying figures in question and the varying roles that they play do cohere sufficiently to allow us to conclude that Second Temple Jews did often think of God as having one or another particular figure distinguished from all the rest of the divine retinue and functioning as the unique agent of God's purposes, a kind of *vizier* or field-marshal.

---

22. I use the expressions "God-discourse" and "discourse" about God with no technical nuances such as invoked by some modern philosophers. I simply mean to designate the statements made about God in New Testament writings.

23. See, e.g., Bauckham, *Jesus and the God of Israel*, 221–32. More recently, note his comments in Richard Bauckham, "Devotion to Jesus Christ in Earliest Christianity: An Appraisal and Discussion of the Work of Larry Hurtado," in *Mark, Manuscripts, and Monotheism: Essays in Honor of Larry W. Hurtado*, ed. Chris Keith and Dieter T. Roth (London: Bloomsbury T&T Clark, 2014), 182–86 (176–200).

Bauckham grants something close to this with reference to the portrayal of Wisdom in Proverbs and Wisdom of Solomon, and with reference to Philo's representation of the divine Logos, and in the references to figures in a few other Jewish texts.[24] But Bauckham insists (and, on this matter, rightly as I see it) that the portrayal of Wisdom as God's chief agent is a literary personification of God's own wisdom, not really a separate being. As for Philo's Logos, this seems essentially to be Philo's way of picturing how God can be both fully transcendent and also really acting and revealed (in a measure) within creation and to human understanding. So for Philo the Logos also is not really a separate being.

But I think that Bauckham errs then in claiming that none of this is of any relevance as evidence for the chief-agent category. To put the matter briefly, it seems to me that these texts reflect and draw upon a notion that God has a chief agent, as a way of depicting figuratively (in these instances) the meaning or function of personified divine Wisdom and divine Logos in relation to God. That personified Wisdom and the Logos are literary and figurative entities does not invalidate the claim that the texts are evidence and expressions of an ancient Jewish chief-agent notion. Indeed, if anything, it seems to me the opposite is the case. As I see matters, the literary and conceptual personifications presuppose and reflect the basic idea in question.

Space does not permit us to consider other evidence, and my purpose here is not really to argue the matter at length. Instead, on the working premise that there was a chief-agent category in ancient Jewish tradition, I want to urge that this is fully compatible with Bauckham's emphasis on "divine identity." To be sure, in earliest Christian texts Jesus is uniquely associated with God in creation, sovereign rule, and redemption, and in this sense I agree that we can say that Jesus is included within "divine identity." But Jesus's particular role in this divine identity is not simply as God's general partner; instead, Jesus's status/role is always defined with reference to God, more specifically as the unique agent of God. So, for example, Jesus is the one *through whom* all things were made (by God), and the one *through whom* the world is redeemed (for God, e.g., 2 Cor. 5:19; Rev. 1:5-6). Jesus is the "Son *of God*," "the Image *of God*," "the Word *of God*," shares "the 'form' *of God*," and has been appointed ruler *on God's behalf* (e.g., 1 Cor. 15:20-28). In short, it seems to me that Jesus is included within the "divine identity" specifically as God's unique chief-agent! So, I repeat, why must we choose between "divine identity" and "chief-agent"

---

24. E.g., he also finds "the idea of a single vicegerent of God" in the archangel in *Joseph and Asenath* (14:8-9), the Spirit of truth/Prince of light/Michael in some Qumran texts (e.g., 1QS 3:15-4:1) (Bauckham, *Jesus and the God of Israel*, 160).

categories, when they seem to me to complement each other, and they both seem to be reflected in the relevant texts?

Certainly, the depiction of Jesus in relation to God seems to exceed any prior example of "principal-agent" figures. For example, personified Wisdom cooperates in creation (e.g., Prov. 8:22-31), but has no stated role in redemption. In a Qumran text (11QMelchizedek) the mysterious Melchizedek figure seems to be God's field-marshal in the eschatological battle, but has no stated role in creation or general governance of the world. Similarly, the mysterious "Chosen One" of the Similitudes of *1 Enoch*, though designated from the beginning of creation, functions solely as the eschatological agent of divine judgment and salvation (e.g., *1 Enoch* 48:1-7). But New Testament texts posit Jesus as chief-agent in all of God's major defining actions and purposes. We could say, thus, that in the New Testament Jesus is *the* chief-agent *par excellence*.

Moreover, and still more crucially, in distinction from all other examples of chief-agent figures, Jesus is accorded a programmatic place in earliest Christian devotional practice. So, as I have proposed a number of times, on the one hand, the Jewish chief-agent tradition provided earliest Jewish believers with a basic conceptual category in which to accommodate the exalted Jesus alongside God. On the other hand, the early Christian appropriation of the chief-agent notion also involved a distinctive and astonishing "mutation" in which Jesus is treated as rightful recipient of cultic devotion.

My second question (the answer to which is not dependent on the previous one) is whether Bauckham gives an adequate explanation for *how* and *why* Jesus was (in Bauckham's terms) included within the "divine identity" so rapidly and so early in the "post-Easter" period. By all accounts, including Bauckham's own, this was a remarkable and unparalleled development. Bauckham refers to the early and novel uses of certain biblical texts, particularly Psalm 110, as being involved.[25] This is, of course, rather clear and is a point made by a number of other scholars as well.[26] Also, there are the fascinating instances where biblical texts that originally referred to YHWH were applied to Jesus (e.g., Rom. 10:13), as analyzed cogently by Capes.[27] But is it sufficient to point

---

25. Bauckham, *Jesus and the God of Israel*, 173-76.

26. E.g., David M. Hay, *Glory at the Right Hand: Psalm 110 in Early Christianity* (Nashville: Abingdon, 1973); William R. G. Loader, "Christ at the Right Hand—Ps. CX.1 in the New Testament," *New Testament Studies* 24 (1978): 199-217; Martin Hengel, "'Sit at My Right Hand!' The Enthronement of Christ at the Right Hand of God and Psalm 110:1," in *Studies in Early Christology* (Edinburgh: T&T Clark, 1995), 119-225.

27. David B. Capes, *Old Testament Yahweh Texts in Paul's Christology*, Wissenschaftliche Untersuchungen zum Neuen Testament 2/47 (Tübingen: Mohr Siebeck, 1992).

to the innovative uses of these biblical passages in earliest Christian circles; or is it not also necessary to ask what in turn prompted, drove, and shaped this remarkably creative selection and interpretative activity? The very extent and nature of the exegetical novelty involved surely suggests something particular to these early Christian circles as the impetus.

To my mind, the most likely answer to why certain texts were so central and why they were so distinctively interpreted is that among these earliest believers there were powerful experiences of revelatory force that conveyed certain new convictions about Jesus's exalted status. On the basis of these convictions early (Jewish) believers then energetically searched their scriptures for further understanding.[28] I do not see, for example, any indication that the familiar exegetical processes operative in ancient Jewish tradition would ever have produced by themselves the notion that Psalm 110:1 depicted the heavenly exaltation of Jesus (or any other figure), or (still more so) that Isaiah 45:22-25 actually refers to two figures, and depicts the universal acclamation of Jesus as Lord "to the glory of God the Father."[29] Instead, I suggest that earliest believers came to these and other biblical texts on the basis of the astonishing conviction that God had exalted Jesus to heavenly glory and now demanded that he be reverenced, this conviction erupting from religious experiences that struck believers with revelatory effect.

From Bauckham's discussion, one could get an impression of a much more sober and perhaps even sedate exegetical activity.[30] At least there is no indication of anything much different from other Jewish reading approaches of the time. Whereas, it seems to me that we must imagine what I have called a kind of "charismatic exegesis" (to borrow a term from David Aune), the biblical texts searched *on the basis of a guiding conviction that arose, not simply from the texts but from revelatory experiences.*[31] To be sure, these revelatory experiences could well have included sudden new insights into biblical texts that presented themselves with the force of revelation. My point is that

---

28. I develop this claim in Larry W. Hurtado, "Two Case Studies in Earliest Christological Readings of Biblical Texts," in *All That the Prophets Have Declared: The Appropriation of Scripture in the Emergence of Christianity*, ed. Matthew Malcolm (Milton Keynes, UK: Paternoster, 2015), 3-23.

29. Indeed, Psalm 110 is scarcely cited or alluded to in Second Temple Jewish texts outside the New Testament, and the same goes for Isa. 45:22-25.

30. See, e.g., Bauckham, *Jesus and the God of Israel*, 33-51.

31. David E. Aune, "Charismatic Exegesis in Early Judaism and Early Christianity," in *The Pseudepigrapha and Early Biblical Interpretation*, ed. James H. Charlesworth and Craig A. Evans (Sheffield: Sheffield Academic, 1993), 126-50.

early believers did not likely derive their distinctive use of certain biblical texts simply by poring over them and applying scribal methods of exegesis of the time.[32] Perhaps the novel exegesis of biblical texts evident in Qumran writings, which likewise is widely thought to have been prompted and guided by revelatory (or "mystical") experiences (maybe including experiences of the Teacher of Righteousness), may give us something of a phenomenological analogy.[33]

My final question is whether Bauckham is correct to contend (as he now seems to do) that the inclusion of Jesus as co-recipient (with God) of cultic worship is adequately understood historically as a "corollary" of Jesus's inclusion in the "divine identity."[34] Stated as such, the move to treat Jesus as worthy of cultic worship could be taken as essentially developing via a theological inference. That is, if I understand Bauckham correctly, he seems to pose a kind of syllogistic logic operative in the earliest Jewish circles of believers that may be summarized in the following propositions: (1) God is worshiped because God is the universal creator and sovereign, i.e., on account of God's "divine identity"; (2) Jesus is included in this "divine identity"; and so (3) Jesus can/should be worshiped too.

I have some serious hesitations about this proposal for several reasons. My first reason is that I really do not see clear New Testament evidence that the worship of Jesus emerged as a "corollary" of Jesus being included in the "divine identity." That is, I see no New Testament text indicating that the worship of Jesus emerged as a legitimate thing to do as the result of a process of formulating devotional implications of Jesus's exaltation. Instead, it seems to me that the closest we get to an explanation or justification for worshiping Jesus is the claim that God has exalted him to share in divine glory and now *requires Jesus to be worshiped*. As I read Philippians 2:9-11, for example, God has highly exalted Jesus and has given him the superlative name, with the clear

---

32. James L. Kugel, "Early Jewish Biblical Interpretation," in *The Eerdmans Dictionary of Early Judaism*, ed. John J. Collins and Daniel C. Harlow (Grand Rapids: Eerdmans, 2010), 121-41 (with bibliography).

33. Note, e.g., the remarkable identification of a mysterious "Melchizedek" figure as the "Elohim" of Ps. 82:1 in the Qumran text *11QMelchizedek*. Jonathan G. Campbell, *The Exegetical Texts* (London: T&T Clark, 2004), gives an introduction to scriptural interpretation in the Qumran texts. On the religious ethos of the Qumran sectaries, see, e.g., James R. Davila, "Exploring the Mystical Background of the Dead Sea Scrolls," in *The Oxford Handbook of the Dead Sea Scrolls*, ed. Timothy H. Lim and John J. Collins (Oxford: Oxford University Press, 2010), 433-54.

34. Cf. Bauckham, *Jesus and the God of Israel*, 153-81.

divine intention that Jesus should now be reverenced as "*Kyrios*," thereby glorifying God (as reflected in the *hina* in v. 10). In Revelation 5:1-13, "the Lamb" is conferred with the sealed book by God, signaling divine approval, and the acclamation given to him by all the heavenly court is in gratitude for his sacrificial redemptive work (esp. vv. 9-10). In John 5:22-23, likewise, it is God ("the Father") who now requires that Jesus ("the Son") be given the same honor that is due to God.[35]

Moreover, I cannot easily see that Jewish believers would have amended so readily and programmatically their devotional practice in the "dyadic" direction of including Jesus as a second, distinguishable recipient by some sort of theological inference or logic. To my mind, Jewish concerns to avoid compromising the uniqueness of the one God were simply too strong to make this credible.

I also do not see evidence in the ancient Jewish sources that there was the sort of logic that seems to be presumed in Bauckham's proposal. Bauckham has argued for an analogy that "proves the rule" in the references to the obeisance/reverence given to the "Chosen One" in the Similitudes of *1 Enoch* (esp. 48:5; 62:6, 9), but I do not find his reading of these texts persuasive.[36] In *1 Enoch* 62:6, 9, those reverencing the Chosen One are the "mighty kings" who are to be conquered, and so their action simply seems to me the obeisance typically offered by the vanquished to the victor. This is hardly a cultic setting or action, and hardly indicative of any real collective worship practices by the elect, whether in heaven or on earth. As for *1 Enoch* 48:5, I submit that the immediate context makes it clear that the worship there is actually focused on God, and the "Chosen One" functions simply as the earthly figure before whom, and under whose auspices, worship is offered to God.

In sum, it seems to me that the inclusion of the risen/exalted Jesus in the devotional practice of early Jewish believers really was novel, and so I contend that it could have emerged in Jewish circles only on the strong and novel conviction that *God now required it*. I repeat that I cannot see that the inclusion of Jesus as co-recipient of their worship was a kind of liturgical experiment, or an innovation ventured on the basis of an established theological syllogism. I hope that I do not distort what Bauckham means, and I welcome his correction if I have. But it seems to me that his relegation of the worship of Jesus to the status of a "corollary" of his "divine identity" category involves radically

---

35. I think it also relevant that Heb. 1:6 portrays God as requiring the angelic host to worship "the firstborn."

36. Cf. Bauckham, *Jesus and the God of Israel*, 169-72.

underestimating the strength of devout Jewish concerns about worship (an apparent shift from the emphasis in Bauckham's earlier works). I think that it also fails to do justice to the momentous development represented by the eruption of the "dyadic" devotional pattern that so quickly characterized earliest Christian circles.

But, in addition to posing these questions about Bauckham's treatment of Jesus being included in the "divine identity," I also want to offer a suggestion. As I have proposed in an earlier publication, not only is Jesus's significance typically defined in the New Testament with reference to God, God is also identified with reference to Jesus.[37] To cite here a few sentences from that earlier publication,

> the glory of "God" and the triumph of "God's" purposes are so closely linked [in the NT] with Jesus as to make Jesus essential to them. That is, arguably, "God" is thereby redefined in a significant degree with reference to Jesus.[38]

Both in the way that God is referred to, and in the way that God is to be worshiped, the New Testament makes Jesus so central that we can say that God is "inseparably connected to Jesus, and theological reflection on 'God' must now reflect the prominence and eschatological centrality of Jesus."[39] Illustrative of this, compare the references to "the God of Abraham, Isaac and Jacob" (e.g., Exod. 3:6, 15) and "the God of Israel" (Josh. 24:2) with Paul's references to "the God and Father of our Lord Jesus Christ" (e.g., Rom. 15:6).

So, in addition to saying (with Bauckham) that Jesus is included within the "divine identity," we should perhaps also say that in the New Testament the "divine identity" is adjusted with reference to Jesus. Bauckham has himself made a somewhat similar point:

> For the early Christians, the inclusion of the exalted Jesus in the divine identity meant that the Jesus who lived a truly and fully human life from conception to death, the man who suffered rejection and shameful death, also belonged to the unique divine identity. What did this say about the divine identity? . . . The profoundest points of New Testament Christology occur when the inclusion of the exalted Christ in the divine identity entails the inclusion of the crucified Christ in the divine identity, and the christo-

---

37. Hurtado, *God in New Testament Theology*, esp. 65–71.
38. Hurtado, *God in New Testament Theology*, 69.
39. Hurtado, *God in New Testament Theology*, 71.

logical pattern of humiliation and exaltation is recognized as revelatory of God, indeed as the definitive revelation of who God is.[40]

Bauckham's comments take us further in a more reflective theological direction than my own, perhaps more modest, point, which is simply that the New Testament references to God typically also refer to Jesus, and vice versa.[41] I hasten to add that any New Testament redefining of God with reference to Jesus did not involve positing a deity different from the God of Israel and the Old Testament. That would take us in the direction of Marcion.[42] Instead, the biblical deity, YHWH, the God of Abraham, Isaac, and Jacob, is also now known as "the God and Father of our Lord Jesus Christ." But I think it is fair to say that the New Testament emphasis on Jesus's centrality comprises the view that any description of God apart from reference to Jesus is inadequate, and any worship of God that bypasses Jesus is also inadequate.

Conclusion

In concluding this brief (and so unavoidably somewhat cursory) engagement with a couple of Bauckham's contributions to the historical understanding of earliest Christology, I want to underscore primarily their significance. It is only a minority of scholars whose work singles them out as prominently associated (and credited) with certain ideas and particular contributions to scholarly study, and Bauckham is certainly one of those. His insightful study of the worship of Jesus in Revelation has been confirmed by others, and has had continuing positive effects in the subsequent highlighting of the historical importance of the inclusion of Jesus along with God as co-recipient of worship. His subsequent emphasis on the inclusion of Jesus in the "divine identity" has likewise proven stimulating, and in my view can be a helpful way of capturing succinctly central features of early Christological discourse. As will be clear in the preceding comments, I also think that there is room for further discussion and development in this proposal, and I look forward to Bauckham's further participation in this intriguing matter.

40. Bauckham, *Jesus and the God of Israel*, 33. I thank my PhD student, Joshua Coutts, for reminding me of this passage in Bauckham's book.
41. I sense also in Bauckham's comments his continuing resonance, and evident sympathy with, Jürgen Moltmann, *The Crucified God* (London: SCM, 1974).
42. See now Sebastian Moll, *The Arch-Heretic Marcion*, Wissenschaftliche Untersuchungen zum Neuen Testament, 250 (Tübingen: Mohr Siebeck, 2010).

"The Agent of the King Is Treated as the King Himself": Does the Worship of Jesus Imply His Divinity?

Philip Alexander

I

In the ongoing and lively debate on Christology there is an argument deployed by those on the high side that can be put as follows. Jews by the time of Jesus were strict monotheists, at least in the sense that they believed that there was only one true God, that God alone was to be worshiped: to worship any being other than the one true God was to commit the cardinal sin of idolatry. From early on in the Christian movement Jesus's followers offered him worship. Therefore they must have regarded him as God. Put syllogistically: only God was to be worshiped. Jesus was worshiped. Therefore Jesus was God. This argument is by no means new. It figures prominently, for example, in H. P. Liddon's Bampton Lectures for 1866, published under the title *The Divinity of Our Lord and Saviour Jesus Christ*, which even for its time was seen as conservative and traditional, but it has recently been revived and restated with considerable force.

I offer this essay as an affectionate tribute to a dear friend from whom I have learned a lot. It reflects the kind of discussions we used to have when he was a colleague at Manchester, as we shared a car into the university, or put the theological world to rights after Sunday lunch at our place. I am sure he will have an answer to my points. Indeed he may think he has already answered them. I have read carefully what he has to say. The fact that I go over again ground that he has to some degree already covered simply means that I am not totally convinced by his statement of the case so far. There is still, I think, more work to be done. Given the space available I cannot footnote all my claims. I have written for an audience that knows the relevant primary and secondary literature, and will be able to supply for themselves the necessary references.

II

A key piece of evidence for this argument has been found in a trope of early Jewish literature in which someone offers worship to a being other than God and is roundly rebuked for it. So Revelation 22:8–9: "I John am he who heard and saw these things. And when I heard and saw them, I fell down at the feet of the angel who showed them to me; but he said to me, 'You must not do that! I am a fellow servant with you and your brethren the prophets, and with those who keep the words of this book. Worship God.'" This looks pretty cut-and-dried. But is it? Several caveats spring to mind.

First, what is the literary and rhetorical function of this statement? I have called it a trope, because it is a motif that recurs particularly in apocalyptic texts. Here it contains a clear proposition: "Worship God [alone]," but how much theological weight is this meant to bear? The very fact that the motif is repeated in a certain type of text raises the possibility that it may serve fundamentally as a stylistic device, introduced primarily because it is regarded as a typical motif of this genre of text. Though it would be odd to claim that it has *no* propositional force, one must nevertheless be a little cautious about assuming that it is making a strong and definitive theological statement. The fact that it recurs not infrequently may not be an indication that the doctrine it ostensibly states was widespread, but simply that it has become a literary *trope*, and that, therefore, we should avoid pressing it too hard, and making it do *too much* theological work.

Second, if we *do* take it in a strong theological sense then it is hard not to construe it as polemical: it is directed at fellow Jews who are charged with worshiping angels. But if this *is* its theological function, then it weakens an important premise of the main argument, in that it shows that *some* Jews did indeed offer "worship" to beings other than God. Now those Jews may have vehemently denied that they were *worshiping* angels, and even more vehemently denied that they were blurring the distinction between angels and God, but to their critics they were indulging in acts that suggested they were. I shall return to this point presently.

That there were groups in early Judaism who offered to angels forms of veneration that some regarded as tantamount to worship is well known. Instances of our trope are cited from later Hekhalot literature, and here the polemical context is reasonably clear, because there is good evidence that the angelology of the Hekhalot circles was seen by some rabbinic authorities as endangering the unity of God, as postulating the existence of a "Second Power." The introduction of the trope into Hekhalot texts might be part of the rabbinizing redaction that this literature has undergone, or it may be a kind of ironic self-correction by the mystics themselves. They may in effect be saying: "Yes, we are happy to repeat this, because we are not, in fact, endangering the unity of God. The veneration we offer these angels is not the same as the worship we offer to God." Little is to be gained from simply amassing *testimonia* stretching from Second Temple times to the Middle Ages which express the trope. Each text has to be carefully weighed and set in its historical context—whether Christian or Jewish. For purposes of the Christological argument we are concerned with here, only those references which are from the first century or earlier should have any weight. The later attestations may have got tangled up with the later Christological debates, and this would complicate the picture. In other words, the later attestations should not be treated as straightforwardly neutral evidence for the purposes of this particular argument, but as part of a debate the history of which the whole exercise is trying to elucidate.

One of the most important developments in recent study of late ancient Judaism has been the realization that it was almost as torn by controversy about the nature of God as was contemporary Christianity.[1] At the time that Christianity was arguing about the divinity of Christ, some in Judaism were arguing about the divinity of high archangels such as Metatron. Whether or not the two debates were in some way linked remains a moot point, but that they were running side by side can now no longer be in any doubt. On the Christian side binitarianism and then trinitarianism became orthodoxy. On the Jewish side an "Arian" solution seems to have become more or less the norm, that is to say, there is a high archangel who is, in effect, a Second God (though some would have balked at using that language), but he is subordinate to the one true God in power and authority and lies outside the godhead.[2] It is necessary to bear these debates in mind when we assess the later attestations of our trope, to avoid falling into circular reasoning.

---

1. This subject has been discussed by Daniel Boyarin among others. See his essays, "Beyond Judaisms: Metatron and the Divine Polymorphy of Ancient Judaism," *Journal for the Study of Judaism in the Persian, Hellenistic, and Roman Periods* 41 (2010): 323–65, and "Is Metatron a Converted Christian?" *Judaïsme Ancien—Ancient Judaism* 1 (2013): 323–65, and the abundant bibliography cited there.

2. In the medieval Qabbalah, Metatron does appear in some speculation to become part of the godhead. In other words a full-blown binitarianism emerges, as opposed to the ditheism of the earlier Hekhalot tradition.

III

The apocalyptic trope of an *angel interpres* rejecting acts of worship may not, then, offer as direct and compelling evidence for the argument as seems at first sight to be the case. But there are other problems. The argument makes two assumptions that are questionable. The first is that there was a universal belief in early Judaism that there was only one God. So fundamental was this belief that we can safely assume that all Jews subscribed to it, and, moreover, that belief was totally accepted also by the Gentiles who joined the early Christian movement, many of whom came from polytheistic cultures. Quantification is important here. Some might want to argue that we don't have to assume that monotheism was *universal* among late Second Temple Jews for the argument to work. It would be sufficient to demonstrate that monotheism was widespread, but the argument, when stated in this form, has unquestionably been weakened. The move from the quantifier "all" to the quantifier "some" constitutes a big step in logic. Second, certain acts constitute "worship" which by universal consent should be offered to God alone, and, therefore, if we find people holding the monotheistic view of God performing those acts, then they must logically regard the one to whom they offer them as God. The acts, *qua acts*, irrespective of the intention of the actors, define the one to whom they are offered as God, and if he is not God, then the worshipers have committed the cardinal sin of idolatry.

IV

Let us analyze these propositions in turn. First, where do we find the evidence for monotheism in ancient Judaism? There is, on the face of it, ample evidence but on closer inspection it turns out to be problematic. The problems are illustrated by the Decalogue, the most obvious place to start:

> You shall have no other gods before me. You shall not make for yourself a graven image, or any likeness of anything that is in heaven above, or that is in the earth beneath, or that is in the waters under the earth; you shall not bow down to them or serve them; for I the Lord your God am a jealous God, visiting the iniquity of the fathers upon the children to the third and fourth generation of those who hate me, but showing steadfast love to thousands of those who love me and keep my commandments. (Exod. 20:3-6; cf. Deut. 5:7-10)

"The Agent of the King Is Treated as the King Himself"

That seems clear enough, and has been clear to many of us since these words were instilled into us from childhood with a strong monotheistic interpretation. But two points should be borne in mind. First, even if the meaning is that there is one and only one God, and that he alone should be worshiped, historically speaking there is ample evidence that this represented only one strand of early Israelite religion. We must be careful not to extrapolate from law to reality. Law prescribes what ought to happen, not what actually happens, and, indeed, the way in which this particular legislation is formulated strongly hints that the law was not universally observed: there were those who from the legislator's standpoint did worship "other gods" beside Yahweh—a view borne out by other passages in Tanakh and by the archaeological record.[3] The Decalogue represents only one strand of early Israelite religious thought—the deuteronomic—but we are surely long past the time when we can simply assume that that strand is orthodoxy or even that it totally dominated early Judaism. I would accept that it did achieve a kind of normativity by late Second Temple times, but other, opposing strands of thought did not simply vanish. The evidence of apocalypticism and even later rabbinic theology, down to the medieval Qabbalah, of belief in high, quasi-divine, angelic figures, can be construed historically speaking as a continuation of early Jewish "polytheistic" tendencies, and there is no obvious reason why early Christology cannot be seen as part of this tradition. Within this tradition the worship of beings other than God is conceivable. Early Judaism was a theologically and religiously complex phenomenon and we must be careful not to oversimplify it.[4]

Second, quite apart from this historical argument, it has to be recognized that the meaning of the words we have quoted from the Decalogue is not as obvious as is sometimes supposed. Exodus 20:3-6 taken in isolation is not necessarily a statement of *monotheism*. Rather, it can be read as an assertion of *henotheism*: it does not deny the existence or reality of other gods, but claims an exclusive relationship between Yahweh and Israel, on the grounds that it was he, and not another god, who had rescued them from Egypt, and this

---

3. For the archaeological evidence, see O. Keel and C. Uehlinger, *Gods, Goddesses, and Images in Ancient Israel* (Edinburgh: T&T Clark, 1998). More evidence has come to light since this survey was published. These gods were probably worshiped *alongside* Yahweh.

4. It should be borne in mind that within even outright polytheistic systems there is normally a hierarchy of the gods—one high god to whom all the others are subordinate. The development within late Greek polytheism is instructive. In some circles the traditional gods were seen as simply satraps of the God Most High. It is not easy to distinguish this polytheism from the picture presented in late ancient Judaism and Christianity of the one supreme God reigning in heaven, surrounded by a retinue of angels.

obligated Israel to worship him alone. Indeed the precise wording, especially the problematic *'al panay* (LXX *plēn emou*), seems to favor this interpretation. It might be argued that in the context of the canon as a whole, which in various places stresses that Yahweh is the creator of the world, a monotheistic reading of the commandment comes naturally. But again a caveat is in order. It is doubtful if we can find full-blown monotheism in the later philosophical sense of the term anywhere clearly articulated in the Bible. Monotheism as it has been understood from the medieval schoolmen onwards is predicated on the premise that God is the ultimate cause of all things, and that implies *creatio ex nihilo*. But where is the doctrine of *creatio ex nihilo* in Scripture? Not in Genesis 1. At least since the time of Rashi it has been well understood that the complex syntax of the opening sentence of that passage implies that chaotic primordial matter preexisted God's act of creation there described, and creation then has to mean the imposing of order on chaos, rather than the bringing into being of all things out of nothing. This understanding is in keeping with the apparent etymological sense of the verb *bara'*, which seems to mean "cut," or "hew," and thus presupposes the preexistence of matter that is shaped. Thus what we have here is *prima facie* a doctrine of the preexistence of matter, which some later theologians, Maimonides for example, would reject as incompatible with strict monotheism.

But so what? Inert, chaotic matter can hardly be a "god," even though it is unoriginated and shares with God preexistence. It is not sentient, it does not possess will, it does not make moral demands. So there is still only one God in any meaningful sense of that term. What we are talking about is analogous to the relationship between a potter and the clay that he molds into a vessel. The potter and the clay clearly belong to different orders of being. This is a reasonable point, but again a caveat. We must be careful not to impose too easily modern ontological categories on ancient thought. There were certainly ancient cosmogonies that divinized primordial chaos. It was a god with whom the Creator engaged in combat and had to subdue to create the world (as in Marduk's conflict with Tiamat), and traces of this idea can still be found in the Hebrew Bible. Indeed, we may have echoes of it in the word *tehom* ("the abyss") in Genesis 1:1, though they are faint, and heavily demythologized. And what is the mysterious *ruakh 'elohim* (divine spirit/wind) that seems to be part of the primeval chaos? The language here has surely overtones of divinity. There are, then, two primeval elements that are coeval with God: "chaos" (which seems to be regarded as watery in nature) and "spirit/wind" (which is airy in nature), and this is not compatible with *creatio ex nihilo*, or with monotheism in any strict sense of the term as now understood.

"The Agent of the King Is Treated as the King Himself"

If it is argued that Exodus 20:3–6, which we discussed earlier, has to be read in its canonic context, then we must also allow this in the case of Genesis 1. As the *locus classicus* on creation, all other references to God making the universe have to be read in the light of it. They can be seen as implicitly or explicitly referring to it. But if Genesis 1 does not teach *creatio ex nihilo*, why should we suppose that *they* do? So deeply embedded is the doctrine of *creatio ex nihilo* now in Jewish and Christian theology that it has become automatic for modern readers to assume that when Scripture refers anywhere, in either the Hebrew Bible or the New Testament, to God's creation of the world, it means creation *out of nothing*. Hebrew *bara'* and Greek *ktizein* mean *creare ex nihilo*. But this is not necessarily the case. The same argument seems to hold good for the reception of Genesis 1 in Second Temple texts: there is not a single text that unequivocally states the doctrine of *creatio ex nihilo*, or is incompatible with a doctrine of the preexistence of primeval matter.

It should be noted that God's *sole* agency in creating the world is also not completely clear in Genesis 1. At first sight it seems obvious: God is the subject of all the verbs of making—till we come to the problematic *na'aseh* in verse 27, "Let us make man." Who is Elohim talking to here? That we have a *pluralis majestatis*—he's talking to himself!—is implausible, as, of course, historically speaking, is the Christian claim that we have an allusion here to the Trinity. It might be suggested that the plural is a sort of slip of the pen. Behind Genesis 1 stands a more polytheistic view of creation which the author is revising in a monotheistic direction. He really meant this in a monotheistic sense. But this is speculation. Another way of looking at it would be to say that he was not as worried about maintaining God's sole agency in creation as later theologians have been. We should also recall passages such as Proverbs 8, which assigns Wisdom—Wisdom that is treated, not necessarily metaphorically, as a sentient being—a role in the creation of the world. The relationship of this primordial Wisdom to God is not clarified. Did it exist eternally with him? Is it the first-created being, created precisely to act as an agent in creation? How careless of a monotheist not to make this clear!

V

Exodus 20:3–6 is a classic proof-text also for the second supposition that underlies the argument under review, viz., that God alone should be the recipient of worship. It implies that the corollary of God being the only God is that he alone should be worshiped, and that worship of anyone or anything else constitutes idolatry. In other words, all the main premises of the argument are present in this one text. Text after text in Tanakh presents idolatry as one of the most heinous sins that Israel could commit, and here idolatry receives its classic definition: it is "bowing down and worshiping other gods." The aspect of idolatry is important for the argument. If the early Christians worshiped Jesus and did not regard him as God, then they were breaking what by their day was surely one of the strongest taboos in Israel. The text seems clear. But is it? There are ambiguities around what constitutes a forbidden "image" and what constitutes "worship" that need to be addressed.

Let us take first the problem of the image. Is the command against making images distinct from the command not to bow down to them? In other words, you should not make an image whether or not you intend to bow down to it. Or are the two injunctions effectively one—you shall not make an image *in order to* bow down to it, but, by implication, if you make it for nonreligious purposes, e.g., purely as decoration, that is permitted? The latter, liberal interpretation of the text opens the way for figurative art. The former stringent interpretation excludes the possibility of all realistic representation of nature in any medium or in any form, whether in the round or drawn on a flat surface. It leaves the possibility only of abstract, geometric forms, or of calligraphy, as in classic Islamic art. It is hard totally to divorce the two statements. Why would anyone forbid the making of an image unless at least, whatever the intention, a risk was perceived to exist that it *might* get worshiped, and so become an idol: it could provide a *temptation* to idolatry. It is a question of putting a fence around the law. A prohibition of *making* images on its own, totally divorced from the interdiction on *worshiping* them, makes little sense. Perhaps the point is that God alone has the right to create and to replicate forms. He is permitted to make an image and a likeness of himself, as when he made man, but it is not permitted for humanity to make an image of a man. In some obscure way this could be seen as an attempt to imitate and to rival God's acts—to play God. But if this is the point, then it is very obscurely expressed.

If there is, as seems more likely, a close connection between the making of the images and the worshiping of them, then it becomes clear that idolatry is the worship of aspects of creation as gods. These are the "*other* gods" mentioned earlier. They become Yahweh's rivals, and this explains his "jealousy" and "zeal," and the punishment he feels obliged to mete out to those members of his covenant people who give to others the devotion he regards as due to him alone. But suppose the image is meant not as an image of *another* god, but of Yahweh himself, the one true God? Is bowing down and serving that forbidden? What's wrong with such an aid to worship? From this text it is not obviously clear that this would be forbidden. We know that other gods were imported into ancient Israel from the surrounding nations and worshiped through images, but there also seem to have been attempts to represent Yahweh the God of Israel as well, though this was opposed in some prophetic circles.[5] A compromise may have been to represent Yahweh aniconically. Though aniconism was occasionally found in other ancient Near Eastern religions, it came to be seen as characteristic of early Judaism—something that marked it out from the rich visual imagery of the surrounding cultures. Aniconism basically took two forms: (a) minimal iconism, where the deity is represented by an abstract form (e.g., a block or a pole) devoid of distinctive, living features; and (b) absolute aniconism, where the deity was represented by an absence, such as an empty throne. This was how Yahweh was represented in the Tabernacle and the Temple. He was visualized by the space framed by the wings of the cherubim and the *kapporet* of the Ark of the Covenant. This was his throne. It was here that the cloud of glory, which symbolized his presence in the sanctuary, was thought to reside. It was here that the most solemn rituals were offered to him.[6]

People were surely capable of taking this as a *representation* of God, as an aid to worship accommodated to the limitations of their embodied state. God was in his heaven, far above the earth, but for purposes of worship they needed to localize him in a house and in a space where they could go and commune with him, individually and communally. The prophets in their denunciation of idols have knockabout fun with gods who cannot move or do anything for themselves, and may end up as firewood and used to cook a meal. But the polemics are superficial. Few image-users in antiquity would surely have been so dumb as to suppose that the little figurine in their house, or even the majestic statue in the great temple, was *actually* their god, rather than a *representation* of their god. It is true that we have an ancient tradition of animating statues of the gods, as in the Egyptian ceremony of the "opening of the mouth," but this does not invalidate the basic point, viz., that people were perfectly capable, on reflection, of distinguishing between the image and the god it

---

5. See the announcement (December 2015) of the discovery on the Ophel of a Hezekiah *bulla* with a winged solar disc and ankh symbols. It is highly probable that the solar disc, though iconographically Assyrian in origin, is here used as a symbol of the God of Israel, extending his protecting wings over the king. Is this idolatrous?

6. See further my essay, "Reflections on Word versus Image as Ways of Mediating the Divine Presence in Judaism," in *The Image and Its Prohibition in Jewish Antiquity*, ed. Sarah Pearce, Journal of Jewish Studies Supplement Series 2 (Oxford: Journal of Jewish Studies, 2013), 10–27.

represented. "Opening the mouth," and similar acts of statue animation, were fundamentally acts of consecration that inaugurated the image's social role as a religious icon. Those very prophets who objected to physical, visual representations of God, because they inevitably used aspects of the created order to depict the transcendent creator of all things, were happy enough to use *verbal* images and even *verbal* pictures to represent that same being—he was a king, a judge, a father, an "Ancient of Days," and so on. It took a long time before Judaism finally realized that these were just as problematic, because human language is as bound to the created order as any visual image. Where this is important for our present purposes is that though acts of worship may be performed before the representation of the god, they are not really being offered to it, and those acts carry no implication as to the ontological status of that representation. The worship is being offered not to the image but to the god who stands behind it. To use a well-known distinction formulated by later supporters of images as aids to worshiping the one true God: the image is *venerated*, but only God is *worshiped*. We will return to this point later.

VI

This brings us to the second question. What is meant by worship, and is it something that is only offered to God? It should be noted that there is no abstract word in the Decalogue for "worship." The concept of worship is defined by two actions: "bowing down" and "serving." "To bow down" means to prostrate oneself, and it was common in ancient Israelite worship: it was a gesture of humility and submission. The verb "to serve" is also a common verb, but here, in context, it must refer to the sort of service that one would give specifically to a god—the bringing of offerings, praying, praising, and petitioning. The nearest that ancient Hebrew gets to a word for worship is *'avodah*—service, but because the word is vague and can be used in all sorts of nonreligious contexts, later Hebrew added the divine name (*'avodat ha-Shem*) to distinguish this type of service from other service. *'Avodat ha-Shem* is the closest Hebrew gets to our general concept of worship. What this linguistic development makes clear is that *'avodah* neither in biblical nor later Hebrew usage denotes an act exclusively reserved for God.[7] A similar semantic

---

7. The fact that the hof'al form of the root *'bd*, rather than the qal, appears to be used in the Masoretic Text of Exodus 20:5, does not affect our argument here. It is clearly not a mistake: see Deut. 5:9; 13:3; Exod. 23:24.

ambiguity inheres in the English "worship." Though in contemporary English "worship" is basically something that applies only to God, save when it is hyperbolically transferred to humans ("he worshiped her" in the sense that he treated her like a god), in older English it could be used quite properly of humans—"the worshipful company of haberdashers," or "your worship" as a title of respect for someone of high social standing, or the 1662 Book of Common Prayer marriage service in which the groom says to the bride, "with my body I thee worship."

"Serving" and, indeed, "bowing down" are actions that are not exclusively directed toward God.[8] But if this is the case, then if there *is* any difference in quality between the acts when directed toward God and when directed toward others, it does not inhere in the acts themselves but in the *mind of the actor*. But the actor must already have made up his or her mind as to the nature of the being toward whom the acts are directed before he or she performs them. The acts in themselves change nothing. This is a point that iconoclasts of all ages find it hard to grasp. Because the acts from an observational point of view are identical in the case both of God and beings that are not God, they complain that in directing them toward others the actors are deifying them. And if the actors assert they are doing no such thing and are perfectly capable of distinguishing God from that which is not-God, the iconoclast tends then to fall back on complaining that they are setting a bad example, and may lead weaker brethren astray. If this analysis is right, then it should be obvious that the acts themselves cannot alter the nature of the being toward whom they are directed. It should equally be obvious that it is impossible to infer from the acts themselves what is the precise status in the minds of the actors of the being toward whom they direct the acts. If they "worship" a being, it does not necessarily follow that they regard that being as in itself divine.

VII

In ancient Hebrew culture the person to whom, besides God, obeisance and service were most obviously due was the king. One way of explaining this would be to suppose that both terms denote actions that by custom an inferior gives to a superior, and since God and the king both belong to the category of "superior beings," then both are fitting objects of "bowing down" and "service." That may, in general, be the case, but there may be more to it specifically in

---

8. See the standard Hebrew lexica.

the case of the king. The king, as the anointed of the Lord, is owed the reverence due to his Master. This principle is encapsulated in the famous rabbinic dictum which I have quoted in the title of my paper: *'Eved melekh ka-melekh*—the servant of the king is as the king himself.[9] In rabbinic thought this dictum is applied to anyone acting as an agent of another. The agent has the same authority and deserves to be treated in the same way as the principal who sent him. That the king was Yahweh's representative on earth is deeply embedded in the ancient Israelite ideology of kingship. This can be seen in the royal psalms and in the application of the language of kingship to God himself. The idea that God is a king is often thought of as a transference to God of a human institution, but in ancient royal ideologies it was viewed the other way round: kingship descended from the gods. Kings are the earthly representatives of the heavenly king. This ideology was, of course, to die hard: Charles I lost his head defending it. But if the king is God's representative and agent on earth, then he is arguably owed the sort of reverence that is God's due, not in his own right, but as God's *agent*. The current debate on New Testament Christology has failed to see the importance of the concept of agency, and what is or is not entailed in the claim that Jesus was God's agent, perhaps even his unique agent, in the sense that he was tasked to do things within the purposes of God that no other agent was tasked to do.

The idea of the king as the agent of God makes another point that is of crucial importance for the present argument, namely that one cannot jump, so to speak, from agency to ontology. If one observes someone offering obeisance and service to the *agent* of God, one cannot assume that the person regards that agent as belonging to the same order of being as God. The king is human, God is divine—two quite different orders of being. It is arguable that there was a tendency in some circles to blur this ontological distinction between God and his royal agent. This can be seen in Egyptian royal ideology, where the king is regarded as himself a god on earth. There may be hints of this even in ancient Israelite thought—as when the king is addressed as God's son. But I don't think this language in ancient Israel ever clearly went beyond the metaphorical. The king remained a mortal, human figure—albeit of exalted status because of his association with God. God works in the world through agents. A human, a demon, an angel, an animal could be one of those agents, but these all clearly belong to different orders of being, not only from God, but from each other.

---

9. See Bavli Qiddushin 41b; Bavli Shavucot 47b; Genesis Rabbah (ed. Theodor-Albeck) 16.5. For a discussion of this in terms of legal agency see Menachem Elon, *Jewish Law: History, Sources, Principles*, 2 vols. (Philadelphia: Jewish Publication Society, 1995), 1:342–43.

"The Agent of the King Is Treated as the King Himself"

The *nature* of the work carried out by the agent of God on his behalf does not fundamentally alter the conclusion that agency carries no ontological implications, though it may define the status of the agent in the scheme of things—the more important the act, the higher the status of the agent. The act might even be considered as something uniquely divine, but even that does not have ontological implications for the agent, and does not mean that the agent must belong to the same category of being as God. One might argue that God alone will redeem his people at the end of history, that if *he* does not act, redemption will not happen. But this surely does not have to mean that he will appear in person as a *deus ex machina*. That the work is uniquely his is not compromised by the fact that he may choose to realize it through agents. This is, of course, precisely what traditional Jewish theology claims. The most important of the eschatological agents is the Messiah, but traditional Jewish theology regards him as human, and even in those cases where he is seen as superhuman, for example as some sort of angel, he is not identical with God. Indeed, the concept of agency fundamentally implies a distinction. It would be a curious redundancy of language to describe someone as acting as an agent of himself.

So too with the creation of the world. Creation of the world is uniquely divine work, but God may choose to realize it through some agent—the Logos, his Memra, or an angel distinct from himself. The divine uniqueness of the work is not thereby compromised, but neither is any ontological status for the agent automatically entailed, save that it can hardly be human, since humans did not exist till the end of the creative process. Actually this last statement is not as self-evident, on reflection, as it may at first appear. The term "creation" is a little slippery. There is a Jewish theological view that humanity is God's agent in completing the work of creation. God has left the world in a state of potentiality precisely to co-opt humanity as his co-worker to complete it, and the work of creation does not reach finality till humanity does so. In completing God's work by fulfilling the *mitzvot,* pious Jews "belong to the identity of God" (for this phrase see below), but they are not ontologically divine. Some rabbinic sources go out of their way to state that God was not helped by angels or other agents to create the world. But this has almost certainly a polemical context, and may be aimed *inter alia* at the Christian view of Christ's agency in creation. But, starting possibly with Proverbs 8, it was perfectly possible within Judaism to hold that God first created an agent through whom he created the world. This view is not incompatible with strict monotheism. Within the early mystical literature we find reference to the *Yotzer Bere'shit* (the Creator) who seems precisely to be the agent through whom God created the world. If the orthodoxy of these texts is deemed problematic, what about philosophers such as Maimonides who assigned to the Active Intellect, whom they designated in traditional Jewish language as an "angel," a role in creation? Was Maimonides not a monotheist? This agent, whoever he may be, because of the nature of the act he performs, must be endowed with powers capable of producing the effects he is meant to produce, but he does not have to be ontologically identical with God, or belong to the godhead.

VIII

So agency is a term of relation and, in itself, carries no ontological implications. All that granted, things are said about Christ as an agent of God in early Christian writings—work is attributed to him—that raise ontological questions. This is what the Christian debates of the fourth century demonstrated with great clarity, and why they borrowed from Greek thought the ontological categories of substance and nature, to resolve them. It has been suggested that the concept of identity is more appropriate as the principal category for understanding Jewish monotheism, than that of divine nature. I would be prepared to concede that this might well be a useful way of characterizing prephilosophical monotheism, but I would still argue that the ontological question cannot in the end be dodged. It was a weakness of the early Christologies that they did not address it properly, and that is why one could not advance them as they stand as adequate today and ignore the clarifications attempted in the fourth century. Let us suppose that we can sum up early Christology by saying that it asserts that "Jesus belongs to the unique identity of God." There is an ambiguity here that cries out for clarification. Identity, as any mathematician or logician will readily testify, is an ambiguous concept, and one obvious way of resolving its ambiguities is to clarify the ontology implied in the relationship it postulates. Does "x is identical with y" mean that x and y are one and the same, i.e., x and y are two terms for the same, single entity (they are *homoousios*)? Or does it mean that x and y belong to the same category or class, though they are discrete members of that class (they are *homoiousios*)? Or does it mean that because x acts as y's agent and with y's authority, we can treat x, in the sphere within which he acts, as identical with y, though they may be two different individuals that belong to two different orders of being?[10]

10. On all this see Richard Bauckham, *Jesus and the God of Israel: God Crucified and Other Studies on the New Testament's Christology of Divine Identity* (Grand Rapids: Eerdmans, 2008),

"The Agent of the King Is Treated as the King Himself"

It is striking how exegetical the Christological debates of the fourth century were. Athanasius, Arius, and the others were seeking to clarify and harmonize the various sometimes conflicting statements the New Testament makes about the relationship of Jesus to God, to hold them harmoniously together within a coherently structured theology, and they correctly saw that this had to be done in terms of ontology. Central to that ontology had to be a clear distinction between necessary being (God) and contingent being (the creatures whom God created and sustains). Once adequate conceptual tools were in place, then the job of clarifying Jesus's relationship to God could properly begin. What all sides came to recognize was that this was essentially an ontological question that could not be postponed indefinitely. But once the ontological genie was out of the bottle, it could not be put back in again. There is a strong continuity between the earliest Christologies and the Christologies of the fourth century: the latter emerge from a sustained attempt to clarify the former and iron out the problems they raise but leave unresolved. Basically two main clarifications were proposed. Arius argued that Christ as Son of God was a created being, though of immense power and status, who was neither consubstantial nor coeternal with God. Athanasius argued that Christ as Son of God was coeternal and consubstantial with God; he was absolutely and fully divine. Which of these is the correct understanding of the New Testament evidence? The short answer is that it is impossible to say, because the New Testament writers never raised the question in this form, or, if they did, they never did so with sufficient precision, because they lacked an adequate technical vocabulary with which to do so. Though the two views have profoundly different theological implications, arguably *both* are compatible with the New Testament evidence. But this only underscores how provisional, how under-

---

6–7. Bauckham writes: "As Vanhoozer notes, '"Identity" is, of course, susceptible to several meanings: numeric oneness, ontological sameness, and the personal identity of self-continuity'" (K. J. Vanhoozer, "Does the Trinity Belong to a Theology of Religions? On Angling in the Rubicon and the 'Identity' of God," in *The Trinity in a Pluralistic Age*, ed. K. J. Vanhoozer [Grand Rapids: Eerdmans, 1997], 47). The last is the meaning employed here. Reference to God's identity is by analogy with human personal identity, understood not as a mere ontological subject without characteristics, but as including both character and personal story (the latter entailing relationships). These are the ways in which we commonly specify "who someone is" (6n.6). Now there is no doubt that the identity of God in terms of what he does, the acts that identify him as who he is, is biblical and has been proposed before (e.g., G. Ernest Wright, *The God Who Acts: Biblical Theology as Recital* [London: SCM, 1964]), but I'm not persuaded it gets us very far Christologically. So Christ belongs to God's story. But don't we all? Relationship is implied, but what is the nature of that relationship? This needs to be clarified ontologically.

developed New Testament Christology is. The ontological question has to be raised and has to be answered.

IX

Let me conclude by summarizing the main points I have tried to make in this brief essay.

We should be very cautious about treating the recurrent motif in early Jewish and Christian literature of an angel rejecting worship from a human and telling him to worship God alone as a strong *theologoumenon* meant to do hard theological work. It may be, in most cases, little more than a literary and rhetorical trope.

Amassing long strings of instances of the trope, stretching from late Second Temple times to the Middle Ages, proves little, if it is indeed a trope. Only those which predate the early Christologies can be used as evidence. The later attestations may well be bound up in the very Christological issues we are trying to clarify. If this is the case, then there is a real danger of falling into circular argument.

If there *is* a theological force in the trope, then it is almost certainly *polemical*, but that immediately weakens the argument it is meant to bolster, because it implies that there *were* Jews who worshiped beings other than God. That this was the case is attested by independent literary evidence stretching from biblical times down to the Middle Ages.

The claim that Jews were universally monotheistic by the first century is problematic also because the meaning of the term "monotheistic" here is ambiguous. For very good reason the medieval schoolmen saw that the doctrine that there is one and only one God had to be predicated on the simultaneous assertion of a doctrine of *creatio ex nihilo*. The latter was a necessary corollary of the former. But it is hard to find an adequate statement of a doctrine of *creatio ex nihilo* in either Judaism or Christianity before late antiquity. General statements such as "God created all things" will not do, since they are equally compatible with the idea that creation involves the ordering of preexistent chaotic matter, which seems to be the original meaning of Genesis 1:1.

Just as the term "monotheism" is ambiguous, so is the term "worship." Worship in the Decalogue is defined by two acts, "bowing down" and "serving," but it is clear that those acts can be offered to beings other than God, e.g., the king. Phenomenologically speaking, intention is an important element of worship. Someone may offer obeisance and service to a being other than God, but not regard that being as in any sense on a par with God. They may make a sharp distinction in their own minds between that being and God. The actions may be from an observational point of view indistinguishable, but their meaning in the mind of the person who performs them may be quite different when offered to God and when offered to the king. This distinction was later expressed as a distinction between "veneration" and "worship," but the distinction is in the mind of the actor and depends on his or her *a priori* assumptions about the being to whom they are offered. The worshiper's view on this cannot be inferred from the actions themselves, which are ambiguous.

The concept of idolatry, which plays a part in the argument, is also "slippery." The argument gains strength if we can assume that by the first century idolatry was regarded by all Jews as a sin: it had become a universal taboo. So it is unthinkable that the early Jewish Christians would have committed this sin if they did not regard Jesus as God. That idolatry was abhorrent to many Jews is beyond question (and some were prepared to give their lives to avoid it), but what qualifies as idolatry is not as straightforward as is often supposed. Fundamentally it is the worship of the images of *other gods*. But it is not so clear that worshiping an image of the one true God falls under the taboo. God *was* represented in ancient Judaism, both visually (often aniconically) and by verbal pictures. Jews who employed images to aid their understanding and worship of God were perfectly capable, as were Gentiles (*pace* the rather trivial prophetic critique), of distinguishing between those images and the gods they represented.

Not enough attention has been paid to the concept of agency. An agent can be offered the same respect as the principal whom he represents (as in the case of the king as God's representative on earth), but the agent and the principal who sent him may belong to different orders of being (as, again, in the case of the king and God). If Christ is the agent, indeed the supreme agent, of God's purposes in the world, then that carries in itself no implication as to his nature, and certainly does not imply that he belongs to the same order of being as God, still less that he *is* God. Agency per se carries no ontological implications.

That said, the ontological implications of what the early Christians said about Jesus need to be clarified. His relationship to God is close and strong: he is clearly "identified" with God, but what does this identification mean? It needs to be clarified in ontological terms. The ontology of the relationship cannot be "fudged" forever. This was what the later Christological debates correctly understood. The Arian and the Athanasian positions attempt to clarify and harmonize the unclear and sometimes conflicting Christological statements in Scripture. Arguably *both* are compatible with those statements (though there may be other theological reasons for favoring one view over the other). The early Christologies never adequately addressed the ontological question, and for that reason cannot, just as they are, ignoring the later clarifications, be made the basis of Christology today.

Christianity without Paul

James D. G. Dunn

1. Introduction

I have sometimes thought of myself as a Paulinist, or more precisely as a Paulinist Christian. The reason is obvious: Paul was one of the main shapers of Christianity, his letters form a central part of the New Testament, and they provide a clearer, fuller, and more integrated theology than any of the other New Testament writings. So recently, somewhat to my own surprise, I found myself asking, What would the New Testament look like without Paul? What would Christianity look like without Paul? In particular, Paul was known and refers to himself as "an apostle to the Gentiles" (Rom. 11:13). So the question arises, What would the Jesus movement have become without Paul? Is it possible that, without Paul, Christianity would have remained a Jewish sect, a sect of Judaism? I ask the question, of course, not out of any idea of dispensing with Paul—quite the contrary, in fact. The thought is rather that a careful pursuit of this question would be a way of indicating how central to the definition and self-understanding of Christianity are Paul, the mission he gave himself to, and the letters he wrote. Not least, it seemed like an appropriate line of investigation to pursue in honor of one who has shed more light on the beginnings of Christianity than almost all his contemporaries.[1]

It is no good asking such a question, What would Christianity have looked

---

1. I quickly realized that to include debate with other scholars in the footnotes would stretch this essay to an unacceptable length. I confess that the resulting freedom to expound and argue directly from the text and without detailed debate has been rather enjoyable!

like without Paul?, with reference to third-generation Christians like Clement and Ignatius, since the question depends for its meaningfulness on the fact that Christianity had already spread widely into the Gentile world. And what is in question is precisely whether the Jesus movement would have spread into the Gentile world without Paul. Of course, there are indications of the Jesus movement having spread as far as Rome, quite apart from Paul—and of there being a strong representation of non-Jews in their number (Rom. 16).[2] But the question still arises whether these non-Jewish groupings of believers in Jesus would have flourished and linked up with other such groups in the Roman Empire apart from Paul, that is, apart from his work and apart from the churches he founded elsewhere.

Of course there were other missionaries—in particular, 1 Peter is addressed to north Turkey (1 Pet. 1:1). But in the agreement of which Galatians 2:1-10 informs us, Peter's missionary work was to focus on the circumcised, that is, on Jews and proselytes; so it is no surprise that 1 Peter is addressed explicitly to "the exiles of the dispersion/diaspora." And according to the same agreement, it was Paul to whom was given the responsibility for a Gentile mission (2:9). So, again the question arises: Without Paul, would there have been a Gentile mission, or, more definitively, a substantive mission which would have made Christianity a substantively Gentile religion? Did Paul in effect transform what was a basically proselytizing messianic Jewish mission into something else?

Of course, we should not forget Barnabas, who is regarded as Paul's partner in the Gentile mission, according to Galatians 2:9. But the following paragraph (2:11-14) indicates that the boundary-mission in Antioch (properly so-called from the opening of Acts 13), following a strong rebuke from James in Jerusalem (2:12), resolved to restrict that mission by insisting that Gentile converts should observe the Jewish food laws. That is, the insistence of Peter, Barnabas, and the others was in effect that Gentile converts should be regarded as and should regard themselves as proselytes. In contrast, it was Paul who insisted that the boundaries round Judaism had to be stretched, to recognize Gentile believers as full participants in the new movement, and full participants without their taking on the distinctively Jewish practices and rites. Faith in Christ, and faith alone, was what made a Gentile a Christian. He saw the issue to be of a piece with what had already been agreed in Jerusalem regarding circumcision. In contrast, those who demanded continuing observation of the

---

2. Of the more than twenty greeted in Rom. 16, three are listed as Jews (Andronicus, Junia, and Herodion—vv. 7, 11), and Aquila, Prisca, Mary, Rufus, and his mother were probably also Jews (vv. 3, 6, 13). But the full list is predominantly Gentile.

Christianity without Paul

food laws Paul refers to as "those from circumcision" (2:12). That is, in Paul's judgment, they were in effect going back on what had been agreed in Jerusalem. They were in effect insisting that what was happening in Antioch should be seen as simply a proselytizing mission. And to Paul's horror and outrage they evidently persuaded not only Peter, but also all the other (believing) Jews in Antioch, including even Barnabas, to follow suit. This was a decisive episode in the earliest history of Christianity—the insistence that in effect the Jesus movement should not regard itself as a different movement from Judaism—messianic Judaism, certainly, but still Judaism. The obvious conclusion was that Gentile converts to the new movement were proselytes to Judaism.

Since Paul does not indicate that his rebuke of Peter was successful, or that the church in Antioch reverted to the practice of Jew and Gentile eating food together without reference to the Jewish food laws, the practice which the unnamed who "came from James" had evidently condemned, the likelihood must be that Paul's rebuke of Peter was unsuccessful from Paul's point of view.[3] In the event, the church in Antioch probably continued to observe the Jewish food laws as a defining mark of their identity. And Paul, it would seem, in effect ignored the self-definition of the new movement established in Antioch (as a Jewish movement winning proselytes) and headed off to develop his own Gentile (nonproselyte) mission in Asia Minor, Macedonia, and Greece.

That mission, of course, was immensely successful in winning converts. That mission, indeed, could be said to have established the non-distinctively-Jewish character of the new movement, that is, of Christianity (that is, requiring neither circumcision nor observation of the Jewish food laws). In which case, the questions arise again: If Paul had fallen in line with the persuasion and practice of Peter, would a proselytizing mission have been so successful? Would Gentiles have been so attracted by such a mission as they were by Paul's mission following his failure in Antioch? And without Paul would the new movement have remained an essentially Jewish movement seeking to win proselytes to Judaism?

2. The Non-Pauline New Testament Literature

How do the other New Testament writings contribute to this discussion? The fundamental problem, of course, is that they were all written after Paul, and

---

3. Gal. 2:15-21 should probably be read as the argument that Paul wished he had used in the unsuccessful confrontation with Peter.

so reflect the situation of emerging Christianity in the wake of his own mission. Is it possible to ask with any hope of a clear answer, what would they have said, were it not for Paul?

a. Take the evidence of Matthew and Mark, for example. It is most likely that the discussion of clean and unclean in Mark 7 reflects Paul's own firm stand on the subject. Mark's rendition of Jesus's teaching, that "[t]here is nothing outside a person that by going in can defile, but the things that come out are what defile" (Mark 7:15), seems to reflect Paul's own firm belief that "nothing is unclean in itself" (Rom. 14:14). So Mark's own interpretation which he adds, "Thus he (Jesus) declared all foods clean" (Mark 7:19), may well, indeed, probably does reflect Paul's own beliefs on the point, and the way that Mark interpreted Jesus's own teaching in the light of Paul's. This is probably confirmed by Matthew's version of the same teaching. For the Matthean parallel to Mark 7:15 reads somewhat differently: "It is not what goes into the mouth that defiles a person, but it is what comes out of the mouth that defiles" (Matt. 15:11). The transformation of the emphatic language of Mark is striking: the "nothing . . . can" words have been omitted; and Mark's interpretive addition, "Thus he (Jesus) declared all foods clean," has likewise disappeared. The effective abolition of the laws of clean and unclean (in Mark) has become (in Matthew) a simple exhortation that what one says is more defiling than what one eats. In this case, the likelihood is that Mark reflects the kind of teaching and fellowship practice which had already become common in the churches Paul had set up; whereas Matthew reflects a more Jewish Christianity for whom observance of the Jewish law was still of prime importance.

This likelihood is strengthened by two other passages in Matthew. One is the very strong reaffirmation of the law in Matthew 5:17-20, where Jesus explicitly states, "I have not come to abolish the law or the prophets" and insists that breach or relaxation even of one of the least of the commandments was unacceptable.[4] And the other is the passage in which Jesus gives instruction to the twelve (disciples) for mission: "Go nowhere among the Gentiles, and enter no town of the Samaritans, but go rather to the lost sheep of the house of Israel" (Matt. 10:5-6). In other words, despite the universal commission with which Matthew closes his Gospel, "Go therefore and make disciples of all

---

4. Note also how concerned Matthew was to warn against *anomia*, "lawlessness" (7:23; 13:41; 23:28; 24:12), a word distinctive of Matthew, clearly indicating his own and the Gospel's loyalty to the law. Similarly indicative is his addition to Mark 13:18 ("Pray that it may not happen in winter") to read "Pray that your flight may not be in winter or on a Sabbath" (Matt. 24:20).

Christianity without Paul

nations" (28:19), his addition of "teaching them to obey everything that I have commanded you" (28:20) is probably a sufficient reminder that obedience to the law, as interpreted by and in the light of Jesus, was still of first importance. In other words, in Matthew's view Gentile converts could still be regarded and should regard themselves as proselytes.

Is there any influence of Paul to be discerned here? And if we should rather speak of a reaction to Paul, the question may be posed whether Matthew is a more accurate reflection of the influence and impact of Jesus apart from Paul. And would Matthean Christianity itself have become a universal religion apart from Paul? Would the schism with Judaism implicit or under way in Matthew[5] have become complete, would the movement for whom Matthew speaks have become an independent and thriving movement, as became the case with Pauline Christianity? Or rather would it have become one of those spinoffs from Judaism which either died away or were subsequently reabsorbed into rabbinic Judaism? This, of course, is the question which hangs over the non-rabbinic forms of Judaism which in the last decades of the first century and early decades of the second were distinct from the Pharisees and from what rabbinic Judaism became.[6] But insofar as Matthew belongs to this category, the same question arises: whether Matthean Christianity could have sustained itself in interaction with post–70 rabbinic Judaism, or was it inevitable that in itself (quite apart from what was happening as the outcome of Paul's mission) it would have grown into a fully independent movement?

b. If we turn to the writings of Luke, not dissimilar questions arise. Of course, Luke was probably the companion of Paul in much of his mission work.[7] So a question like this—What would Luke have recorded, or have had to record, apart from Paul?—is probably too unrealistic to pursue very far. Nevertheless, if the issue is the Jesus movement apart from Paul, it is possible to probe at least a little. The fact is that Luke goes out of his way in Acts to set out Paul in some parallel to Peter.[8] But that very feature raises the question whether Luke

---

5. See further my *The Partings of the Ways* (London: SCM, 1991; 2nd ed. 2006), §8.5.

6. Trypho, in Justin Martyr's *Dialogue with Trypho*, can be regarded as a diaspora Jew not yet heavily influenced by the emerging rabbinic Judaism of Palestine and Syria. And see further under §3 below.

7. As indicated most noticeably by the "we" passages in Acts: 16:10-17; 20:6-15; 21:1-18; 27:1–28:16.

8. Miracles of judgment (5:1-10; 13:11); remarkably similar initial sermons (2:14-36; 13:16-41); healing of a man "lame from birth" (3:2; 14:8), evoking wonder from the crowd (3:9-11; 14:11-13, 18), and providing opportunity to preach (3:12-26; 14:14-17).

was trying to boost the image and memory of Peter by comparing him with Paul. Which then raises the further question whether Peter would have been portrayed as so effective a missionary had Luke not set out to make that comparison.

(i) It is of course the case that Luke attributes the major breakthroughs of the early mission to Peter. It is Peter, with John, who confirms the success of Philip's mission to the Samaritans in Acts 8. And it is Peter who makes the great breakthrough in taking the good news of Jesus to the Roman centurion, Cornelius. The fact that Luke devotes to this episode a chapter and a half (Acts 10:1–11:18) indicates the importance which Luke attached to the story. But then, according to the same Luke, after his imprisonment by Herod and release by angelic agency in Acts 12, Peter in effect disappears from the ongoing story — somewhat dismissed with the brief and mysterious conclusion, "He left and went to another place" (12:17).

(ii) Of course, Peter reappears in Acts 15 as one of the two principal figures, recalling precisely the precedent he himself had set with the conversion of Cornelius (15:7–11). The other principal figure is James the brother of Jesus, who is portrayed as in effect the chairman of the consultation in Jerusalem, and who, as such, sums up the conclusions of the consultation (13:13–21). Paul and Barnabas are given only brief mention as narrating their success in Gentile mission (13:12). So, although Luke goes on to devote the second half of his account of Christianity's beginnings to the mission of Paul, it is surely significant that he in effect boosts the role played by Peter, and in effect diminishes the breakthrough which Paul's mission actually achieved.

(iii) Notable also is the fact that Luke in effect draws a veil over Paul's confrontation with Peter in Antioch. He never mentions the Antioch incident (Gal. 2:11–14), on which Paul himself placed so much evidence in justifying his law-free mission to Gentiles (2:15–21).

So, should we say that Luke was trying to boost the image of Peter? He ignored Peter's insistence (according to Gal. 2:11–14) that the mission on which they were engaged (Paul as well as Barnabas) was a Jewish mission, seeking to win proselytes. And in effect he attributed to Peter the initial Gentile breakthrough which Paul achieved (Acts 13–14 coming after Acts 10–11). But if we strip away that motivation, and focus only on Peter's own view of the enterprise, are we not led to the conclusion that Luke's portrayal of *Peter* is drawn to a substantial extent from what we know of *Paul's* mission? And if that is the obvious inference, then how much of mission as mission to Gentiles can be attributed to Peter? Alternatively expressed, was the conversion of Cornelius more to be described and understood as the

Christianity without Paul

affirmation of a devout proselyte's (10:2) acceptance within the Jesus movement rather than as the breakthrough to full-scale Gentile mission, such as we attribute to Paul? Certainly the mission attributed to Peter prior to the Cornelius episode is not framed in terms of a Gentile breakthrough (9:32–43). And in the Jerusalem conference the conclusion drawn by Peter is still in terms of legal requirements which Gentile converts should be asked or required to observe (15:19–21).

Nor should we forget that Paul's mission thereafter is still set out in characteristic Jewish terms: first to the synagogue;[9] and Paul's own readiness to practice and observe the law.[10] Although fully accepting the outcome of Paul's final return to Jerusalem (21:17–26:32), Luke seems anxious to portray Paul as still a respectful Jew. The affirmation, "I am a Jew," which Luke attributes twice to Paul's self-confession (21:39; 22:3), comes across as much more assertive of Paul's Jewish status than Paul's own affirmations such as 1 Corinthians 9:20 ("To the Jews I became as a Jew") and Galatians 3:28 ("There is no longer Jew or Greek"). Of course Acts narrates Paul's "turn to the Gentiles" on several occasions,[11] and does not hesitate to portray "the Jews" as Paul's chief antagonists on several occasions.[12] But Luke also makes a point of recording that the Jews of Rome had heard no negative reports of Paul and wanted to hear from him regarding the new Jesus "sect" (Acts 28:21–22), and he makes no attempt to exclude the Roman Jews from the "all who came to him" to hear him teaching about Jesus from his fade-out picture at the end of Acts (28:30–31).

So, if Luke took such pains to retain and reinforce the image of the self-confessed "apostle to the Gentiles" (Rom. 11:13) as a Jew, is it fair to ask whether the earliest Christian movement would have developed a Gentile mission without Paul? After all, there is a significant difference between the acceptance of a God-fearer like Cornelius, which could be counted as in effect an extension of proselyte status, and the all-out Gentile mission of Paul, which wholly dispensed with the characteristic Jewish identity markers of circumcision and food laws. So it is not a senseless question to ask: What would the early Christian movement have become without Paul? Did he in effect force open a door which otherwise would have remained shut? Without Paul would what we think of as the earliest Christian mission have gone beyond a proselytizing

---

9. Acts 13:14; 14:1; 17:1–2, 10; 18:4; 19:8.
10. Acts 18:18; 21:26; 22:3; 25:8.
11. Acts 13:46; 18:6; 28:28.
12. Acts 13:45, 50; 14:2, 19; 17:5, 13; 20:3, 19.

mission? Would it have ever expanded beyond the status of a Jewish "sect"? It is noticeable that Luke uses this word ("sect") to describe the Jesus movement (Acts 24:5; 28:22), noticeable in that he uses the same word to describe the Sadducees (5:17) and the Pharisees (15:5; 26:5), and indeed has Paul using the same word to describe his own affiliation as a believer in Jesus (24:14). Was it, then, precisely that sect status, and the possibility of the new movement continuing as a sect of Judaism, like the sects of Sadducees and Pharisees, which Paul's Gentile mission in effect destroyed? But without Paul . . . ?

c. And what about the Fourth Gospel? That is interesting in this discussion precisely because it does not evidence much if any influence from Paul. Is it fair, then, to ask whether it indicates and expresses what the Jesus movement might have become without or apart from Paul? Here the interest lies precisely in what John does with classic elements of what Judaism had been and of what became Judaism in the second century and beyond. The key consideration is that he presents Jesus in effect as the fulfillment of historic Judaism. He is the only New Testament writer to use the word "Messiah" (*Messias*) of Jesus (John 1:41; 4:25); that Jesus fulfilled the historic messianic hopes of Jew and Samaritan was a key point for the Fourth Evangelist. It is the "water reserved for the Jewish purification rites" which is transformed into wine (2:1-11). In 2:19-22 Jesus plays with the image of the Jerusalem Temple, which had already been destroyed when John most probably wrote his Gospel. The point is not so much that Jesus is recalled as contrasting his own body with the Temple. Rather, he portrays his own body, his resurrected body, as in direct continuity with the Temple. At the heart of the point being made by John is the continuity with Temple-centered Judaism now bereft of its Temple, a continuity that Jesus's resurrection would achieve.

Likewise in the conversation with the Samaritan woman at the well, when Jesus speaks of "worship in Spirit and truth" (4:23), the point is not that such worship shows the worship in Jerusalem and Gerizim to have been wrong. It is rather a matter of older hope and practice being fulfilled, as the woman indicates (4:25). It is a spirit of continuity and climax more than of rejection and abolition which is expressed here. Similarly with the language and spirit of the Passover in chapter 6. There is a deeper and fuller reality which comes to effect through Jesus's death. But it can still be richly expressed in Passover ritual and language. Similarly in chapter 8, the point is not that Abraham has been superseded and that descent from him no longer matters. It is rather that Jesus is in continuity with and the climax of what Abraham signified (8:56). Similarly in chapter 10 the sheep and shepherd imagery, so beloved in the

Christianity without Paul

(Jewish) scriptures, is fulfilled in Jesus, the Feast of Dedication resonating in Jesus and his teaching.

Had the ways (of Judaism and Christianity) already parted? Some think so. The negative references to "the Jews" can certainly be seen as evidence of such a split[13]—a Jesus movement which no longer saw itself within Judaism, its participants no longer as fellow worshipers with the Jews. A fair reading of John's Gospel, however, must take account also of the fact that there are other references to "Jews."[14] There are Jews who remain unclear as to whether Jesus is the Messiah, Jews who can still be persuaded. John, it would appear, thought that he could still win them to faith in Jesus. So it would seem to be a fairer reading of John to infer that John saw the believers in Jesus as Messiah as still within rather than already outside the traditions of Judaism.

The point is nicely brought to focus in John's use of the term *aposynagōgos*, "out of/expelled from the synagogue."[15] The threat is clear: that some Jews had been or were in danger of being expelled from the synagogue. Or to be more precise, that some at least of the Jewish followers of Jesus had been or were in danger of being expelled from the synagogue. Which brings us back to the fact that post–70 Judaism, in a turmoil because of the destruction of the Temple, was fairly diverse, with not only Pharisees still functioning as exponents of their faith, but also those who understood their Judaism particularly in apocalyptic, but also other expressions of Jewish faith.[16] When the Pharisees began in effect to restrict the definition of Judaism to what was in fact one form of pre–70 Judaism, rabbinic Judaism, what happened to the other forms? John's Gospel gives us a partial answer to that question. For it implies that while "the Jews" (= what was to become rabbinic Judaism) rejected the teaching of the believers in Jesus, there were other Jews who were still open to it. Johannine Christianity, in fact, can be fairly categorized as one of the forms of Judaism which rabbinic Judaism sloughed off since the rabbis in effect regarded themselves as the sole representatives of Judaism properly so called.

So it can be fairly argued that Johannine Christianity saw itself as a climactic form of Israel's faith and practice, as the eschatological realization of what Israel had hoped and looked for throughout its high and low times. The

---

13. E.g., John 5:16, 18; 6:41; 7:1, 13; 8:48, 52, 57–59; 9:22; 10:31–33; 11:8.

14. E.g., John 4:22; 6:52; 7:11–12; 10:19–21; 11:36; 12:11.

15. John 9:22; 12:42; 16:2.

16. The Christian apocalypse, the Revelation of John, can be most closely matched in the writings of the period with the Jewish apocalypses of 2 Baruch and 4 Ezra. Note also the Testamental literature, e.g., the Testament of Moses.

heirs of the Pharisees at the turn of the first/second century wanted to say that their own self-understanding of these hopes was decisively different; the ways had already parted. From their perspective, for Judaism to reaffirm itself in the wake of the Temple's destruction, it was in effect necessary to slough off all other forms of first-century Judaism which challenged or confused the Pharisaic self-understanding of Judaism. That included the Jesus movement, which saw itself as the fulfillment or eschatological realization of Israel's faith and hope, that is, Johannine Judaism. Which leaves the question hanging: Without the Pauline Gentile mission, would the Johannine movement have become an international expression of a faith essentially different from Judaism?

d. Even more than the Fourth Evangelist, the writer to the Hebrews presents the new faith in Jesus the Christ as the climax and fulfillment of Israel's faith and hopes. It is precisely the continuity of God's purpose in creation and in salvation, the continuity between what God said to the/our[17] fathers and what he said in/by his son, which the writer chooses to emphasize in his opening words (Heb. 1:1-2). The impression is reinforced by the way the writer repeatedly quotes scripture (Israel's scriptures) to show that they have been and are being fulfilled in and by Jesus.[18] For the sake of Abraham's descendants Jesus became like his brothers (fellow Jews) in every respect in order that he might minister on their behalf as "a merciful and faithful high priest in the service of God, to make a sacrifice of atonement for the sins of the people" (2:17). He is not set in antithesis to Moses, but more in parallel (3:2): Jesus represents the builder of the house (God), but Moses represents the house built; Christ is the son in God's house, and Moses is a servant in the same house (3:3-6). Similarly, the writer wants his readers to see Israel's testing time in the wilderness prior to entry into the promised land as representative of the trials and anticipations of their own entry into the promised rest (3:7-4:11).

Of course, the main thrust of Hebrews is to portray Israel's wilderness experience as foreshadowing and typifying the experience of its readers. Christ is the high priest, and because his priesthood is of the order of Melchizedek, who was "without father, without mother, without genealogy, having neither beginning of days nor end of life" (7:3), his priesthood transcends that of

---

17. The inclusion of "our" ("our fathers"), whether original or introduced later, strongly suggests that the letter itself evoked that sense.

18. Direct quotation of the Hebrew scriptures is more intense, particularly in the opening chapters, than elsewhere in the New Testament.

Aaron. It is Jesus whom the writer identifies as the one addressed in the otherwise mysterious words of Psalm 110:4: "You are a priest forever, according to the order of Melchizedek" (7:17). His death too transcends the atoning sacrifice which used to be offered in the Jerusalem Temple. The point is of such importance for the author that he saw no difficulty in portraying both Jesus as the sacrificing priest *and* Jesus's death as the sacrifice offered by himself. There is continuity here, much more than any thought of discontinuity—transcendence, yes, but not abolition. Without the whole biblical system of priesthood and atoning sacrifice, Jesus's death would make no sense. More than any other New Testament writing, without the Old Testament Hebrews would make no sense.

Similarly the strong motif of the new covenant, introduced in 7:22 and dominant through chapters 8 and 9, is drawn entirely from Jeremiah 31:31–34 (Heb. 8:8–12). The point, of course, is that the ancient hope of Israel has found its fulfillment in Christ. The thought is more of continuity and completion rather than of abrogation and obsolescence.[19] That the author of Hebrews regards the buildup to the new covenant in positive terms is surely confirmed by his strong affirmation of Noah, Abraham, Moses, Gideon, and the rest as heroic precedents of the faith which he commends to his readers (ch. 11). His concluding affirmation that God had no intention of making such heroes of Israel's history perfect "apart from us" (11:40) should not be falsely turned round to affirm Hebrews' intention to bring his readers to perfection "apart from them"!

The unbroken continuity of God's saving purpose, from Abel to Abraham, and from Moses to the present, is at the heart of Hebrews' exposition. He (I assume a male author) could not have conceived of a worshiping group of Jesus followers which disowned that continuity or disregarded it. More than any other New Testament writing, Hebrews' self-consciousness could be characterized as the continuity and climax of Israel's history and hope. The writing is often characterized as written for those who were dismayed, their faith threatened by the destruction of the Jerusalem Temple. Not unfairly, since it is the continuity of their faith with Israel's history, the completion of that story in Jesus, which the writer was chiefly concerned to bring out. It is hard to

---

19. Too many modern translations render *palaioein* in 8:13 as "declare/treat as obsolete" (W. Bauer, *A Greek-English Lexicon of the New Testament and Other Early Christian Literature*, 3rd ed. of BAGD, rev. by F. W. Danker [Chicago: University of Chicago Press, 2000], 751). That is too strong, since it diminishes too much the degree of continuity which is central to the argument of Hebrews. "Renders old/out of date" would accord more with the principal thesis of Hebrews. Similarly in 10:9, should not *anairein* be rendered simply as "take away," rather than "destroy"?

imagine that he would have wanted or been happy with a response which turned its back on Israel's history and hope.

e. The only other non-Pauline writings in the New Testament which we need consider now are the letter of James and the Revelation of John.[20] For James is arguably the most Jewish of all the New Testament writings, the only New Testament writer to use the term "synagogue" for assemblies of Jesus-followers (James 2:2). Two features are of particular importance here. One is that James is the clearest example in the New Testament of the genre of Jewish wisdom literature, classically expressed in the biblical book of Proverbs.[21] The other is the striking degree to which James draws not only on classic Jewish wisdom but also on Jesus's own wisdom teaching.[22] That is to say, Jesus is remembered and celebrated in the letter of James as a teacher of Jewish wisdom. In other words, James can be regarded as a good example of what Christianity might have been and might have continued as apart from Paul. It is noticeable that Christ is mentioned specifically only twice (1:1; 2:1), though James also refers to "the coming of the Lord" (5:7) and speaks of anointing the sick "in the name of the Lord" (5:14). But this makes the character of James all the more striking: that Jesus is remembered by James primarily as a teacher of wisdom and for his wisdom teaching.

There is also the intriguing interaction with, and implicit rebuke of, one of the most distinctively Pauline emphases—that justification is reckoned to faith apart from works (as in Gal. 2:16). In what can only be regarded as some contrast with Paul's teaching, James insists that "faith without works is dead" (James 2:14-26). One can well see that no contradiction need be reckoned here, since Paul also insists that "faith working through love" is "the only thing that counts" (Gal. 5:6). Nevertheless, it is hard not to juxtapose James 2:14-26 with Galatians 2:16, and just as hard to avoid drawing the inference that James represents a reaction to Paul's essential gospel message, a reaction which must have been shared by many Jewish believers in Jesus.

This all becomes more intriguing when we recall that James was regarded

---

20. 1 Peter is too Pauline in character, that is, too much influenced by Paul, to be considered as an example or evidence of what might have been apart from Paul.

21. For details of passages where James echoes or quotes Jewish wisdom, particularly passages from Proverbs and ben Sira, see my *Christianity in the Making*, vol. 2, *Beginning from Jerusalem* (Grand Rapids: Eerdmans, 2009), 1133.

22. Note James 1:5 (Matt. 7:7/Luke 11:9); 2:5 (Matt. 5:34/Luke 6:20b); 4:9 (Matt. 5:4/Luke 6:21b); 4:10 (Matt. 23:12/Luke 14:11); 5:1 (Luke 6:24-25); 5:2-3a (Matt. 6:20/Luke 12:33b); 5:12 (Matt. 5:34-37).

as the chief figure among the leadership of the Jerusalem believers (Gal. 2:1–10; Acts 15:13–21). Should the letter of James, then, be seen as an expression of what the Jesus movement might have become, or perhaps better, of how the Jesus movement might have remained, apart from Paul? Did Paul in effect change what was a Jewish revival or renewal movement into something else— something bigger, yes, but also something different on crucial self-defining points, something growing away from its Jewish roots? Christianity, but no longer messianic Judaism?

Revelation deserves at least a brief mention. For Paul is more or less irrelevant to it. The apocalypse of John could have been written and circulated in complete disregard of Paul. Paul is never mentioned explicitly, and implicit allusion to him or his work is not really evident. Even though the letters written to churches (Rev. 2–3) include letters written to a church he founded (Ephesus), and even though the other six churches were probably established as offshoots of the churches founded by Paul, there is no allusion to Paul or any of his works or writings. The references to "those who call themselves Jews" (2:9; 3:9) certainly have echoes with some of Paul's fiercer statements.[23] But the fuller references themselves should not be missed: "those who call themselves Jews, and are not, but are a synagogue of Satan" (2:9); "those from the synagogue of Satan who call themselves Jews, and are not but tell lies" (3:9). Here, it should be noted, are not dismissals of Jews as such. The dismissal is of those who in the author's view cannot make a justifiable claim to be Jews. The implication is that to be a Jew is good. Those who are dismissed are criticized for misleadingly or falsely claiming the status of Jews. The writer evidently regarded the gospel as he understood it as in direct continuity with the religion of the Jews, presumably, as the eschatological fulfillment of Jewish hope and expectation. Jews who quarreled with that were at best misguided. Here, in other words, is still an intra-Jewish dispute. The Christian apocalypse can be fairly regarded as one of the Jewish reactions to the catastrophe of 70 CE, an apocalyptic reaction which emerging rabbinic Judaism similarly tried to slough off with the other post–70 apocalypses.

In conclusion, then, what has emerged is the fascinating picture of a Jewish movement, the Jesus movement, which, apart from Paul, could be reckoned simply as part of the diverse Judaism in the second half of the first century, an expression of eschatological Judaism which was increasingly sloughed off by emerging rabbinic Judaism in the second century of the common era.

---

23. Particularly 1 Thess. 2:14 and 2 Cor. 11:24.

3. Paul

At this point we should, at last, bring Paul himself into the discussion. What would Christianity have been or become without Paul? Of course, Paul is integral to what Christianity became. But since Paul is not so integral to Christianity as Jesus is, it is not impossible to imagine the impact or influence of Jesus apart from Paul. Paul, of course, was almost certainly the major influence in directing the new movement's gospel to Gentiles. So it can hardly be an unfair question to ask whether the new movement would have directed itself so emphatically in a Gentile direction without Paul. We certainly cannot exclude the question, If Paul played such a crucial role in the development of the Jesus movement into historic Christianity, would the Jesus movement, apart from Paul, have naturally transposed itself into the predominantly Gentile religion that it became?

The uncomfortable historic fact is that Jewish Christianity was or became a branch of Christianity which was in effect sloughed off in the process of Christianity's development, already in the second century. We know from literature of or referring to the second-century period that there were several forms of Jewish Christianity—Ebionites, Nazoreans, and Elkesaites in particular. These are regarded by the patristic Christian writers as schismatic, and it is probably fair to describe them as left behind in the development of mainstream Christianity. There is unclarity of course on various aspects of these movements. But the impact of Paul was certainly one of the key factors in setting, for example, the Ebionites over against the mainstream Christianity of the fathers. Irenaeus describes the Ebionites in these terms:

> They use the Gospel according to Matthew only and repudiate the apostle Paul, saying that he was an apostate from the Law. . . . [T]hey practise circumcision, persevere in the customs which are according to the Law and practise a Jewish way of life, even adoring Jerusalem as if it were the house of God. (*Adv. haer.* 1.26.2)[24]

Origen also notes that the Ebionites "do not accept the letters of Paul" (*C. Celsum* 5.66); similarly Eusebius notes that the Ebionites rejected all the epistles of the Apostle, "whom they called an apostate from the Law" (*HE* 3.27.4); and similarly Jerome, that they "rejected Paul as a transgressor of the Law" (*In*

---

24. The quotations are from A. F. J. Klijn and G. J. Reinink, *Patristic Evidence for Jewish-Christian Sects*, Supplements to Novum Testamentum 36 (Leiden: Brill, 1973).

Matth. 12.2).²⁵ And the probable source underlying the pseudo-Clementine, identifiable in *Recog.* 1.27–71,²⁶ has no qualms in identifying Saul/Paul as "a certain hostile person" who disputed with James and then threw him from the top of the stairs, leaving him for dead (70.1–8).

The question naturally arises, Why was Paul so disparaged in such strongly Jewish, albeit Jewish-Christian circles? And the answer is clear: that it was primarily Paul's attitude to and teaching on the (Jewish) law which proved so offensive to such Jewish believers in Jesus. As Irenaeus says, Paul was regarded as "an apostate from the law." In the period following the destruction of the Jerusalem Temple, we know that the law became the critically self-defining feature of the Judaism which survived and which slowly spread through the eastern Roman Empire. In that circumstance, the one who had relaxed the claims of the law on participants of the Jewish sect venerating Jesus was bound to be regarded with suspicion and derision. Paul in effect became the breakpoint for Jewish Christianity in relation to the broader, more Gentile-dominated Christianity. Which brings us back to our key question: whether the Jesus movement would have become the Christianity of Clement, Ignatius, etc. without Paul. What would the Jesus movement have become without Paul?

It is not as though Paul himself was unaware of the danger his mission threatened to his messianic Judaism. His early letter to the Galatians clearly signaled the danger. Some slackness regarding circumcision might have been acceptable (Gal. 2:1–10). But the further readiness of Paul to disregard the food laws, even against the strong urging of Jerusalem, had already made a breach within the new movement (2:11–14). And in his subsequent self-defense Paul had not hesitated to deny and dismiss the importance of law-keeping. For Paul to characterize law-keeping as "a yoke of slavery" (5:1) must have been surprising and offensive to most Jews. And to set Spirit and law in such sharp antithesis (5:16–23) must have puzzled and angered his Jewish readers. It is not out of order to ask how Paul's letter to Galatia would have been regarded when news of it came to the Jerusalem believers. And if Paul had indeed lost in the confrontation in Antioch, as seems most likely, his vigorous and rather rude (5:6) response was likely to be read as a signal that with Paul's Gentile mission the ways had already parted—parted, that is, not between the Jesus movement and Judaism so much as parted between the Jesus movement in Palestine and the Gentile mission of Paul.

It can certainly be argued that in his subsequent letter to Rome Paul ex-

---

25. I draw here from my *Christianity in the Making*, vol. 3, §45.8a.
26. See further *Christianity in the Making*, vol. 3, §§40.6g and 45.8d.

pressed himself more carefully, and probably hoped to rebuild some of the bridges with his ancestral Judaism which his Galatian epistle had disregarded and indeed seemed to break down. Thus it is that Paul repeatedly reminds his readers or audiences that the good news is for Jew (first) but also for Greek.[27] He insists that Jews have not been disadvantaged by the gospel (3:1-2). He argues the case for seeing Abraham, rightly understood, as providing the model of saving faith (ch. 4), argued more carefully than the more contentious version of Galatians. He seeks to clarify what he sees to be the real function of the law (chs. 7-8) and insists that love of neighbor is the fulfilling of the law (13:10). And in chapters 9-11 he sets the Gentile mission within the overall divine plan, climaxing as intended in the salvation of all Israel. It is the Paul of reconciling Romans, then, who should feature in Jewish/Christian dialogue, rather than the Paul of the offensive Galatians.

Was it too late? Was the damage done by Paul's failure in Antioch, by his more intensive mission to Gentiles, and by his somewhat intemperate defense in his letter to Galatia already in effect beyond repair? The fact that Paul's subsequent attempt to heal the breach with Jerusalem by bringing the collection, made at his instigation by his Gentile churches for "the poor among the saints in Jerusalem" (Rom. 15:26), was virtually ignored by Luke cannot but be significant.[28] As also the fact that Luke records no support for Paul from Jerusalem believers during his two-year imprisonment and trials in Jerusalem. That silence is surely a disturbing precursor of the anti-Paulinist attitudes of the Jewish-Christian sects indicated earlier in this section. The somewhat unpleasant fact, then, is that the anti-Pauline attitude expressed by such branches of early Christianity was probably rooted in the reactions to Paul's Gentile mission during its pre-70 flourishing. Paul's abrasive promotion of his mission to Gentiles and the reactions to that law-free mission among Jewish believers are probably sufficient to explain why a Christianity which honored Paul highly was bound to become more and more detached from its Jewish roots.

4. Conclusion

So the question emerges again: Without Paul and apart from Paul would the Jesus movement have become separated from its maternal Judaism? Would

---

27. Rom. 1:16; 2:9-10; 3:29; 9:24; 10:12.
28. Luke records Paul as mentioning the collection, but as "alms to my nation" (Acts 24:17) without further clarification, and says no more on the subject.

what became Christianity have remained a renewal movement within Judaism, an eschatological movement to be sure, and as such drawing in proselytes no doubt, but not a predominantly Gentile movement or a new religion? If we owe Christianity's universal character in such large part to Paul, do we also have to acknowledge that his universalizing mission was what in the event caused the schism between Judaism and Christianity? His vision of an eschatological Judaism, with arms wide open to Gentiles, but shorn of its distinctively Jewish marks of circumcision and food laws, was bound to be a bridge too far for most Jewish Christians, was it not?

PART 2

TEXTUAL STUDIES

God Put Jesus Forth: Reflections on Romans 3:24–26

N. T. Wright

When Paul writes a particularly dense clause, sentence, or paragraph the temptation for interpreters is to focus all their attention on the precise words he is using, and the precise relationship in which they stand to one another. These are of course vital. Without them, the door to eisegesis stands wide open. But this necessary microscopic focus often gets in the way of, or even replaces altogether, the equally important task of understanding the contribution made by the passage to the larger unit of thought within which it occurs. Sometimes the latter task will shed fresh light on the former. I believe this is the case with one of Paul's densest formulations: the statement of the meaning of the death of Jesus in Romans 3:24–26. I offer these reflections with gratitude to a friend and colleague who has done as much as any, and more than most, to reshape the contemporary discussion of how the early Christians understood who Jesus was and what he had achieved.[1]

---

1. Richard Bauckham and I got to know one another as members of the Church of England's "Doctrine Commission" in the late 1980s, discussing the doctrine of salvation; hence, I trust, the appropriateness of this contribution. Among his more recent gifts of friendship was his recommendation to me of a Japanese research student, Norio Yamaguchi, whose St Andrews doctoral dissertation (*Sacrifice, Curse and the Covenant in Paul's Soteriology* [2015]) I gladly acknowledge as the source of some of the key reflections in what follows (though Dr. Yamaguchi has not seen this and bears no responsibility for the use I have made of his work). I am grateful to Max Botner and Raymond Morehouse for their help with this article, though they too are exonerated from any responsibility for my views.

Introductory Considerations

The microscopically focused problems of this passage are well known. There are the three main loadbearing nouns: *hilastērion, apolytrōsis,* and above all *dikaiosynē* itself, which appears to tie these verses closely to the opening of the paragraph in 3:21-22. There is the meaning and possible interrelation of the two clauses in the middle of verse 25, *dia tēs pisteōs* and *en tō autou haimati*. There is the meaning of the double phrase that straddles the end of verse 25 and the start of verse 26, *dia tēn paresin tōn progegonotōn hamartēmatōn en tē anochē tou theou.* And there is of course the central question for this passage: granted that Paul is clearly claiming that "justification" is accomplished for Jews and Gentiles alike by means of the death of Jesus, why does he think the death of Jesus has that effect, and what overtones is he building in to this statement?

We do not need to rehearse the answers routinely given to these questions. Commentaries, monographs, and articles provide this in profusion, showing among other things that there is no agreement in sight.[2] Even when something of a partial consensus seems to be emerging, at least in some quarters, it is still by no means clear how the overall flow of thought actually works. I think, for instance, of the way in which *hilastērion* is linked with the Day of Atonement, but without much sense of why Paul would allude to this ceremony at this, obviously crucial, point in his argument. And though it is almost universally admitted that verses 25 and 26 refer to God's *own* "righteousness," rather than to a status somehow granted to believers, it remains unclear (a) what Paul understands as the content of this divine "righteousness," (b) whether the same meaning holds for the phrase *dikaiosynē theou* in 3:21-22—and, by extension, in 1:17, and also (c) how precisely this divine "righteousness" is displayed in the death of Jesus. Though Paul must be allowed to use similar phrases in subtly different ways, if there is a way of assigning the same overall meaning to all these passages then such a way must have a *prima facie* claim to strength.[3]

---

2. Among the fullest recent English-language commentaries, I note R. Jewett, *Romans: A Commentary* (Minneapolis: Fortress, 2007). Among recent monographs, I note almost at random J. R. Treat, *The Crucified King: Atonement and Kingdom in Biblical and Systematic Theology* (Grand Rapids: Zondervan, 2014); and J. J. Williams, *Christ Died for Our Sins: Representation and Substitution in Romans and Their Jewish Martyrological Background* (Eugene, OR: Pickwick, 2015); see too the important collection of articles in J. Frey and J. Schröter, eds., *Deutungen des Todes Jesu im Neuen Testament,* 2nd ed. (Tübingen: Mohr, 2012). All these contain substantial bibliographies of other recent work.

3. My own earlier reflections on this passage can be seen in various places, e.g., my

God Put Jesus Forth

The latter problem—of the meaning of the divine "righteousness" in 3:25–26 in particular—alerts us to an older discussion that continues to rumble on in the literature. It was clear already to exegetes like Rudolf Bultmann that 3:25–26 was referring to the divine *faithfulness to the covenant*, to the covenant (that is) with Israel. But because it was assumed a priori that Paul would not have wanted to speak positively about Israel's covenant, and that he might actually have regarded it as something to be positively argued against, a different approach was taken. The hypothesis was advanced, developed, modified, and is still repeated in various forms that in this passage Paul has embedded a pre-Pauline "Jewish Christian" formula, which he has modified in line with his own different point of view. This kind of move belongs with an older *Sachkritik*—the attempt to improve what Paul actually wrote in the light of what we assume he "really" meant or "must have meant"—which, as I have argued elsewhere, ought to arouse suspicion.[4] That is not to deny that Paul is capable of quoting pre-Pauline formulae, or that he may have done so in this case; it is only to say that since Paul himself is after all an early "Jewish Christian," and since as we shall see there are good reasons for ascribing to him the view that in Jesus the God of Israel has been true to his covenant, the attempt to save Paul from "covenant theology" by means of such a hypothesis lacks conviction. (Nor is such a hypothesis necessarily helped by pointing out that some words and phrases here are unique in his letters. More or less every chapter in Paul has unique elements. Again, this is not to say that Paul is not quoting earlier formulations; merely that we should assume, especially in a dense summary, that he means exactly what he has written.)

The normal way of contextualizing the paragraph 3:21–26 is to regard the problem being addressed as universal human sin and the divine wrath it necessarily provokes. Since that is how Paul sums up the whole previous section in its opening (1:18) and its closing (3:19–20), repeating the latter point in 3:23, this seems reasonable. The emphasis on "sin" will be strengthened by the reading I am proposing. But this obvious point has given rise to the widespread

---

Romans, New Interpreters Bible 10 (Nashville: Abingdon, 2002), here at 468–77; *Justification: God's Plan and Paul's Vision* (London: SPCK; Downers Grove, IL: IVP, 2009), ch. 7; and *Paul and the Faithfulness of God* (hereafter *PFG*) (London: SPCK; Minneapolis: Fortress, 2013), at various points. Sharp eyes will observe that I have changed my mind on some issues.

4. See my *Paul and His Recent Interpreters* (London: SPCK; Minneapolis: Fortress, 2015), e.g., 33, 82, 177, 199. For the hypothesis see, e.g., E. Käsemann, *Commentary on Romans* (London: SCM, 1980), 91–101, with older literature; Jewett, *Romans*, 268–93, depending particularly on D. A. Campbell, *The Rhetoric of Righteousness in Romans 3.21–26* (Sheffield: Sheffield Academic, 1992).

assumption that this is the *only* real problem Paul is addressing, so that the overall argument is assumed to run something like this: (a) all sinned, incurring the divine wrath, (b) Jesus died, taking the divine wrath on himself, (c) all can now be justified. At a popular level this is often expounded in what is known familiarly as "the Romans Road," a simplified "gospel message" for popular usage. In more formalized and traditional Reformed theology (as for instance in the Westminster Confession) this is systematized into a "covenant of works" in which God makes an implicit covenant with the whole human race, consisting of an absolute moral standard to be obeyed, which would result in "righteousness," i.e., moral goodness. All humans fail the test, but Jesus's death (and, in some Reformed theories, his perfectly obedient life) meets the standard on their behalf, so that "righteousness" is now available for all—still within the same "covenant of works." The complex formulations of verses 24 to 26 are then made to say something about "penal substitution," whether in the traditional "satisfaction" theory (as in Anselm, the theory that God's infringed honor, and his consequent and necessary wrath against sinners, was "satisfied" in the death of Jesus) or some other, but always with the meaning that Jesus bears a punishment in order that sinners, both Jewish and Gentile, do not. This is frequently linked with the apparent sacrificial overtones in verse 25 (the *hilastērion*, and the blood of Jesus), on the assumption that sacrifices, for instance those associated with the Day of Atonement, were being killed in substitution for sinful Israel.

Before we look at the wider context, which I shall suggest tells a rather different story, we note three problems with readings of this type. First, the animal sacrifices in Leviticus and elsewhere, including those associated with the "Day of Atonement," were not regarded, in the original texts or subsequently, as receiving *punishment* (the death penalty, no less) in the place of the sinful worshipers. Since this will be central to our argument later on, we had better develop this point just a little.[5] The "Day of Atonement" was the moment in the ancient Israelite calendar when, according to Leviticus 16 and 23, the sins of Israel were to be confessed and solemnly set aside. A complex ritual is prescribed in the Torah, focused among other things on the High Priest sprinkling the sacrificial blood on top of, and in front of, the Ark of the Covenant (the sacred box in which the covenant documents were stored). In Hebrew the

---

5. On the "Day of Atonement" see recently, e.g., D. Stökl ben Ezra, *The Impact of Yom Kippur on Early Christianity: The Day of Atonement from Second Temple Judaism to the Fifth Century* (Tübingen: Mohr, 2003); J. Sklar, *Sin, Impurity, Sacrifice, Atonement: The Priestly Conceptions* (Sheffield: Sheffield Phoenix, 2005); T. Hieke and T. Nicklas, eds., *The Day of Atonement: Its Interpretation in Early Jewish and Christian Traditions* (Leiden: Brill, 2013).

lid of the Ark, designated as the place where YHWH would meet with his people, was called the *kapporet* (Exod. 25:17–22). Precisely what was understood by this term remains a matter of debate, with the older meaning "cover" or "covering" being strongly challenged in recent research, and the noun being instead connected with *kipper*, "cleanse" or "purge." The blood of the "sin offering" "acts as a ritual detergent" to purify the sanctuary, in order that the place on earth where the divine glory comes to dwell (Exod. 40:35) may be kept pure, maintaining not only the covenantal link between God and Israel but also the very fabric of the cosmos, the joining of heaven and earth.[6] The word *kapporet* was rendered in the LXX as *hilastērion*, and was innovatively translated into English in the sixteenth century as "mercy-seat," perhaps reflecting the German *Gnadenstuhl*, though the lid of the Ark was not a "seat" in the modern sense (the sense was more like describing the heart as "the seat of the emotions"), and strictly speaking it was the place, not simply of "mercy," but of both "meeting" and "cleansing"—God *meeting* with his people, and the priest *cleansing* the sanctuary from the defiling effects of the past sins of Israel with the sprinkled blood of the sacrifice. We should note in addition that the English word "atonement" is itself problematic: it does not correspond to any one Hebrew or Greek term (the "Day of Atonement" itself is *Yom Kippur*, the "day of cleansing"), nor indeed to any single German word (*Versöhnung* can carry a range of meanings, overlapping in some but not all ways with the English "atonement").[7] We must beware of importing much later ideas about "atonement" into passages where the English word "atonement" happens to occur in English translations of the Bible, whether Old Testament or New. We can easily be misled into supposing that in ancient Israel, or among the early Christians, what we have come to mean by "atonement" was common coin. Anachronism is all too easy at a point like this, and will distort or even subvert the fine-tuned meanings in the New Testament itself.

Anyway, the important part of the ancient Israelite sacrificial ritual was not the killing, which did not in any case take place on the altar. The killing was simply the prelude to the release of blood, symbolizing the animal's life, which was then used as the all-important cleansing agent, purging or cleansing the sacred place and its furniture, and the worshipers, and thus enabling the all-holy God to meet with his people without disastrous results.[8] The place of

---

6. See, e.g., S. E. Balentine, "Day of Atonement," in *The New Interpreter's Dictionary of the Bible*, vol. 2, ed. K. D. Sakenfeld et al. (Nashville: Abingdon, 2007), 42–45; J. Milgrom, *Leviticus 1–16* (New York: Doubleday, 1991), 1014, 1079–84; Sklar, *Sin, Impurity*, 44–45.

7. The German for "Day of Atonement" is *Versöhnungstag*.

8. For the possible link here with the idea of "ransom" see Sklar, *Sin, Impurity*, 154–57.

that meeting was precisely the *kapporet*, the place of cleansing or purgation. There is nothing here about punishment, and neither the older meaning of "covering" nor the recent scholarly consensus concerning "purgation" carries that implication. The only time in Leviticus when an animal has sins confessed over its head, the animal in question—the so-called "scapegoat"—is precisely *not* sacrificed; it is, after all, impure and would not be suitable as an offering. It is driven out into the wilderness. Even though later traditions indicate that the person leading the goat into the wilderness would then kill it by pushing it over a cliff—presumably lest it find its way back and so pollute the people or the sanctuary again—such killing, even supposing it took place, had to do with symbolically removing the sins, not with punishing the goat on behalf of the people. The first point, then, is that it is a mistake to suppose that the sacrificial language of Romans 3:25 will support any variety of "penal substitution" at this stage of the argument. (Perhaps I should make it clear that I do believe some form of "penal substitution" to be present in, for instance, Romans 8:1–4, where God's condemnation of "sin" in the Messiah's flesh means that there is "no condemnation" for those who are "in him." But this is in a different context, and requires quite separate treatment.)

The second problem with readings of the type I have mentioned is found in Romans 5:8–10. Here it appears that being "justified by [the Messiah's] blood" and "being saved from anger (or 'wrath')" are two quite different things, the latter being entailed by, but not identical to, the former:

> This is how God demonstrates his own love for us: the Messiah died for us while we were still sinners. How much more, in that case—since we have been declared to be in the right by his blood—are we going to be saved by him from God's coming anger! When we were enemies, you see, we were reconciled to God through the death of his son; if that's so, how much more, having already been reconciled, shall we be saved by his life.[9]

Here it seems clear that "declared to be in the right by his blood" is a summary of what Paul thinks he has argued in 3:24–26; and "being saved from God's anger" *is a different event*. The former takes place in the present time (3:21, 26); the latter, in the future, as in 1 Thessalonians 1:10 and 5:9. (It is true that for Paul the divine wrath is "revealed" in the present time, but as I have argued

---

9. All quotations from the New Testament are taken from N. T. Wright, *The Kingdom New Testament: A Contemporary Translation* (San Francisco: HarperOne, 2011)—in the UK, *The New Testament for Everyone* (London: SPCK, 2011).

elsewhere what is presently revealed is the certainty of *future* wrath, as in Romans 2:1–16.[10]) Whatever Paul is saying about sins and the death of Jesus in 3:24–26, it cannot be that he is speaking there about "the wrath" being poured out, or satisfied, in that event. Were that to be the case, 5:9 would not be an a fortiori argument, as Paul seems to think it is, but a tautology: having been saved from the wrath, we shall be saved from the wrath. No: 3:24–26 is seen in hindsight, from 5:9, as the *prerequisite* for being "saved from wrath," but it is not a description of how that rescue-from-wrath takes place (e.g., by the "wrath" being poured out on Jesus instead).

The third problem with readings of the type I have outlined is that when we meet the theme of the divine *dikaiosynē* in Israel's scriptures it is primarily *covenantal*. It refers to the divine covenant faithfulness.[11] To be sure, this faithfulness to the covenant includes the appropriate covenantal punishment when Israel is disobedient, but it will go on to restoration after punishment. This is the whole logic of Isaiah 40–55, Daniel 9, and other passages, with Deuteronomy 27–32 standing in the background, as in many Second Temple texts.[12] This is not at all to deny that in 3:19–20 Paul has summed up the problem of universal sin in terms of the law court: "The purpose of this is that every mouth may be stopped, and the whole world may be brought to the bar of God's judgment. No mere mortal, you see, can be declared to be in the right before God on the basis of works of the law. What you get through the law is the knowledge of sin." As we shall see, however, this law-court setting must not be played off against a "covenantal" setting. The purpose of the covenant, as far as Paul at least was concerned, was precisely to put everything right at last; and one major feature of the covenant seems to have been that it provided the context within which the covenant God would engage in "lawsuits" with his people.[13] But with that we are ready at last to step back from 3:24–26, indeed from 3:21–26, and to look at the larger context within which Paul has placed this seminal statement.

---

10. See *PFG*, 764–71.

11. This continues to be contested in some quarters, and really requires a long demonstration for which there is no space here. For a start, see *PFG*, 795–815.

12. For all this, see *PFG*, ch. 2.

13. The idea of the "covenant lawsuit" has been controversial in the study of Israel's scriptures, but however misleading the label in some respects there are passages (e.g., Isa. 1:2–20; Hos. 4:1–3; Amos 3:1–15) that use covenantal language to frame an indictment that God brings against Israel. For an older study, see, e.g., H. B. Huffmon, "The Covenant Lawsuit in the Prophets," *Journal of Biblical Literature* 78 (1959): 285–95; for a recent survey, R. M. Davidson, "The Divine Covenant Lawsuit Motif in Canonical Perspective," *Journal of the Adventist Theological Society* 21, no. 1/2 (2010): 45–84.

The Larger Context

Romans has suffered from being made to bear the weight of being the adopted "systematic theology" of the Reformation churches in particular. This has had several exegetically damaging effects, notably on the reading of chapters 9–11; but within the first four chapters, our present focus, there are two serious issues to note.

The first is that Romans 1–4 was not designed to be a complete statement of "how sinners get justified." For that—to look no further!—one would need some account of the work of the Spirit, which Paul provides in the equivalent passage in Galatians 3 but (apart from 2:29) does not mention in the first four chapters of Romans.[14] As I have argued elsewhere, a good many lines of argument in Romans 1–4 continue into chapters 5–8 (and indeed beyond, though that is mostly outside our present view). In particular, the eschatological scenario sketched in 2:1–16 looks ahead to chapter 8. When, in 3:21–4:25, Paul speaks of the *present* "justification" of those who believe, this is the bringing into the present of the verdict to be announced in the future in 2:1–16, but it is only with chapter 8 (though sketched preliminarily in 5:1–11) that he shows how that future verdict is arrived at for those "in the Messiah." Though the style of argumentation in chapters 5–8 is quite different from that of chapters 1–4, this should by no means be taken to indicate that chapters 1–4 were meant to stand on their own.

The second problem is that the eagerness to grasp the point of universal sin in 1:18–3:20 has blinded readers to what is in fact being said in 2:17–24 and then in 3:1–9. I have expounded this at length elsewhere and here simply summarize.[15]

The key point is that the person Paul is addressing as "the Jew" in 2:17 is not saying, "Well, all right, the Gentiles are sinful, but I and my fellow Jews have the Torah so we are not guilty like they are." That reading has been almost universally assumed, but it is demonstrably wide of the mark—and putting it right has an almost immediate effect, first on 3:1–9 and then on 3:21–26 and indeed 3:27–31. No doubt, as in Jesus's parable of the Pharisee and the tax collector, there were some of Paul's contemporaries who would have said, "But

---

14. On this, see my "Justification by (Covenantal) Faith to the (Covenantal) Doers: Romans 2 within the Argument of the Letter," in *Doing Theology for the Church: Essays in Honor of Klyne Snodgrass*, ed. R. A. Eklund and J. E. Phelan Jr. (Chicago: Covenant Publications; Eugene, OR: Wipf & Stock, 2014), 95–108.

15. See my *Pauline Perspectives* (London: SPCK; Minneapolis: Fortress, 2013), ch. 30 (originally published in *Journal for the Study of Paul and His Letters* 1, no. 2 [2012]: 3–28).

we are the exception." However, when the passage is read in this way then it appears—as commentators have not been slow to point out—that Paul's response seems very weak, since the citation in 2:21–23 of theft, adultery, temple-robbery, and law-breaking can hardly apply to *all* Jews. Certainly the Paul of Philippians 3:4–6 would have rejected all those charges. But that was not the subject at issue. The real point is clear in 2:19–20, which rehearses, not the supposed moral achievement of the Jewish people, but their *vocation within the divine plan*:

> Supposing you believe yourself to be a guide to the blind, a light to people in darkness, a teacher of the foolish, an instructor for children—all because, in the law, you possess the outline of knowledge and truth.

We know from Paul's repeated references to Isaiah 49 that he was very familiar with the chapter, which declares that Israel's "servant"-vocation is to be "the light to the nations, that my salvation may reach to the end of the earth" (Isa. 49:6). When he summarizes the whole message of Romans in 15:8–9—a passage to which we shall return—we see the subtle balance, maintained ever since 1:16 ("to the Jew first, and also, equally, to the Greek"):

> The Messiah became a servant of the circumcised people in order to demonstrate the truthfulness of God—that is, to confirm the promises to the patriarchs, and to bring the nations to praise God for his mercy.

This represents Paul's way of putting a belief that was widespread among Jews of the Second Temple period: when Israel's God finally does what he has promised Israel he will do, then this will affect the whole world.[16] God is, after all, the creator of all people. Often, of course, the effect in question will be judgment rather than mercy, but the note of mercy, of welcome, is there not only in Isaiah (and not only in chapter 49) but also in the Psalms, such as those quoted by Paul in Romans 15:9, 11, and obviously in other psalms such as 45 or 72. For Paul, of course, it is the Messiah himself who has been the fulfillment of Israel's destiny. But in 2:17–24 *he agrees with "the Jew" that Israel's vocation was indeed to be the light to the nations*. That was the divine call, and it was and is irrevocable. Paul is not arguing against a Jew who is saying, in effect, "I am an exception to the rule of universal sin." He is addressing a Jew who is saying "Yes, the world is indeed in a mess; but the Jewish people, armed with Torah,

---

16. See esp. *PFG*, 783–95.

are God's chosen answer to this problem; we are charged with the divine vocation to be the means of sorting out this mess, of putting the world right." And Paul basically agrees with this. This has been so unexpected in many traditions of reading that Paul's plain words have been overlooked. The passage offers a classic statement of the well-known Jewish belief—variously expressed, but common across many traditions—that God's call of Abraham and his family was designed to put right what was wrong with the world. Paul is *not* saying, as some commentators have imagined, "You are a bigot, imagining yourself to be morally superior."[17] He is saying, "You believe that God has called you—has called Israel as a whole—to be the light of the world." And Paul affirms that belief. "The Jew" whom he is addressing is correct. That is indeed the vocation of Israel.

Paul's problem is then exactly the same as the problem articulated again and again by Israel's ancient prophets: the vocation has not worked out the way it might have done, because Israel has gone wrong. This is not a new charge. There is no "Christian hindsight" involved here. The prayers of penitence in Ezra 9, Nehemiah 9, and Daniel 9 said it all. The "curse" of Deuteronomy had come into force: Israel had been exiled; and, as in Daniel 9, the exile had been extended from seventy years to 490.[18] Paul quotes Isaiah 52:5, echoing Ezekiel 36:20 as well: "Because of you, God's name is blasphemed among the nations." The non-Jewish nations were supposed to look at Israel and *praise* Israel's God. Instead, they look at Israel and blaspheme his name.

Paul then sharpens the critique by supposing for a moment (2:25-29) that God can and will summon Gentiles into his family, making them a people who really do keep the law. What he means by this is not our present concern. But this highlights the question that is already on the table from 2:17-24: If this was the divine plan, what has become of it? If God called and commissioned Israel to be the light to the nations, how will that plan now go forward? If God established his covenant through Abraham and Israel as the means by which the world would be made right, but if the covenant people have let him down, is God now going to abandon the covenant with Israel and do things by a different route?

At this point the normal reading of Romans—reflecting the normal view of the church—has been to answer: Yes! God has parked his broken covenant

---

17. Jewett, *Romans*, 221, 223 and elsewhere refers to the imaginary "Jew" of 2:17 as "the pretentious bigot." This continues the long and disturbing German tradition of regarding "the Jew" as "the type of *homo religiosus*."

18. On "extended exile" see *PFG*, 139-63; and the forthcoming volume edited by J. M. Scott, *Exile: A Conversation with N. T. Wright* (Downers Grove, IL: IVP).

with Israel in a side-road somewhere and has completed the journey by other means. He has replaced the covenant with Israel with his own direct intervention through Jesus. In theological language, "incarnation" has taken the place of "election"—a mistake all the easier to make in that Paul does indeed believe in incarnation. For him, however, the incarnate Son *is also Israel's Messiah*, and it is exactly that explosive fusion of roles that forms the heart of his theological vision. But this is to run ahead of ourselves. The normal reading of Romans—incorporating some version of the "covenant of works"—imagines that, for Paul, God has indeed put the covenant with Israel to one side and has accomplished salvation by a different route. But Paul's answer to the question is resolutely different to this common one: No! God has not abandoned the covenant. "Let God be true, and every human being false!" (3:4). Or, in more detail:

> The Jews were entrusted with God's oracles. What follows from that? If some of them were unfaithful to their commission, does their unfaithfulness nullify God's faithfulness? Certainly not! (3:2b–4a)

God has not given up on his plan to bring light to the world through Israel. And his "faithfulness" to that plan *is exactly what is meant by "God's righteousness,"* as 3:5 makes clear: literally translated, the start of that verse reads, "But if our unrighteousness establishes God's righteousness. . . ." This sets the tone.

Paul thus arrives at the conclusion of the first major section of Romans (1:18–3:20) with two problems to solve, not just one. First, there is still of course the underlying issue of idolatry and injustice (as in 1:18), and plain old "sin" (as in 3:9, 20, 23). That is clear. It hasn't gone away. It hasn't been displaced by all this talk of the covenant, of Israel's vocation—though nor should we forget that the problem with "sin" is not just the breaking of moral laws but the failure to grasp the truly human vocation and so to reflect God's glory into the world: "all sinned, *and fell short of God's glory"* (3:23). But, second, there is the problem of God's faithfulness to the covenant. Faced with the problem of sin (1:18–2:16), God promised, and established this by his covenant with Abraham, that he would rescue the world from its plight through that covenant. It would be very strange if God were to make solemn promises to rescue the world through Israel and were then to respond to Israel's faithlessness by being, himself, faithless *to those specific promises*. More especially, the question of "God's faithfulness" or "God's righteousness" has a serious impact on the question of how universal sinfulness is to be addressed. This is not simply, as it were, a problem for God ("has he been true to his word?"); nor is it simply a problem for Israel. It is a problem for the whole human race ("If God has committed himself to rescuing the world through the Israel-covenant, and if Israel has not played its part in this arrangement, how then will God rescue the world?"). This comes to sharp focus in Romans 3:1–9, as we saw a moment ago, and especially 3:2–5.

That is the long backdrop to our present very difficult passage—to 3:21–26 in general, also to 3:27–31, and in particular to the statement of Jesus's death in 3:24–26. And when we put 2:17–3:20 together with chapter 4, we discover that our key passage is flanked on *both* sides by expositions of God's covenant purposes, of the divine plan to rescue the world from sin through Abraham and his family. As I have argued in detail elsewhere, Romans 4, like Galatians 3 in its way, expounds the original covenant with Abraham (in Genesis 15) in terms of God's plan to give Abraham a worldwide family marked out by *pistis* ("faith" or "faithfulness"). Paul's point is that in and through the Messiah, and his death and resurrection, God has done what he promised Abraham he would do.[19]

We can come even closer: 3:27–31 is all about the coming together of Jew and Gentile, circumcised and uncircumcised, on the basis of *pistis*, "faith"— which looks like a further fulfillment of the hints Paul dropped in 2:25–29. *The whole passage from 2:17 to 4:25 is all about God's covenant with Israel and about the way in which that covenant was God's designed means of reaching out to rescue the whole world.* And—before we even probe into any specifics—we must therefore assume that 3:21–26 is highly likely to be saying something about how God has been faithful to the plan to save the world through Israel, and how that has worked out in rescuing all humans from the underlying plight of sin. When, therefore, we note that 3:25–26 seems to be speaking of the divine covenant faithfulness, this ought to be an indication, not that Paul is quoting earlier "Jewish Christian" formulations which he is then anxiously modifying, but that this is indeed what the whole passage is about. *God's faithfulness to the covenant with Israel, even granted the large-scale failure of Israel as a whole, will result in the rescue of the whole sinful world.* This is what we ought to assume that the passage will be about. And we will not be disappointed.[20]

In fact, we will find that all sorts of things come much clearer on this approach than on the normal ones. In particular, it will highlight two things:

---

19. See "Paul and the Patriarch," in *Pauline Perspectives*, ch. 33, originally published in a slightly shorter version in *Journal for the Study of the New Testament* 35, no. 3 (2013): 207–41.

20. I have argued elsewhere (Wright, *Romans*, 549–85) that this theme is then developed extensively in Rom. 7:7–8:11, itself developing 5:20.

the role of the faithful Messiah, and God's dealing with the longstanding problem of Israel's previous failure. Neither of these, of course, makes much sense within the normal reading of the passage, focused on a putative "covenant of works." They are routinely swept aside by those who continue to read the passage that way.[21] But both of them are essential components of what Paul is actually saying. In more detail, there are four points that, granted the whole argument so far, we might assume Paul to be making. First, God has been faithful to the covenant with Abraham, the covenant through which the sin of the world is to be dealt with and people from every nation are brought to praise the God of Israel. (That this is one of Paul's own ways of summarizing his argument is clear from Romans 15:8–9.) Second, in order to do this God has somehow fulfilled his purpose to rescue the world *through Israel*; that is the purpose to which Paul has declared that God will be "true" even if all human beings have let him down. Third, the result must be that the problem of universal sin (1:18–2:16) is dealt with, allowing a forgiven worldwide family to come into existence. Fourth, this means that God must somehow have put aside the long, dark history of Israel's rebellion and sin, the years of "exile"—as well as the long, unregistered history of non-Jewish idolatry, injustice, and wickedness. These four things are indeed central to the passage.

One more point of considerable relevance must be added to the mix before we address the central passage itself. At the end of chapter 4, summing up the long argument from 3:21 until that point, Paul suddenly mentions the death and resurrection of Jesus in an explicit formula, in a way he has not done in the letter up to this point:

> But it wasn't written for [Abraham] alone that "it was calculated to him." It was written for us as well! It will be calculated to us, too, since we believe in the one who raised from the dead Jesus our Lord, who was handed over because of our trespasses and raised for our justification. (Rom. 4:23–25)

Like so many statements in Paul and elsewhere, this is of course a dense and formulaic summary. It does not spell out what exactly is meant by "handed over because of our trespasses." One could spend quite a bit of time trying to second-guess what lies under that phrase, as also the final one, "raised for our justification." But two things stand out, since this short passage seems to be

---

21. On the now-extensive debate about *pistis Christou* see, e.g., M. F. Bird and P. M. Sprinkle, eds., *The Faith of Jesus Christ: Exegetical, Biblical and Theological Studies* (Milton Keynes, UK: Paternoster, 2009).

drawing together, and making explicit, what has been said in 3:21–4:25 as a whole, particularly here the way in which the Abrahamic covenant is fulfilled through the messianic events. These two things will send us back to 3:24–26 with a somewhat better chance of attaining clarity.[22]

First, Paul is explicitly echoing Isaiah 53. In 53:12 the "servant" was "handed over because of our sins"—not exactly the same phrase ("sins" rather than "trespasses"), but functionally equivalent. That verse sums up the whole fourth Servant Song (52:13–53:12), rather as Romans 4:24–25 sums up 3:21–4:25 as a whole. This increases the likelihood that a reference to the Servant may lie behind 3:24–26 as well.

Second, this phrase therefore indicates that Jesus's servant-like death (and then his resurrection, declaring him to be God's Son as in 1:3–4 and therefore declaring his people to be in the right, as here) was the way in which God completed the long-range covenantal promise he had made to Abraham.[23] In Genesis 15:13–16 God told Abraham that, though his promised family would be slaves for a long time, he would bring them out of slavery and give them the Promised Land. In the long narrative of Israel's scriptures, this was of course fulfilled in the events of the first Exodus. But when the covenantal curse had fallen, and the Jewish people found themselves in exile in Babylon—and when, after several of them had returned and rebuilt the Temple, they were still by their own admission "slaves in our own land"[24]—then the hope for a "new Exodus," a new Passover, became fused with the hope, as in Isaiah 40–55 or Daniel 9, for a full and final atonement, a "dealing with sin" that would bring about the ultimate "return from exile." When, therefore, we transpose the promises of Genesis 15 into the Second Temple period, what we have is the hope for two things simultaneously: for a new Passover that would also be the ultimate Day of Atonement, the moment of forgiveness of sins and covenant renewal.[25] And, remembering the promises echoed in 2:19–20, the whole point of this—dealing with Israel's own long entail of sin—was that this would also be the means by which the light would shine on the Gentiles, by which the "oracles" with which Israel had been "entrusted" (as in 3:2) would at last be passed on and received with joy.

This, then, is the larger context within which we must read 3:21–31 and particularly 3:21–26 with its dense statement about the death of Jesus. The

---

22. See further Wright, *Romans*, 502–5.

23. See again Rom. 15:8, where Paul describes Jesus as the *diakonos* to the "circumcised," to fulfill the promises made to the Patriarchs.

24. Neh. 9:36.

25. This is the fundamental insight of Dr. N. Yamaguchi, as in the first note above.

God Put Jesus Forth

underlying problem of universal idolatry, injustice, and sin is compounded by the covenantal problem that Israel was called to be the means by which this problem would be solved, and Israel has—according to Israel's own scriptures—failed to deliver on that vocation. Paul's answer to this double problem in 3:21-26 is that in Jesus, Israel's Messiah, Israel's God has provided what was needed *both* to complete Israel's vocation after all *and thereby* to deal with the problem of sin. And this complex but coherent analysis of where the argument has got to by 3:20 will result, I think, in shedding fresh light on some of the traditionally problematic words and phrases in 3:24-26 in particular.

Romans 3:21-26

The first point to notice is one I have spelled out in detail in chapter 10 of *Paul and the Faithfulness of God*. When Paul declares in 3:21 that the *dikaiosynē theou* has been displayed in the gospel events, and when he repeats in verses 25 and 26 that God has displayed his *dikaiosynē*, the *primary* meaning he has in mind throughout is that God has been faithful to the covenant with Israel, and thus, through Israel, to the world. We cannot ignore, as many have done, the occurrence of *theou dikaiosynē* in 3:5, so close to 3:21 (and with nine of the intervening sixteen verses being a catena of biblical quotations). Nor can we ignore the emphasis in verses 25 and 26, which it is generally agreed is on God's faithfulness to the covenant.[26] The high probability is that 3:21 and 3:22 fit into this framework, rather than stepping outside to talk about something else. In other words, in 3:21 Paul is referring to the *dikaiosynē* which is displayed the more brightly by contrast with Israel's *adikia* (3:5a), that is, the "covenant faithfulness" spoken of in terms of God's *pistis* in 3:3 and his being *alēthēs* in 3:4. But the *secondary* meaning Paul has in mind, as in 2:17-24, is that this covenant always expressed God's intention to deal with the problem of worldwide sin. The law court in which the judge of all will put all things right at last (3:6) is the law court of Israel's God; the point of the covenant, as in 2:19-20, always was to sort out the problem of 1:18-2:16. In other words, we ought already to know, as we read 3:21, that Paul is now intending to expound the way in which God has been faithful to the covenant with Israel *and has thereby* dealt with the problem of universal human sin.

---

26. Even Cranfield, who elsewhere resists this reading of *dikaiosynē theou*, accepts it here: C. E. B. Cranfield, *A Critical and Exegetical Commentary on the Epistle to the Romans*, vol. 1 (Edinburgh: T. & T. Clark, 1975), 211.

If the *dikaiosynē theou* is interpreted in this way throughout the passage, then the two other vital nouns immediately gain a fresh context and thereby a much greater clarity. What is needed, according not only to Genesis 15 but to Isaiah and other prophets, is a new Exodus: in other words, a "redemption," an *apolytrōsis*, a new Passover.[27] That is what Paul offers in 3:24: the *apolytrōsis* which is "in Messiah Jesus." This brings Paul into the same territory as Luke, for whom the hope of the *lytrōsis* of Jerusalem (2:38), or of Israel (24:21), with which we should compare Isaiah 52:9, was part of the framing device for understanding the significance of Jesus's entire career and death; or of Mark, whose *lytron anti pollōn* (10:45) is often heard as an echo of Isaiah 53:10-12. Such echoes are presumably intended also by Paul, since, as we saw, when he sums up the argument of chapters 1–4 in 4:25, he offers one of his most obvious echoes of Isaiah 53: "[he] was handed over because of our trespasses." But we should beware of moving at once from discerning an Isaiah reference here to concluding that Paul is endorsing the normal "covenant of works," focusing on the traditional "penal substitution" or "satisfaction." Paul, like Isaiah, is thinking in terms of a *new Exodus*. "Redemption" is not, as so often imagined, just a miscellaneous metaphor taken from the slave-market.[28] As far as the Israelites were concerned, Egypt had been the ultimate slave-market, and God had redeemed them from there. As so often, we must beware of exchanging a word full of Jewish narratival overtones for a flattened-out metaphor that would then contribute to other kinds of narrative. And Passover was of course the ultimate covenant-fulfilling event. This is what God had promised Abraham. When the Exodus happened, those promises were explicitly recalled (Exod. 2:24). This "redemption" is then to be found "in the Messiah": he is the place where it happens, and the location therefore where people must come, the reality into which they must be incorporated—as in chapter 6!—if they are to benefit from his accomplishment. The sign that they are incorporated is the same as the sign of his work: *pistis*, "faith" or "faithfulness." That is why, in 3:22, Paul declares that "God's covenant justice comes into operation through the faithfulness of Jesus the Messiah, for the benefit of all who have faith." Faith is the Messiah-badge, the sign that one is "in the Messiah," sharing in the fruits of the "redemption" accomplished in him.[29]

---

27. On the "Exodus"-associations of *apolytrōsis* see, e.g., B. Byrne, *Romans* (Collegeville, MN: Liturgical Press, 1996), 132, with copious references.

28. See, e.g., Treat, *The Crucified King*, 186: "Paul interweaves three different metaphors from three different spheres of life," namely law court, commerce, and cult.

29. On "faith," "faithfulness," and the way in which the *pistis* of the believer is the mark that links one to the *pistis* of the Messiah, see *PFG*, 406, 839–40, 848–49, 931, etc.

But—and this is actually the point of Isaiah 53 as well—if there is to be a new Exodus it will be achieved *through God dealing with Israel's sins*; through, in other words, something like a new "Day of Atonement." Passover was not itself a sin-forgiving festival; but when Israel was languishing in the prolonged exile that resulted from sin, the necessary "new Exodus" could only come, as Isaiah 40–55 states so clearly, by sins being dealt with (e.g., Isa. 40:1–2). We see the same combination in the Last Supper traditions, including as here of course the mention of "blood," which the present context strongly suggests is "the blood of the new covenant," corresponding to the "blood of the covenant" in Exodus 24:8 (and also perhaps, though I think this less likely, to the blood of the Passover lamb). What all this suggests—this narrative of God's faithfulness to the covenant, so that Israel, in the person of the Messiah, is at last able to bring the intended rescue to the whole world—is that Paul quite deliberately declares that the new Exodus has occurred *because* God put forward the Messiah to be the *hilastērion*, the place and the means of dealing with Israel's sins. The strong allusion to the "Day of Atonement" in Romans 3:25, then, is not simply one powerful Jewish image among many. It belongs exactly at this point in the narrative, the point where the indictment of Israel outlined in 2:17–3:20 reaches its height. It is always precarious to try to figure out how a first-century Jew might have understood the inner rationale of Jerusalem's sacrificial cult, but we can stay on the sure ground of the Levitical regulations. As we saw earlier, this is not the moment when Israel's sins were *punished*; it is the moment when they were *set aside*, when the divine provision of sacrificial blood purged the sanctuary from the pollution that would otherwise have made it impossible for the divine glory to dwell there.

With that, we come at last, with due caution, to the difficult but vital passage 3:24–26 itself. The whole passage, starting near the end of verse 22, is a single sentence in the Greek, though for ease of understanding we break it up into its component parts:

> For there is no distinction: all sinned, and fell short of God's glory—and by God's grace they are freely declared to be in the right, to be members of the covenant, through the redemption which is found in the Messiah, Jesus. God put Jesus forth as the place of mercy, through faithfulness, by means of his blood. He did this to demonstrate his covenant justice, because of the passing over (in divine forbearance) of sins committed beforehand. This was to demonstrate his covenant justice in the present time: that is, that he himself is in the right, and that he declares to be in the right everyone who trusts in the faithfulness of Jesus.

Here the role of the Messiah and his death, summarized in 4:24-25, is obviously central, and the main point Paul is making ought not to be in doubt. God *has* been faithful to the covenant he made with Israel, the promise that through Israel he would redeem the world; and the way in which he has been faithful is through *the faithfulness of the Messiah*, sent forth by God himself (as in 8:3) to perform this role.[30] The Messiah has been *the representative faithful Israelite*, and this whole train of thought explains why the idea of the Messiah's faithfulness is not a strange or distorting notion, as some have protested, but is vital for the underlying logic. God promised to save the world through Israel, and the messianic death and resurrection of Jesus is the way in which he has done this. The whole argument only makes sense, of course, if Paul assumes (a) that Israel's vocation was somehow to rescue the world, as in 2:19-20; (b) that Israel's Messiah represents Israel; and therefore (c) that the Messiah's own faithfulness-to-death *can be seen as the effective covenant faithfulness of Israel* which was required, but which had been lacking, in 3:2-3. Israel as a whole was unfaithful; God has provided the Messiah as the faithful Israelite. That is how the problem of universal sin is now dealt with. When we put the promise of divine glory in 5:2 alongside the loss of that glory in 3:23, we can suggest that Paul has in mind as well the divine provision whereby the cosmos itself is healed, a conclusion strongly confirmed by 8:18-25.

The new Passover, then, is also, as in Isaiah, Jeremiah, Ezekiel, and Daniel, the real "return from exile," which means the real "forgiveness of sins." The great "feast" and the great "fast" are held together. That is what Paul now describes. He does so in three interlocking ways, but first we notice the heavy emphasis, by a repetition very unusual in Paul, on the fact that through these events God has demonstrated his faithfulness to the covenant—the great theme of the letter, stated in 1:16-17 and underlying all that comes after, not least chapters 9-11. His whole point is not that Jesus somehow persuaded God to do something he might not otherwise have wanted to do. Rather, he stresses that, in the messianic events, God demonstrated his own covenant faithfulness. He unveiled it in action. We note the repeated emphasis on the display of God's *dikaiosynē*, his "covenant justice" or his "being in the right" (these being variant English translations of the same Greek root):

---

30. I regard 3:22, providing as it does the answer to the problem of 3:1-5, as the strongest argument for taking *pistis Christou*, in the present passage at least, to refer to the faithfulness of the Messiah. One can only avoid this point, I think, by an atomistic exegesis that refuses to see the longer threads of Paul's argument.

God put Jesus forth as the place of mercy, through faithfulness, by means of his blood. He did this *to demonstrate his covenant justice*, because of the passing over (in divine forbearance) of sins committed beforehand. This was *to demonstrate his covenant justice* in the present time: that is, that *he himself is in the right*, and that he declares to be in the right everyone who trusts in the faithfulness of Jesus. (3:25-26)

One does not normally accuse Paul of heavy-handed repetition. Usually, we have the opposite problem: he is going so fast that he takes for granted, and so leaves out, steps in his argument which are obvious to him but which we have to fill in as we go, panting along behind him and trying to keep up. When he labors the point like this we should sit up and take extra notice. *The point of the Messiah's death, within the present argument, is that it demonstrates, in action, the faithfulness of God to his covenant plan.* The Messiah's death accomplishes what God planned to do and said he would do. Somehow, the Messiah's faithful death *constitutes* the fulfillment of the Israel-shaped plan: or, to put it another way (since Paul, like all the early Christians, had thought everything through again backwards, in the light of the resurrection), when God called Abraham he had the Messiah's cross in mind all along. Since, as we have seen, one place in Israel's scriptures where that divine plan is concentrated is in Isaiah 53, and since Paul, summing all this up briefly, alludes to that chapter in 4:24-25, we would be right to assume that that statement of Israel-faithfulness, of servant-faithfulness, of crucified-Messiah-faithfulness, is under the present passage as well. The new Passover is accomplished through the event that ends the exile by dealing with sin. Israel's covenantal vocation is thus accomplished.

Within this unveiled covenant justice, then, and within the overarching statement that *God himself* "put Jesus forth," are the three elements. First, God put Jesus forth *as the place of mercy*. This phrase is an attempt to catch at least some of the significance of the Greek word *hilastērion*. Those who have approached this passage in terms of the "covenant of works" have tended to take this in its distantly possible sense of "a means of propitiation," that is, the means by which divine anger is turned away.[31] That is certainly the sense it seems to have in 4 Maccabees 17:22. That has then generated long-running arguments about "propitiation" and "expiation," as many sensitive souls, anx-

---

31. The classic case for this was made by L. L. Morris, "The Meaning of *Hilastērion* in Romans 3:25," *New Testament Studies* 2 (1955-56): 33-43, discussed by most subsequent commentators.

ious about the apparently pagan idea of an angry god punishing an innocent victim, have tried to avoid any such implication.³² But this is not where the weight of the short paragraph falls, and that long-running debate can distract our attention from what Paul really wants to emphasize. As I have insisted, the vital sequence of thought is not, "we all sinned; God punished Jesus instead; problem solved," but rather "God promised to rescue the whole world through Israel; the crucified Messiah has been faithful to that purpose; therefore sinners, Jew and Gentile alike, can be justified freely." That still, of course, leaves open the question of *how* the Messiah's faithful crucifixion achieved the intended purpose. But it reframes that question and throws it in a different direction.

In particular, there are two signs here that Paul does *not* intend these verses as a statement of how the punishment deserved by sinners—the "wrath" of Romans 1:18–2:16—was meted out on Jesus instead. The first one we have already mentioned: though he is here talking about justification in the present time (note "but now" in 3:21 and "in the present time" in 3:26), when we get to 5:9 we find him saying that, because we are "justified by his blood"—which must be intended as a summary of our present passage, 3:24-26—we can be confident that we *shall* be saved from "the wrath" in the future. (The best sense that can be made of the otherwise strange phrase "justified by his blood" is, I think, to take "justified" in its covenantal meaning—"reckoned to be within the covenant"—and the "blood" as the "blood of the covenant," in this case of course the renewed covenant, as in 1 Corinthians 11:25.) It looks, therefore, as though whatever is going on in 3:24-26 it cannot be the meting out of divine wrath on Jesus. In Romans 8:3-4 Paul speaks of God condemning sin in the Messiah's flesh, so that there is "no condemnation" for those who are "in the Messiah." That is speaking of the *final* day of judgment. This penal substitution, framed carefully by Paul in terms of the long story of Israel and the strange work of the Law (Rom. 7:1–8:11), is the truth toward which, I believe, the "propitiation" readings of 3:24-26 are straining. But by reading it back into the present passage such treatments distort both the passage and the doctrine.

Second, Paul specifically says that God's fulfillment of the covenant involved him "passing over" former sins, in his *anochē*, his "forbearance." (If there is a reference here to "Passover" it is very oblique. "Passing over" and "Passover" are of course very close in English, but there is no equivalent link

---

32. One of the best ways of retaining "propitiation" here while avoiding the caricature is that of Cranfield, *Romans*, 217: "God ... purposed to direct against His own very Self in the person of his Son the full weight of that righteous wrath which [sinners] deserved."

God Put Jesus Forth

in the Greek.) In the normal "covenant of works" approach, interpreters have looked at this passage for an account of how sins were *punished*. But the whole point of *anochē* is that sins are *not* punished. In Romans 2:4, Paul asks his imaginary interlocutor whether, in his arrogance, he is despising "the riches of God's kindness, forbearance and patience," which were supposed to lead one to repentance. Punishment is what would happen later, if this opportunity were missed: "by your hard, unrepentant heart you are building up a store of anger for yourself on the day of anger" (2:5). It is possible—and many interpreters have suggested this—that Paul is here suggesting that sins (either Israel's sins specifically or the sins of all people) had never to this point been punished as they deserved, but that now, in the Messiah's death, that punishment was at last being meted out. That would then lead to a reading of verse 26 in which God is "righteous" in the sense of "having at last punished sins properly," while simultaneously "justifying" the one who is *ek pisteōs Iēsou*. But this is not, as I suggested earlier, how the logic of the Day of Atonement actually works. The sacrificial blood that is sprinkled on, and in front of, the *kapporet* is not a sign of an animal being punished vicariously on behalf of the people. It is, rather, the means whereby the sanctuary is cleansed from uncleanness so that the covenant may be refreshed and access to the divine presence assured, with God and his people meeting at the "mercy-seat," as in Exodus 25:22. That Paul has something like this in mind may appear from Romans 5:1–2, which again employs the language of the cult: being justified by faith, Paul declares, "we have peace with God through our Lord Jesus the Messiah," and "through him we have been allowed to approach, by faith, into this grace in which we stand; and we celebrate the hope of the glory of God." That—with an allusion back to the divine "glory" that was lost with universal sin in 3:23—continues the theme of the sanctuary: the hope for the divine glory is the hope for the ultimate return of YHWH to his people. We may go so far as to say that, had Paul wished to talk about punishment being diverted from other people on to Jesus, it would have been unthinkable for him to use the language of the Day of Atonement. That is not what that ceremony was about. What seems to have happened is that, at a time in church history when the rationale for the sacrifices and offerings of the ancient cult was not understood, but when society and theology were focused rather heavily on "honor," "rights," and so forth, and particularly "righteousness" seen simply as "moral goodness," the sacrificial language Paul was employing, which actually fitted like a glove the train of thought from 2:17 onward, was taken to refer to vicarious punishment. It is not that sins are heaped up during the *anochē* of God so that they can then be *punished*. They are allowed to accumulate and are then *purged* by the blood of the covenant, so that they can be "passed over," and thus can no longer pollute the sanctuary. The way is then open for all people, Jew and Gentile alike, to meet the creator God at the mercy-seat. The fact that this conclusion coheres rather well with a central argument in the letter to the Hebrews, and also with the regularly drawn implication of the rending of the temple veil in the synoptic passion narratives, ought in my view to be seen as a strength: this appears to be very early common Christian tradition, woven here by Paul into his specific argument about the covenant faithfulness of God.

The present passage then looks similar to what Paul is reported as having said in Athens about the time of ignorance in which the nations blundered about in idolatry and folly:

> That was just ignorance; but the time for it has passed, and God has drawn a veil over it. Now, instead, he commands all people everywhere to repent... (Acts 17:30)

Paul is not, then, arguing in Romans 3 that God has *punished* former sins, whether of Israel or the Gentiles; certainly not that he has punished them in Jesus. There is no mention here of such a punishment then exhausting the divine wrath. As we just saw, that would leave 5:9 looking very odd. Paul says, rather, that God has chosen to overlook the "former sins." The assumption here must be, I think, that he is referring to Israel's former sins: God is faithful in the Messiah to the covenant *through Israel for the world*, and to that end he has pushed Israel's "former sins" to one side. The ultimate "Day of Atonement" has "purged" them with the blood of the renewed covenant. Attempts to lift these verses out of their context in Romans, and make them serve a subtly different purpose, distort them. This distortion, being made central to some entire theological schemes, has I think resulted in distorted readings of Romans as a whole.

There is an analogy here with Galatians 3:13-14, a passage that has also suffered from being forced to speak its lines on the wrong stage. The topic is not "how sinners get saved," but "how the promises to Abraham reach their Gentile destination."[33] There is indeed substitution. The Messiah is cursed, and the curse hanging over his people is removed. But the context is not the "covenant of works." It is what we might call "the covenant of vocation." By standing in for his people, the Messiah overcomes the covenantal failure of Israel and enables the promises to reach their destination.

---

33. See N. T. Wright, *The Climax of the Covenant* (Edinburgh: T&T Clark, 1991; Philadelphia: Fortress, 1992), ch. 7.

What then is Paul saying in Romans 3? He is clearly identifying Jesus with the *hilastērion*, and seeing Jesus's blood in terms of the blood that is sprinkled on and in front of the Ark, as Israel's sins are set aside once more.[34] This, though striking and dramatic—nowhere else is Jesus identified with a piece of temple furniture—makes exactly the point that is needed *granted the argument that runs from 2:17 through chapter 4*. Israel had been faithless to the divine vocation to bring blessing to the nations; but Israel's failure is dealt with in the proper way, by the reality to which the Day of Atonement had always pointed. The Messiah, in his faithful death, had very specifically accomplished the purpose for which Israel had been called, and at the same time had "purged" with his own blood the past sins which God was now overlooking—or, to put it the other way, had purified with his blood the implicit heaven-and-earth sanctuary where the divine glory was to dwell. And all this was demonstrating, as Paul says again and again, *the righteousness of God*, that is, God's faithfulness to his covenant promises. He himself is in the right—that is, he has been true to the covenant, including its penal clauses about exile as a result of sin and its promises of ultimate restoration and renewal; and, within that renewal, he justifies those who are rooted in the faithfulness of Jesus and who reflect that faithfulness in their own faith (as in 3:22). In all this, aligning the Messiah himself with the *kappōreth* makes sense in one particular way. The Messiah is, in Paul's mind, the unique place where Israel's God really does meet with his people. The Messiah embodies Israel, as the king who sums up his people in himself and whose faithfulness stands in for their faithlessness. But this Messiah, as far as Paul is concerned, also embodies Israel's God himself, come to rescue his people. Paul has fused together the vocation of Israel on the one hand and the intentions of Israel's God—that he would return in person to rescue his people—on the other.[35]

This coming-together is rendered operative "by means of his blood." (In

---

34. The major research in this area is that of D. P. Bailey, "Jesus as the Mercy Seat: The Semantics and Theology of Paul's Use of *Hilastērion* in Romans 3:25" (PhD diss., Cambridge University, 1999), summarized briefly in *Tyndale Bulletin* 51, no. 1 (2000): 155–58. Bailey makes a strong case for taking the word here to indicate the *kappōreth*, but without drawing all the conclusions I am proposing. He does, however, note suggestively the LXX of Exod. 15:13, when, celebrating the events of Passover and Exodus, Miriam sings that God, in his *dikaiosynē*, is guiding to his sanctuary the people "whom you redeemed," *hon elytrōsō*, thus producing a combination of themes very close to Rom. 3:21–26 (Bailey in *Tyndale Bulletin* summary, 157).

35. This conclusion is, I think, very close to Richard Bauckham's argument in *Jesus and the God of Israel* (Grand Rapids: Eerdmans, 2008), 32–57, though Bauckham does not there discuss our present passage.

a literal translation this would read "in his blood," but "in" in Greek often means "by means of," and this is best here. Some translations link "through faith" with "in his blood" [as in, "by faith in his blood"], but that seems not to be Paul's meaning. It seems best to take "through faith" as meaning "through faithfulness" and as referring to Jesus's own "faithfulness," as in 3:22.) This is clearly a reference to Jesus's death as a sacrifice, and hence also—though this would take us too far afield—to Jesus's life as the means of ultimate salvation, as in 5:10b. But that idea, as we have seen, does not indicate that Jesus is being punished for someone else's sin. That is not how sacrifices were understood. I suspect—though with the density of expression this is impossible to prove—that as well as the Day of Atonement Paul may have in mind here the inauguration of the covenant in Exodus, where the "blood of the covenant" was sprinkled on the people (Exod. 24:7–8). The *hilastērion* was, after all, the lid for the Ark of the Covenant, and here again the overarching covenantal context draws together the relevant themes. The covenant purposes of God *for* Israel, and *through* Israel for the world, were at last established, with Jesus's own blood as the blood of the new covenant. (If Paul intends a reference here to the Eucharist, as in 1 Corinthians 11:25, it remains very oblique.) In other words, *Jesus, as Israel's Messiah, is the place where, and the means by which, God's covenant purposes and Israel's covenant faithfulness meet, merge, and achieve their original object*. Israel's past sins, the faithlessness that had apparently thrown the covenant into jeopardy, had been passed over, while the purpose of the covenant was gloriously fulfilled in dealing with the problem of 1:18–2:16 and so creating, as implicitly in 2:25–29, a worldwide justified people. The "covenant of vocation"—Israel's vocation, to be the light of the world—was fulfilled.

This passage does not, then, focus on the point that most of us, including myself in earlier writings, have assumed. Paul is not simply offering a roundabout way of saying "We sinned; God punished Jesus; we are forgiven." He is saying, "We all sinned; God promised Abraham to save the world through Israel; Israel was faithless; but God has put forth the faithful Messiah, whose death has been our Exodus from slavery because it has dealt with sins." That larger context is vital and non-negotiable. This is where I want to insist that if we take what Paul says out of its Jewish context—and, ultimately, out of its Jewish eschatological context, replacing that with a Platonized vision of the "goal"—then we will end up with a pagan view of the "means." That has happened, again and again. It is time to put things back as they should be. Yes, when Paul sums it all up at the end of chapter 4 he quotes Isaiah 53 as his way of saying, in a nutshell, what he has here said more fully; and that should hint that other meanings, too, are not far away. Isaiah 53, after all, does indeed offer the idea of a "substitute" who is punished for the people's sins. But this takes place in the context of Israel's vocation, Israel's exile-because-of-sins, and especially of the promise that "the arm of YHWH" will come in person to deal with the problem (Isa. 51:9; 52:10; 53:1). The "sins" are the sins of the "servant people," which have resulted not only in their exile but in the failure of the divine plan to make Israel the light of the nations. Within this context, and only within this context, we can find the note of "propitiation." This is not the simplistic "propitiation" that has given western theology so much trouble. It means what it means within the Isaiah-context, the Abraham-context, the Israel-for-the-world context. Take it out of that context, as has often been done, and we are left with something much more like the normal pagan model of a malevolent deity placated by an innocent victim.[36]

That, indeed, is the hostage given to fortune by 4 Maccabees 17:22, which some have hailed as providing the clue to Paul's meaning here.[37] Throughout that book the author is mounting an explicit and sustained attempt to render the Jewish tradition of the martyr-stories (as found in 2 Maccabees) into a pagan register. Little sense is left of the larger covenant story of God, Israel, and the world. The promise of resurrection, so prominent in 2 Maccabees, has been omitted. All the themes in Isaiah that Paul so carefully builds in to his picture are left to one side. What I think may have happened—certainty on a point like this is impossible—is that the author of 4 Maccabees was on the one hand distantly echoing some elements of Israel's scriptural heritage, and on the other hand eager to present the Jewish martyrs to a pagan audience as dying a noble death on behalf of their country, and that he has therefore combined those two strands, producing a mixture neither fully scriptural nor completely pagan. What has happened in the more recent western Christian tradition, I suggest, is that with the assumed "goal" of a Platonized "heaven" has gone a more thorough paganization of the "means." It is in ancient Greece and Rome, not in Israel, that we find plentiful evidence of people being sacrificed, or giving their lives in battle, to save others, usually because of the need to placate an angry deity.[38] This is not Paul's view. Romans 1–4 has been read with little or no attention to the theme of the divine covenant with Israel, and through Israel for the world. Other ideas, particularly the popular image of

---

36. This theme is amply documented in, e.g., M. Hengel, *The Atonement: A Study of the Origins of the Doctrine in the New Testament* (London: SCM, 1981), 4–32.

37. Recently, e.g., J. J. Williams, *Christ Died for Our Sins: Representation and Substitution in Romans and Their Jewish Martyrological Background* (Eugene, OR: Pickwick, 2015), summing up arguments advanced by the author in various other monographs and articles.

38. Details in, e.g., Hengel, *The Atonement*, 4–32.

"God punishing Jesus," envisaged as a separate, noncovenantal abstraction, have come in to take the place of that all-important theme. Many distortions have resulted, not only through that teaching itself but through teachings which, in reaction against the distorted view, have proposed equally unsatisfactory alternatives.

So what, in this view, had actually happened by 6 pm on the first Good Friday? If Romans 3:21–26 was all we had to go on to answer that question, what might we say? First, we would say that the age-old covenant plan of the creator, to rescue humanity and the world from sin and death through his covenant people, had been accomplished. The new Passover took place, in fulfillment of God's promises to Abraham. Second, we would say that this had been accomplished by God himself, in his act of covenant faithfulness (for which the shorthand is of course "love," though in the present argument Paul reserves that word for Romans 5:6–11 and 8:31–39), drawing together Israel's vocation and his own deepest purposes in the faithful death of the Messiah. (Clearly, the relationship between God and Jesus needs further explication; Paul here takes this for granted.) Third, as befits a "passover" moment, we would say that people of all sorts—Jew and Gentile alike—are now free, free from past sins, free to come in to the single covenant family. They are "freely declared to be in the right." Fourth (and here Paul stands alongside the four Gospels, the letter to the Hebrews, the first letter of Peter, and the book of Revelation), the new Passover also functions as the dealing with sins through which exile is undone. This is where Passover and the "Day of Atonement" meet and merge. Fifth, and at the heart of it all, we have Israel's representative Messiah "handed over because of our trespasses," in the sense intended in Isaiah 53.

Nothing vital in traditional western understandings has been lost through this approach. What has been lost is the paganized vision of an angry God looming over the world and bent upon blood. What Paul gives us instead, here and throughout his writings, is the Jewish vision of the loving, generous creator God, giving his own very self for the life of the world.

This is certainly not a complete statement of "atonement." It is not even a complete, or comprehensive, statement of all the things that Paul understands to have taken place in Jesus's death. But as usual we must remind ourselves that Romans is not, in that sense, a "systematic theology" in which all the basic theological topics are laid out in summary form. Nor is Romans 3:24–26 an attempt to say everything Paul might want to say about "the atonement." As with every other time when Paul mentions Jesus's death, these verses do the job he wants them to do within their larger context. The larger context is the faithfulness of God to his covenant with Abraham and Israel, which is also his covenant *through* Abraham and Israel for the wider world. That faithfulness, through which the Israel-purpose is fulfilled and the world-salvation purpose accomplished, has now been unveiled in action. Once we liberate Romans 3:21–26 from the burden of trying to say "everything about the cross," it too experiences its Exodus. It is free to make its own point in its own way, and thereby to contribute vitally to the larger argument of the letter as a whole.

Jesus the Baptist: The First Temptation of Christ

Sean M. McDonough

Over the last few decades, Richard Bauckham has reinvigorated the study of John's Gospel with a series of innovative essays.[1] Central to his project has been a reclamation of the historical orientation of John's work. Far from being a form of self-talk therapy for a putative Johannine community, the Gospel is instead what it purports to be: a story about Jesus. One of the more intriguing aspects of this history is the account of Jesus's baptizing ministry in John 3 and 4, which has attracted increased attention in the last few decades.[2] Those who have paid closest attention to the passage have argued strongly for its historical

---

1. See, e.g., the collection *The Testimony of the Beloved Disciple* (Grand Rapids: Baker, 2007).

2. See esp. R. T. France, "Jesus the Baptist?" in *Jesus of Nazareth: Lord and Christ*, ed. Joel Green and Max Turner (Grand Rapids: Eerdmans, 1994), 94–111. Paul W. Hollenbach devotes significant attention to the question in his "The Conversion of Jesus: From Baptizer to Healer," *Aufstieg und Niedergang der römischen Welt*, ed. H. Temporini and W. Haase (Berlin: De Gruyter, 1972–), 2.25.1:196–219, as do Robert Webb ("John the Baptist and His Relationship to Jesus," in *Studying the Historical Jesus*, ed. Bruce Chilton and Craig A. Evans [Leiden: Brill, 1994], 179–229, esp. 219–26) and Jerome Murphy-O'Connor ("John the Baptist and Jesus: History and Hypotheses," *New Testament Studies* 36 [1990]: 359–74). See also C. H. Dodd (*Historical Tradition in the Fourth Gospel* [Cambridge: Cambridge University Press, 1963], 279–87, esp. 286) and Raymond Brown (*The Gospel according to John I–XII* [Garden City, NY: Doubleday, 1966], 150–55).

Earlier drafts of this paper were read at the Boston Theological Institute New Testament Colloquium and the St. Andrews Conference on the Gospel of John and Christian Theology. My thanks to all who offered comments and critiques in those sessions.

veracity,[3] while even Historical Jesus scholars who treat the matter much more cursorily still seem to regard it as a plausible account.[4] What has not been brought to the fore, however, is the significance of the passage for the fourth evangelist himself. When the relevant texts in John are read against the first-century Jewish milieu and the synoptic tradition, they provide critical insights into the fourth evangelist's understanding of Jesus's early career. Rather than being an awkward parenthesis in the Gospel, the accounts offer an essential introduction into the nature of Jesus's distinctive messianic vision.

1. Historical Significance

For the purposes of our argument, one need only acknowledge that, whatever we might make of it, the fourth evangelist appears to believe the baptizing ministry of Jesus actually happened. This alone would justify locating it within the broader contours of first-century Judaism to see what light that context may shed on the texts in John 3 and 4. As noted above, however, the historicity of this material has in fact attracted widespread scholarly support.[5] The absence of the baptizing account from the synoptic tradition is not necessarily a problem. John Meier argues that the synoptic writers might well have been scandalized that Jesus had a copycat baptizing ministry. The "criterion of embarrassment" would enhance the historical plausibility of John's account.[6] One might also argue that the synoptic writers, while not necessarily embarrassed

---

3. All the authors mentioned in the previous note support the historicity of the baptizing ministry.

4. See, e.g., David Strauss, who states, "As, however, the rite of baptism was introduced by John, and we have reason to believe that Jesus, for a time, made that teacher his model, it is highly probable that he and his disciples also practiced baptism, and hence that the positive statement of the fourth gospel is correct" (*The Life of Jesus Critically Examined*, ed. Peter Hodgson, trans. George Eliot [Philadelphia: Fortress, 1972], 325). Paula Fredriksen adopts a similar tone: "If we can rely on John 3:22 . . . Jesus also baptized, at least for a while; but clearly that activity was not as central a part of the mission, and it left no trace in the synoptics at all" (*Jesus of Nazareth, King of the Jews* [New York: Knopf, 2000], 192).

5. See esp. Webb, "Relationship to Jesus," 219–20. While there may be lingering doubts about anything in John being considered historical, Jerome Murphy-O'Connor's words (written precisely about our passage) are to the point: "The facile skepticism of an earlier generation with regard to ostensibly historical and geographical information in the Fourth Gospel has fortunately given way to a genuinely critical approach" (Murphy-O'Connor, "John and Jesus," 366).

6. John P. Meier, *A Marginal Jew: Rethinking the Historical Jesus*, vol. 2, *Mentor, Message, and Miracles* (New York: Doubleday, 1994), 120–22.

by the account, nonetheless thought that including it might diminish the effect of seeing the dynamic power of the Spirit active in the healings and exorcisms. What better way to clarify the point that Jesus baptizes *in the Spirit* than by focusing on the works of the Spirit and omitting references to water baptism? In any event, the baptizing ministry in the Fourth Gospel is not the kind of random bit of teaching, or stylized miracle story, that might easily slip into a life of Jesus. It is a very specific, and a rather puzzling, description of a unique practice. One would have to provide compelling arguments to explain why John, or anyone else, would have made it up.[7]

Ablutions and immersions were of course a longstanding and integral part of Jewish life.[8] Various cleansing rituals were prescribed in the Old Testament, from bathing to remove the impurity of bodily emissions to the sprinkling of water containing the ashes of the red heifer for cleansing corpse impurity. Additional washings, like the washing of the hands before meals, are also attested for our period.[9] The Dead Sea Scrolls offer some very suggestive comparative material. In his detailed study of Qumran immersions, Robert Webb concludes that, in addition to the expected type of Old Testament purificatory immersions, the community also practiced initiatory immersions that moved a candidate "from an impure non-Israelite to a pure Israelite."[10] The Scrolls make it clear, however, that this ritual is useless without a concomitant change of heart and lifestyle (e.g., 1QS 2:25–3:9). While we cannot be entirely sure if this type of initiatory immersion originated at Qumran, it does fit well with the sect's self-perception as the true spiritual temple. Spiritual and ritual uncleanness need to be remedied before entering this spiritual temple, hence the call for repentance and immersion. Eschatologically oriented texts like Ezekiel 36:25 were no doubt crucial in the emergence of these practices: "I will sprinkle clean water upon you, and you shall be clean from all your uncleanness, and from all your idols I will cleanse you" (author's translation). (It is hardly a coincidence that the vision of the eschatological temple follows soon after this promise.)

---

7. Cf. Brown, who states, "There is no plausible theological reason why anyone would have invented the tradition that Jesus and his disciples once baptized" (*Gospel according to John I-XII*, 155).

8. See, e.g., Lev. 8:6 (the consecration of Aaron and his sons); Lev. 14:8 (cleansing of lepers); Lev. 15:1-31 (those having or coming into contact with various bodily discharges). They were also an integral part of Greco-Roman religion; see, e.g., the discussion in Walter Burkert, *Greek Religion*, trans. John Raffan (Cambridge, MA: Harvard University Press, 1985), 75-79.

9. E.g., Matt. 15:2.

10. Webb, *John the Baptizer and Prophet*, Journal for the Study of the New Testament Supplement Series 62 (Sheffield: JSOT Press, 1991), 162.

The parallels with John's baptism are illuminating. I am again inclined to accept Webb's conclusions. Let me quote him at length:

> As a corporate body, these prepared ones constituted the eschatological community of the true, remnant Israel, and it was the baptism which prepared them, and so initiated them into this community. . . . John's baptism, as a rite which mediated forgiveness, indicated that the usual means of forgiveness, the temple cultus, had been made invalid, probably by the actions and policies of the temple establishment. Thus, John's baptism functioned as a protest against the perceived abuses by the temple establishment.[11]

John the Baptist's group, of course, appears to have been much less regimented than the community at Qumran, and insofar as these things may be distinguished, he seemed more concerned with general ethical transformation than with detailed ritual and communal regulations. Some may also wish to debate whether John consciously intended to replace the temple. Nonetheless, the broader theme of the *renewal of Israel*, which was marked by *initiatory immersion*, holds true in both cases. We would anticipate that Jesus's baptizing would follow the same basic pattern.[12]

At this point a critical question emerges. Was Jesus's baptizing ministry simply a continuation of John's ministry? Did he even carry it out under John's auspices?[13] If this is the case, the significance of Jesus's baptizing is relatively easy to discern—it will be more or less the same as that of John. The problem then becomes, why did he *stop* baptizing? Since the Gospels do not give an abundance of evidence on this point, scholars have advanced various theories based on the broader distinctions between John and Jesus. Paul Hollenbach argues that Jesus abandoned baptism after the unexpected success of his healing and exorcizing ministry, which triggered a radical change in his whole approach to life and ministry. (He goes so far as to say that Jesus "thus appears to be astonished by his exorcisms.")[14] Jesus was no longer looking forward to the kingdom, like John, but was in fact participating in it. Webb endorses this general point and adds the notion of Jesus's sense of prophetic call as another

---

11. Webb, *John the Baptizer*, 216.
12. See esp. Ben F. Meyer, *The Aims of Jesus* (London: SCM, 1979), 122–24.
13. As affirmed by Murphy-O'Connor, "John and Jesus," 362.
14. Hollenbach, "The Conversion of Jesus," 211. Meier raises pertinent concerns about this psychologizing approach (*Marginal Jew*, 124–25).

factor in his new style of ministry.[15] For Murphy-O'Connor, the precarious economic situation of many in Galilee may have been "instrumental in causing Jesus to give the mercy of a gracious God priority over the demands of the Law."[16] Ben Meyer, meanwhile, believes that Jesus "saw the arrest of John as closing an initial, limited, distinct phase in the scheme of divinely willed fulfillment events."[17]

These are all significant points, and the elements of discontinuity between John and Jesus must be accounted for. But the accounts above do not deal sufficiently with three important considerations. First, we will argue in detail below that the fourth evangelist does in fact provide a plausible explanation for the cessation of Jesus's Judean baptizing ministry. One may ascribe this to Johannine theology, but it at least provides us with one first-century explanation of the phenomenon. Second, while the arguments do make sense of the differences in tenor between Jesus and John, they do not necessarily demand the conclusion that Jesus must have abandoned the practice of baptism itself. This leads to the third point: Is it even certain that Jesus *did* stop baptizing during his career? R. T. France has made a convincing argument that Jesus continued baptizing as the normal way of bringing people into his movement.[18] In brief, France says that an ongoing ministry of baptism makes sense on the one hand of Jesus's continuity with John, and his ongoing relationship with John's disciples; and on the other hand, with the early church's practice of baptism. The latter point is particularly forceful. France summarizes his point in comments on the Great Commission: "Rather than introducing a new rite, oddly reminiscent of John's practice which, *ex hypothesi*, Jesus had earlier deliberately abandoned, the risen Jesus is in fact simply instructing his followers to continue with the practice which has throughout his ministry been the normal and expected visible form of 'disciple making.'"[19]

Nothing in Jesus's later ministry seems to demand the cessation of baptism per se. Whatever differences he may have had with John, Jesus was still demonstrably calling for a renewal of Israel. He calls twelve disciples, he pro-

---

15. Webb, "Relationship to Jesus," 224-26.
16. Murphy-O'Connor, "John and Jesus," 374.
17. Meyer, *Aims of Jesus*, 129.
18. France, "Jesus the Baptist?" 105-7. Murphy-O'Connor affirms that Jesus baptized in Galilee, although he later stopped ("John and Jesus," 368-74). He makes the salient point (also noted by France) that this would account for Herod's supposition that Jesus was John the Baptist *redivivus* ("John and Jesus," 372).
19. France, "Jesus the Baptist?" 109.

claims forgiveness of sins far from the temple grounds, he initiates a radical reenvisioning of what it means to obey Torah. All of this proceeds from a new understanding of what Israel is. Employing the rite of baptism would be a perfectly natural way of expressing such a renewal in the early first century.[20] It might evoke images of the creation waters, the deliverance of the Exodus, and the conquest of the land. If France is correct, the effort to account for Jesus turning his back on baptism as such is unnecessary. Baptism was a broadly applicable symbol of renewal, and could be employed both as a symbol of preparation for God's kingdom (John) or as a symbol of participation in God's kingdom (Jesus and the early church).

When we discuss renewal movements, however, we also need to consider the overtly military uprisings (or would-be uprisings) of people like Theudas, the Egyptian prophet, and others. The line between these uprisings and the movements of John and Jesus is not as readily perceptible as is sometimes imagined. Theudas is described by Josephus (*A.J.* 20.5.1 §97) not as a mere military leader, but as a self-proclaimed prophet, whom Josephus describes as a *goēs*, translated, probably correctly, as an "impostor," but also susceptible to the rendering "sorcerer." Such labels, of course, would be placed upon Jesus during or after his ministry. The idea of a great crowd (*ochlon*) going out to the Jordan with Theudas resonates with the crowds thronging to John and Jesus in their baptizing ministries (see especially Luke 3:7, which uses *ochlois*). The eventual fate of Theudas again does not differ from that of John and Jesus.

If we look for a moment at some of the other revolutionary movements in the first part of the century, we find more items of interest. In describing assorted revolutionary "deceivers," Josephus begins by contrasting them with the *sicarii*: these desert revolutionaries have "cleaner hands," albeit equally harmful intentions (*B.J.* 2.13.4 §258). They claim divine inspiration and persuade their followers that in the desert they would be given "signs of deliverance" or freedom, *sēmeia eleutherias* (2.13.4 §259). Their activities are seen as *apostaseōs . . . katabolē*, the foundation of a rebellion (2.13.4 §260). One may perhaps give the benefit of the doubt to Josephus, who condemns them with the word, and Felix, who assaults them with the sword, and assume that they really were up to no good in the desert. But the quite vague and sometimes even positive terms employed by Josephus, combined with very religious language of "signs of deliverance" and "pure hands," make one wonder if these

---

20. See, e.g., Meyer (*Aims of Jesus*, 125) and N. T. Wright (*Jesus and the Victory of God* [Minneapolis: Fortress, 1996], esp. 198–220).

movements would have looked very much like the efforts at renewal undertaken by John and Jesus, at least on the surface.[21]

The point is not that Jesus or John secretly intended a military uprising. But in terms of *popular associations*, it is obvious that the wilderness in general, and the wilderness around the Jordan in particular, was steeped with the memories of the Exodus and Conquest. Thus any movement of renewal, however peaceable it might be, was subject to being understood as a call to overthrow the authorities in Judea.[22]

More pointedly, it could be understood broadly as a *messianic* movement to overthrow the authorities. If we can leave aside the myriad conceptions that have accumulated around the idea of Messiah in the Christian era, we are left with the basic idea of an anointed leader, usually a political figure, and more particularly an anointed leader fulfilling the promises made to David in places like 2 Samuel 7. In the religiously charged atmosphere of first-century Judea, it is difficult to imagine someone leading a revolt who could *not* claim some type of anointing from God. While some may regard it as a later gloss, it is still worth recalling the question of the Pharisees to John the Baptist in John 1:25: "Why, then, are you baptizing, if you are not the Christ, nor Elijah, nor the Prophet?" "You are here in the Jordan, proclaiming a new day for Israel—you surely must have some special authorization for doing so? Perhaps you are the anointed leader some have been expecting—or at least some sort of forerunner like Elijah or the Prophet?" (author's translation). The assumption in this text is that a likely identification of a desert-dwelling herald of renewal is an anointed one, or *the* anointed one. The later claims of Theudas, the Egyptian prophet, and nameless others do nothing to undercut this assumption.

We conclude, then, that the baptizing ministry of Jesus was looking toward some sort of a renewal or restoration of Israel. Given the clear associations with John's ministry, the thrust of Jesus's later teaching, and the teachings of the early church, we would presume that this was a nonviolent call for renewal, focusing on spiritual revivification and a concomitant exhortation to high ethical standards. We might speculate about an exodus from the dominion of sin, a conquest of spiritual enemies, or even a re-creation, with a new person rising out of the creation waters. At the same time, whatever Jesus's

---

21. Cf. Wright, *Jesus*, 150–55.

22. And, we might add, of the rest of Palestine. Many authors note the political overtones of Herod's arrest of John the Baptist. See, e.g., Murphy-O'Connor ("John and Jesus," 368–69) and Webb ("Relationship to Jesus," 206–10). For a convenient overview of issues surrounding revolt see N. T. Wright, *The New Testament and the People of God* (Minneapolis: Fortress, 1992), 170–81.

intentions might have been, his baptizing ministry was liable to be understood as the same sort of "preparation for rebellion" we saw elsewhere in early Judaism. This latter observation holds the key, I believe, for the cessation of at least this phase of Jesus's baptizing ministry, as will emerge more clearly in our discussion of the Gospel evidence.

2. Significance in John

This much we may say from the general historical background. If we wish to go beyond this, we will need to examine closely John 3 and 4 within the flow of John's Gospel and against the backdrop of the synoptic tradition. Obviously the relationship of John and the synoptics is a world unto itself in the scholarly debate, and there is insufficient space to resolve that question here.[23] Our argument requires only two things: that John expected his readers to be conscious of the basic outline of Jesus's career as depicted in the synoptics; and that he would specifically expect them to be aware of the sequence of Jesus's baptism, temptation, and return to Galilee. This does not require that John necessarily knew the synoptics as we now have them. One could make do with a pre-synoptic tradition that would have been commonly known in the early church and off of which John could play.[24] Similarly, one could grant John full knowledge of Mark, Matthew, and Luke, or of Mark only, with the possibility of some information that also appears in Matthew and Luke.[25] The working

---

23. D. Moody Smith provides a convenient summary of the debate in *John among the Gospels* (Minneapolis: Fortress, 1992).

24. At a minimum, for instance, one might hold with J. Louis Martyn that John was influenced by the "traditional melodies" in the early church, assuming that the baptism-temptation-return to Galilee complex was a widely recognized one (*History and Theology in the Fourth Gospel* [New York: Harper & Row, 1968], xx). Even Ernst Haenchen's very cautious approach ("the single Evangelist with which John has frequent contact—and that is not close—is Luke") could conceivably accommodate our argument, if the above assumption is granted (*John: A Commentary on the Gospel of John*, 2 vols., trans. R. W. Funk [Philadelphia: Fortress, 1984], 1:75).

25. According to Smith, many of the church fathers accepted John's knowledge of the synoptics (*John among the Gospels*, 10). Bauckham makes a persuasive case for John's engagement with Mark ("John for Readers of Mark," in *The Gospels for All Christians*, ed. R. Bauckham [Grand Rapids: Eerdmans, 1998], 147-71). Other combinations are possible, e.g., Streeter's contention that John used Mark and Luke but not Matthew (*The Four Gospels* [London: Macmillan, 1930], 424-25); cf., more cautiously, C. K. Barrett (*The Gospel according to Saint John*, 2nd ed. [Philadelphia: Westminster, 1978], 45-56), and D. A. Carson (*The Gospel according to John* [Grand Rapids: Eerdmans; Leicester: IVP, 1991], 51).

theory of this essay will be the latter: that John knew Mark,[26] and that he may well have been aware of elements appearing in Matthew and Luke. (For the sake of convenience we may refer to this loosely as the "synoptic tradition," recognizing the caveats listed above.)

Since the story of Jesus's baptizing is missing from the synoptics, it is obviously impossible to compare accounts as we might with the feeding of the five thousand. But it is possible to see where this story fits in terms of synoptic chronology. In the Fourth Gospel, Jesus starts baptizing after his own (implied) baptism at John's hands (1:32-34), at the same time as the reintroduction of John the Baptist to the narrative (3:23), and just before his departure to Galilee (via Samaria; 4:3). It is our contention that John is mirroring the synoptic complex of baptism-temptation-return to Galilee, with one significant difference: in place of the temptation narratives, we find the narratives concerning Jesus's baptizing ministry.

The first element in the complex, the baptism, does not appear explicitly in John but is clearly indicated in 1:32-34. That the baptism of Jesus is only implicit in the text does not present a major problem. The baptism of Jesus was so solid a part of the tradition that John could assume his readers knew it.[27] The interplay of John and Jesus is sufficient for a reader to know where he or she stands in the standard chronology. Nor is the presence of intervening material (1:35-3:21) between the allusion to the baptism and the baptizing ministry a fatal objection to our thesis. The reintroduction of John at 3:23 keeps Jesus's baptizing ministry squarely in the context of his relationship with John, so that the reader can still make the connection with the synoptic complex of baptism-temptation-return to Galilee. It is hardly unusual for John to insert unique material into the familiar flow of Jesus's story (most notably in the account of Lazarus just prior to Jesus's triumphal entry). Moreover, the inter-

---

26. Cf. Barrett's remark: "anyone who after an interval of nineteen centuries feels himself in a position to distinguish nicely between 'Mark' and 'something much like Mark,' is at liberty to do so" (45).

27. See, e.g., R. Schnackenburg, *The Gospel according to John*, 3 vols., trans. Kevin Smyth (New York: Seabury, 1980), 1:27; Bauckham, "John for Readers of Mark," 154. As for the question of why the evangelist omits the baptism of Jesus, but includes the baptizing of Jesus, Dodd's comments are helpful: "It would no doubt be congenial with his [sc. the fourth evangelist's] general attitude to represent Jesus, not as receiving baptism from John, but as himself administering it, in so far as the incarnate Logos must be thought of as always active and never merely passive" (Dodd, *Historical Tradition*, 286). The latter part may be a bit overstated, but the essential insight is sound. We would only underscore that this redactional choice finds its power precisely in the fact that the evangelist realizes his readers will already know Jesus has been baptized by John.

vening material is critical for helping the reader trace the contours of the transition from John to Jesus (on which see below).

It remains to determine whether the departure for Galilee in 4:3 is the same one signaled in Mark 1, Matthew 4, and Luke 4. This is not self-evident, since Jesus shuttles back and forth frequently between Jerusalem and Galilee in John's Gospel. While not self-evident, however, it is readily demonstrable. In Mark and Matthew, the news of John's imprisonment triggers Jesus's return to Galilee. The Fourth Gospel deals with John's imminent demise in its own way—"He must increase, but I must decrease" (3:30), arguably the final words of the Baptist in the Fourth Gospel. Almost immediately after this statement we have the account of Jesus's departure for Galilee. (The statement in John 3:24, "John had not yet been put into prison," might seem to disrupt this line of reasoning, since it has sometimes been taken as a correction of Mark's chronology. But Bauckham has demonstrated that John is instead enabling his readers to locate the first sections of the narrative [John 1:19–4:43] *between* Mark 1:13 and 1:14.[28]) Furthermore, after a characteristically Johannine detour, this time through Samaria, we have a clear sign that the fourth evangelist is tracking the synoptic account of Jesus's ministry in Galilee. The words "for Jesus himself bore witness that a prophet does not have honor in his own home" (John 4:44) are most naturally taken as a reference to Jesus's rejection at Nazareth, with Luke 4:24 being perhaps the most interesting parallel, coming as it does at the very beginning of his public ministry (cf. Mark 6:1-4). Thus in John, Jesus's final scene before the departure for Galilee is the baptizing ministry. In the synoptics, the final scene before the departure is the temptation narrative.

The baptizing ministry of Jesus, then, takes place at the critical juncture where the baton is handed from John to Jesus. It is in light of this that we might try to make sense of the curious note in 4:2: "not that Jesus baptized, but only his disciples." This has generally been viewed as indisputable evidence for later redaction within the Gospel, and it may be hard to persuade someone otherwise. But these apparently glaring contradictions are a double-edged sword. On the one hand, one needs to posit a redactor who is willing to tamper with

---

28. Bauckham, "John for Readers of Mark," 154–55. Bauckham notes that the *public* ministry in Galilee does not occur until John 4:45 (this is to be distinguished from the miracle at Cana in the presence of the disciples). Brown, while affirming the problems of chronology, concedes: "It is true that the Synoptics do not tell us exactly when John the Baptist was arrested, so that all that John has narrated might have occurred before the official opening of the Galilean ministry" (*Gospel according to John I-XII*, 153). Bauckham's argument serves to support just this point.

the received texts with something bordering on reckless abandon. But one must also imagine that this same person failed to notice the problem back in chapter 3, where the trouble started, and only caught up with it several verses later.[29] Granted, many things can happen in the course of textual transmission, and one can imagine scenarios in which 4:2 could have slipped in where it is now. But it is precisely in the "obvious" cases that the most careful attention is required.

Are there any grounds for believing that the admittedly peculiar disclaimer is an integral part of the narrative rather than a later insertion? I believe that there are. In the synoptics, two things need to happen in the transition from John the Baptist to Jesus. First, one needs to show *continuity* between John and Jesus; and second, one needs to show *advancement* from John to Jesus.[30] This is partly achieved in the dialogues surrounding the scenes of Jesus's baptism, but it is also done in the accounts of Jesus's early ministry. Jesus *echoes* John with the call to repentance (Mark 1:15; Matt. 4:17). He *advances* beyond John in his assertion that the kingdom of God is now at hand; the good news is there to be embraced, and it is demonstrated by mighty works of healing and exorcism.

In the Fourth Gospel, the evangelist may be achieving the same goal by different means. The continuity with John is emphasized not by having Jesus echo John's words, but by having Jesus echo John's actions. Jesus, like John, calls for a renewal of Israel, symbolized by baptism. Hence there is a need to identify Jesus with the baptizing ministry. At the same time, the fourth evangelist signals the *advancement* represented by Jesus's ministry. He does this not simply by stressing the numerical superiority of Jesus's baptizands, which might only serve to make Jesus *primus inter pares*. Instead, he points out in 4:2 that Jesus himself had set his sights beyond simply baptism. The delay until 4:2 allows time for the theme of continuity to be established, while the disclaimer serves to shock the reader into the realization that Jesus has his sights set on much more than a Judean baptizing ministry. The numerous references to Jesus baptizing *in the Spirit* signal the precise nature of the advancement of Jesus's ministry, and distance him from the actual sprinkling or immersion, thus keeping the spiritual focus intact. This is reinforced by the surrounding material in chapters 1–3: John's disciples now follow Jesus (1:35-51); Jesus brings the new wine of the kingdom (2:1-12); Jesus re-centers worship around himself (2:13-25); Jesus comes to give the life-giving spirit (3:1-21). The note concern-

---

29. Haenchen notes at least this part of the problem (*John*, 218).
30. France speaks in a similar vein (see esp. "Jesus the Baptist?" 108-9, 110-11).

ing the dispute between John's disciples and a Jew (there is no need for an emendation) in 3:25–36 fits here as well. John's circle remains enmeshed in discussions concerning ritual matters, while Jesus stands, as it were, above the fray. His hands are not only clean, but dry.

3. Baptism and Temptation

Whatever one makes of these arguments concerning 4:2, the correspondence in chronological flow between John and the synoptics should be established. Jesus is baptized, Jesus baptizes, and Jesus goes back to Galilee. In the synoptics, Jesus is baptized, Jesus is tempted, and Jesus goes back to Galilee. Does this conspicuous absence of the temptation story in John, and its replacement with the baptizing accounts, enhance the reader's understanding of John's Gospel?[31] Is there a meaningful connection between the temptation narratives and the story of Jesus the Baptist?

There is such a connection, and it lies in messianic activity; in particular, in *conspicuous* messianic activity. In the synoptics, Jesus is arguably tempted to display his messianic authority for all to see and to sweep the world before him, gaining the rule of the world without the need to go to the cross. To demonstrate this, we do not need to rely on uncertain parallels to the works of the Messiah in later rabbinic literature.[32] A much better approach is to note the clear parallel between Jesus's temptations and the temptations faced by Israel in the wilderness wanderings. It is hard to dispute that Jesus is portrayed in the synoptics as recapitulating Israel's experience, with the significant distinction that Jesus passes the test that ancient Israel failed. This Spirit-led triumph sets the scene for a reenvisioning of what Israel is.[33] What label would be best for a figure who represents the nation in his own person, and who goes on to reconfigure the nation around himself? What better than the Messiah, the anointed one of God?

---

31. Note that Barrett includes the temptation in a list of synoptic incidents known by John that nonetheless did not make it explicitly into his Gospel. Others include the virgin birth, the transfiguration, and the agony in the garden (*Saint John*, 51). He understands the truth of the temptation narrative to be expressed in the climactic conflict against Satan on the cross (John 12:31; Barrett, *Saint John*, 53).

32. E.g., the prophecy that the Messiah would reveal himself on the roof of the temple (*Pesiq. Rabbati* 36 [162a]), discussed and dismissed by I. Howard Marshall in *Luke*, New International Greek Testament Commentary (Grand Rapids: Eerdmans, 1978), 173.

33. Meyer, *Aims of Jesus*, 240.

The fact that Jesus is portrayed as the Messiah, and that he is tempted, is sufficient to label these as "messianic temptations." The case for this is strengthened when we recognize the echoes of Psalm 2 in the devil's offer to give Jesus the kingdoms of the world, if Jesus will only worship him. "Ask of me, and I will make the nations your heritage, and the ends of the earth your possession." As Joel Green puts it, "The devil proposes to displace God as Jesus' benefactor."[34] Satan is putting forward an alternative vision of how to be Israel's Messiah, one based on self-satisfaction (the bread), self-display (the temple), and self-aggrandizement on a cosmic scale (the kingdoms of the world). What is more, Satan's messiah can get all of this without the suffering that has already made its presence felt in Matthew and Luke—the crown is to be had without the cross. The only requirement is to worship the devil rather than God.[35]

It is this same temptation to messianic self-aggrandizement and display that faces Jesus throughout John's Gospel, and in particular in the case of the baptizing ministry. We have already argued that renewal movements would naturally have some messianic element, whether in hope or in fulfillment, since you need an anointed leader to usher in the full-scale renovation of the nation. The promises to David and his descendants (2 Sam. 7, etc.) are too thoroughly rooted in the Hebrew Bible to be ignored by those interested in renewal. Thus, when Jesus begins baptizing, it is likely that people—including discerning readers of the Fourth Gospel—will begin to wonder whether he is in fact laying claim to this anointed role. The ingredients for a mass movement along the lines of Theudas were there: a charismatic leader; a large and apparently pliable populace eager for a change; the promise of divine blessing on their efforts; and some easily accessible villains in Jerusalem—the religious aristocracy, represented by the Pharisees (John 4:1-3), and the Roman government. Jesus's own intentions, at this juncture, take a back seat to public perception.

The point is not simply that the time is not right for the revelation of Jesus's messianic authority, or that he is avoiding his inevitable demise at the hand of the Jerusalem authorities. Seen in light of the synoptics, the problem in the Fourth Gospel is less that Jesus will fall prey to the Pharisees at the wrong time, and more that Jesus will triumph over the Pharisees in the wrong way, that he will become the Messiah the people want rather than the one they need. Such a retreat from militant messiahship surfaces even more visibly in

---

34. Joel Green, *The Gospel of Luke*, New International Commentary on the New Testament (Grand Rapids: Eerdmans, 1997), 194.

35. See Wright's comments (*Jesus*, 458-59).

John 6:15, where the crowds wish to seize Jesus and make him king after the feeding of the five thousand.[36] It also resonates with Jesus biding his time beyond the Jordan in the spot John was baptizing (John 10:40) before his final "strike" on Judea in the raising of Lazarus and his withdrawal to "the country near the wilderness" before the triumphal entry. All of this is the latter-day David's wilderness time before the ascent to Zion's throne.[37]

4. Conclusion

Based on the conscious parallels in chronology, and the thematic convergence of conspicuous messianic display, it appears that the baptizing ministry of Jesus as depicted by John is a deliberate counterpart to the synoptic temptation narratives. In John's view, Jesus was indeed tempted early on in his ministry to display his messianic power and authority in a very visible way. But this temptation was not simply a private "spiritualized" or "apocalyptic" encounter with the devil. While we are not given a reason to suspect that John would deny the validity of the synoptic temptation narratives, John chooses to focus on the very public temptation faced by Jesus: the temptation to turn his successful baptizing ministry into a messianic tour de force, a confrontation with the powers-that-be in Jerusalem. Jesus instead abandons this highly charged venue for baptism (though not necessarily abandoning the practice itself) and withdraws to Galilee, a much less visible spot for messianic endeavor.

Thus, in this instance at least, the usual perspective on John and the synoptics must be stood on its head. It is John who concerns himself with public

---

36. There may be echoes of the synoptic temptation narratives here as well—miraculous bread in the desert. It is perhaps worth noting that John uses the verb *anachoreō* here, which is precisely the verb Matthew uses for Jesus's withdrawal to Galilee after the temptation in the wilderness (and the verb Matthew uses for Jesus's withdrawal to a lonely place after the execution of John the Baptist).

37. Pulling back from the messianic limelight also features in 2:23–25 and 5:13. Even the superficially disturbing fact that Jesus appears to go back on his original intention—Should he baptize or not? Why begin and then stop (at least in Judea)?—would be fully in keeping with the rest of the Fourth Gospel. In chapter 2, he declares that his time has not yet come, as if he would prefer the now-nonalcoholic festivities to proceed as is. Of course, he ends up changing the water to wine, which becomes "the beginning of his signs," a manifestation of his glory that leads to belief. In chapter 7, he explicitly denies that he will go up to the feast in Jerusalem, but he does go, albeit in secret. Despite the caricature of the Johannine Jesus as an all-controlling Superman, the actual Jesus of the Fourth Gospel finds himself continually responding to the reactions of those around him.

history, while the synoptics give us a more private, spiritualized account of Jesus's early ministry. Jesus's spiritual or existential crisis is mirrored in the exigencies of first-century Jewish politics. The Fourth Gospel's account only takes on its full resonance when heard against this historical backdrop, as well as the synoptic tradition. It may also cause us to stand Albert Schweitzer's well-known dictum on its head. In John's Gospel, Jesus does not come to us as one unknown. He comes as one very well known, a charismatic leader gathering hordes of disciples in the desert of Judea. He is a visible player in the religious life of Judea, well along the bright path to messianic success as popularly understood. But he retreats from that path and takes a longer and darker way, and it is that choice that will define his ministry. The *via crucis* leads to Galilee.

Giving the Kingdom to an *Ethnos* That Will Bear Its Fruit: Ethnic and Christ-Movement Identities in Matthew

Philip F. Esler

Richard Bauckham's career in biblical interpretation has been remarkable for the sheer scale of his productivity, creativity, penetrating historical and exegetical insight, and theological suppleness. A longstanding interest of Professor Bauckham has been to explain how the early Christ-movement understood Christ against the Second Temple context, including his insistence on its "early high Christology," a view with which I am essentially in agreement. One of the theological centers of Matthew's Gospel is his emphasis on the continuing presence of Christ with those who have faith in him (see, for example, Matt. 1:23; 10:40; 18:20; 25:31–46; and 28:20). This is a dimension of the Matthean perspective surely rooted in and nourished by that early high Christology.

In this essay, which I am honored to be able to contribute to Professor Bauckham's *Festschrift*, I seek to trace certain dimensions of the impact that this belief in Christ had on the way that Matthew construed and presented the identity of the Christ-movement and its membership to the audience for whom he was writing. My focus is on Matthew 21:43: "Therefore I tell you, the kingdom of God will be taken away from you and given to an *ethnos* bearing its fruit." This verse conjures up two sharply delineated groups, namely, the people referred to as "you" on the one hand and those referred to as an *ethnos* on the other. My argument here is that this verse goes right to the heart of the meaning Matthew intended for his original audience, especially the critical

---

An earlier version of this essay was presented at the British New Testament Conference at the University of Edinburgh on September 4, 2015.

relationship between Judeans and non-Judeans in the Christ-movement. It does this by adumbrating the new identity for human beings that has opened up in consequence of Christ's life, death, resurrection, and ongoing presence with those who believe in him. In part 1 of this essay I will set out theoretical perspectives, focusing on identity, necessary for the task. In part 2 I will consider general features of Matthew's Gospel in light of these perspectives. In part 3 I will situate Matthew 21:43 within the broad Matthean pattern thus proposed.

1. Theoretical Perspectives on Identity

Identities: Personal and Social

Recent decades have seen an explosion of research into identity across many disciplines.[1] The word "identity," however, only came into general use through the writings of the psychoanalytic theorist Erik Erikson, especially with his 1959 work *Identity and the Life-Cycle*.[2] For Erikson personal identity "was located deep in the unconscious as a durable and persistent sense of sameness of the self," whatever vicissitudes one might encounter in life. Erikson had in mind the identity of an *individual person*, so that identity, or rather "self-identity," in this sense is closely tied to properties of uniqueness and individuality.[3]

Yet there is another, quite different, meaning of identity, which relates to the social, not the personal. Here identity refers to qualities of sameness, where persons associate themselves, or are associated by others, with groups or categories expressed through common salient features.[4] These groups take many forms: families, sports teams, army units, religions, ethnic groups, or nation-states, to name a few.

Driving an interest in group identity in the last thirty years has been the prominence of certain phenomena, notably the outbursts of violence involving various groups such as Arabs and Kurds in Iraq, Tamils and Sinhalese in Sri

---

1. The founding of the journal *Identity: An International Journal of Theory and Research* in 2001 indicates that interest in the concept had become very lively even by the turn of the millennium.

2. E. H. Erikson, *Identity and the Life-Cycle* (New York: W. W. Norton, 1959).

3. Reginald Byron, "Identity," in the *Encyclopedia of Social and Cultural Anthropology*, ed. Alan Barnard and Jonathan Spencer (London and New York: Routledge, 1996), 292.

4. Byron, "Identity," 292.

Giving the Kingdom to an Ethnos *That Will Bear Its Fruit*

Lanka, Unionists and Nationalists in Northern Ireland, Hutus and Tutsis in Rwanda, and the various constituent peoples of the former Yugoslavia. More recently the rise of radical Sunni jihadism has led to murderous onslaughts on other religious groups, such as Yazidis, Shia Muslims, and Christians. Being a member of groups like these can often get you killed. A collection of essays published in 2007 and entitled *Identity Matters* and subtitled *Ethnic and Sectarian Conflict* focuses on the connection between certain kinds of group identities and conflict.[5]

The Kurds

To explore the issues, let us consider one particular group, the Kurds. They have the misfortune to occupy territory that is spread over four nation-states: Iran, Iraq, Syria, and Turkey, the core of which, located in northern Iraq, they call Kurdistan. There may be as many as thirty million people in the world who identify as Kurds. From the Islamic period onward, the Arabs applied the name "Kurd" to Iranian nomadic tribes. More recently the word has become one of proud self-ascription. Over the last few centuries much of the territory inhabited by the Kurds has been controlled politically by the Ottomans, then by the British after World War I, and then by the state of Iraq.

Many Kurds occupy an autonomous region in northern Iraq. Some wish to establish a nation-state on their territorial homeland and memorialize their struggle to achieve this, especially by reference to the heroes of the cause. Saddam Hussein, pursuing the interests of "Arab" Iraq, killed hundreds of thousands of them. Most Kurds speak Kurdish, a northwestern Iranian language. About two-thirds of Kurds are Sunni Muslims. But some are Shia Muslims, Christians, Yazidis, and members of other groups. Like many Middle Eastern cultures, they practice patrilineal patterns of kinship.[6] Diane King, a recent ethnographer among the Kurds, comments:

> In patriliny, a man's generative power is cumulative, and both during his lifetime and in successive generations becomes attached to his reputation. The descendants through males of a particular man constitute a patrilin-

---

5. James L. Peacock, Patricia M. Thornton, and Patrick B. Inman, eds., *Identity Matters: Ethnic and Sectarian Conflict* (New York and Oxford: Berghahn, 2007).

6. See Diane E. King, *Kurdistan on the Global Stage: Kinship, Land and Community in Iraq* (New Brunswick, NJ: Rutgers University Press, 2014), 38.

eage. Some patrilineages trace their origins to particularly noteworthy men, and others to ordinary men.[7]

Among the Kurds, as elsewhere, patrilinearity results in an emphasis on the necessity of premarital virginity for women.[8] All Kurds enter into patron and client relationships.[9] There are distinctive Kurdish cultural patterns in areas such as music,[10] dance, and carpet-weaving.

The Meaning of Ethnic Identity vis-à-vis Religious Identity

It makes good sense to follow Diane King in describing Kurdish identity as "ethnic." The currently dominant understanding of ethnicity dates from a 1969 essay by Norwegian anthropologist Fredrik Barth. Barth rejected the "primordial" approach that viewed ethnic groups as constituted by a set of cultural features. Instead, their sense of themselves as a group interacting with other groups came first and cultural *indicia* (frequently changing over time) were employed, as a boundary, to express that group identity. Characteristic of an ethnic boundary was to permit some forms of interaction but to proscribe others. Ethnicity was thus a field of self-ascription and self-identification used by certain groups to organize their relationships with other groups.[11] But this left hanging the question of what social features could be deployed to maintain an *ethnic* boundary. Barth himself noted that an ascription of someone to a social category was ethnic in character "when it classifies a person in terms of his basic, most general identity, *presumptively determined by his origin and background.*"[12] John Hutchinson and Anthony Smith provided a repertoire of such features, which we must treat as diagnostic, not constitutive of ethnic identity, to accord with Barth's approach:

(1) a common proper name to identify the group;
(2) a myth of common ancestry;

---

7. King, *Kurdistan*, 67.
8. See King, *Kurdistan*, 117-19.
9. See King, *Kurdistan*, 39.
10. Even in the very recent past, playing Kurdish music could be dangerous: see King, *Kurdistan*, 58.
11. Fredrik Barth, "Introduction," in *Ethnic Groups and Boundaries: The Social Organization of Culture Difference*, ed. Fredrik Barth (London: George Allen & Unwin, 1969), 9-38.
12. Fredrik Barth, "Introduction," 13 (emphasis added).

(3) a shared history or shared memories of a common past, including heroes, events and their commemoration;
(4) a common culture, embracing such things as customs, language and religion;
(5) a link with a homeland; and
(6) a sense of communal solidarity.[13]

The Kurds possess all of these features. But so, too, do Tamils and Sinhalese, Unionists and Nationalists in Northern Ireland, Hutus and Tutsis, and Serbians and Kosovans. Considering the conflicts that have occurred between such groups, we see the wisdom of Stefan Wolff's observation that, "Empirically, it is relatively easy to determine which conflict is an ethnic one: one knows them when one sees them."[14] Often the possession of land lies at the heart of disputes between ethnic groups, a subject well addressed in Monica Toft's 2005 work *The Geography of Ethnic Violence*.[15] Sometimes, as with the Kurds, conflict between ethnic groups over land entails which one will be able to institute a polity, that is, to create a nation-state, in the territory.

What about religion in this context? The difficulties of defining religion are well known, which is not to say that its meaning is completely elastic. In addition, there is a growing awareness, stemming from the arguments of scholars such as Wilfred Cantwell Smith and Bruce Malina,[16] that "religion" designates a stand-alone institution of a kind not found in the ancient world, where religious phenomena tended to be embedded in ethnic, political, or domestic contexts. There is, admittedly, far less objection to speaking of "religious" phenomena in the first century CE. It is enough to state that while not all religions make reference to the supernatural and to human interaction with it, the religious identities in view here are all focused on a belief in a god or gods and with practices in which such a belief is embodied. Since, in the Hutchinson and Smith list, religion features as one aspect of one of six indicators, a common culture, ethnic identity is more inclusive than religious identity.

13. John Hutchinson and Anthony Smith, "Introduction," in *Ethnicity*, ed. John Hutchinson and Anthony Smith (Oxford: Oxford University Press, 1996), 3–14, at 6–7.
14. Stefan Wolff, *Ethnic Conflict: A Global Perspective* (Oxford: Oxford University Press, 2006), 2.
15. Monica Duffy Toft, *The Geography of Ethnic Violence: Identity, Interests, and the Indivisibility of Territory* (Princeton: Princeton University Press, 2005).
16. Wilfred Cantwell Smith, *The Meaning and End of Religion* (Minneapolis: Fortress, 1991 [1962]), and Bruce Malina, "Religion in the Imagined New Testament World: More Social Science Lenses," *Scriptura* 51 (1994): 1–26, and "Mediterranean Sacrifice: Dimensions of Domestic and Political Religion," *Biblical Theology Bulletin* 26 (1996): 26–44.

Sometimes, however, religion can be a very prominent aspect of ethnic identity, as Claire Mitchell has shown for Protestantism in Northern Irish Unionism.[17] Nevertheless, while ethnic and religious identities can overlap, they are very different in character. Thus Kurds can be Sunni or Shia Muslims, Yazidi or Christians. Serbians can be Serbian Orthodox, Catholics, Protestants, or atheists. Saddam Hussein, a Sunni Muslim, persecuted ethnic Kurds in the name of "Arab" Iraq whatever their religion. In the Netherlands today, Muslim migrants from various North African countries negotiate between their original and adopted Dutch ethnic identities and their religious identity.[18] Ethnic and religious identities are different and separable yet impact each other in various ways. They may be fluid and dynamic, but they do have a distinctive content and are not infinitely malleable. Accordingly, they should not be assimilated to each another.

Ethnicity and "Race" Contrasted

Ethnicity is admittedly a constructed social concept. As British social psychologist Hanna Zagefka has noted: "Ethnic cleavages are socially constructed by a practice that can be analysed and deconstructed." But, in advocating a position of moderate constructivism, she rightly insists that this does not mean that ethnic identities are entirely fabricated.[19] For these identities are "real" in the sense "that they form an important part of people's *psychological* realities." While a belief that a whole people descend from one ancestor is unlikely to be empirically true, "a *myth* of common descent is a powerful part of people's social realities."[20]

The language of "race" is very different. It originated from pseudoscientific attempts in the eighteenth and nineteenth centuries to categorize human beings on the basis of observable, inheritable, physical characteristics and then to arrange those categories hierarchically, with "white" "races" like

---

17. See Claire Mitchell, "Behind the Ethnic Marker: Religion and Social Identification in Northern Ireland," *Sociology of Religion* 66 (2005): 1–22, and "The Religious Content of Ethnic Identities," *Sociology* 40 (2006): 1135–52.

18. See Maykel Verkuyten and Borja Martinovic, "Social Identity Complexity and Immigrants' Attitude toward the Host Nation: The Intersection of Ethnic and Religious Group Identification," *Personality and Social Psychology Bulletin* 38 (2012): 1165–77.

19. Hanna Zagefka, "The Concept of Ethnicity in Social Psychological Research: Definitional Issues," *International Journal of Intercultural Relations* 33 (2009): 228–41, at 230.

20. Zagefka, "Ethnicity," 231 (emphases original).

Giving the Kingdom to an Ethnos *That Will Bear Its Fruit*

"Anglo-Saxons" and "Aryans" at the top and allegedly inferior "races" under them.[21] While these categories were social constructs, absurd fabrications in fact, they were devised by people who believed that they had a firm foundation in biology. Since Nazi anti-Jewish ideology was a direct expression of such thinking, not surprisingly "race" fell out of favor after World War II. The word "race" should not be used to describe an ancient or modern group. "Race" can never escape from its origins so as to lose its noxious character of social categorization based on inherited physical characteristics. "Race" language today still carries this connotation of biological determinism. It is a type of social construct very different from ethnicity.[22]

In her 2005 work *Why This New Race: Ethnic Reasoning in Early Christianity*, Denise Kimber Buell, however, while acknowledging these problems with "race," insists on using it as an alternative to "ethnic group":

> Far from seeking to rehabilitate the concept, I use it precisely because of the damage this modern concept has wrought and continues to wreak. If we want to get beyond race, we have to grapple with how it informs historical interpretation even when it is excluded. By provocatively using race interchangeably with ethnicity in this book, I am challenging readers to be accountable to the terms we use for interpreting cultural differences in antiquity.[23]

While others may, I cannot accept this position.[24] By parity of reasoning, should we smack our misbehaving children in supermarkets rather than admonish them so as to alert others of the evil of smacking, or laugh uproariously at funerals to warn people that such behavior is inappropriate, and so on? We show our disapproval of "race" by expressly disavowing it to describe ancient or modern groups, not by embracing it.

---

21. See Hannah Franziska Augstein, ed., *Race: The Origins of an Idea, 1760–1850* (Bristol, UK: Thoemmes Press, 1996).

22. So Stephen E. Cornell and Douglas Hartmann, *Ethnicity and Race: Making Identities in a Changing World*, 2nd ed. (Thousand Oaks, CA: Pine Forge Press, 2007), 26–34, but query why they continue to use the word in any positive sense at all.

23. Denise Kimber Buell, *Why This New Race: Ethnic Reasoning in Early Christianity* (New York: Columbia University Press, 2005), x–xii.

24. The notion of "race" is accepted, for example, by David G. Horrell, "'Race,' 'Nation,' 'People': Ethnic Identity Construction in 1 Peter 2:9," *New Testament Studies* 58 (2011): 123–43 and elsewhere.

PHILIP F. ESLER

Actual and Fictive Identities

I turn now to the distinction between actual and fictive identities. Anthropologists define actual or true kinship either in terms of blood ties, that is, consanguinal kinship, or ties by marriage, that is, affinal kinship. Fictive kinship, conversely, refers to the practice of employing the language of kinship in relation to people with whom one has a relationship but not by blood or marriage. The distinction remains useful in settings where kinship is consanguinal or affinal in spite of the recent reassessment of kinship in anthropology and the rise of broader notions of "interrelatedness" to cover more complex situations than were allowed for when the concept of kinship was originally developed.[25]

Stephen Cornell and Douglas Hartmann have described the process of "ethnicization," meaning "the making of an ethnic group." Ethnicization "is the process by which a group of persons comes to see itself as a distinct group linked by bonds of kinship or their equivalents, by a shared history, and by cultural symbols that represent . . . the 'epitome' of their peoplehood. It is the coming to consciousness of particular kinds of bonds: the making of a people."[26] Here they are talking about the creation of an *actual* ethnic identity. The formation of Kurdish ethnic identity over the last century or so is an example of ethnicization. So too was the development of a Nabatean ethnic identity when North Arabian nomads moved into what is now Jordan and established a viable state there in the period 400 BCE to 106 CE.

This leaves open, however, the question of whether some of the features of ethnic identity might be deployed by other groups in fictive ways; this would not make such a group ethnic, but would reveal ways in which ethnic discourse can be reapplied fictively, or even symbolically or metaphorically, in other settings. The notion of fictive ethnicity is, indeed, used by Étienne Balibar to describe the way in which the community instituted by the nation-state, in the process of idealizing its politics, adopts ethnic features to contribute to the formation and maintenance of that community.[27] Might a religious group,

---

25. For an important reassessment of kinship, see David M. Schneider, *A Critique of the Study of Kinship* (Ann Arbor: University of Michigan Press, 1984). For more recent discussion, see Jane Carsten, ed., *Cultures of Relatedness: New Approaches to the Study of Kinship* (Cambridge: Cambridge University Press, 2000).

26. Cornell and Hartmann, *Ethnicity and Race*, 35.

27. Étienne Balibar, "The Nation Form: History and Ideology," in Étienne Balibar and Immanuel Wallerstein, *Race, Nation, Class: Ambiguous Identities*, trans. Chris Turner (London and New York: Verso, 2002), 86-106, at 96-97.

Giving the Kingdom to an Ethnos *That Will Bear Its Fruit*

while always remaining a religious group, also deploy ethnic signifiers fictively to build or maintain its identity?

2. Matthew in the Broad

Judean Ethnic Identity in the First Century CE: Evidence from Josephus

We will now pursue these issues with respect to Matthew's Gospel in its ancient Mediterranean context. The best evidence for *Ioudaioi* having an identity that was ethnic in character comes from the *Contra Apionem* of Josephus, written in the late first or early second century CE.[28] In defending his people against an attack by Apion, Josephus mentions about fifty groups in the Mediterranean world that are recognizably ethnic. He uses the words *genos, ethnos,* and *laos* as generic descriptors for these groups, including the *Ioudaioi*. He presents his people not as unique but as an example of this type of group, such as when he speaks of the *ethnē* of the Judeans, the Phoenicians, and the Syrians.[29] This does not stop him presenting them as an admirable instance of such a group.

The word *genos*, which in this text is by far the most common group designation, is linked to the verb *gennaō* and is best translated "descent-group." The word "race" is a mistranslation of *genos*,[30] not least because of the sheer anachronism involved. In the use of *genos* we see the importance of origins in ethnic identity. Josephus provides details of many ethnic groups in the first-century Mediterranean, including the *Ioudaioi*. These details can be compared with the Hutchinson and Smith list of diagnostic features, which thus provides a level playing field for the purposes of comparison, especially as between the Judeans and other ethnic groups.[31]

With the exception of the Hycsos, all these groups are named after their ethnic homeland. Those who insist today on translating *Ioudaioi* as "Jews" therefore give this people a name that has a form unique among the numerous ethnic

---

28. Philip F. Esler, "Judean Ethnic Identity in Josephus' *Against Apion*," in *A Wandering Galilean: Essays in Honour of Sean Freyne*, ed. Zuleika Rodgers, with Margaret Daly-Denton and Anne Fitzpatrick McKinley (Leiden: Brill, 2009), 73–91.

29. Josephus, *Contra Apionem* 1.19 §137.

30. The word *genos* is translated as "race" by Buell, *Why This New Race*, 1.

31. This is a preferable approach to the exceptionalist process of isolating Judean identity with reference to certain indicators and treating it as different from all others, as John Barclay does in his *Flavius Josephus: Translation and Commentary,* vol. 10, *Against Apion* (Leiden: Brill, 2006).

groups of their world. Such exceptionalism is driven by reasons unrelated to the historical realities of the first century CE. Moreover, it is contradicted by the way in which Josephus himself understands his people's name: at one point he quotes with approval a saying attributed to Aristotle to the effect that the Judeans take their name from the land Judea.[32] I am attracted to the thought that we honor the memory of first-century Judeans—that magnificent and chosen people—by naming them in a form as close as possible to how they named themselves.

Once we acknowledge the reasons for translating *Ioudaios* as Judean in an ethnic sense in the *Contra Apionem*, the text from the first century CE with the most abundant evidence on the point, it is only by special pleading that we would translate the word as "Jew" in any other texts from this period, including the New Testament. It is occasionally suggested in scholarly circles resistant to the arguments for replacing "Jews" with "Judeans" for the first-century CE situation that *Ioudaioi* should be translated "Judeans" only when the reference is to people actually living in Judea (the alleged "geographic" designation); for all the rest, "Jews" should be used. This view, however, represents a misunderstanding of the ancient evidence. *Ioudaioi* meant ethnic Judeans, from wherever they hailed (the name was ethnic, not "geographic," even though it stemmed from their ethnic homeland). *To indicate Judeans who actually lived in Judea, a periphrasis was needed.* Thus, when at one point Josephus is describing Judeans coming to Jerusalem from various parts of the world, including Judea, he refers to these latter as "the membership of the people from Judea itself."[33] A similar approach is taken by Luke. In Acts 2 he describes how "there were Judeans living in Jerusalem, pious men from every *ethnos* under heaven" (v. 5). Among them were those who dwelled in Judea (v. 9). In saying all this I am not forgetting that while *Ioudaioi* was used by outsiders to describe Judeans and by themselves when other ethnic groups were in view, they also had a purely ingroup designation, *Israēlitai*.

It is interesting to compare the Judeans with the Kurds. They have in common a homeland situated at the intersection of other powerful peoples, with a resultant struggle to control their land. Recent Kurdish history can, in fact, be compared with the story told in 1 Maccabees, which is not that of Judeans under threat from an empire, but that of their struggle against several ethnic groups to establish a polity on their ancestral land.[34] In both cases the

32. Josephus, *Contra Apionem* 1.22 §179.
33. Josephus, *Judean War* 2.3.1 §43; for a general discussion and this translation, see Philip F. Esler, *Conflict and Identity in Romans: The Social Setting of Paul's Letter* (Minneapolis: Fortress, 2003), 71-72.
34. This was the subject of an essay I delivered at the SBL Conference in Atlanta in No-

Giving the Kingdom to an Ethnos *That Will Bear Its Fruit*

religious aspect was only one aspect of a larger ethnic identity. Whereas Kurdish identity embraces several types of religious expression, Judean identity was strongly tied to one. This accords with how Herodotus's description of Greek identity included the fact of their having the shrines of gods and the sacrifices in common.[35] They also share the social pattern of patrilinearity.

Major consequences for interpretation flow from the recognition of the *Ioudaioi* as an ethnic group. Above all, it means that the use of "Judaism" to describe the social entity in scope is a category error. For first-century CE Judeans were not adherents of a religion (a difficult concept for the ancient world anyway, as noted above) that we might call "Judaism." Rather, they were members of an ethnic group with a common culture (Hutchinson and Smith's fourth indicator of ethnicity) that included a strong cultic or religious dimension. This common culture aspect of their ethnic identity is referred to by Paul as *Ioudaismos* in Galatians 1:13 and 14. The continued use of "Judaism" as a catch-all expression for the identity of *Ioudaioi* in the first century CE inevitably impedes our understanding of the historical realities of the period.

To anticipate my later discussion, however we categorize the identity of the Christ-movement—religious, socio-religious, or whatever—it is not ethnic. Accordingly, it is very different in kind from the ethnic identity of the Judeans. The identities of Judeans and Christ-followers were not symmetric to each other, like apples and oranges, but asymmetric. The popular metaphor of the parting of the ways, with its scene of two entities of the same type coming to a fork in the road and separating, misleadingly perpetuates this false notion of two symmetric identities.

Judean Ethnic Identity in Matthew 1–2

Matthew 1 and 2 plunge us directly into Judean ethnic identity.[36] The genealogy in 1:2–17 summarizes this people's myth of common ancestry, in typical patri-

---

vember 2015, in the Construction of Christian Identities Seminar: "The Birth of the Maccabean Ethnic State: Ethnic Groups not 'Empire' in the Meaning of 1 Maccabees."

35. See Herodotus, *History* 8.144.2, cited and discussed by Dennis C. Duling, "Ethnicity, Ethnocentrism, and the Matthean *Ethnos*," in his *A Marginal Scribe: Studies in the Gospel of Matthew in a Social-Scientific Perspective*, Matrix: The Bible in Mediterranean Context (Eugene, OR: Cascade, 2012), 288–328, at 296–97.

36. See Philip F. Esler, "Rival Group Identities in the Matthean Gospel: Evidence from Matthew 1–2 and 23," in *Conception, Reception, and the Spirit: Essays in Honor of Andrew T. Lincoln*, ed. J. Gordon McConville and Lloyd K. Pietersen (Eugene, OR: Cascade, 2015), 26–29.

lineal terms, beginning with Abraham. For first-century CE Judeans, this ancestry was a physical reality, not a myth, which is why John the Baptist attributes to the Pharisees and Sadducees the thought that "We have Abraham as our father" (Matt. 3:9). In a similar way, the ancient Greeks (Hellenes, living in Hellas) regarded themselves as descended from an eponymous ancestor, Hellen. As mentioned above, even from his anti-primordial perspective Fredrik Barth acknowledged that ethnicity was presumptively determined by a person's origin and background.

After the genealogy, Matthew describes the conception and birth of Jesus Christ in terms replete with features of the common Judean culture (1:18–25). An angelic messenger deflects Joseph from acting in accordance with the customs of this patrilineal and patrilocal society by divorcing his betrothed when she is discovered to be pregnant before they have come together. The angel addresses him as "Joseph son of David," thus designating him with respect to his descent from an illustrious ancestor in a manner typical of ethnic identity. The angel instructs Joseph to name the child Jesus, "because he will save his people (*laos*) from their sins" (1:21). This is the first of fourteen instances of *laos* in Matthew, a word that describes an ethnic group, not a religion.

We soon learn that Jesus was born in Bethlehem in Judea (2:1). Judea was the homeland (which is ethnic indicator [5] above) of Judeans—whether they actually lived there or in diaspora communities—who were named after that land just like all other ethnic groups of the time. Moreover, this is an ethnic group having a polity in the form of a kingdom, with its king, Herod, in his capital, Jerusalem (2:1). Wise men from the east visit Herod in Judea looking for the one who has been born "king of the Judeans (*tōn Ioudaiōn*)" (2:2), the name for the group used by outsiders. Soon afterwards, however, we have the first use of the ingroup word for the land and people: Israel (2:6).

The Judean Ethnocentrism of Matthew's Jesus and Its Transformation

A surprising feature of the Matthean Gospel is that it initially presents a Jesus who is ethnophobically Judean in relation to foreigners.[37] The word *ethnikos*, "foreigner," in this context meaning "a non-Judean," occurs three times in this

---

37. For a detailed argument, see Philip F. Esler, "Judean Ethnic Identity and the Matthean Jesus," in *Jesus—Gestalt und Gestaltungen: Rezeptionen des Galiläers in Wissenschaft, Kirche und Gesellschaft: Festschrift für Gerd Theissen*, Novum Testamentum et Orbis Antiquus, ed. P. von Gemünden, D. G. Horrell, and M. Küchler (Göttingen: Vandenhoeck & Ruprecht, 2013), 193–210.

Gospel, at Matthew 5:47, 6:7, and 18:17, each time on the lips of Jesus. In the first two cases Jesus negatively stereotypes foreigners: he is critical of them for only greeting their brothers (5:47) and, more derisively, accuses them of verbose babbling while praying (6:7). At 6:32 he again targets the *ethnē* ("foreign peoples"; "foreigners"), accusing them of being anxious about material things. This is one of fifteen instances of *ethnos* in this Gospel, which have been well discussed by Dennis Duling.[38] All of them are applied to ethnic groups with the sole exception, as we will see, in Matthew 21:43.

These examples of the Matthean Jesus using derogatively the expressions *ethnikoi* and *ethnē* cohere with his initial position toward his ministry as embedded in and focused on ethnic Judeans. They accord with his saying to the twelve as he sends them off, "Do not go off onto the road of the *ethnē* nor enter a city of the Samaritans; go rather to the lost sheep of the house of Israel" (10:5), and with his statement later that "I was not sent except to the lost sheep of the house of Israel" (15:24).

In Matthew's Gospel Jesus remarkably learns through his experience of the deep faith of non-Judeans that he must also extend his mercy to them. These foreigners are the centurion of Capernaum in Matthew 8:5–13 and the Canaanite woman in 15:21–28. Let us briefly consider the former passage. Having heard with astonishment the centurion's statement that Jesus need only say the word and his servant will be healed, Jesus says:

> "Truly, I say to you, not even in Israel have I found such faith. I tell you, many will come from east and west and sit at table with Abraham, Isaac, and Jacob in the Kingdom of Heaven, while the sons of the Kingdom will be thrown into the outer darkness, where there will be weeping and gnashing of teeth." (8:10–12)

The context of the story, with Jesus making a point to illustrate a non-Judean's faith, necessitates that the many who will come from the east and the west must comprise or at least include non-Judeans.[39] These non-Judeans will be dining with Abraham, Isaac, and Jacob, who were the first three figures mentioned in the genealogy in Matthew 1:2, the progenitors of the Judean people. It is precisely with these three primary figures in the establishment of Judean

---

38. Matt. 4:15; 6:32; 10:5; 10:18; 12:18; 12:21; 20:19; 20:25; 21:43; 24:7 (bis); 24:9; 24:14; 25:32; and 28:19. See Duling, "Ethnicity, Ethnocentrism, and the Matthean *Ethnos*," 300–302.

39. *Contra* W. D. Davies and D. C. Allison (*A Critical and Exegetical Commentary on the Gospel according to St. Matthew*, vol. 2, *Matthew VII–XVII* [Edinburgh: T&T Clark, 1991], 28), who argue that those from east and west are "unprivileged Jews."

identity that Matthew describes non-Judeans sitting down to dine in the kingdom of heaven. Luke does not have this feature in the parallel passage (Luke 13:28–29). Accordingly, Matthew depicts table-fellowship in the kingdom of heaven, not only between Judeans and non-Judeans of a sort prohibited to first-century Judeans,[40] but also involving the very founders of Judean identity. The shared meal embodies a new form of group identity that transcends the boundaries of ethnicity. This is Jesus's vision for the future, however much he may be focusing upon ethnic Israel during his own ministry. I will argue later that the circumstance that Jesus adds to this—that the "sons of the kingdom" will be cast out—connects this passage closely with Matthew 21:43.

Matthew 8:5–13 is one of several passages in the Gospel where Jesus points to the future, including after his death and resurrection, and indicates that there are many interactions with ethnic groups to come. Matthew 28:19–20 provides the programmatic expression of this position when Jesus directs his followers to "Go therefore and make disciples of all peoples (*ethnē*), baptizing them in the name of the Father and of the Son and of the Holy Spirit, teaching them to observe all that I have commanded you; and lo, I am with you always, to the close of the age." He envisages that in the future the Christ-group will embrace people of all ethnic groups, and the inclusion of Abraham, Isaac, and Jacob from Matthew 8:11 means that they and no doubt other representatives of the Judean ethnic group will be present.

But before the end his followers will experience persecution and bear witness to the peoples (*ethnē*; 10:18). In the end-time, *ethnos* will rise against *ethnos* (24:7) and his followers will be hated by all *ethnē* for his sake (24:9). But the gospel will be proclaimed to the whole world as a witness to all the *ethnē* (24:14). At the last judgment (25:31–46), all the *ethnē* will be assembled before the Son of Man and he will separate people (*autous*) from one another, like a shepherd separating sheep from goats (25:32). A long formula quotation, Matthew 12:18–21 quoting

---

40. See Philip F. Esler, *Galatians*, New Testament Readings (London: Routledge, 1998), 93–116. Stephen R. Turley (*The Ritualized Revelation of the Messianic Age: Washings and Meals in Galatians and 1 Corinthians* [London: Bloomsbury, 2015], 107) has disputed my view that Judeans refrained from eating with non-Judeans on the basis that it presupposes Judean and non-Judean as antithetical and fails "to see intermediate possibilities, such as 'God-fearers.'" Turley's view, however, founders on the necessity, as Fredrik Barth has shown, for ethnic boundaries to involve prescriptions and proscriptions and not some fusion of characteristics. This social reality suggests that allowing non-Judeans into synagogues did not lead to their being invited to meals, for which there is direct first-century CE evidence in the Judean antagonism to Peter dining with Cornelius, even though he was a God-fearer (Acts 10:1–2; 11:1–3).

Giving the Kingdom to an Ethnos That Will Bear Its Fruit

the first servant passage of Isaiah 42:1–4,[41] states both that the *ethnē* will hope in his name (Matt. 12:21) and that he will announce judgment to the *ethnē*.

The Nature of Christ-Movement Identity in Matthew

This analysis prompts the question: How best can we understand the nature of the Christ-movement identity shared by Matthew's audience, wherever he wrote his Gospel? As indicated at the outset of this essay, to ask this question is to consider the impact of belief in Christ and his abiding presence on the group identity (with all that entails) of Matthew and his audience. The paramount observation is that such identity cannot have been Judean ethnic in character, simply because it comprised members from various ethnic groups. For a group that combines representatives of different ethnic identities of necessity ceases to be ethnic. The critical ethnic boundaries lose their claim on the members in the context of their new, common ingroup identity.

Thus Matthew specifies that the *ethnē* will hope in his name (12:21), that the gospel will be preached to all *ethnē* (28:19), and that all the *ethnē* will be judged, with some people among them saved (25:32). More importantly, Matthew envisages table-fellowship between Judean and non-Judean. Although the passage concerning the centurion describes such fellowship in the kingdom of heaven (8:11), that it is paradigmatic for the movement emerges later, in the discourse on the difficult brother in Matthew 18. In verse 17 Jesus says that if the wayward brother "refuses to listen to them, tell it to the *ekklēsia*; and if he refuses to listen even to the *ekklēsia*, let him be to you as an *ethnikos* and a tax collector." Clearly the man is to be expelled from the community. Yet note what this entails. For serious misbehavior, identities that are disregarded on entry to the community (including those of non-Judeans [like the centurion and the Canaanite woman] and tax collectors [like Matthew in Matt. 9:9–13]) are reinstated to eject the miscreant. Whereas beforehand there was fellowship with such people, afterward there was not.

Ignatius's letter to the Smyrneans offers very early support for this view on the composition of the Matthean group. In a section probably dependent on Matthew (1:1–2),[42] Ignatius refers to the saints and believers of Jesus

---

41. This quotation would repay closer attention; Craig S. Keener (*A Commentary on the Gospel of Matthew* [Grand Rapids: Eerdmans, 1999], 361) suggests Matthew is translating freely from the Hebrew.

42. See John P. Meier, "Matthew and Ignatius: A Response to William R. Schoedel," in *Social History of the Matthean Community: Cross-Disciplinary Approaches*, ed. David L. Balch

"whether among Judeans or non-Judeans (*ethnē*) in the one body of his church." Ignatius understands Matthew to depict an *ekklēsia* comprising Judeans and non-Judeans. Such a unified entity conflates the *ethnē* in Matthew 28:19–20 and the three references to *ekklēsia* in Matthew 16 and 18.

No single epithet captures the identity of the Christ-movement, and "religious" or "socio-religious" are probably as good as we will get. I hesitate to speak of the Christ-movement as a "religion" because of the arguments of Wilfred Cantwell Smith and Bruce Malina (mentioned above) that this word suggests a separate institution of a kind unknown in the ancient world. Nevertheless, as noted earlier, the religious identities in view here are those focused on a belief in a god or gods and with practices in which such a belief is embodied, and such was the core of the Christ-movement identity.

Matthew sharply, indeed savagely, distinguishes between Judean and Christ-movement identities in chapter 23.[43] In verse 30 Jesus attributes to the scribes and the Pharisees the sentiment, "If we had lived in the days of our fathers, we would not have taken part with them in shedding the blood of the prophets," and here we are again confronted with the centrality of physical descent for Judean ethnic identity. In verse 31 Jesus turns their self-ascription as descendants of such ancestors on its head, saying: "Thus you bear witness against yourselves, that you are the sons of those who murdered the prophets." Soon after, he emphatically affirms the depth of their evil in a manner that continues the notion of physical descent: "You snakes, progeny (*gennēmata*) of vipers, how will you flee from the judgment of hell?" (v. 33). We have already seen the importance of *genos*, physical descent for Judeans at this time. That the scribes and Pharisees would recognize that Jesus was casting a slur on their ethnic ancestry is clear from an earlier passage, when John the Baptist says:

> "You progeny (*gennēmata*) of vipers! Who warned you to flee from the coming anger? Bear fruit worthy of repentance and do not presume to say to yourselves, 'We have Abraham as our father'; for I tell you, God is able from these stones to raise up children to Abraham." (Matt. 3:7b–9)

John appreciates that their likely riposte will involve an assertion of their *Abrahamic* ancestry. The force of the progeny-of-vipers slur is that they are not even Judean, but ophidian.

(Minneapolis: Fortress, 1991), 178–86, at 180–82, for the case for Ignatius being dependent on Matthew here.

43. Philip F. Esler, "Intergroup Conflict and Matthew 23: Towards Responsible Interpretation of a Challenging Text," *Biblical Theology Bulletin* 45 (2015): 38–59.

Giving the Kingdom to an Ethnos *That Will Bear Its Fruit*

On the other hand, in Matthew 23:8–12 we find two perfectly balanced sets of statements describing the identity of Christ-followers. We learn that they have one teacher and one guide (Jesus) and that they should call no man father on earth, because they are all brothers and they have a father who is in heaven. Ethnic descent from ancestral fathers is not part of their identity. Fictive kinship of brothers and sisters under God in the presence of Jesus most certainly is.

The Rupture between Ethnic Judeans and Matthean Christ-Followers

Such a Christ-movement identity bears heavily upon whether Matthew's community was, to quote the current formulation, *intra muros* or *extra muros* "Judaism." Reformulated in line with the discussion above, the question becomes: Was Matthew's community still part of the Judean ethnic group or not? Two factors mean that that question must be answered in the negative. First, they were members of a movement in which Judeans and non-Judeans engaged in joint table-fellowship of a sort prohibited among first-century CE Judeans as threatening the ethnic boundary.[44] Second, Matthew expressly and polemically differentiates Christ-movement identity from Judean identity in chapter 23. This indicates a fundamental rift between these two asymmetrical identities.

The Gospel contains many signs of this estrangement. One is the repeated expression "their synagogues" or "their synagogue."[45] Another is the statement that the story that the disciples stole Jesus's body has been spread round among Judeans (*Ioudaioi*) until the present (28:15). This is the only redactional use of *Ioudaioi* in Matthew, the other instances originating with non-Judeans.[46] Although *Ioudaioi* is anarthrous here, that does not dispel the impression that they are an outgroup for Matthew's audience. Other evidence for the split comes from Matthew's attitude to the Mosaic law. Although scholars such as David Sim argue that Matthew's community was Torah-observant, I prefer the views of those such as John Meier and Paul Foster for the opposite conclusion.[47] The highpoint of Sim's case, the teaching about the law in Matthew 5:17–20,

---

44. Esler, *Galatians*, 93–116.
45. See Matt. 4:23; 9:35; 10:17; 12:9; and 13:54.
46. Matt. 2:2; 27:11, 29, and 37.
47. See David C. Sim, *The Gospel of Matthew and Christian Judaism: The History and Social Setting of the Matthean Community* (Edinburgh: T&T Clark, 1998) on the one hand, and John P. Meier, *Law and History in Matthew's Gospel*, Analecta Biblica 71 (Rome: Biblical Institute, 1976), and Paul Foster, *Community, Law and Mission in Matthew's Gospel*, Wissenschaftliche Untersuchungen zum Neuen Testament 177 (Tübingen: Mohr Siebeck, 2004).

really involves Matthew's protesting too much in a situation where his community is rightly being accused of breaching the Torah because of its mixed table-fellowship. The trivial penalty for breaking the law and advocating its breach—being called least in the kingdom of heaven (5:19), so that you are still there but have a seat at the back (!)—solidifies this impression.

3. Matthew 21:43

Matthew 21:43 occurs in the midst of the parable of the vineyard and the tenants (21:33–46) and is based on Mark 12:1–12. Matthew follows Mark reasonably closely in 21:33–46 except for his addition of verses 41b, 43, 44 (where the text is uncertain), and 45. Commentators on the passage all note that the parable contains allegorical dimensions.[48] It is, for example, difficult to avoid the view that the vineyard is Israel (not least because of its debt to Isa. 5:1–7); the householder is God; the tenants are Israelites; the earlier messengers are the prophets; and the son is Jesus. One area of debate is whether the tenants are the people of Israel or the leaders of Israel. In favor of the latter option, strongly championed by Matthias Konradt,[49] is that Matthew redactionally states that the chief priests and Pharisees recognized that Jesus was speaking about them (Matt. 21:45). Whether, however, all connection with the Israelite people can be excluded, as Konradt insists,[50] seems doubtful, especially as two chapters later Matthew will note that it is Jerusalem who kills the prophets and stones those sent to her (23:37). Ultimately not a great deal turns on this, since the real interest in Matthew 21:43 is less on who, precisely, the tenants are than on the identity of the *ethnos* to whom the kingdom of God will be given.

As noted above, every other instance of *ethnos* in this Gospel refers to an ethnic group and usually occurs in the plural. The singular form appears only at 24:7 ("*ethnos* will rise against *ethnos*") and here in 21:43. Often the word refers to non-Judean ethnic groups (4:15; 6:32; 10:5; 10:18; 20:19; 20:25), but on a few occasions the plural, *ethnē*, probably includes Judeans as well (24:14; 25:32; 28:19). What then of *ethnos* in Matthew 21:43?

The most likely referent for the word is the Christ-movement in general. It is unlikely to refer to the leaders of the movement since that would privilege

---

48. This affects whether it originates with Jesus or was composed by a Christ-follower later.

49. Matthias Konradt, *Israel, Church, and the Gentiles in the Gospel of Matthew*, Baylor-Mohr Siebeck Studies in Early Christianity, trans. Kathleen Ess (Waco, TX: Baylor University Press, 2014), 172–93.

50. Konradt, *Israel*, 183.

Giving the Kingdom to an Ethnos *That Will Bear Its Fruit*

them in a way that is alien to Matthew's understanding of their role (23:8–12). Yet this movement was not ethnic in nature, especially since it embraced a variety of ethnic groups. And using a word with ethnic connotations in relation to the Christ-movement could not and did not convert its religious or socio-religious identity into an ethnic identity. Nor is it appropriate to refer to the movement as "a third race."[51]

To understand what is going on here we need to refer back to the issue of actual and fictive identities. As already noted, an important dimension of Christ-movement identity in Matthew is that of fictive kinship: the members are brothers and sisters under their heavenly father (Matt. 18:15; 23:8–9). Such language allowed the Christ-movement and Matthew to utilize the family, the most powerful social institution in their world, in the service of strengthening the sense of relatedness among the members.

While commentators have struggled with the meaning of *ethnos* in Matthew 21:43, the likely solution is that the evangelist is invoking another dominant social institution, the ethnic group, *again fictively*, to attract to the Christ-movement some of the sense of belonging shared by co-ethnics. I stress that this is a fictive use; the religious identity of the Christ-movement does not become an actual ethnic identity in the process. Rather, Matthew is, with considerable daring, redeploying the language of ethnicity in a different context and to serve a very different identity. Given that his audience was likely separated from ethnic Judeans, using this word provided a form of symbolic compensation for the loss. A good translation for *ethnos* is simply "a people."

Matthew is not alone in the use of ethnic language fictively in a non-ethnic setting. In Galatians 3 Paul runs the extraordinary argument that Christ-followers (not Judeans) are the descendants of Abraham.[52] In 1 Peter 2:9 there is another appropriation of the collective memory of Israel when the author quotes Exodus 23:22 (LXX) to the effect that his addressees are a chosen *genos*, a royal priesthood, a holy *ethnos*, a *laos* set apart. By this citation the 1 Peter author is not creating an ethnic identity for his audience,[53] but is applying these ethnic designators *fictively* for the purpose of solidifying and legitimating their *religious* identity.

There is one other aspect of the use of *ethnos* in Matthew 21:43 worth noting. Trilling argued that there must have been an old *ethnos* in view as a

---

51. As does Graham N. Stanton, *A Gospel for a New People: Studies in Matthew* (Edinburgh: T&T Clark, 1992), 11–12, 151–52; Davies and Allison, *Matthew*, 1:23.

52. See Philip F. Esler, "Paul's Contestation of Israel's (Ethnic) Memory of Abraham in Galatians 3," *Biblical Theology Bulletin* 36 (2006): 23–34.

53. As argued by David Horrell, "'Race,' 'Nation,' 'People,'" 123–43.

counterpart to the new *ethnos*.[54] This seems likely here. The leaders of the Judean *ethnos* are having the kingdom taken away from them. The situation comes close to the prediction of Jesus in Matthew 8:12 that the "sons of the kingdom" will be cast into the outer darkness.

4. A Final Point

While I have argued for very different, indeed asymmetrical, Judean and Christ-movement identities being represented in Matthew, with 21:43 marking a high point in their differentiation, I am not suggesting that Judeans or Jews (their spiritual and often physical descendants) after them had or have been superseded. I take my lead from Paul in Romans 11:25–32. The Jews are the chosen people, still loved by God who never revokes his promises. Ultimately they will be saved, and I do not consider that such an outcome will depend on their acceptance of Christ. As a Roman Catholic, I am happy to note that this sentiment, which formed the conclusion of my original presentation of this essay on September 4, 2015, is very similar to the position expressed soon afterwards by the Vatican in its recent statement on Catholic-Jewish relations published to celebrate the fiftieth anniversary of the seminal Vatican II document *Nostra Aetate*.[55]

---

54. Wolfgang Trilling, *Das Wahre Israel: Studien zur Theologie das Matthäusevangeliums* (Munich: Kösel, 1964), 63, 65.

55. *"The Gifts and the Calling of God Are Irrevocable" (Rom 11:29): A Reflection on the Theological Questions Pertaining to Catholic-Jewish Relations on the Occasion of the 50th Anniversary of* Nostra Aetate (No. 4), promulgated by the Holy See on December 10, 2015.

Mark's Gospel for the Second Church of the Late First Century

Bruce W. Longenecker

When Richard Bauckham launched the book *The Gospels for All Christians*, the study of the Gospels shifted significantly.[1] The common stranglehold of reading a Gospel narrative in reference to a specific community's situation was broken. Still valid, of course, is the consideration of whether certain situations known and experienced by the evangelists may have influenced their presentation of the remembered Jesus, for certainly that was the case to one degree or another. But whatever tendency there might have been to confine the evangelists' agendas to their respective communities is now considered an eccentric interest. If the Gospels really were written with the expectation that they would circulate widely among early Christian communities of the Mediterranean basin, then each of the evangelists must have been writing to address not a single community's experience but a more generalized matrix of Christian experience.

Twenty years or so after *The Gospels for All Christians* was published, Ramsay MacMullen's book *The Second Church* appeared, with its focus advertised by its subtitle: *Popular Christianity A.D. 200-400*.[2] In that work, MacMullen demonstrated that Christian identity in the third and fourth centuries revolved around two somewhat separate poles, and in different proportions. Some Christians formed their identities through the influence of "the estab-

---

1. Richard Bauckham, ed., *The Gospels for All Christians: Rethinking Gospel Audiences* (Grand Rapids: Eerdmans, 1997).

2. Ramsay MacMullen, *The Second Church: Popular Christianity A.D. 200-400* (Atlanta: Society of Biblical Literature, 2009).

lished church"—which roughly corresponds to the theologically informed ecclesiastical voices evident in the extant literature of the "patristic" period. For others, Christian identity was more in alignment with "the second church"—that is, those whose Christian commitment was mixed with a significant dose of "pagan" assumptions and practices, and the very ones whom representatives of the established church frequently sought to address and, in fact, correct. In the third and fourth centuries, and much to the dissatisfaction of clerical members of the established church, ordinary Christians were often only "half-converted." MacMullen demonstrates this in a number of ways, not least in the practice of Christian banqueting with the dead. Christians of the second church often celebrated the dead in meals that, occurring within cemeteries, permitted the spirits of the deceased to participate in those rituals alongside the living. The pagan practice of embedding vertical pipes into graves so that sustenance could be fed to the departed below was carried on in the burial practices of the second church, allowing the living celebrants to maintain favor with the spirits of the deceased.

When he does the math, MacMullen arrives at percentages for the two churches in the third and fourth centuries, with the established church composed of 5 percent of Christians and the second church composed of 95 percent of Christians. We might wonder about the robustness of MacMullen's percentages, but his general case is sound. Many who espoused a Christian identity did so in ways that often were out of line with the expectations of the clerical leaders of Christian circles. And even if MacMullen's percentages are adjusted somewhat, his case demonstrates that the figure for the second church must certainly have been very large when compared to the established church of the third and fourth centuries.

But if that is the case for the third and fourth centuries, should we imagine the situation to be much different for the second, or even the first century? Anyone who has ever read Paul's critique of Corinthian Jesus-followers in 1 Corinthians or the critique of Christians in Pergamum, Thyatira, Sardis, and Laodicea in Revelation 2–3 will see the point. First-century Christians were at times not all that different from their non-Christian neighbors. Even when Jesus-devotion was adopted, it seems not always to have gone very deep. Often a simple veneer of Jesus-devotion was placed over layers of non-Christian identity. The "apostolic voice" of the first century is often addressed to people such as this.

In fact, precisely this situation is evidenced in the material remains of Pompeii. As I have argued recently, a combination of previously unnoticed artifacts and previously misinterpreted artifacts permits us a glimpse of Jesus-devotion in that first-century town.[3] A victim of Mount Vesuvius's eruption in 79 CE, Pompeii includes within its material remains nearly two dozen artifacts testifying that Jesus-devotion had infiltrated the town's walls. Moreover, those artifacts usually reveal why Jesus-devotion was attractive among a small cohort of Pompeians. Quite simply, Jesus-devotees in Pompeii sought protection from evil through the crucified-but-resurrected deity. Their devotion to a deity who had died but had risen in power provided them with a new apotropaic hope—a hope that their lives would be enhanced in the present and would continue past death.

As expressions of this hope, they incorporated depictions of the cross of Jesus at vulnerable points in the security systems of their residences.[4] One cross articulated their attraction to Jesus explicitly. It was embedded on the wall of one residence in the form of an announcement, "he lives" (*vivit*). Another cross seems to have been constructed in order to "riff off" the cult of the Egyptian deity Isis, who was well known to enhance life in the present and to provide the continuance of life after death. If Isis can give life to her devotees both in this world and in the next, the same must be true for Jesus Christ, whose rising gives to his followers both empowerment in life and over death. Most of the Pompeii crosses of Jesus-devotion were placed at liminal points in the spaces of houses or neighborhoods, and served to bring apotropaic protection to those devoted to the risen deity in whom death had been defeated. The phrase "deliver us from evil [or 'from the evil one']" (Matt. 6:13) is precisely the register of these first-century artifacts of Jesus-devotion. A deity of power was a deity worthy of devotion.

There may have been more to it than that simple equation, but the artifacts themselves do not lend themselves to much more. Those who devoted themselves to the crucified but risen deity were seemingly simple and ordinary folk—a baker and his family, shop workers, a cloth dyer and his household, a slave by the name Meges, and a few other otherwise inconsequential people. These people may have known nothing, or next to nothing, about the Jewish scriptures. They probably had very little educational training. They probably had not enjoyed rhetorical training of any kind. They may have had no penchant for theological intricacies. They probably did not see themselves as key players in a mission strategy to preach the "good news" throughout the Med-

---

3. See my *The Crosses of Pompeii: Jesus-Devotion in a Vesuvian Town* (Minneapolis: Fortress, 2016).

4. On the cross as a pre-Constantinian symbol of Jesus-devotion, see my *The Cross before Constantine: The Early Life of a Christian Symbol* (Minneapolis: Fortress, 2015).

iterranean basin. Instead, they were probably just everyday people who had learned (perhaps from a Christian in Puteoli, Rome, or elsewhere) of the "power of God for salvation" (Rom. 1:16). Perhaps they had heard that nothing could separate them from their deity—"neither death, nor life, nor angels, nor rulers, nor things present, nor things to come, nor powers, nor height, nor depth, nor anything else in all creation" (Rom. 8:38-39). Pompeians, like almost everyone else in the first century, feared the power of evil all around them. Pompeian Jesus-followers, however, adopted devotion to Jesus Christ in order to "abound in hope by the power of the Holy Spirit" (Rom. 15:13). For them, the cross of Christ symbolized power precisely because, as one leading apostle had contended, "it is the power of God" (1 Cor. 1:18; cf. 1:17; 2:4; 4:19; 5:4; 6:14; 2 Cor. 4:7; 6:7; 10:4), the power over dangerous spiritual forces. This is because Jesus Christ "was crucified in weakness, but lives by the power of God," so that his devotees "will live with him by the power of God" (2 Cor. 13:4). Philippians 3:21 captures the sentiment perfectly: "He will transform the body of our humiliation that it may be conformed to the body of his glory, by the power that also enables him to make all things subject to himself."

I have used the apostle Paul's words here, not to imply that Pompeian Jesus-devotees had ever heard them specifically, but to illustrate that words spoken in one context might easily spin off in a somewhat different direction, especially when unaccompanied by the larger context of the apostolic voice. And if we imagine that the second church was far more widespread in the first century than simply Pompeii, it becomes abundantly clear why it became imperative for the apostolic voice to be strongly articulated in the Christian literature of the late first century.

One of those articulations of the apostolic voice is the Markan Gospel. In what follows, I want to track how that Gospel might have had traction in relation to the second church of the late first century. Regardless of whether it was written in the second half of the 60s or the first half of the 70s, the Gospel of Mark seems to have circulated among early Jesus-groups of the Mediterranean basin in the late first century—as testified by the fact that both the Matthean and the Lukan Gospels made extensive use of it. In other words, the date of its early circulation corresponds precisely to the last days of Pompeii's existence as a vibrant Greco-Roman urban center and one in which we may well see evidence of the second church of the late first century.

In what follows, however, I will not attempt an exercise of "hearing the Markan Gospel in Pompeii." Such an approach would give the exercise far too specific a reference point for our purposes. Instead, the register of Jesus-devotion in Pompeii (as noted above) can guide us in understanding what the second church might have looked like in Mark's day. And in that regard, it is the apotropaic power of the crucified-but-risen deity that stands at the forefront of our reading exercise.

The second church may have taken root in indigenous settings where the story of Jesus was itself somewhat fragile in its content. Perhaps some incarnations of the second church knew only the very basics about the deity who had been crucified and raised to life in power. The second church may have had a handful of stories about Jesus working miracles of power—healing the ill, casting out demons, and overcoming the forces of nature. It may have known that these things happened in and around the problematic region of Judea in the recent past. And it may have known that a small number of Jesus-devotees were gathering to worship this new deity in groups dotted around the Mediterranean basin. But the second church of the late first century may not have known much more than that. There were no established *bioi* about his life that it could consult. There were only a few eyewitnesses who could testify to his life, and those eyewitnesses were extremely rare in the urban centers of the Greco-Roman world.[5] Consequently, for the second church, the easiest way to think of the story of Jesus might have been to compare it to the story of the Egyptian deity Isis raising her husband Osiris to life—as evidence from Pompeii seems to suggest.[6] Moreover, there is no reason to think that the second church of the late first century restricted its devotion solely to Jesus Christ. As part of its strategies for survival in a dangerous world, the second church might simply have added Jesus Christ to its list of important deities to whom one might wisely adopt some (nonexclusive) allegiance.

Scholars continue to debate the primary audience of the Markan Gospel. Was it written especially for Christians in Rome during or subsequent to Nero's persecution of Christians in that city in the second half of the 60s?[7] Or was it written especially for Christians in Syria during or subsequent to the Jewish revolt against Rome in 66–70? No doubt the debate is important. But however we answer that question, we need not say that the Markan evangelist had only one situation in view. If his Gospel really was written "for all Christians," and

---

5. And on this issue, see, of course, Richard Bauckham, *Jesus and the Eyewitnesses: The Gospels as Eyewitness Testimony* (Grand Rapids: Eerdmans, 2008).

6. On this, see my *The Crosses of Pompeii*, ch. 7.

7. I am unpersuaded by the recent effort to list this persecution as a "myth," as in Brent D. Shaw, "The Myth of the Neronian Persecution," *Journal of Roman Studies* 105 (2015): 73–100. For an early response demonstrating the deficiencies of this argument, see Larry Hurtado's blog of December 14, 2015, https://larryhurtado.wordpress.com/2015/12/14/nero-and-the-christians.

if a good sector of the early Jesus movement in the late first century looked somewhat like the second church of Pompeii, the Markan Gospel must have had something to say to that sector of his potential audience. In what follows, I will outline a few simple observations in this regard.

Framing Jesus

The first thing to note is that the Markan Gospel begins and ends in conjunction with the interests of the second church. Of course, those sections contain material that runs along a trajectory that at times differs from the interests of the second church, but there is plenty within the frame of the Markan Gospel to give its narrative some traction within the second church.

Unlike the later canonical Gospels, for instance, there is no birth narrative, and there is no eternal generation of the Logos. Although later canonical evangelists preferred to preface the story of Jesus with notable theological preamble, the Markan story immediately connects with the second church in establishing that this story is about power. In fact, within the first fifteen verses of the narrative, the Markan evangelist establishes that Jesus's story is all about suprahuman power that has never been previously available. So John the Baptizer, who is himself a popular, powerful, and puzzling figure, proclaims at the start: "The one who comes after me is more powerful than I am" (1:7). The followers of this very powerful deity (who is soon to come onto the stage of the story) are promised that they have available to them something called "the Holy Spirit" (1:8). The divine power that sponsors all this adds his imprimatur to all of this ("You are my son, with you I am well pleased"). In fact, this deity tears open the heavens and sends a divine spirit upon Jesus Christ (1:10–11). Divine power that commands the elements of nature—now that is certainly impressive, attractive, and much needed in a world where evil powers are threatening. So, before we hear anything from Jesus himself, we hear about a forty-day period in which he withstood the influence of Satan, the powerful force for evil within this world. Even "wild beasts" did not destroy him during those forty days, and angels gave him assistance. And when we finally hear from Jesus himself, he proclaims "good news" about the arrival of a new kingdom (1:14–15).

All these features of the Markan narrative would have immediately caught the attention of the second church of the late first century. There is much that the second church might not have grasped in this initial section. It might well have missed the significance of Isaiah and his writings, the Jordan River, the wilderness, and even the imprisonment of John the Baptizer. But it would have heard enough to affirm its own expectation that allegiance to this powerful deity is well placed.

The second church also knows that this powerful deity died and was raised to life. In fact, these features of his story were what attracted the second church to him in the first place. And the Markan Gospel does not disappoint them on that score. In its final scene, "a young man" (perhaps one of the angels who attended him in the wilderness?) says to three women at his tomb, "You are looking for Jesus of Nazareth, who was crucified. He has been raised" (16:6).

Of course, by that point in the narrative, the second church is to recognize that things are not quite the way it had imagined them before hearing the fuller story. But for now it is enough to notice that the Markan Gospel captures the attention and interests of the second church by linking the story of Jesus to power that it frames at both its beginning and its end. It is in the middle where the important work of the Markan Gospel is done for the second church. But there is plenty to keep the interest of the second church before we get there.

Power Like Never Before

Past the introductory paragraphs, the Markan Gospel carries on in much the same way that it began. The second church would be greatly enamored with the story for long stretches. Before the hearer gets through what we know as the first chapter of Mark, the second church finds Jesus doing all the things it loves and expects of him: exorcising a demon from a possessed man ("He commands even the unclean spirits, and they obey him," 1:27); expelling illness (probably understood by the second church to be demonically induced) from Peter's mother-in-law ("the fever left her," 1:31); going throughout the region "casting out demons" (1:39); and healing a man of leprosy ("the leprosy left him," 1:42; leprosy would have been understood as induced by evil powers). Little wonder, then, that "people came to him from every quarter" (1:45). This is precisely why the second church itself has "come" to Jesus: protection from the clutch of fearful spiritual powers that have the potential to undermine the goodness of life. The second church knows precisely what is going on within the narrative, and sees itself in the narrative image of those people who came to Jesus from every quarter.

Next the second church sees a paralytic carried to Jesus on a stretcher, only to walk away on his own two feet after Jesus says the words, "Stand up, take your mat and go to your home" (2:11). No wonder all who saw it said, "We have never seen anything like this!" (2:12), and no wonder a crowd "gathered around him" because of his power (2:13)—just like the second church is doing.

The second church may get a little lost for a while at this point. The second half of what we know to be Mark 2 is not directly about overcoming spiritual forces; instead, it has more to do with controversies with the leaders of the people. But the second church finds itself back on familiar ground soon enough, when it hears Jesus commanding a man with a withered hand to "stretch out your hand," at which point "his hand was restored" (3:5).

Hearing that different kinds of leaders now joined together in a conspiracy that sought "to destroy him" (3:6), the second church might understand that the parts of the storyline that they haven't quite understood thus far are actually quite important after all, because it is the leaders who will orchestrate Jesus's death, and that is good news, because Jesus Christ will live again and give power to his followers in inordinate ways after that. So the second church sees irony in the leaders' efforts to remove him, and it is keen to watch their unfolding role within the story.

The irony is heightened by the fact that the people themselves were enamored with this powerful deity: "a great multitude from Galilee followed him" (3:7), people "in great numbers from Judea, Jerusalem, Idumea, beyond the Jordan, and the region around Tyre and Sidon" (3:8). Like the second church, these people followed him because they had heard about "all that he was doing" (3:8). The second church understands precisely the interests of these wise people; they were concerned for their own well-being, and they wanted their lives to be enhanced by the power of Jesus Christ. These people are narrative representatives of the second church itself. No wonder Jesus's power is reinforced at this point within the narrative: they came to him because "he had cured many, so that all who had diseases pressed upon him to touch him" (3:10). Even "the unclean spirits . . . fell down before him" whenever they saw him (3:11). All this is smooth sailing for the second church of the late first century.

And the same is true when the second church hears Jesus call followers to him and give them power, including the power "to cast out demons" (3:15). Meanwhile, the combination of crowds and power continues to dominate. Knowing precisely why "the crowd came together again" in such great numbers "that they could not even eat" (3:20), the leaders are foregrounded again, as the ones who will manipulate things in order for Jesus to die and be resurrected. Those leaders focus precisely on the very interests of the crowds in the narrative and the second church of the late first century: that is, they oppose Jesus by focusing on his power over malevolent spiritual forces: "By the ruler of the demons he casts out demons," they say stupidly (3:22). Trouncing them by revealing the stupidity of their remark, Jesus explicitly frames the clash of spiritual power in ways that play off of his success against Satan at the beginning of the narrative (i.e., 1:14): "No one can enter a strong man's house and plunder his property without first tying up the strong man; then indeed the house can be plundered" (3:27). If spiritual power over fearful evil forces is called plundering the house of the strong man, the second church is all in favor of that plunder. This, after all, is the sum total of what Jesus-devotion is all about.

Along the way, a few features of the narrative have slipped off the radar of the second church, and that might happen again in what we know as Mark 4. There, Jesus speaks in riddles about seed. Clearly the deity of the second church is wise and has much that is of interest to say. He clearly thinks that he has special things to offer his followers, even though many others refuse to participate in those things.

This sense is immediately reinforced after Jesus is done speaking in riddles. An exciting sea story captures the attention of the second church, with the chaos of the sea threatening to destroy the lives of those in the boat. Nature is at her worst. But the second church gets what it wants when it hears that Jesus "rebuked the wind, and said to the sea, 'Peace, be still.'" The second church might notice that the word Jesus speaks to calm the tumultuous sea is the same word he spoke to the demon in the very first exorcism recounted in the narrative (Greek: *phimōthēti*, 1:25; *pephimōso*, 4:39). Perhaps the forces of evil have stirred up this disaster-in-waiting. But Jesus's power harnesses the chaotic forces unleashed on the natural world, whether that chaos is evidenced in demonic possession or in threats of disaster. The second church loves this sentence: "Then the wind ceased, and there was a dead calm" (4:39). Is there no limit to this deity's power? The second church knows what the disciples don't know when they ask themselves, "Who then is this, that even the wind and the sea obey him?" The second church knows that he is a deity who triumphed over death and, as the disciples have now poignantly discovered, brings protective power to his followers.

For the second church, the next episode reinforces the point. They hear about a man whose humanity is barely evident since the demonic Legion has taken over his personality in a thousand manifestations. The story is fascinating in itself, but the second church is unsurprised by the result of Jesus's encounter with the man: the demonic power is exorcised and the man returns to full health and humanity. The oddity is that the man's neighbors are afraid of this powerful miracle worker, so they "beg Jesus to leave their neighborhood" (5:17). The second church itself may have experienced a similar resistance to Jesus, driven by fear that devotion to Jesus might be detrimental to the well-being of society. But the second church finds a much more sensible response to Jesus in the man who had been saved from evil possession; he "begged him [Jesus] that he might be with him" (5:18). When the man tells others "how much Jesus ['the Lord' of 5:19] had done for him," everyone "was amazed" (5:20)—a response affirmed by the second church.

The next stories are just as splendid. For twelve years a woman has been hemorrhaging blood, and no doctor could heal her. Surely a demon was behind this trick of the body. But when she reached out to touch even just the hem of Jesus's garment, "immediately her hemorrhage stopped; and she felt in her body that she was healed of her disease" (5:29). This is the deity worshiped by the second church—one from whom power proceeds (5:30). And it is a power over death, as the second church knows, since he is the resurrected deity who gives life to his followers. This is reinforced in the two-part story of the girl who died when she was twelve (5:21–24, 35–43). When Jesus brings her back to life, the second church watches the people join in with its own assessment of Jesus: they "were overcome with amazement" (5:42).

That amazement contrasts with the reaction of Jesus's hometown neighbors. They resent his wisdom and the "deeds of power" that were "being done by his hands" (6:3). It is those "deeds of power" that the story focuses on in Jesus's exchange with his townspeople: "he [Jesus] could do no deed of power there, except that he laid his hands on a few sick people and cured them" (6:5).

More fortunate were other villages. Jesus sent his twelve followers out in twos, and "gave them authority over unclean spirits" (6:7), with the result that "they cast out many demons, and anointed with oil many who were sick and cured them" (6:13). That is the Jesus beloved by the second church of the late first century—one whose divine power offered protection against evil and malady.

The second church hears the story of Herod Antipas's beheading of John the Baptizer through the lens of Herod's identification of Jesus with John. "When Herod heard of it, he said, 'John, whom I beheaded, has been raised'" (6:16). Although others also imagined that Jesus was inhabited by the spirit of John the Baptizer, that interpretation includes an ominous note in relation to Herod himself. The presence of the spirit of a beheaded man is a fearful thing to the one who beheaded him, especially if the beheading was unjust. Herod fears Jesus because he knows Jesus has power (6:14), and he imagines that Jesus's power will be targeted against him as the vengeful spirit of John returns to exact its revenge on Herod himself. The story of the beheading of John is intriguing to the second church because it highlights the all-important issue of Jesus's power and places it in yet another frame of reference. Although Herod's interpretation of Jesus's power was deficient, his recognition of Jesus's immense power was not.

The story continues with the disciples returning to Jesus after casting out demons and curing the sick. Like the second church, many people are attracted to Jesus's power, so that "a great crowd" gathers to him and his disciples. Hungry, the crowd is fed through the miraculous power of Jesus, because he "had compassion for them" (6:34). The second church has placed faith in that compassion for its own protection. That is precisely what the next episode emphasizes: when his followers are about to die in a storm at sea, Jesus appears, gets into the boat with them, and the storm is settled (6:47–51). Since the disciples failed to understand that the feeding miracle was about divine protective power (6:52), the second church contents itself that it understands more about Jesus's power than his first disciples. What an irony that those who had wielded Jesus's power earlier in the narrative were the same ones who failed to understand its tremendous limitlessness. What a contrast between the disciples, who didn't quite understand the extent of the power that was on tap, and the crowds who "rushed about that whole region and began to bring the sick on mats to wherever they heard he was . . . , [laying] the sick in the marketplaces, and begged him that they might touch even the fringe of his cloak; and all who touched it were healed" (6:55–56). These are the people with whom the second church identifies—the insightful, everyday, ordinary folk who know a good thing when they see it.

For a short while, the narrative begins to take on a slightly different character, with a fairly lengthy section on a dispute between Jesus and the leaders (7:1–15), which overspills into instruction to the disciples (7:17–23). The second church doesn't feel the need to understand all the nuances of the dispute about purity in these sections, although they are happy that an explanation is provided for them regarding the importance of certain practices for those curious leaders called the Pharisees (7:3–4).

The second church is then happy to get back to familiar territory with yet another exorcism episode, with the simple punchline that the demon was gone from its victim (7:30). Next comes the healing of a deaf mute, an episode that concludes with the crowd being "astounded beyond measure" and saying, "He has done everything well; he even makes the deaf to hear and the mute to speak" (7:37). This is capped off with yet another miraculous feeding, in which Jesus has "compassion for the crowd" (8:2) and provides for the needs of all who have followed him (8:1–10).

A short section follows in which Jesus has little time for people who don't understand what he's about—something about loaves of bread and attending to need, which is good enough for the second church (8:11–21). At least in this section Jesus makes fools of the Pharisees who ask for a sign—haven't they been watching all the mighty deeds he has been doing! The second church feels secure in their knowledge of who Jesus is. When he asks his disciples, "Do you not yet understand?," the second church knows that it does. And it is rewarded with yet another healing—a blind man in this case (8:22–26), although curiously the powerful transformation takes two stages to implement before the man is able to see "everything clearly" (8:25).

Stuck in the Middle

Anyone who has studied the Markan Gospel knows what the second church is about to encounter now that it has reached the middle of the narrative. The second church has had no trouble buying into the storyline of the Markan Gospel right up to the middle of chapter 8. Over and over again the second church has seen its powerful deity doing things it expects him to do for Jesus-devotees who are faithful to him. I have followed fairly closely the second church's imagined responses to the first half of the Markan Gospel in order to illustrate how frequently that narrative plays into the interests of the second church. But, as we know, things are about to change for the second church in its first encounter with the Markan Gospel.

This happens in the second half of chapter 8. There, the storyline takes an unexpected shift for the second church. Although grand identities are discussed in relation to Jesus (8:28–29), this deity of power says the strangest things to his devotees: they are to "deny themselves and take up their cross and follow me" (8:34), and they are called to "lose their life" (8:35). The tease that some will live to "see that the kingdom of God has come with power" is splendidly placed just after these puzzling, dire pronouncements (9:1). The second church is catching a glimpse of the intertwining of those off-putting pronouncements with the motif of power. If his disciples are to "lose their life," is this really a deity of power? The very next episode assures the second church that that remains the case. The second church learns that their deity was "transfigured" (9:2), so that "his clothes became dazzling white, such as no one on earth could bleach them" (9:3). An impressive deity, indeed! Despite the odd twist that the narrative has taken in its discussion of taking up the cross and losing one's life, the second church knows it is still accessing the same narrative when the divine voice from heaven reiterates much of what it had said in the introductory verses, now saying, "This is my Son, the Beloved; listen to him" (9:7). Perhaps there is more good stuff about power in the following episodes, as there had been after the divine voice from heaven last spoke.

Sure enough, the second church is not disappointed even in this. After a short section predicting the death and resurrection of Jesus (which the second church already knew about before hearing the narrative), a long and intriguing episode has Jesus back doing what the crowd (9:14–15) and the second church want from him—casting out evil spirits (9:14–29). When the demon left his victim looking as if he were dead, "Jesus took him by the hand and lifted him up, and he was able to stand" (9:27). The second church feels the story is back on track again, and Jesus's pronouncement about his impending death and resurrection (9:30–32) confirms that this story is all about him and the power over death that he will bestow on his devotees.

From this point onward, however, the second church encounters regular intervals in which pesky aspects of the story are intertwined with the aspects that have so much appeal for the second church. There is much throughout the rest of the story that could be assimilated into a second church point of view. This includes the following episodes: people casting out demons in the name of Jesus (9:38–41); Jesus predicting events that were soon to happen to him and being proved right (11:1–6; 14:12–16); the people praising Jesus (11:7–10); and Jesus trumping the leaders who seek to destroy him, adding irony to the narrative of his death and resurrection (11:27–12:27; 12:35–40; perhaps also 12:28–34, with a different tone). But intertwined with those features of the story are other dimensions that nestle in alongside the powerful Jesus and require the second church to consider its allegiance to Jesus in new ways—this includes both what allegiance might look like in practice and the very character of their allegiance.

In terms of what allegiance to Jesus looks like, the second church has to grapple with how the Markan Gospel presents Jesus's own demands on his followers. This includes statements of inverted honor (e.g., "Whoever wants to be first must be last of all and slave of all," 9:35), and statements about the urgency of proper allegiance lest punishment should await (e.g., "it would be better for you if a great millstone were hung around your neck and you were thrown into the sea," 9:42; cf. 9:43–48). Such weightiness in proper allegiance even includes realigning one's attitude toward such practical matters as divorce and remarriage (10:2–12)—the place in the narrative where the second church can no longer pretend that Jesus is just a powerful deity without much claim on their lives. Evidently Jesus's power requires a radical revision of expectations and lifestyle. This "requirement of revision" is reinforced in the very next episode, when Jesus expects a man who "had many possessions" to "give the money to the poor" after having sold off all of his possessions (10:21–22; cf. 10:17–27). Driving the point home further is Jesus's third prediction about his impending death and resurrection (10:32–35), which pivots directly into a repetition of the point that true greatness among Jesus's followers involves becoming "a slave of all" (10:35–41), in obedience to the one who serves others by giving up his own life. This form of greatness is embodied by the poor widow, who is commended by Jesus for giving "everything she had, all she had to live on" (12:41–44). If devotees of the deity Isis expected life to be enhanced in the present, the Markan Gospel makes no promises to devotees of Jesus Christ (except in terms of gaining a new fictive family of support; 10:28–31). Jesus-devotion might even include ominous prospects, such as those outlined in Mark 13:9–13:

> As for yourselves, beware; for they will hand you over to councils; and you will be beaten in synagogues; and you will stand before governors and kings because of me, as a testimony to them. . . . Brother will betray brother to death, and a father his child, and children will rise against parents and have them put to death; and you will be hated by all because of my name. But the one who endures to the end will be saved.

The second church would know of such things happening—not least, perhaps, in the Neronian persecution against Christians. But the second church probably never imagined that its own Jesus-devotion, when properly configured, might put them on a similar course. The Markan Gospel raises precisely such a prospect for the second church.

Why would they permit their comfortable allegiance to take such a nosedive in comfort levels? Why shouldn't they simply redirect their Jesus-devotion, channeling their devotional energies to deities like Isis, who promised enhanced life in the present and a life beyond death? Isn't that all that the second church is looking for? Why would the second church maintain its devotion to a deity of power whose devotees faced an uncertain future?

The Markan Gospel supplies the answer. In a nutshell, the point is encapsulated in the phrase, "Whoever welcomes me welcomes not me but the one who sent me" (9:37). Who is "the one who sent me"? The sender is to Jesus as "Father" (8:38; 14:36), just as Jesus is to him as "Son" (1:11; 9:7; cf. 3:11; 5:7; 13:32; 15:39). We have heard the voice of this divine Father on two previous occasions, and it is the voice of the deity who is able to rip open the heavens (1:10). The power exerted by Jesus has its ultimate origins in a deity who has barely appeared within the storyline at all. But his influence is everywhere, for this is the deity who created the whole of creation (13:19). The second church had no doubt heard that Isis controlled Fate, since such claims were spreading like wildfire throughout the second half of the first century.[8] But in light of the Markan Gospel, the second church is faced with counterclaims. The one who oversees creation in its course is the deity whom Jesus calls "Father." The second church hears this fresh news in awe and wonder (13:24–27):

> The sun will be darkened, and the moon will not give its light, and the stars will be falling from heaven, and the powers in the heavens will be shaken. Then they will see "the Son of Man coming in clouds" with great power and glory. Then he will send out the angels, and gather his elect from the four winds, from the ends of the earth to the ends of heaven.

Perhaps the second church is forced to consider whether its devotion to other deities alongside Jesus Christ is the right strategy after all. The second church might not, in fact, understand everything about "the desolating sacrilege" (13:14), but it might pick up on the implication that the deity of creation does not share his power and authority with others. "Heaven and earth will pass away, but my words will not pass away," notes Jesus (13:31). Only the one whom Jesus calls "Father" knows the full course of creation's future (13:32). But Jesus does know that he himself, as "the Son of the Blessed One," will play a central role in that future: "You will see the Son of Man seated at the right hand of the Power, and coming with the clouds of heaven" (14:61–62).

What an irony, then, that the characters in the stories fall away from their allegiance to the one who is "seated on the right hand of the Power." The disciples' various forms of denial, desertion, and betrayal (14:17–52, 66–72) are illustrations of flawed Jesus-devotion, whether it be halfhearted or self-seeking, or both.

But what is most noticeable to the second church is the way that the crowds shift their allegiance as well. Throughout the first half of the narrative, the crowds were narrative representatives of the second church—eager to benefit

---

8. The script of an initiation ceremony into the Isis cult from the first century BCE–CE (found in a room off the sanctuary of Isis in Kyme) makes the point well. It includes these words, spoken by Isis: *egō to himarmenon nikō emou to heimarmenon akouei*, or "I conquer Fate; Fate listens to me" (Laurent Bricault, *Recueil des Inscriptions concernant les Cultes isiaques* [Paris: De Boccard, 2005], 302/0204). Isis has power over Destiny and can change what might happen in the future, to the benefit of her devotees.

from Jesus's power on any and every occasion.[9] Something happens toward the end of the second half of the narrative, however. Whereas the crowds praise Jesus (11:7–10) and their attraction to Jesus restrains the leaders in their efforts to do away with him (14:1–2), eventually the crowds become hostages to the leaders' machinations. Being motivated by "jealousy" against Jesus's popularity with the crowds, the leaders ironically stoke up the crowds in order to enlist them as pawns in a manipulative power-grab. As a consequence, the crowds bark their command that Pilate should crucify Jesus (15:11–14). Of course, the second church is glad that Jesus was crucified, since that leads to his victory over death. But the irony for the second church is that their narrative representatives have played a part in bringing about that tragedy—placing them in much the same category as Jesus's betrayer, about whom Jesus said, "It would have been better for that one not to have been born" (14:21). Now the second church distances itself from the crowd that has for so long represented it within the narrative. In the process, the second church might begin to reconfigure its Jesus-devotion. In his riddle about the sower and the seed, Jesus had described the seed sown on rocky ground as ones who "have no root, and endure only for a while; then, when trouble or persecution arises on account of the word, immediately they fall away" (4:16–17). Along similar lines, the crowd seems to have had little root; enduring for only a while, it fell away. The second church might now start to rethink its self-identity in relation to Jesus's pronouncement against the seed sown on rocky ground, beginning to distance itself from the deficient crowd that had served for so long as the narrative representatives of the second church.

Another narrative feature might help to foster this adjustment in the self-understanding of the second church—that is, the observation of the centurion at the moment of Jesus's death: "Now when the centurion, who stood facing him, saw that in this way he breathed his last, he said, 'Truly this man was God's Son'" (15:39). The second church hears this as a true statement, since this is the way Jesus has been described by those with suprahuman insight throughout (1:11; 3:11; 5:7; 9:7; 13:32). But the second church also knows that this valid observation requires a significant infill of content in order to be properly understood. The centurion is much like the second church at the start of the process of hearing the Markan Gospel—he knows some impressive basics about Jesus, but his knowledge is also underdeveloped and, therefore, deficient in itself. At this point in its hearing of the narrative, the second church knows that, unless the rest of the Markan Gospel's theological emphases are imported

---

9. The crowds would also listen to his teachings—themselves life-giving words, to the consternation of the leaders of the people.

into the centurion's observation, that observation remains lacking in much-needed theological nuances—much like the convictions of the second church itself prior to its hearing of the Markan Gospel.

In Sum

In the preceding sections of this essay, I have managed only very cursory observations on how the story of the Markan Gospel might have impacted the second church of the late first century. The reading has been simple and un-refined, and has not made use of specialized narratological methods (e.g., differentiating the implied author from the narrator; postulating the ideal or authorial audience; etc.). No doubt, weaknesses abound as a consequence. But despite the inevitable weaknesses, I hope to have demonstrated how the Markan Gospel might have been accessed by the fairly unrefined second church of the late first century.

In the process of this simple reading, some features of the Markan Gospel have been underplayed, precisely because I imagine that the second church might not have fully appreciated them on the first reading of the narrative. These include structuring techniques (e.g., intercalation, chiasm, etc.), double-entendres (e.g., "the way" in Mark 8–10; the two healings of blind men in relation to Mark 8–10; *egō eimi*; etc.), and important theological motifs (e.g., the significance of the Gentile mission; the intricacies within the divine identity; the function of scriptural citations and echoes; etc.). Many things lie in waiting for further encounters with the Markan Gospel, precisely because, as my simple and unrefined reading suggests, the second church was itself probably rather simple in its expectations of what Jesus-devotion involved.

In the course of this exercise, there seem to be very few episodes in the Markan Gospel that do not impact on the interests of the second church.[10] Almost all of the Markan episodes have significance for the second church agenda in one of at least two ways. First, throughout the first half of the Gospel especially, the Markan Gospel ensures that the second church finds its interests on display within the story's episodes, thereby attracting the second church into the folds of the storyline. By the time it is reading Mark 8, the second

---

10. In only a few places is the story told seemingly for its own merits, without any particular spin toward the second church. One example of this might be the crucifixion and burial of Jesus (15:21–47). In other instances, the second church might be unsure of the purpose of an episode, only to find its significance upon further hearings. One example of this might be the parables of the seed in Mark 4.

church has already bought strongly into the story. The second church tracks with the story with great ease throughout the first half of the Gospel. The sense of ownership is high; this story belongs to the second church.

The second way in which the Markan Gospel has significance for the second church runs against the grain of the first. For throughout the second half of the Gospel especially, the Markan Gospel frequently challenges the second church. Adopting allegiance to Jesus Christ is not simply a tool to enhance one's life, nor is it something that can simply be added to other layers of devotion. The Markan Gospel forces the second church to grapple with its understanding of what it means to adopt Jesus-devotion. Should it comply with the narrative contours of the Markan Gospel, the second church will start the process of revising its devotion to Jesus—rethinking its expectations and realigning its practices. When "the ideal second church" hears the Markan Gospel, it first grows so addicted to the narrative of the powerful Jesus that it then cannot legitimately detach itself from the storyline once the challenges start seeping in from various angles.[11] In the process of engaging with this story, the ideal second church learns that it is to become nonexistent.

The Markan Gospel sets itself up as a legitimate form of the good news. The episode of the anointing of Jesus by the woman with costly ointment suggests as much: "Wherever the good news is proclaimed in the whole world, what she has done will be told in remembrance of her" (14:9). The second church might not have heard this story previously. Whatever formulation of Jesus's life the second church might have had before, it was not, then, the good news of the apostolic voice. With the arrival of the Markan Gospel, however, the second church has received a legitimate form of good news about Jesus Christ, including the challenge to recognize that the good news is not always good, at least when assessed in terms of self-protection and self-enhancement— the very things that fostered the early growth of the second church in the second half of the first century. The Markan Gospel harnesses those interests and, without denying them, turns them inside-out, rechanneling them along different lines, to the point of calling the second church out of existence altogether. Presumably the Markan evangelist would want the same for the second church of the early twenty-first century—itself widespread, and a form of Jesus-devotion from which no one is immune.

---

11. The Matthean and Lukan Gospels especially carry on the task begun by the Markan evangelist, recounting stories of challenge and intertwining them with enhanced Christological and soteriological storylines. The Johannine Gospel takes all this to a new level altogether, but not without precedent in the earlier canonical Gospels.

The Book of Revelation and the Hekhalot Literature

James R. Davila

The book of Revelation and the strange collection of revelatory texts known as the Hekhalot literature share a striking number of parallels. Both focus on visionary travel to heaven to gain revelations before a celestial throne room modeled after the vision of the heavenly realm in the book of Ezekiel. Both also present scenarios involving the divine judgment of Rome and the Roman emperor, again containing many similar features. Revelation is a late first-century CE Christian work, and the Hekhalot literature was composed from late antiquity to the Geonic era, with editing continuing into the Middle Ages, so anything like a direct connection between them seems on the face of it unlikely.[1] Nevertheless, there is some evidence that the Hekhalot texts drew

---

1. All translations from the book of Revelation are my own from the Greek text. Major manuscripts of the Hekhalot literature were published by Peter Schäfer et al. in *Synopse zur Hekhalot-Literatur*, Texte und Studien zum Antiken Judentum 2 (Tübingen: Mohr Siebeck, 1981). Many fragments of Hekhalot texts from the Cairo Geniza were published by Schäfer in *Geniza-Fragmente zur Hekhalot-Literatur*, Texte und Studien zum Antiken Judentum 6 (Tübingen: Mohr Siebeck, 1984). An edition of the *Shiʿur Qomah* texts, which focus on the features of the imagined gigantic body of God, has been published by Martin Samuel Cohen in *The Shiʿur Qomah: Texts and Recensions*, Texte und Studien zum Antiken Judentum 9 (Tübingen: Mohr Siebeck, 1985). All translations of material from the Hekhalot literature are taken from

---

It is my pleasure to dedicate this essay to my colleague Richard Bauckham, whose work has contributed so much to the study of early Christianity and ancient Judaism. A draft of this essay was presented at the annual meeting of the Society of Biblical Literature in the Early Jewish and Christian Mysticism Section in November of 2008.

at times on much earlier material, perhaps even going back to Second Temple times.² The parallels between the book of Revelation and the Hekhalot literature have never been thoroughly collected and explored.³ Endless details in the two are comparable, but it seems most productive to concentrate on patterns of shared parallels rather than individual details, so this essay concentrates on what I regard to be the most interesting such patterns, and it offers some very preliminary reflections on their possible significance.⁴

1. John and the Merkavah Mystics

John gives us a protracted account of his visionary experiences. But unlike the Hekhalot literature and some of the other ancient Jewish apocalypses, he gives us almost no information about the process he underwent to achieve the vi-

---

James R. Davila, *Hekhalot Literature in Translation: Major Texts of Merkavah Mysticism*, Supplements to the Journal of Jewish Thought and Philosophy 20 (Leiden: Brill, 2013) and are cited by the paragraph or column and line numbers used therein. General bibliography and a basic orientation to the Hekhalot texts can be found in chapter one of that book. The following special abbreviations are used here: *HR*: *Hekhalot Rabbati* (§§81-121, 152-73, 189-277); *HZ*: *Hekhalot Zutarti* (§§335-75, 407-26); *MM*: *Ma'aseh Merkavah* (§§544-96); *Youth*: the *Youth* text. From the Cairo Geniza: G8 (the Ozhayah Fragment). For an excellent English translation of *3 Enoch*, see Philip Alexander, "3 (Hebrew Apocalypse of) Enoch," *Old Testament Pseudepigrapha*, ed. James H. Charlesworth (New York: Doubleday, 1983, 1985), 1:223-315.

2. It is generally agreed that some of the Hekhalot traditions go back to late antiquity (the third to sixth centuries CE) and some specialists argue that some go back to the Tannaitic period or even the Second Temple period. For discussion and bibliography see Davila, *Hekhalot Literature in Translation*, 14-16, 41-42, 162-63, 192-94, 248, 304-5.

3. David Halperin has important prolegomena in *The Faces of the Chariot: Early Jewish Responses to Ezekiel's Vision*, Texte und Studien zum Antiken Judentum 16 (Tübingen: Mohr Siebeck, 1988), 87-96. I have collected parallels to Revelation and to the Hekhalot literature in the Qumran Songs of the Sabbath Sacrifice and 4QBerakhot in *Liturgical Works*, Eerdmans Commentaries on the Dead Sea Scrolls 6 (Grand Rapids: Eerdmans, 2000), 46-47, 91-93, and passim in the relevant chapters. But I have not analyzed the collected parallels in any critical detail and I generally did not compare Revelation and the Hekhalot literature to one another.

4. Both Revelation and the Hekhalot literature contain numerous "merkavah hymns," songs whose setting is the heavenly realm, especially the divine throne room. These have many interesting points of comparison and contrast and they deserve a full-scale analysis on their own. I have set them aside here for future treatment. The most recent substantial analysis of Revelation's hymns is by Steven Grabiner, *Revelation's Hymns: Commentary on the Cosmic Conflict*, Library of New Testament Studies 511 (London: Bloomsbury T&T Clark, 2015). See therein for earlier bibliography.

The Book of Revelation and the Hekhalot Literature

sionary state and whether it involved the use of any ritual techniques. But he does give us two important hints when in Revelation 1:10a he reports that these experiences commenced while "I was in the spirit (*en pneumati*) on the Lord's day." Within the book of Revelation, John tells us three more times that he was "in the spirit" at the beginning of a new vision (4:2; 17:3; 21:10). This phrase can have a number of meanings,[5] but the one that best fits this context is to be in a state of prophetic inspiration, and this meaning is well attested in Septuagint Greek[6] and the Greek of the New Testament and related literature.[7] The wording of Revelation 1:10b also consciously imitates that of Ezekiel 3:12 (where while being lifted up by the spirit Ezekiel hears a loud voice behind him), implicitly identifying John's experience with Ezekiel's spirit-inspired vision.

The phrase "on the Lord's day" is generally understood to refer to Sunday, commemorated by the early Jesus movement as the day of Jesus's resurrection.[8] So Revelation 1:10 tells us that John entered a state of visionary prophetic inspiration at a time explicitly flagged as of cultic significance.[9] Although one

---

5. In the biblical and related Greek relevant here, the sense usually involves the agency of or participation in the divine spirit, often specified as "holy spirit" (e.g., John 1:33; Rom. 8:9; 15:16) etc. (e.g., "spirit of God," Ezek. 11:24). For this sense see, e.g., Isa. 4:4 (the Lord's judgment); Zech. 4:6 (Zerubbabel); Ps. Sol. 17:37 (the future king); Matt. 12:28 (Jesus's power of exorcism); John 4:23-24 (the worship of true worshipers); 1 Tim. 3:16 (the vindication of Christ); and the passages cited in the next two notes. The phrase can also refer to a wind (Ps. 48[47]:8[7]); a human spirit (Qoh. 7:9; 8:8; Gal. 6:1); human (royal) breath (Isa. 11:4); possession by an unclean spirit (Mark 1:23; 5:2); and an allegorical meaning of scripture (*Barn.* 10:2, 9; cf. 13:5).

6. See Greek 2 Esd. 19:30; Zech. 1:6; 7:12; Ezek. 37:1; and perhaps Mic. 3:8. The mention of Elijah's spirit seems also to refer to this prophetic inspiration in 2 Kings 2:9 (cf. Luke 1:17). Cf. David's spirit in 1 Chron. 28:12 in the context of v. 19.

7. See Matt. 22:43 (// Mark 12:36 "in the holy spirit"; cf. *Barn.* 12:10-11); 1 Cor. 14:16; Eph. 3:5 (and perhaps 2:22?); *Barn.* 9:7; 14:2; *Did.* 11:7-9, 12; *Gos. Naz.* frag. 15; *Acts Paul* 9. See further, R. H. Charles, *A Critical and Exegetical Commentary on the Revelation of St. John*, International Critical Commentary, 2 vols. (Edinburgh: T. & T. Clark, 1920), 1:22; J. Massyngberde Ford, *Revelation: Introduction, Translation and Commentary*, Anchor Bible 38 (Garden City, NY: Doubleday, 1975), 70; Robert H. Mounce, *The Book of Revelation*, New International Commentary on the Old Testament (Grand Rapids: Eerdmans, 1977, rev. ed. 1997), 55; David E. Aune, *Revelation 1-5*, Word Biblical Commentary 52 (Dallas: Word, 1997), 82-83.

8. Charles, *Revelation of St. John*, 1:22-23; Ford, *Revelation*, 382; Mounce, *Book of Revelation*, 55-56; Aune, *Revelation 1-5*, 83-84.

9. In *Barn.* 14:2 the state of being "in the spirit" is also tied to an ascetic ritual (prolonged fasting) in the case of Moses; John tells us that true worshipers worship "in the spirit" (4:23-24); and the devout are exhorted to "pray at every opportunity in the spirit" in Eph. 6:18 (cf. Jude 20, "pray in the holy spirit"), so this state is at least sometimes associated with ritual praxis.

should not make too much of this, there are hints that John may have engaged in ritual preparation for his vision, as did the Hekhalot practitioners in the Hekhalot texts and the biblical prophets in the fictional narratives of the ancient Jewish apocalypses.[10]

John's experience also has a number of specific parallels to the experiences of the Hekhalot practitioners. His book opens by asserting that it is a revelation from God, mediated by an angel "to show His slaves the things that must happen soon," things to which John bears witness (Rev. 1:1-2), as he was commanded by the Lord (Rev. 1:11). Likewise, at the beginning of the throne vision of chapter 4, he is told that he will be shown "the things that must happen after these (present) things" (Rev. 4:1). The *Hekhalot Rabbati* opens by introducing the songs by which the practitioner may bind himself to God so as to descend and ascend safely[11] and to stand near the throne of God "to see whatever they do before the throne of His glory and to know whatever shall happen in the future in the world" (*HR* §81). At the beginning of the account of the ten martyrs (on which more below), an edict of Rome against certain Jewish sages leads R. Nehuniah ben HaQanah to order his disciple, R. Ishmael, to descend to the chariot, where the angel Suriah, the Prince of the Presence, grants him a vision of the heavenly deliberations and negotiations with the hostile angel Samma'el behind the scenes of the persecution (*HR* §§107-10). R. Ishmael then returns "and made known this testimony from before the throne of glory" (§111). Likewise, later in the work, the practitioners are sternly warned, "The decree of heaven is against you, descenders to the chariot, unless you say what you have heard and unless you testify to what you have seen" in the practitioners' visionary experiences (*HR* §169). And in a paradigmatic instructional account of the descent to the chariot we are told, "And all the descenders to the chariot ascend and are not harmed; rather they see all this violence and descend safely and they come and they stand and testify to the fearsome and confounding sight, the like of which is not in all the palaces of kings of flesh and blood" (*HR* §216). Indeed, God

---

10. For the use of ritual in the ancient Jewish apocalypses see James R. Davila, "Ritual in the Jewish Pseudepigrapha," in *Anthropology and Biblical Studies: Avenues of Approach*, ed. Louise J. Lawrence and Mario I. Aguilar (Leiderdorp: Deo, 2004), 158-83, esp. 178-80; idem, "The Hekhalot Literature and the Ancient Jewish Apocalypses," in *Paradise Now: Essays on Early Jewish and Christian Mysticism*, ed. April Deconick, Society of Biblical Literature Symposium Series 11 (Atlanta: Society of Biblical Literature, 2006), 105-25, esp. 122.

11. Paradoxically, the Hekhalot literature often refers to the ascent to God's throne ("chariot") as a "descent" and the return descent as an "ascent." Therefore a common name for the Hekhalot practitioners in the texts is "descenders to the chariot."

longs for the practitioners to make the descent. He asks, "When will the descender descend to the chariot? When will he feast his eyes on the majesties on high? When will he hear the end of salvation? When will he see *what eye has not seen* (Isa. 64:4)? When will he ascend and report to the seed of Abraham who loves Him?" (*HR* §218). Like the descenders to the chariot, John undertakes a perilous visionary journey, guided by angels, in which he learns heavenly secrets about the current persecution by and imminent fall of Rome, and he returns to testify to these secrets to his community.

John's visionary experiences also find parallels in the *Hekhalot Zutarti*. The visions of the book of Revelation may broadly be set beside a description of the Hekhalot practitioners presented as a series of rhetorical questions in *HZ* §349(//§361), which begin, "And what mortal man is it who is able . . . ?" Like the practitioner, John is able to "ascend on high." He can also "search out the inhabited world" in his world-encompassing visions that range from Asia Minor to Jerusalem to Rome to the river Euphrates and beyond. He can "walk on the dry land" when he measures the Temple of God in chapter 11. He can "gaze at His splendor" and "know the lightning" in the throne vision of chapter 4. He has "a vision of what is above" in chapters 4–5 and elsewhere and although he may not strictly speaking "descend below," he does have "a vision of what is below" in his glimpses of the abyss in 9:1–2 and 20:1–3. He is able "to know the explanation of the living," for example, in the risen Christ's admonitions to the seven churches in chapters 2–3, "and to see the vision of the dead" in the episode with the righteous souls under the altar in 6:9–11 and in the scene of the final judgment in chapter 20. He is not explicitly "transformed by His glory" so as "to walk in rivers of fire," although his apparent near proximity to the dangerously splendorous and fiery celestial realm (e.g., in chapter 4) may imply some manner of temporary transformation into an angelic state. He does not "ride on wheels" (in a fiery chariot?), "recite His praise," "combine letters" in theurgic recitations, or "recite the names," although he does witness the angels and glorified saints reciting praise (e.g., 4:8–11; 7:9–12; 14:2–3), and he is aware of the power of names, especially divine ones (2:17; 3:12; 19:16). Likewise, in *HZ* §366 (//§496), R. Akiva reports that, like John, "I had a vision of and I observed the whole inhabited world and I saw it—what it is." Like John, he "ascended," although explicitly "in a wagon of fire," while John's means of ascent is not specified. R. Akiva "gazed on the palaces of hail" and John saw "heavy hail" in the celestial temple (Rev. 11:19; cf. Ps. 18:13–14 [EVV 18:12–13]). R. Akiva also saw something unintelligible "that sits on the burning sea," while John saw a mountain of fire cast into the sea (Rev. 8:8).

JAMES R. DAVILA

2. Jesus, the Youth, and Metatron

The presentation of the exalted Christ in the book of Revelation has some notable parallels with two exalted angels in the Hekhalot literature. The Youth is the celestial high priest who serves in the heavenly tabernacle, and the angel Metatron is the deified patriarch Enoch, who was taken into heaven and transformed into an enthroned archangel so exalted that he could be mistaken for a second god. These two angels are identified with one another in some traditions, but there is good reason to believe that they were originally separate.[12]

The Youth is described in a passage in a Hekhalot Geniza fragment (G8 2b 13b-17) and in some *Shi'ur Qomah* manuscripts (the *Youth* text). The theophany in G8 describes him in terms similar to Jesus in Revelation. The Youth's "eyes ki[ndle like to]rches and his eyeballs kindle like lamps" and "the sun is poured from the belt in front of him." John's "one like a son of man" has "eyes like a flame of fire" and "his face shines like the sun" (Rev. 1:14, 16; cf. Dan. 10:5-6). The Youth is crowned, and the "one like a son of man" in Revelation 14:14 (who may be Christ, at least in the final form of the text) wears a golden crown.[13] The Youth wears a robe that "is like the robe of his King," meaning, apparently, that like God's robe, it is written all over with the Tetragrammaton (cf. *HR* §102). In Revelation 19:16, Jesus wears a robe on which is inscribed the name "King of kings and Lord of lords." The splendor and adornment of the Youth are like those of God and—like the Ancient of Days in Daniel 7:9— John's "one like a son of man" has head and hair that are "white as white wool, like snow" (Rev. 1:14). The visionary is told that the Youth "takes hold of [you] by your hand and seats you on his lap" as he has others before. Likewise, Jesus tells his followers, "The one who conquers, I will grant to him to sit with me on my throne" (Rev. 3:21).[14]

---

12. I have made the case for their separate origin in "Melchizedek, the 'Youth,' and Jesus," in *The Dead Sea Scrolls as Background to Postbiblical Judaism and Early Christianity: Papers from a Conference at St. Andrews in 2001*, ed. James R. Davila, Studies on the Texts of the Desert of Judah 46 (Leiden: Brill, 2003), 248-74, esp. 258-61.

13. For more on the scriptural background of "the one like a son of man" in Revelation, see Charles, *Revelation of St. John*, 1:27-31; Charles A. Gieschen, *Angelomorphic Christology: Antecedents and Early Evidence*, Arbeiten zur Geschichte des antiken Judentums und des Urchristentums 42 (Leiden: Brill, 1998), 246-52. On Revelation 14:14 see Charles, *Revelation of St. John*, 2:19-20; Ford, *Revelation*, 250; Mounce, *Book of Revelation*, 277-78; David E. Aune, *Revelation 6-16*, Word Biblical Commentary 52B (Dallas: Word, 1998), 800-801.

14. See Aune, *Revelation 1-5*, 261-62, for some literary background to this verse. The perspective of the Hekhalot texts offers one answer to his question, "How many can occupy a single throne at one time?" (262). Two can, if one sits on the lap of the other.

The Book of Revelation and the Hekhalot Literature

Both the Youth and Jesus exhibit features belonging to angels and features belonging to God, although these features overlap in the two figures only partially. And the implications of the similarities to God are treated quite differently. The Hekhalot visionary is warned, "Do not abase yourself to him," just as John is admonished twice not to fall down before an angel (Rev. 19:10; 22:8-9),[15] but he does fall at the feet of the risen Christ and is not reproached for it (1:17). Apparently the glorious appearance of the Youth could lead to him being mistaken for a divine being, but he was actually no more than an exalted angel. John's risen Christ is a more complicated figure to whom obeisance was appropriate.

The figure of Metatron, who is described in *3 Enoch* 1-16/§§1-20, is likewise more complex than that of the Youth. Like Jesus, Metatron is a mortal man exalted to heaven. He bears the name "the lesser YHWH" (*3 En.* 12:5/§15); he is, like Jesus, enthroned (*3 En.* 10:1-2/§13; cf. Rev. 3:21; 7:17; 22:1, 3); and the other angels prostrate themselves before him (*3 En.* 4:9/§6; 14:5/§18).[16] Like Jesus he wears a robe and a crown (*3 En.* 12:1-3/§15). And Enoch's knowledge of the secrets of the universe (*3 En.* 11/§14) seems comparable to the knowledge of the Christ who grants revelations to John. In addition, after being misidentified by the arch-heretic Elisha ben Avuyah as a second power in heaven, Metatron was dethroned (*3 En.* 16/§20). Elsewhere I have raised the possibility that the erased contours of a Metatron cult may be visible in the surviving text of *3 Enoch*.[17] Be that as it may, the Christ of Revelation shares with both the Youth and Metatron many details of theophanic splendor, enthronement, and other elements of deification with Metatron and, with the Youth alone, the ability to enthrone his followers.[18]

---

15. The exhortation not to fall down before an angel is a motif in ancient visionary literature, found also in *Apoc. Zeph.* 6:11-15 and *Ascen. Isa.* 7:18-22.

16. Note that angels *stand* before the Youth while with him they worship God (*Youth* 14, 30-31). The living creatures put their faces to the ground during the heavenly liturgy (*Youth* 42), but they are honoring God, not the Youth.

17. "Of Methodology, Monotheism, and Metatron: Introductory Reflections on Divine Mediators and the Origins of the Worship of Jesus," in *The Jewish Roots of Christological Monotheism. Papers from the St. Andrews Conference on the Historical Origins of the Worship of Jesus*, ed. James R. Davila, Carey C. Newman, and Gladys S. Lewis, Journal for the Study of Judaism in the Persian, Hellenistic, and Roman Periods Supplement Series 63 (Leiden: Brill, 1999), 3-18, esp. 15-18.

18. The origins of the Youth and Metatron have been much-debated topics in recent years. Daniel Boyarin has offered a reconstruction of the origins of both, starting with traditions found in the Parables of Enoch, and tracing their development into the early rabbinic period: "Beyond Judaisms: Metatron and the Divine Polymorphy of Ancient Judaism," *Journal for the*

3. The Celestial Throne Room

Both the Hekhalot practitioners and John describe visions of the celestial throne room which draw heavily on the visions in Ezekiel 1 and 10, as well as Isaiah 6:1-6 and Daniel 7:9-10. God is enthroned there, and the scenes draw on the rainbow (Ezek. 1:28), the gems (Ezek. 1:16, 26; 10:1, 9), the lightning (Ezek. 1:4), and the fire (Ezek. 1:13, 27; 10:2, 6) of Ezekiel's vision. In Revelation, John comes before the throne, around which a rainbow shines and the occupant of which resembles gems. From the throne issue lightning and thunder, and before it flame seven torches, which are identified as the seven spirits of God (4:2-5). Many of the same elements appear in the description of the throne scene in *HZ* §356: before the throne are gems, spirits, thunderclaps, and lightning bolts; "the letters of His name" are "like the splendor of the rainbow in the cloud"; and God's feet rest on, among many other things, torches of fire. The throne itself speaks in Revelation 16:17; 19:5; 21:3 as the throne of God does frequently in the Hekhalot literature (e.g., *HR* §§99, 251; *HZ* §§348, 423; *MM* §552).

Ezekiel's "firmament like a spring of terrible ice" (1:22) becomes "(something) like a glass sea resembling crystal" in Revelation 4:6 and in the *Hekhalot Zutarti* the floor of the sixth palace, which the unwary Hekhalot practitioner might mistake for myriads of waves of water and perish (*HZ* §338[//344//671]-

---

Study of Judaism in the Persian, Hellenistic, and Roman Periods 41 (2010): 323-65. Peter Schäfer has argued that the Metatron tradition as found in *3 Enoch* was written with full awareness of late antique Christian theological teachings about Jesus and constituted a direct response and challenge to those teachings, offering Enoch/Metatron as a divinized redeemer figure, savior, and heavenly judge, who was not preexistent and did not die a shameful death before his exaltation. See Schäfer, *The Origins of Jewish Mysticism* (Tübingen: Mohr Siebeck, 2009), 315-27, 330; idem, *The Jewish Jesus: How Judaism and Christianity Shaped Each Other* (Princeton: Princeton University Press, 2012), 103-49. This is a very interesting suggestion, but it is not clear to me why these hypothetical late antique Jewish circles would take exception to Jesus, a preexistent redeemer who died a salvific death, yet would accept Metatron as a divinized human savior who bore the name of God, and even offer the latter as a viable alternative to Jesus. The solution to the problem does not seem adequate to me. Moreover, the figure of Enoch/Metatron in *3 Enoch* clearly has his roots in the Son of Man of the Parables of Enoch, and this implies that the figure developed over a considerable period of time between the Second Temple period and late antiquity. Schäfer's suggestion cannot be ruled out, but it awaits verification with more data about the circles he postulates. The parallels with the book of Revelation collected here could even be taken as further support for his theory, but I hesitate to take them as such, since the parallels do not form a pattern that implies the direct influence of Revelation on *3 Enoch*.

The Book of Revelation and the Hekhalot Literature

§339[//345//672]).[19] Ezekiel's living creatures, cherubim, and ophannim (wheels) are for the most part kept separate from one another and from Isaiah's seraphim in the Hekhalot literature,[20] whereas they are amalgamated in Revelation 4 into a single type of being, called the four living creatures, who have features of all four (Rev. 4:6b-8). Notably, the living creatures of Revelation recite the trisagion of the seraphim (Rev. 4:8), as do the living creatures in *HR* §§101 and 273. The twenty-four elders are some sort of angelic or angelified figure, whether the glorified patriarchs of Israel and the twelve apostles or the angels over the twenty-four priestly courses or something else.[21] They are perhaps paralleled by the "princes of the peoples of the world" on whom the Youth dispenses his splendor in the *Shi'ur Qomah* throne scene (*Youth* 23-24). The elders wear crowns, as angels often do in the Hekhalot texts, and in their worship they remove the crowns and cast them before the throne as they sing praises to God (Rev. 4:4, 10-11). In *HR* §190 the living creatures also fall down before God and remove their crowns while invoking God's mercy on Israel in song. Likewise in *3 Enoch* 18:1-23/§§23-28, the entire hierarchy of angels remove their crowns and fall prostrate in series. The four living creatures and the twenty-four elders fall before the Lamb while holding golden bowls filled with incense, "which are the prayers of the saints" (Rev. 5:8). In *HR* §163 God declares that the voices of Israel at the times of daily prayer ascend before him "as a soothing odor," echoing the terminology used of sacrifice in Leviticus 1:9, 13, 17, etc. Likewise "salted incense" is a term used to describe the praise of God in the hymn in *HR* §251.

In addition, the heavenly realm in the Hekhalot literature is populated with dangerous armored angels who ride fire-breathing horses, carry swords and bows, and inhabit a region of fire, blood, and hail (*HR* §§213-15; cf. Zech. 1:8). In Revelation the horsemen of the apocalypse (Rev. 6:2-8), the angels of the seven trumpets (esp. Rev. 8:7), the angels of the heavenly temple (Rev. 11:19; 14:17-20), and the angels who accompany Christ at the apocalyptic battle (Rev. 19:14) have similar features. The heavenly temple of Revelation contains a "tent of testimony" (15:5), which brings to mind the "tabernacle of the Youth" in *Youth* 39.

---

19. Ford, *Revelation*, 73-74; Mounce, *Book of Revelation*, 122-23; Aune, *Revelation 1-5*, 296-97; Halperin, *Faces of the Chariot*, 93-100, 199-210, 231-38, 247-49.

20. The cherubim, living creatures, and ophannim appear frequently, e.g., *HR* §§100, 101, 103, 119, 161, 170-71, 198, 236, 245, 247, 250; *HZ* §411; *MM* §§559, 590, 593, 594; G8 2b 43. (These passages mention all three together. They are often mentioned separately as well.) The seraphim are mentioned much less frequently, e.g., *HR* §§268-69; *HZ* §420; *MM* §595.

21. Charles, *Revelation of St. John*, 1:128-33; Ford, *Revelation*, 72-73; Mounce, *Book of Revelation*, 121-22; Aune, *Revelation 1-5*, 287-92.

4. The Fall of Wicked Rome

Finally, the book of Revelation and an episode in the *Hekhalot Rabbati* that retells the legend of the ten martyrs[22] both present gloating fantasies of the humiliation and destruction of Rome. Revelation tells us that the end of the dragon, or Satan, will be to be cast from heaven with his angels for persecuting the saints (Rev. 12:7-9, 12). Likewise Samma'el, the wicked patron angel of Rome, is to be slaughtered and hurled down with all the princes of the kingdoms on high for persecuting Israel (*HR* §108). In Revelation 13:1-2, 5-8, the dragon gives the beast, who is widely regarded to be a Roman emperor (Rev. 17:11),[23] authority, and the beast in turn is given leave to persecute the saints. In *HR* §§108-9, Samma'el reaches an agreement with the heavenly law court that permits him to inspire the apocryphal emperor Lupinus Caesar to persecute the sages of Israel. In Revelation 16 the actions of the dragon and the beast lead to heavenly punishment in the form of the seven bowls of God's wrath, commencing with the infliction of a foul and evil ulcer (*helkos*) on the followers of the beast (16:2). In *HR* §110 God writes the punishments of Rome down on a blank parchment, commencing with a cloud that hovers over Rome and inflicts a raw ulcer (*shekhin poreakh*) on its inhabitants (cf. Exod. 9:10-11; Job 2:7: *shekhin*, LXX *helkos*).[24] Nevertheless, both the followers of the beast (Rev. 16:9, 11) and Lupinus Caesar (*HR* §117-18) refuse to relent (cf. Exod. 9:12).

In Revelation 17:16-18, in accordance with the providence of God, the beast turns on Rome (the great harlot). In *HR* §120, God miraculously replaces

---

22. The very complicated manuscript tradition of *The Story of the Ten Martyrs* has been edited by Gottfried Reeg in *Die Geschichte von den Zehn Märtyrern: Synoptische Edition mit Übersetzung und Einleitung*, Texte und Studien zum Antiken Judentum 10 (Tübingen: Mohr Siebeck, 1985). The relationship of this material to the passage in the *Hekhalot Rabbati* has been thoroughly and sensitively examined by Ra'anan S. Boustan in *From Martyr to Mystic: Rabbinic Martyrology and the Making of Merkavah Mysticism*, Texte und Studien zum Antiken Judentum 112 (Tübingen: Mohr Siebeck, 2005). For the early Byzantine-era cultural context of the Hekhalot version of the story, see Boustan, "Immolating Emperors: Spectacles of Imperial Suffering and the Making of a Jewish Minority Culture in Late Antiquity," *BibInt* 17 (2009): 207-38, esp. 231-37.

23. Charles, *Revelation of St. John*, 2:70-71; Ford, *Revelation*, 281-82, 288-91; Mounce, *Book of Revelation*, 317-18; David E. Aune, *Revelation 17-22*, Word Biblical Commentary 52C (Dallas: Word, 1998), 945-50. There is debate whether the beast is one of the historical emperors, especially *Nero redivivus*, or a future emperor-Antichrist. Some connection with the *Nero rediturus* or *Nero redivivus* myth is usually posited.

24. The plagues of the seven bowls of God's wrath in Revelation are much influenced by the ten plagues of the Exodus. See Charles, *Revelation of St. John*, 2:43-46; Ford, *Revelation*, 265-75; Mounce, *Book of Revelation*, 291-97; Aune, *Revelation 6-16*, 883-90.

Lupinus Caesar with R. Nehuniah ben HaQanah, who takes on the emperor's physical appearance and proceeds to slaughter the military leadership of Rome. In Revelation 18:1, 6, 8, an angel announces the punishment of Rome including plagues and pestilence, paralleling the further plagues and pestilence inflicted on Rome by a second malevolent cloud in *HR* §110. In Revelation 18:9-19, Rome is humiliated before the kings of the earth, the merchants, and the shipmasters. In *HR* §110 Rome's afflictions make her accounted not worth a single coin, and in *HR* §112-13 Lupinus Caesar is humiliated before the officials of his kingdom when his family and the members of his court are thrown down and torn apart by divine decree. Moreover, the bodies are left to lie desecrated and decomposing because the Deep or Abyss (which also figures, as "the Pit of the Abyss," in Rev. 9:1-11 and 20:1-3 as a source of divine judgment) swallows them up when someone tries to collect them for burial, then expels them again when the recovery effort is abandoned. Likewise the corpses of the defeated enemies of the Lamb are left desecrated as food for the birds in Revelation 19:17-18, 21.

Revelation 18:12-13 lists twenty-eight wares of the merchants whose business is now collapsing with the fall of Rome. A similar, briefer list of the riches of Rome ruined by the malevolent cloud is found in *HR* §110. The latter refers to human beings, cattle, silver, gold, fruit, and vessels of cast metal, corresponding more or less to the gold, silver, vessels of bronze and iron, cattle and sheep, and slaves ("human souls") listed in Revelation 18:12-13 (cf. the fruit [*opōra*] mentioned in v. 14). Both lists are influenced by the list of the wares of the merchants of Tyre in Ezekiel 27:12-24, which include silver, human beings, vessels of bronze, wrought iron, foodstuffs, gold, and lambs, rams, and goats. The long list in Revelation constitutes a meticulous critique of the extravagant economic exploitation of the empire by Rome.[25] The function of the list in the *Hekhalot Rabbati* is less obvious. It is clearly meant to encapsulate Rome's wealth, but its dependence on Ezekiel 27 also may hint at criticism of the economic excesses of Roman trade.

In Revelation 18:20, the saints, apostles, and prophets are directed by an angel to rejoice over God's imminent judgment of Rome, while in *HR* §111, R. Ishmael returns from his descent to the chariot with the testimony of the angel Suriah, with the result that all his companions throw a party to celebrate God's coming vengeance on Rome. Finally, in Revelation 19:20 the ultimate

---

25. Richard Bauckham, "The Economic Critique of Rome in Revelation 18," in *Images of Empire*, ed. Loveday Alexander, Journal for the Study of the Old Testament Supplement Series 122 (Sheffield: Sheffield Academic, 1991), 47-90.

fate of the beast is to be thrown into the lake of fire that burns with sulfur.[26] In *HR* §§119–20, in what almost reads as a horrific parody of the *Nero redivivus* myth, Lupinus Caesar is given the physical appearance of each of the ten sages he sentenced to death, then "they threw him into the fire and he was in the asphyxiation within the burning." After one execution, he is resurrected, given the appearance of the next sage, and burned to death again, until he has been executed as each of the ten sages. He is then consigned to a well-deserved eternal torment where he must "taste the taste of flame and fire and the glowing coals of the cherubim, the ophannim, and the holy living creatures in the midst of Gehinnom"[27] (*HR* §119).

5. Conclusions

What should we make of all these parallels, which I have collected above without a great deal of synthetic analysis? Broadly speaking, the common use of both scriptural themes and specific scriptural passages in Revelation and the Hekhalot literature explains many of them. Sometimes the inspiration is thematic rather than relying on the wording of a particular scriptural passage. Visionary and prophetic literature takes it for granted that the visionary or prophet will testify on earth to what he or she has seen. And visionary literature of the Second Temple period and later includes revelations of future events, ascents to heaven, tours of the universe, and tours of the underworld and the realm of the dead. The falls of Satan and Samma'el may be indirectly inspired by the fall of the Day Star in Isaiah 14:12–20 and perhaps of the prince of Tyre in Ezekiel 28. Scriptural traditions about the Deep or Abyss (*tehom*) inform its appearances in both texts, but the development is quite different, with it acting as the agent of God's judgment in the *Hekhalot Rabbati* but appearing as a place that is a source of God's judgment in Revelation.

But often the texts are inspired by specific scriptural passages whose wording they echo. Both Revelation and the Hekhalot literature adapt scriptural theomorphic and angelomorphic traits in their descriptions of an angel (the Youth) or divinized human beings (Enoch and Jesus). But the implications of

---

26. Untypically for apocalypses produced before the fourth and fifth centuries, Revelation narrates the post-mortem torment and damnation of a specific Roman emperor: the beast (widely understood to be Nero). But later descriptions of the fates of specific figures such as Lupinus are presented in lurid detail considerably beyond what we find in Revelation. See Boustan, "Immolating Emperors," 210–21, 227–31.

27. That is, Gehenna.

these echoes are rather different. John forbids human prostration to an angel, but he prostrates himself before Jesus. Enoch/Metatron receives angelic prostration, but he is severely punished when a human being mistakes him for a second power in heaven. Human prostration before the Youth is forbidden, and the angels stand before him as they worship God together.

Likewise there is a shared use of scriptural passages to construct a picture of the divine throne room. Since the details are scriptural, the descriptions are similar in many ways, but the specifics are often quite different. For example, Revelation amalgamates the angelic living creatures, cherubim, and seraphim into a single quartet, while the Hekhalot literature keeps them separate. Elements of the ten plagues of the Exodus also inspire the two descriptions of the projected fall of Rome, but Revelation is more systematic and comprehensive in its use of these traditions. The mercantile trafficking of Ezekiel's Tyre inspires the two descriptions of Rome as well; but again, Revelation uses more of the material and with a better-defined agenda of condemnation. A midrashic development of Ezekiel's "terrible ice" is behind both Revelation's sea of glass and the ethereal paving of the sixth palace in the Hekhalot literature, but only the latter adapts it as a test for the aspiring visitor to the divine throne room.

Both Revelation and the version of the account of the ten martyrs found in the *Hekhalot Rabbati* also show an intense hostility toward Rome. But this hostility arose from somewhat different social situations, of Christians in the first century, and of Jews in late antiquity, both involving a real or perceived persecution by Roman authorities. Given these similar backgrounds, hostility toward Rome and its emperor follows naturally in both cases, as do the lurid fantasies of the emperor's torment and the rejoicing over his imagined downfall and damnation. Moreover, many but not all of the parallels between Revelation and the *Hekhalot Rabbati* explored in section 4 above also appear in the *Story of the Ten Martyrs* on which the latter is more or less based. I say "more or less" because the relationship between them is complex, and the former seems also to have exerted a significant influence on the surviving text of the latter, so we should perhaps not make too much of the use by the *Hekhalot Rabbati* of the other work.[28]

The pattern of parallels between the book of Revelation and the Hekhalot literature is notable and pervasive while at the same time curiously fragmented. They share numerous themes and motifs, but the authors make these themes and motifs entirely their own. They are bricoleurs drawing from sev-

28. See Boustan, *From Martyr to Mystic*, 211–43.

eral common heaps of material. These include trance states, perhaps induced by some ritual praxis; visionary ascent in the tradition of apocalyptic visions; a panorama of the celestial throne room inspired by much the same set of prophetic passages from the Jewish scriptures, including Ezekiel 1 and 10, Isaiah 6, and Daniel 7; mediatorial traditions about angels and deified human beings; and the fantasy of a future divine punishment of Rome, the pagan persecutor of God's people, drawing on the scriptural tradition of the plagues of Egypt and the trade of Tyre. The exegesis of specific motifs in these passages is for the most part independent, although there is some evidence for the sharing of more elaborate midrashic constructions, such as the transformation of Ezekiel's "terrible ice" into a celestial floor.

It is impossible to rule out some genetic influence of the book of Revelation on the much later Hekhalot literature, be it direct literary influence or, more speculatively, an influence bridged by a subterranean ancient Merkavah mystical or visionary tradition. But the evidence collected here offers little support for either possibility. Certainly the broader agendas of these works are quite different. Revelation is an apocalypse that aims to reassure the followers of Jesus that he will soon triumph over the evil Roman persecutors and grant his followers eternal life in heavenly bliss. The Hekhalot texts are instruction manuals for achieving altered states of consciousness that allow the practitioners to translate themselves into the celestial throne room and join in the angelic liturgy and to call down angels and compel them to grant these practitioners supernatural knowledge of Torah or other theurgic powers.

This is a brief and incomplete overview of evidence that deserves more study. Much can be explained by positing two authors in widely separated eras and circumstances who were interested in trance states, the heavenly realm, and traditions about exalted human beings and high angels; who wrote with an intense hostility toward Rome; and who drew on exegesis of many of the same scriptural themes and passages to construct narratives around their interests and viewpoints. It may be that authors sharing these basic interests could independently generate these parallels without any genetic connection between the works or the traditions they drew upon, and the evidence surveyed here suggests that this is a promising explanation of the parallels.

Bibliography

Publications by Richard Bauckham through December 2015

Books (Sole Author)

Bauckham, Richard. *2 Peter, Jude*. Word Biblical Commentary. Nashville: Thomas Nelson, 1983.
———. *Jude and the Relatives of Jesus in the Early Church*. Edinburgh: T&T Clark, 1990.
———. *The Theology of the Book of Revelation*. Cambridge: Cambridge University Press, 1993.
———. *The Theology of Jürgen Moltmann*. Edinburgh: T&T Clark, 1995.
———. *The Fate of the Dead: Studies on Jewish and Christian Apocalypses*. Supplements to Novum Testamentum. Leiden: Brill Academic, 1998.
———. *God Crucified: Monotheism and Christology in the New Testament*. Grand Rapids: Eerdmans, 1999.
———. *James: Wisdom of James, Disciple of Jesus the Sage*. New Testament Readings. New York: Routledge, 1999.
———. *The Climax of Prophecy: Studies on the Book of Revelation*. Edinburgh: T&T Clark, 2000.
———. *God and the Crisis of Freedom: Biblical and Contemporary Perspectives*. Louisville: Westminster John Knox, 2002.
———. *Gospel Women: Studies of the Named Women in the Gospels*. Grand Rapids: Eerdmans, 2002.
———. *Bible and Mission: Christian Mission in a Postmodern World*. Grand Rapids: Baker Academic, 2003.
———. *The Testimony of the Beloved Disciple: Narrative, History, and Theology in the Gospel of John*. Grand Rapids: Baker Academic, 2007.

———. *Jesus and the Eyewitnesses: The Gospels as Eyewitness Testimony*. Grand Rapids: Eerdmans, 2008.
———. *Jesus and the God of Israel: God Crucified and Other Studies on the New Testament's Christology of Divine Identity*. Grand Rapids: Eerdmans, 2008.
———. *Bible and Ecology: Rediscovering the Community of Creation*. Waco, TX: Baylor University Press, 2010.
———. *The Jewish World around the New Testament*. Grand Rapids: Baker Academic, 2010.
———. *The Bible and Politics: How to Read the Bible Politically*. 2nd ed. Louisville: Westminster John Knox, 2011.
———. *Jesus: A Very Short Introduction*. Oxford: Oxford University Press, 2011.
———. *Living with Other Creatures*. Milton Keynes, UK: Paternoster, 2012.
———. *The Bible in the Contemporary World: Hermeneutical Ventures*. Grand Rapids: Eerdmans, 2015.

Books (Coauthor)

Bauckham, Richard, R. P. C. Hanson, et al. *Hermias: Satire des Philosophes Paiens*. Paris: Les Éditions du Cerf, 1993.
Bauckham, Richard, and Trevor Hart. *Hope Against Hope: Christian Eschatology in Contemporary Context*. Grand Rapids: Eerdmans, 1999.
Bauckham, Richard, and Trevor Hart. *At the Cross: Meditations on People Who Were There*. Downers Grove, IL: IVP, 1999.
Bauckham, Richard, and Trevor Hart. *Finding God in the Midst of Life: Old Stories for Contemporary Readers*. Milton Keynes, UK: Paternoster, 2006.

Books (Editor)

Bauckham, Richard, ed. *Scripture, Tradition and Reason: A Study in the Criteria of Christian Doctrine: Essays in Honour of Richard P. C. Hanson*. Edinburgh: T&T Clark, 1988.
Bauckham, Richard, R. T. France, M. Maggay, J. Stamoulis, and C. P. Thiede, eds. *Jesus 2000*. Oxford: Lion, 1989.
Bauckham, Richard, and R. John Elford, eds. *The Nuclear Weapons Debate: Theological and Ethical Issues*. London: SCM, 1989.
Bauckham, Richard, ed. *The Book of Acts in Its Palestinian Setting*. Grand Rapids: Eerdmans, 1995.
Bauckham, Richard, ed. *The Gospel for All Christians: Rethinking the Gospel Audiences*. Grand Rapids: Eerdmans, 1998.
Bauckham, Richard, ed. *God Will Be All in All: The Eschatology of Jürgen Moltmann*. Minneapolis: Fortress, 1999.

Bauckham, Richard, and Carl Mosser, eds. *The Gospel of John and Christian Theology*. Grand Rapids: Eerdmans, 2008.
Bauckham, Richard, Daniel Driver, Trevor Hart, and Nathan MacDonald, eds. *A Cloud of Witnesses: The Theology of Hebrews in Its Ancient Context*. London: T&T Clark, 2008.
Bauckham, Richard, Daniel R. Driver, Trevor A. Hart, and Nathan MacDonald, eds. *The Epistle to the Hebrews and Christian Theology*. Grand Rapids: Eerdmans, 2009.
Bauckham, Richard, James Davila, and Alex Panayotov, eds. *Old Testament Pseudepigrapha: More Noncanonical Scriptures*. Grand Rapids: Eerdmans, 2013.

Articles and Essays

Bauckham, Richard. "Adding to the Church—in the Early American Period." In *Adding to the Church*, papers read at the 1973 Westminster Conference.
———. "The Great Tribulation in the *Shepherd of Hermas*." *Journal of Theological Studies* 25 (1974): 27-40.
———. "Colossians 1:24 Again: The Apocalyptic Motif." *Evangelical Quarterly* 47 (1975): 168-70.
———. "Marian Exiles and Cambridge Puritanism." *Journal of Ecclesiastical History* 26 (1975): 137-48.
———. "Science and Religion in the Writings of Dr William Fulke." *British Journal for the History of Science* 8, no. 28 (1975): 17-31.
———. "The Martyrdom of Enoch and Elijah: Jewish or Christian?" *Journal of Biblical Literature* 95 (1976): 447-58.
———. "Synoptic Parousia Parables and the Apocalypse." *New Testament Studies* 23 (1976-77): 162-76.
———. "The Eschatological Earthquake in the Apocalypse of John." *Novum Testamentum* 19 (1977): 224-33.
———. "Moltmann's Eschatology of the Cross." *Scottish Journal of Theology* 30 (1977): 301-11. Translated as "Moltmanns Eschatologie des Kreuzes" in *Diskussion über Jürgen Moltmanns Buch "Der gekreuzigte Gott,"* edited by Michael Welker, 43-53. Munich: Chr. Kaiser, 1979.
———. "Theologians of Hope: Moltmann and Pannenberg." *Christian Graduate* 30 (1977): 112-13.
———. "Hooker, Travers and the Church of Rome in the 1580s." *Journal of Ecclesiastical History* 29 (1978): 37-50.
———. "The Rise of Apocalyptic." *Themelios* 3, no. 2 (1978): 10-23; reprinted in *Solid Ground: 25 Years of Evangelical Theology*, edited by C. R. Trueman, A. J. Gray, and C. L. Blomberg, 43-68. Leicester: Inter-Varsity, 2000.
———. "The Sonship of the Historical Jesus in Christology." *Scottish Journal of Theology* 31 (1978): 245-60.
———. "Barnabas in Galatians." *Journal for the Study of the New Testament* 2 (1979): 61-70.

———. "Believing in the Incarnation Today." *Evangelical Review of Theology* 3 (1979): 3-10; reprinted in *Christian Graduate* 32 (1979): 15-18.
———. "Reformed Theology and Concrete Churches." *International Reformed Bulletin* 76 (1979): 19-22.
———. "Universalism—A Historical Survey." *Themelios* 4 (1979): 48-54.
———. "Apocalyptic," "Enoch," "Eschatology," "Gabriel," "Jubilees, Book of." In *The Illustrated Bible Dictionary*, edited by J. D. Douglas, Part 1, 73-75, 458, 470-76, 532; Part 2, 821. Leicester: Inter-Varsity, 1980.
———. "The Delay of the Parousia." *Tyndale Bulletin* 31 (1980): 3-36.
———. "The *Figurae* of John of Patmos." In *Prophecy and Millenarianism: Essays in Honour of Marjorie Reeves*, edited by Ann Williams, 107-25. London: Longman, 1980.
———. "History and Eschatology." *The TRACI Journal* (New Delhi) 18 (December 1980): 45-53.
———. "Jürgen Moltmann." In *One God in Trinity*, edited by P. Toon and J. D. Spiceland, 111-32. London: Bagster, 1980.
———. "The Role of the Spirit in the Apocalypse." *Evangelical Quarterly* 52 (1980): 66-83.
———. "The Worship of Jesus in Apocalyptic Christianity." *New Testament Studies* 27 (1980-81): 322-41.
———. "Chiliasmus IV: Reformation und Neuzeit." In *Theologische Realenzyklopädie*, vol. 7, 737-45. Berlin: De Gruyter, 1981.
———. "A Note on a Problem in the Greek Version of I Enoch i.9." *Journal of Theological Studies* 32 (1981): 136-38.
———. "Richard Hooker and John Calvin: A Comment." *Journal of Ecclesiastical History* 32 (1981): 29-33.
———. "The Lord's Day," "Sabbath and Sunday in the Post-Apostolic Church," "Sabbath and Sunday in the Protestant Tradition." In *From Sabbath to Lord's Day: A Biblical, Historical, and Theological Investigation*, edited by D. A. Carson, 221-50, 251-98, 299-310, 311-42. Grand Rapids: Zondervan; Exeter, UK: Paternoster, 1982.
———. "2 Peter: A Supplementary Bibliography." *Journal of the Evangelical Theological Society* 25 (1982): 91-93.
———. "Weakness—Paul's and Ours." *Themelios* 7, no. 3 (1982): 4-6.
———. "The *Liber Antiquitatum Biblicarum* of Pseudo-Philo and the Gospels as 'Midrash.'" In *Gospel Perspectives 3: Studies in Midrash and Historiography*, edited by R. T. France and D. Wenham, 33-76. Sheffield: JSOT Press, 1983.
———. "Recent Literature on the Doctrine of the Holy Spirit." *Epworth Review* 10 (1983): 89-95.
———. "Synoptic Parousia Parables Again." *New Testament Studies* 29 (1983): 129-34.
———. "'Only the Suffering God Can Help': Divine Passibility in Modern Theology." *Themelios* 9, no. 3 (1984): 6-12.
———. "Using the Bible to Do Politics." A series of seven articles in *Third Way* 7/10-8/5 (November 1984-May 1985).

―――. "Enoch and Elijah in the Coptic Apocalypse of Elijah." In *Studia Patristica*, vol. 16, part II, edited by E. A. Livingstone, 69–76. Berlin: Akademie-Verlag, 1985.

―――. "The Fall of the Angels as the Source of Philosophy in Hermias and Clement of Alexandria." *Vigiliae Christianae* 39 (1985): 313–30.

―――. "The Genesis Flood and the Nuclear Holocaust: A Hermeneutical Reflection." *Churchman* 99 (1985): 146–55.

―――. "The Son of Man: 'A Man in My Position' or 'Someone'?" *Journal for the Study of the New Testament* 23 (1985): 23–33.

―――. "The Study of Gospel Traditions outside the Canonical Gospels: Problems and Prospects," "A Bibliography of Recent Work on Gospel Traditions outside the Canonical Gospels." In *Gospel Perspectives 5: The Jesus Tradition outside the Gospels*, edited by D. Wenham, 369–403, 405–19. Sheffield: JSOT Press, 1985.

―――. "The Two Fig Tree Parables in the Apocalypse of Peter." *Journal of Biblical Literature* 104 (1985): 269–87.

―――. "The Apocalypses in the New Pseudepigrapha." *Journal for the Study of the New Testament* 26 (1986): 97–117; reprinted (with minor revisions) in *New Testament Backgrounds: A Sheffield Reader*, edited by C. A. Evans and S. E. Porter, 67–88. Biblical Seminar 43. Sheffield: Sheffield Academic, 1997.

―――. "Approaching the Apocalypse." In *Decide for Peace: Evangelicals against the Bomb*, edited by D. Mills-Powell, 88–98. London: Marshall Pickering, 1986.

―――. "Bibliography: Jürgen Moltmann." *Modern Churchman* 28 (1986): 55–60.

―――. "The Coin in the Fish's Mouth." In *Gospel Perspectives 6: The Miracles of Jesus*, edited by D. Wenham and C. Blomberg, 219–52. Sheffield: JSOT Press, 1986.

―――. "First Steps to a Theology of Nature." *Evangelical Quarterly* 58 (1986): 229–44.

―――. "The Ordination of Women." *Home Words* (January 1986): 8–9, 16; reprinted as a pamphlet: *The Ordination of Women*. London: Movement for the Ordination of Women, 1986.

―――. "Theology after Hiroshima." *Scottish Journal of Theology* 38 (1986): 583–601.

―――. "The Bishops and the Virginal Conception." *Churchman* 101 (1987): 323–33.

―――. "Jesus—God with Us" (with Rowan Williams). In *Stepping Stones*, edited by Christina Baxter, 21–41. London: Hodder & Stoughton, 1987.

―――. "The Parable of the Vine: Rediscovering a Lost Parable of Jesus." *New Testament Studies* 33 (1987): 84–101.

―――. "Review Article: The Old Testament Pseudepigrapha." *Evangelical Quarterly* 59 (1987): 147–52.

―――. "Teología después de Hiroshima." *Selecciones de Teología* 26 (1987): 163–75 (abbreviated version in Spanish of "Theology after Hiroshima").

―――. "Theodicy from Ivan Karamazov to Moltmann." *Modern Theology* 4 (1987): 83–97.

―――. "Anonymous Christianity," "Antichrist," "Apocalyptic," "Cross, Theology of," "Descent into Hell," "Hooker, Richard," "Ignatius of Loyola," "Joachimism," "Küng, Hans," "Lonergan, Bernard," "Millennium," "Moltmann, Jürgen," "Rahner, Karl," "Schillebeeckx, Edward," "Sölle, Dorothee," "Vision of God." In *New Dictionary of Christian Theology*, edited by S. B. Ferguson and D. F. Wright, 31–32, 33–35, 181–83,

194-95, 319-21, 327, 351-52, 373-74, 397-98, 428-30, 439-40, 556-57, 617-18, 651, 710-11. Leicester: Inter-Varsity, 1988.

———. "The Book of Revelation as a Christian War Scroll." *Neotestamentica* 22 (1988): 17-40.

———. "Christology Today." *Scriptura* 27 (1988): 20-28.

———. "Evolution and Creation: (9) in Moltmann's Doctrine of Creation." *Epworth Review* 15 (1988): 74-81.

———. "James, 1 and 2 Peter, Jude." In *It Is Written: Scripture Citing Scripture: Essays in Honour of Barnabas Lindars, SSF*, edited by D. A. Carson and H. G. M. Williamson, 303-17. Cambridge: Cambridge University Press, 1988.

———. "Jesus' Demonstration in the Temple." In *Law and Religion: Essays on the Place of the Law in Israel and Early Christianity*, edited by B. Lindars, 72-89. Cambridge: James Clarke, 1988.

———. "Pseudo-Apostolic Letters." *Journal of Biblical Literature* 107, no. 3 (1988): 469-94.

———. "Tradition in Relation to Scripture and Reason." In *Scripture, Tradition and Reason: A Study in the Criteria of Christian Doctrine: Essays in Honour of Richard P. C. Hanson*, edited by R. Bauckham and B. Drewery, 117-45. Edinburgh: T&T Clark, 1988.

———. "2 Peter: An Account of Research," "Jude: An Account of Research," "The Apocalypse of Peter: An Account of Research." In *Aufstieg und Niedergang der römischen Welt*, ed. H. Temporini and W. Haase, part II, vol. 25, no. 5, 3713-52, 3791-3826; no. 6, 4712-50. Berlin/New York: De Gruyter, 1988.

———. "Facing the Future: The Challenge to Theological and Secular Presuppositions," and "In Place of a Conclusion." In *The Nuclear Weapons Debate: Theological and Ethical Issues*, edited by Richard Bauckham and R. John Elford, 29-46, 213-16, 219-22. London: SCM, 1989.

———. "Ignatius and the Exercises," "The Imitation of Christ," "Francis of Assisi," "The Martyrs," "The Human Jesus," "God in a Human Life," and "The Finality of Jesus." In *Jesus 2000*, edited by R. Bauckham, R. T. France, M. Maggay, J. Stamoulis, and C. P. Thiede, 100-101, 127, 140, 166-67, 204-5, 214-19, 233-35. Oxford: Lion, 1989.

———. "Jürgen Moltmann." In *The Modern Theologians: An Introduction to Christian Theology of the Twentieth Century*, vol. 1, edited by D. F. Ford, 293-310. Oxford: Blackwell, 1989.

———. "Moltmann's Theology of Hope Revisited." *Scottish Journal of Theology* 42 (1989): 199-214.

———. "The Origins and Growth of Western Mariology." In *Chosen by God: Mary in Evangelical Perspective*, edited by D. F. Wright, 141-60. London: Marshall Pickering, 1989.

———. "Theology, Apartheid and Hope" (review article). *Third Way* 12, no. 3 (March 1989): 26-28.

———. "The Conflict of Justice and Mercy: Attitudes to the Damned in Apocalyptic Literature." *Apocrypha* 1 (1990): 181-96.

———. "In Defence of *The Crucified God*." In *The Power and Weakness of God: Impassi-*

bility and Orthodoxy, edited by N. M. de S. Cameron, 93-118. Scottish Bulletin of Evangelical Theology Special Study 4. Edinburgh: Rutherford House Books, 1990.

———. "Early Jewish Visions of Hell." *Journal of Theological Studies* 41 (1990): 355-85.

———. "The Economic Critique of Rome in Revelation 18." In *Images of Empire*, edited by L. Alexander, 47-90. JSOT Supplement Series 122. Sheffield: Sheffield Academic, 1991.

———. "The List of the Tribes in Revelation 7 Again." *Journal for the Study of the New Testament* 42 (1991): 99-115.

———. "Moltmann's Messianic Christology." *Scottish Journal of Theology* 44 (1991): 519-31.

———. "More on Kainam the Son of Arpachshad in Luke's Genealogy." *Ephemerides Theologicae Lovanienses* 67 (1991): 95-103.

———. "The Rich Man and Lazarus: The Parable and the Parallels." *New Testament Studies* 37 (1991): 225-46.

———. "Salome the Sister of Jesus, Salome the Disciple of Jesus, and the Secret Gospel of Mark." *Novum Testamentum* 33, no. 3 (1991): 245-75.

———. "Descent to the Underworld," "Hades, Hell," "Jesus, Worship of," "Jude, Epistle of," "Spirits in Prison," "Virgin, Apocalypses of the." In *The Anchor Bible Dictionary*, edited by D. N. Freedman, 2:145-59; 3:14-15, 812-19, 1098-1103; 6:177-78, 854-56. New York: Doubleday, 1992.

———. "Gospels (Apocryphal)." In *Dictionary of Jesus and the Gospels*, edited by J. B. Green, S. McKnight, and I. H. Marshall, 286-91. Downers Grove, IL/Leicester: InterVarsity, 1992.

———. "The Martyrdom of Peter in Early Christian Literature." In *Aufstieg und Niedergang der römischen Welt*, part II, vol. 26, no. 1, edited by W. Haase, 539-95. Berlin/New York: De Gruyter, 1992.

———. "Mary of Clopas (John 19:25)." In *Women in the Biblical Tradition*, edited by G. J. Brooke, 231-55. Lewiston, NY: Edwin Mellen, 1992.

———. "Recent Books on Christology." *Theology Themes* (Northern Baptist College, Manchester) 1 (1992): 20-21.

———. "A Quotation from *4Q Second Ezekiel* in the *Apocalypse of Peter*." *Revue de Qumran* 59 (1992): 437-46.

———. "The Acts of Paul as a Sequel to Acts." In *The Book of Acts in Its Ancient Literary Setting*, edited by B. C. Winter and A. D. Clarke, 105-52. Grand Rapids: Eerdmans; Carlisle, UK: Paternoster, 1993.

———. "The *Apocalypse of the Seven Heavens*: The Latin Version." *Apocrypha* 4 (1993): 141-75.

———. "Apocryphal Pauline Literature." In *Dictionary of Paul and His Letters*, edited by G. F. Hawthorne and R. P. Martin, 35-37. Downers Grove, IL: IVP, 1993.

———. "The Beloved Disciple as Ideal Author." *Journal for the Study of the New Testament* 49 (1993): 21-44; reprinted in *The Johannine Writings*, edited by S. E. Porter and C. A. Evans, 46-68. Biblical Seminar 32. Sheffield: Sheffield Academic, 1995.

———. "God Who Raises the Dead: The Resurrection of Jesus in Relation to Early

Christian Faith in God." In *The Resurrection of Jesus Christ*, edited by Paul D. L. Avis, 136-54. London: Darton, Longman & Todd, 1993.

———. "Jude, The Letter of," "Peter, The Second Letter of." In *The Oxford Companion to the Bible*, edited by B. M. Metzger and M. D. Coogan, 395-97, 586-88. New York: Oxford University Press, 1993.

———. "Jürgen Moltmann." In *Theologen der Gegenwart*, edited by D. Ford, 272-87. Paderborn: F. Schöningh, 1993.

———. "Moltmann, Jürgen." In *The Blackwell Encyclopaedia of Modern Christian Thought*, edited by A. E. McGrath, 385-88. Oxford: Blackwell, 1993.

———. "Papias and Polycrates on the Origin of the Fourth Gospel." *Journal of Theological Studies* 44 (1993): 24-69.

———. "The Parting of the Ways: What Happened and Why." *Studia Theologica* 47 (1993): 135-51.

———. "Resurrection as Giving Back the Dead: A Traditional Image of Resurrection in the Pseudepigrapha and the Apocalypse of John." In *The Pseudepigrapha and Early Biblical Interpretation*, edited by J. H. Charlesworth and C. A. Evans, 269-91. Studies in Scripture in Early Judaism and Christianity 2, JSPSS 14. Sheffield: JSOT Press, 1993.

———. "The Second Letter of Peter" and "The Letter of Jude." In *The HarperCollins Study Bible*, edited by W. A. Meeks, 2286-91, 2304-6. New York: HarperCollins, 1993.

———. "The *Apocalypse of Peter*: A Jewish Christian Apocalypse from the Time of Bar Kokhba." *Apocrypha* 5 (1994): 7-111.

———. "The Brothers and Sisters of Jesus: An Epiphanian Response to John P. Meier." *Catholic Biblical Quarterly* 56, no. 4 (1994): 686-700.

———. "Jesus and the Wild Animals (Mark 1:13): A Christological Image for an Ecological Age." In *Jesus of Nazareth, Lord and Christ: Essays on the Historical Jesus and New Testament Christology*. Festschrift for I. Howard Marshall. Edited by J. B. Green and M. Turner, 3-21. Grand Rapids: Eerdmans, 1994.

———. "The Nature of Evil: The Unholy Trinity." *Third Way* 17, no. 10 (December 1994): 16.

———. "Se confronter au futur: Le défi aux présuppositions séculières et théologiques." In *Temps et Eschatologie: Données bibliques et problématiques contemporaines*, ed. J.-L. Leuba, 347-71. Paris: Éditions du Cerf, 1994.

———. "God in the Book of Revelation." *Proceedings of the Irish Biblical Association* 18 (1995): 40-53.

———. "Heinrich Bullinger, the Apocalypse and the English." In *The Swiss Connection: Manchester Essays on Religious Connections between England and Switzerland between the 16th and 20th Centuries*, edited by H. D. Rack, 9-54. Department of Religions and Theology, University of Manchester, 1995.

———. "James and the Jerusalem Church." In *The Book of Acts in Its Palestinian Setting*, edited by R. Bauckham, 415-80. Carlisle, UK: Paternoster; Grand Rapids: Eerdmans, 1995.

———. "James at the Centre." *EPTA Bulletin: The Journal of the European Pentecostal Theological Association* 14 (1995): 23-33; also in Society for the Study of Early Christianity (Macquarie University) *Newsletter* 39 (February 2001): 3-7.

———. "James at the Centre: A Jerusalem Perspective on the New Testament: Inaugural Lecture as Professor of New Testament Studies Delivered on 17 March 1994." *St Mary's College Bulletin* 37 (1995): 46–60.

———. "The Messianic Interpretation of Isaiah 10:34 in the Dead Sea Scrolls, 2 Baruch and the Preaching of John the Baptist." *Dead Sea Discoveries* 2 (1995): 202–16.

———. "Politics." In *New Dictionary of Christian Ethics and Pastoral Theology*, edited by D. J. Atkinson and D. H. Field, 669–72. Leicester: Inter-Varsity, 1995.

———. "The Relevance of Extra-Canonical Jewish Texts to New Testament Study." In *Hearing the New Testament*, edited by Joel B. Green, 90–108. Grand Rapids: Eerdmans; Carlisle, UK: Paternoster, 1995. Revised version in *Hearing the New Testament: Strategies for Interpretation*, 2nd ed., edited by Joel B. Green, 65–84. Grand Rapids: Eerdmans, 2010.

———. "Tamar's Ancestry and Rahab's Marriage: Two Problems in the Matthean Genealogy." *Novum Testamentum* 37, no. 4 (1995): 313–29.

———. "Tragedy and Religion." In *"Iris Murdoch's Giffords": A Study of the 1982 Gifford Lectures*, edited by R. Gillies, 41–44. Theology in Scotland Occasional Paper 1. St Andrews: St Mary's College, University of St Andrews, 1995.

———. "Visiting the Places of the Dead in the Extra-Canonical Apocalypses." *Proceedings of the Irish Biblical Association* 18 (1995): 78–93.

———. "Apocalyptic," "Enoch," "Eschatology," "Gabriel," "Jubilees, Book of," "Lazarus." In *The New Bible Dictionary: Third Edition*, edited by J. D. Douglas, N. Hillyer, and D. R. W. Wood, 53–54, 324–25, 333–39, 389, 616, 678–79. Leicester: Inter-Varsity; Downers Grove, IL: IVP, 1996.

———. "James and the Gentiles (Acts 15.13–21)," "Kerygmatic Summaries in the Speeches of Acts." In *History, Literature and Society in the Book of Acts*, edited by B. Witherington III, 154–84, 185–217. Cambridge: Cambridge University Press, 1996.

———. "Josephus' Account of the Temple in *Contra Apionem* 2.102–109." In *Josephus' Contra Apionem: Studies in Its Character and Context with a Latin Concordance to the Portion Missing in Greek*, edited by L. H. Feldman and J. R. Levison, 327–47. Arbeiten zur Geschichte des antiken Judentums und des Urchristentums 34. Leiden: Brill, 1996.

———. "Jürgen Moltmann." In *The Modern Theologians: An Introduction to Christian Theology in the Twentieth Century*, revised ed., edited by D. F. Ford, 209–24. Oxford: Blackwell, 1996.

———. "Kingdom and Church according to Jesus and Paul." *Horizons in Biblical Theology* 18 (1996): 1–26.

———. "Meditation: Good Friday." *Church Times* (4 April 1996): 12.

———. "Millenarianism." In *Dictionary of Ethics, Theology and Society*, edited by P. B. Clarke and A. Linzey, 565–69. London/New York: Routledge, 1996.

———. "The New Age Theology of Matthew Fox: A Christian Theological Response." *Anvil* 13, no. 2 (1996): 115–26.

———. "Nicodemus and the Gurion Family." *Journal of Theological Studies* 46 (1996): 1–37.

———. "The Parable of the Royal Wedding Feast (Matthew 22:1–14) and the Parable of the Lame Man and the Blind Man (*Apocryphon of Ezekiel*)." *Journal of Biblical Literature* 115, no. 3 (1996): 447-64.

———. "The Relatives of Jesus." *Themelios* 21, no. 2 (1996): 18-21.

———. "The Relevance of Revelation." *Catalyst* 22, no. 4 (1996): 1-3.

———. "The *Acts of Paul*: Replacement of Acts or Sequel to Acts?" *Semeia* 80 (1997): 159-68.

———. "Anna of the Tribe of Asher (Luke 2:36-38)." *Revue Biblique* 104 (1997): 161-91.

———. "Apocalypse de Pierre." In *Écrits apocryphes chrétiens*, vol. 1, edited by F. Bovon and P. Geoltrain, 745-74. Bibliothèque de la Pléiade. Paris: Gallimard, 1997.

———. "Apocryphal and Pseudepigraphal Literature," "2 Peter," "Relatives of Jesus." In *Dictionary of the Later New Testament and Its Developments*, edited by R. P. Martin and P. H. Davids, 68-73, 923-27, 1004-6. Downers Grove, IL: IVP, 1997; "2 Peter," reprinted in *The IVP Dictionary of the New Testament*, edited by D. G. Reid, 861-65. Downers Grove, IL: IVP, 2004.

———. "The Book of Ruth and the Possibility of a Feminist Canonical Hermeneutic." *Biblical Interpretation* 5, no. 1 (1997): 29-45.

———. "Egalitarianism and Hierarchy in the Biblical Traditions." In *The Interpretation of the Bible: Historical and Theological Studies in Honour of David F. Wright*, edited by A. N. S. Lane, 259-73. Leicester: Apollos, 1997.

———. "For Whom Were Gospels Written?" "John for Readers of Mark." In *The Gospels for All Christians: Rethinking the Gospel Audiences*, edited by R. Bauckham, 9-48, 147-71. Grand Rapids: Eerdmans; Edinburgh: T&T Clark, 1997.

———. "James, 1 Peter, Jude and 2 Peter." In *A Vision for the Church: Studies in Early Christian Ecclesiology in Honour of J. P. M. Sweet*, edited by M. Bockmuehl and M. B. Thompson, 153-66. Edinburgh: T&T Clark, 1997.

———. "Jesus the Revelation of God." In *Divine Revelation*, edited by Paul Avis, 174-200. London: Darton, Longman & Todd; Grand Rapids: Eerdmans, 1997.

———. "Jürgen Moltmann's *The Trinity and the Kingdom of God* and the Question of Pluralism." In *The Trinity in a Pluralistic Age: Theological Essays on Culture and Religion*, edited by K. J. Vanhoozer, 155-64. Grand Rapids: Eerdmans, 1997.

———. "Moltmann, Jürgen." In *The Oxford Dictionary of the Christian Church*, 3rd ed., edited by F. L. Cross and E. A. Livingstone, 1101. Oxford: Oxford University Press, 1997.

———. "Must Christian Eschatology Be Millenarian? A Response to Jürgen Moltmann" (Tyndale Christian Doctrine Lecture for 1997). In *'The Reader Must Understand': Eschatology in Bible and Theology*, edited by K. E. Brower and M. W. Elliott, 263-77. Leicester: Apollos, 1997.

———. "Qumran and the Fourth Gospel: Is There a Connection?" In *The Scrolls and the Scriptures: Qumran Fifty Years After*, edited by S. E. Porter and C. A. Evans, 267-79. Journal for the Study of the Pseudepigrapha Supplement Series 26; Roehampton Institute London Papers 3. Sheffield: Sheffield Academic, 1997.

———. "Ecologie." In *Dictionnaire critique de Théologie*, edited by J.-Y. Lacoste, 364-65. Paris: Presses Universitaires de France, 1998.

———. "The Future of Jesus Christ (Finlayson Memorial Lecture 1998)." *Scottish Bulletin of Evangelical Theology* 16 (1998): 97-110; reprinted in *The Only Hope: Jesus Yesterday,*

Today, Forever, edited by M. Elliott and J. L. McPake, 203-19. Fearn: Christian Focus Publications; Edinburgh: Rutherford House, 2001.

———. "Jesus and Animals I: What Did He Teach?" and "Jesus and Animals II: What Did He Practise?" In *Animals on the Agenda: Questions about Animals for Theology and Ethics,* edited by A. Linzey and D. Yamamoto, 33-60. London: SCM, 1998.

———. "Jews and Jewish Christians in the Land of Israel at the Time of the Bar Kochba War, with Special Reference to the Apocalypse of Peter." In *Tolerance and Intolerance in Early Judaism and Christianity,* edited by G. N. Stanton and G. G. Strousma, 228-38. Cambridge: Cambridge University Press, 1998.

———. "Lamb," "Lion," "Pillar," "Seven," "Swine." In *Dictionary of Biblical Imagery,* edited by L. Ryken, J. C. Wilhoit, and T. Longman III, 484, 514-15, 645-46, 774-75, 834-35. Downers Grove, IL: IVP, 1998.

———. "Life, Death, and the Afterlife in Second Temple Judaism." In *Life in the Face of Death: The Resurrection Message of the New Testament,* edited by R. Longenecker, 80-95. Grand Rapids: Eerdmans, 1998.

———. "Response to Philip Esler." *Scottish Journal of Theology* 51 (1998): 253-49.

———. "Scripture and Authority." *Transformation* 15, no. 2 (1998): 5-11.

———. "The Scrupulous Priest and the Good Samaritan: Jesus' Parabolic Interpretation of the Law of Moses." *New Testament Studies* 44 (1998): 475-89.

———. "The Worship of Jesus in Philippians 2:9-11." In *Where Christology Began: Essays on Philippians,* edited by R. P. Martin and B. J. Dodd, 128-39. Louisville: Westminster John Knox, 1998.

———. "Approaching the Millennium." *Anvil* 16 (1999): 255-67.

———. "The Decline of Progress and the Prospects for Christian Hope." *Evangel* 17 (1999): 87-95.

———. "Did Jesus Wash His Disciples' Feet?" In *Authenticating the Activities of Jesus,* edited by B. Chilton and C. A. Evans, 411-29. New Testament Tools and Studies 28, no. 2. Leiden: Brill, 1999.

———. "Editorial." *Evangel* 17 (1999): 69.

———. "Eschatology in *The Coming of God,*" "The Millennium," "Time and Eternity." In *God Will Be All in All: The Eschatology of Jürgen Moltmann,* edited by R. Bauckham, 1-34, 123-47, 155-226. Edinburgh: T&T Clark, 1999.

———. "For What Offence Was James Put to Death?" In *James the Just and Christian Origins,* edited by B. Chilton and C. A. Evans, 199-232. Leiden: Brill, 1999.

———. "For Whom Were Gospels Written?" *Hervormde Teologiese Studies* 55 (1999): 865-82. Danish translation: "For hvem blev evangelierne skrevet?" *Ichtys: Menighedsfakultets Stundenterblad* 28, no. 3 (2001): 100-112.

———. "Heinrich Bullinger, l'Apocalypse et les Anglais." *Études Théologiques et Religieuses* 74 (1999): 352-77.

———. "The New Testament Teaching on the Environment: A Response to Ernest Lucas." *Transformation* 16 (1999): 99-101.

———. "A Story through Women's Eyes (Ruth)," "Women's Perspectives in the Gospels," "Understanding Revelation." In *The Lion Handbook to the Bible,* revised ed., edited by P. and D. Alexander, 254, 603, 771. Oxford: Lion, 1999, paperback 2002.

———. "The Throne of God and the Worship of Jesus." In *The Jewish Roots of Christological Monotheism: Papers from the St. Andrews Conference on the Historical Origins of the Worship of Jesus*, edited by C. C. Newman, J. R. Davila, and G. S. Lewis, 43-69. Supplements to the Journal for the Study of Judaism 63. Leiden: Brill, 1999.

———. "All in the Family: Identifying Jesus' Relatives." *Bible Review* 16, no. 2 (2000): 22-31.

———. "Eschatology." In *The Oxford Companion to Christian Thought*, edited by A. Hastings, 206-9. Oxford: Oxford University Press, 2000.

———. "Imaginative Literature." In *The Early Christian World*, edited by P. F. Esler, 791-812. London/New York: Routledge, 2000.

———. "Jude, Letter of," "Peter, Letters of," and "Jewish Christians." In *Encyclopedia of the Dead Sea Scrolls*, edited by L. H. Schiffman and J. C. VanderKam, 409-12, 440, 656-57. New York: Oxford University Press, 2000.

———. "Moltmann, Jürgen (b. 1926)." In *The Dictionary of Historical Theology*, edited by T. A. Hart, 376-78. Carlisle, UK: Paternoster; Grand Rapids: Eerdmans, 2000.

———. "The Qumran Community and the Gospel of John." In *The Dead Sea Scrolls Fifty Years After Their Discovery: Proceedings of the Jerusalem Congress, July 20-25, 1997*, edited by L. H. Schiffman, E. Tov, and J. C. Vanderkam, 105-15. Jerusalem: Israel Exploration Society, 2000.

———. "Stewardship and Relationship." In *The Care of Creation: Focusing Concern and Action*, edited by R. J. Berry, 99-106. Leicester: Inter-Varsity, 2000.

———. "2 Peter," "Jude." In *The HarperCollins Bible Commentary*, revised ed., edited by J. L. Mays, 1175-77, 1184-86. San Francisco: HarperSanFrancisco, 2000.

———. "What If Paul Had Travelled East Rather Than West?" *Biblical Interpretation* 8, no. 1-2 (2000): 171-84; also in J. C. Exum, ed., *Virtual History and the Bible*. Leiden: Brill, 1999.

———. "The Year 2000 and the End of Secular Eschatology." In *Called to One Hope: Perspectives on the Life to Come*, edited by J. Colell, 240-51. Carlisle, UK: Paternoster, 2000.

———. "Apocalypses." In *Justification and Variegated Nomism*, vol. 1, *The Complexities of Second Temple Judaism*, edited by D. A. Carson, P. T. O'Brien, and M. A. Siefrid, 135-87. Tübingen: Mohr (Siebeck), 2001.

———. "The Audience of the Fourth Gospel." In *Jesus in Johannine Tradition*, edited by R. T. Fortna and T. Thatcher, 101-11. Louisville: Westminster John Knox, 2001.

———. "The Future of Jesus Christ." In *The Cambridge Companion to Jesus*, edited by M. Bockmuehl, 265-80. Cambridge: Cambridge University Press, 2001.

———. "Gospel Lesson: Matthew 25:14-30," "Gospel Lesson: Mark 6:30-44, 53-56," "Gospel Lesson: Luke 12:13-21," "Gospel Lesson: John 2:1-11," "Gospel Lesson: John 10:22-30." In *The Lectionary Commentary: Theological Exegesis for Sunday's Texts*, vol. 3, *The Third Readings: The Gospels*, edited by R. E. Van Harn, 147-50, 220-22, 380-83, 489-92, 530-33. Grand Rapids: Eerdmans; London: Continuum, 2001.

———. "James and Jesus." In *The Brother of Jesus: James the Just and His Mission*, edited by B. Chilton and J. Neusner, 100-137. Louisville: Westminster John Knox, 2001.

---. "Prayer in the Book of Revelation." In *Into God's Presence: Prayer in the New Testament*, edited by R. N. Longenecker, 252–71. Grand Rapids: Eerdmans, 2001.

---. "The Restoration of Israel in Luke-Acts." In *Restoration: Old Testament, Jewish and Christian Perspectives*, edited by J. M. Scott, 435–87. Journal for the Study of Judaism in the Persian, Hellenistic, and Roman Periods Supplement Series 72. Leiden: Brill, 2001.

---. "Revelation." In *The Oxford Bible Commentary*, edited by J. Barton and J. Muddiman, 1287–1306. Oxford: Oxford University Press, 2001.

---. "Richard Holloway in the Moral Maze: The Lost Leading the Lost." *Scottish Episcopal Church Review* 8, no. 2 (2001): 26–36.

---. "The Horarium of Adam and the Chronology of the Passion." *Kristianskij Vostok* 4, no. 10 (2002): 413–39. Reprinted in *L'église des deux Alliances: Mémorial Annie Jaubert (1912–1980)*, edited by Basil Lourié, Andrei Orlov, and Madeleine Petit, 39–68. Orientalia Judaica Christiana 1. Piscataway, NJ: Gorgias, 2008.

---. "How Junia Changed Her Sex." *Church Times* (14 June 2002): 9.

---. "Joining Creation's Praise of God." *Ecotheology* 7 (2002): 45–59.

---. "Paul and Other Jews with Latin Names in the New Testament." In *Paul, Luke and the Graeco-Roman World: Essays in Honour of Alexander J. M. Wedderburn*, edited by A. Christophersen, C. Claussen, J. Frey, and B. Longenecker, 202–20. Journal for the Study of the New Testament Supplement Series 217. Sheffield: Sheffield Academic, 2002.

---. "Where Is Wisdom to Be Found? Theological Reflections on Colossians 1:15–20." *Ministry and Theology* 5 (2002): 194–95 (in Korean).

---. "Creation Mysticism in Matthew Fox and Francis of Assisi." In *Mysticism East and West: Studies in Mystical Experience*, edited by C. Partridge and T. Gabriel, 182–208. Carlisle, UK: Paternoster, 2003.

---. "The Early Jerusalem Church, Qumran, and the Essenes." In *The Dead Sea Scrolls as Background to Postbiblical Judaism and Early Christianity: Papers from an International Conference at St. Andrews in 2001*, edited by J. R. Davila, 63–89. Studies on the Texts of the Desert of Judah 46. Leiden: Brill, 2003.

---. "The Eyewitnesses and the Gospel Traditions." *Journal for the Study of the Historical Jesus* 1 (2003): 28–60.

---. "The Final Meeting of James and Paul: Narrative and History in Acts 21,18–26." In *Raconter, interpréter, annoncer: Parcours de Nouveau Testament: Mélanges offerts à Daniel Marguerat pour son 60e anniversaire*, edited by E. Steffek and Y. Bourquin, 250–59. Le Monde de la Bible 47. Geneva: Labor et Fides, 2003.

---. "James." In *Eerdmans Commentary on the Bible*, edited by J. D. G. Dunn and J. W. Rogerson, 1483–92. Grand Rapids: Eerdmans, 2003.

---. "Loving Our Fellow-Creatures: Christians and Animal Rights." In *Encounter with God*, edited by Andrew C. Clark, 74–77. Milton Keynes, UK: Scripture Union, 2003.

---. "The 153 Fish and the Unity of the Fourth Gospel." *Neotestamentica* 36 (2002): 77–88.

---. "The Origin of the Ebionites." In *The Image of the Judaeo-Christians in Ancient Jewish and Christian Literature*, edited by P. J. Tomson and D. Lambers-Petry, 162–81.

Wissenschaftliche Untersuchungen zum Neuen Testament 158. Tübingen: Mohr Siebeck, 2003.

———. "Reading Scripture as a Coherent Story." In *The Art of Reading Scripture*, edited by E. F. Davis and R. B. Hays, 38–53. Grand Rapids: Eerdmans, 2003.

———. "Where Is Wisdom to Be Found? Colossians 1.15–20 (2)." In *Reading Texts, Seeking Wisdom*, edited by D. F. Ford and G. Stanton, 129–38. London: SCM, 2003.

———. "Why Were the Early Christians Called Nazarenes?" *Mishkan* 38 (2003): 80–85.

———. "Biblical Theology and the Problems of Monotheism." In *Out of Egypt: Biblical Theology and Biblical Interpretation*, edited by C. Bartholomew, M. Healey, K. Möller, and R. Parry, 187–232. Milton Keynes, UK: Paternoster; Grand Rapids: Zondervan, 2004.

———. "Freedom in the Crisis of Modernity." In *Public Theology in the 21st Century: Essays in Honour of Duncan B. Forrester*, edited by W. F. Storrar and A. R. Morton, 77–94. London/New York: T&T Clark, 2004.

———. "Fulke, William (1536/7–1589)." In *Oxford Dictionary of National Biography*, vol. 21, edited by H. C. G. Matthew and B. Harrison, 129–31. Oxford: Oxford University Press, 2004.

———. "Interview with Professor Richard Bauckham." In *An Extraordinary Gathering of Angels*, edited by Margaret Barker, 314–15. London: MQ Publications, 2004.

———. "James, Peter, and the Gentiles." In *The Missions of James, Peter, and Paul: Tensions in Early Christianity*, edited by B. Chilton and C. Evans, 91–142. Supplements to Novum Testamentum 115. Leiden: Brill, 2004.

———. "Judgment in the Book of Revelation." *Ex Auditu* 20 (2004): 1–24.

———. "Monotheism and Christology in Hebrews 1." In *Early Jewish and Christian Monotheism*, edited by L. T. Stuckenbruck and W. E. S. North, 167–85. Journal for the Study of the New Testament Supplement Series 263. London/New York: Continuum (T&T Clark), 2004.

———. "The Spirit of God in Us Loathes Envy: James 4:5." In *The Holy Spirit and Christian Origins: Essays in Honor of James D. G. Dunn*, edited by G. N. Stanton, B. W. Longenecker, and S. C. Barton, 270–81. Grand Rapids: Eerdmans, 2004.

———. "Jürgen Moltmann." In *The Modern Theologians: An Introduction to Christian Theology since 1918*, 3rd ed., edited by D. F. Ford and R. Muers, 147–62. Oxford: Blackwell, 2005.

———. "Monotheism and Christology in the Gospel of John." In *Contours of Christology in the New Testament*, edited by R. N. Longenecker, 148–66. Grand Rapids: Eerdmans, 2005.

———. "The Estate of Publius on Malta (Acts 28:7)." In *History and Exegesis: New Testament Essays in Honor of Dr. E. Earle Ellis for His Eightieth Birthday*, edited by Sang-Won (Aaron) Son, 73–87. New York/London: T&T Clark International, 2006.

———. "Messianism according to the Gospel of John." In *Challenging Perspectives on the Gospel of John*, edited by John Lierman, 34–68. Wissenschaftliche Untersuchungen zum Neuen Testament 2/219. Tübingen: Mohr Siebeck, 2006.

———. "Modern Domination of Nature—Historical Origins and Biblical Critique." In

Environmental Stewardship: Critical Perspectives—Past and Present, edited by R. J. Berry, 32–50. London: T&T Clark International, 2006.

———. "The Second Letter of Peter" and "The Letter of Jude." In *The HarperCollins Study Bible: Fully Revised and Updated*, edited by Harold W. Attridge, 2067–71, 2083–85. San Francisco: HarperSanFrancisco, 2006.

———. "Tobit as a Parable for the Exiles of Northern Israel." In *Studies in the Book of Tobit: A Multidisciplinary Approach*, edited by Mark Bredin, 140–64. The Library of Second Temple Studies 55. London/New York: T&T Clark International, 2006.

———. "The Alleged 'Jesus Family Tomb.'" *Case* 11 (2007): 17–20.

———. "Conclusion: Emerging Issues in Eschatology in the Twenty-First Century." In *The Oxford Handbook of Eschatology*, edited by Jerry L. Walls, 671–89. New York: Oxford University Press, 2007.

———. "Eschatology." In *The Oxford Handbook of Systematic Theology*, edited by John Webster, Kathryn Tanner, and Iain R. Torrance, 306–22. Oxford: Oxford University Press, 2007.

———. "Historiographical Characteristics of the Gospel of John." *New Testament Studies* 53 (2007): 17–36.

———. "The Holiness of Jesus and His Disciples in the Gospel of John." In *Holiness and Eschatology in the New Testament*, Festschrift for Alex R. G. Deasley, edited by Kent Brower and Andy Johnson, 95–113. Grand Rapids: Eerdmans, 2007.

———. "James and the Jerusalem Community." In *Jewish Believers in Jesus: The Early Centuries*, edited by Oskar Skarsaune and Reidar Hvalvik, 55–95. Peabody, MA: Hendrickson, 2007.

———. "The 'Most High' God and the Nature of Jewish Monotheism." In *Israel's God and Rebecca's Children: Christology and Community in Early Judaism and Christianity: Essays in Honor of Larry W. Hurtado and Alan F. Segal*, edited by David B. Capes, April D. DeConick, Helen K. Bond, and Troy A. Miller, 39–53. Waco, TX: Baylor University Press, 2007.

———. "Traditions about the Tomb of James the Brother of Jesus." In *Poussières de christianisme et de judaïsme antiques: Études réunies en l'honneur de Jean-Daniel Kaestli et Éric Junod*, edited by Albert Frey and Rémi Gounelle, 61–77. Lausanne: Éditions du Zèbre, 2007.

———. "The Continuing Quest for the Provenance of the Old Testament Pseudepigrapha." In *The Pseudepigrapha and Christian Origins: Essays from the Studiorum Novi Testamenti Societas*, edited by Gerbern S. Oegema and James H. Charlesworth, 9–29. New York/London: T&T Clark (Continuum), 2008.

———. "Creation's Praise of God in the Book of Revelation." *Biblical Theology Bulletin* 38 (2008): 55–63.

———. "Eyewitnesses and Critical History: A Response to Jens Schröter and Craig Evans." *Journal for the Study of the New Testament* 31, no. 2 (2008): 221–35.

———. "The Fourth Gospel as the Testimony of the Beloved Disciple." In *The Gospel of John and Christian Theology*, edited by Richard Bauckham and Carl Mosser, 120–39. Grand Rapids: Eerdmans, 2008.

———. "The Horarium of Adam and the Chronology of the Passion." In *L'église des deux*

Alliances: Mémorial Annie Jaubert (1912-1980). Orientalia Judaica Christiana 1. Edited by Basil Lourié, Andrei Orlov, and Madeleine Petit, 39-68. Piscataway, NJ: Gorgias, 2008.

———. "In Response to My Respondents: *Jesus and the Eyewitnesses* in Review." *Journal for the Study of the Historical Jesus* 6 (2008): 225-53.

———. "James the Brother of the Lord in the Pseudo-Clementine Literature." In *Nouvelles intrigues pseudo-clémentines (Plots in the Pseudo-Clementine Romance)*, edited by Frédéric Amsler, Albert Frey, Charlotte Touati, and Renée Girardet, 303-12. Publications de l'Institut Romand des Sciences Bibliques 6. Lausanne: Éditions du Zèbre, 2008.

———. "The Names on the Ossuaries." In *Buried Hope or Risen Savior? The Search for the Jesus Tomb*, edited by Charles L. Quarles, 69-112. Nashville: B. & H. Academic, 2008.

———. "Response to the Respondents." *Nova et Vetera* (English Edition) 6 (2008): 529-42.

———. "Review of Robby Waddell, *The Spirit of the Book of Revelation*." *Journal of Pentecostal Theology* 17 (2008): 3-8.

———. "The Transmission of the Gospel Traditions." *Revista Catalana de Teologia* 33 (2008): 377-94.

———. "The Bethany Family in John 11-12: History or Fiction?" in *John, Jesus, and History*, volume 2, *Aspects of Historicity in the Fourth Gospel*, edited by Paul N. Anderson, Felix Just, and Tom Thatcher, 185-201. Atlanta: Society of Biblical Literature, 2009.

———. "The Bible and Globalization." In *The Gospel and Globalization: Exploring the Religious Roots of a Globalized World*, edited by Michael W. Goheen and Erin G. Glanville, 27-48. Vancouver: Regent College Publishing/Geneva Society, 2009.

———. "The Divinity of Jesus Christ in the Epistle to the Hebrews." In *The Epistle to the Hebrews and Christian Theology*, edited by Richard Bauckham, Daniel R. Driver, Trevor A. Hart, and Nathan MacDonald, 15-36. Grand Rapids: Eerdmans, 2009.

———. "The Eyewitnesses in the Gospel of Mark." *Svensk Exegetisk Årsbok* 74 (2009): 19-39.

———. "Jesus, God and Nature in the Gospels." In *Creation in Crisis: Christian Perspectives on Sustainability*, edited by Robert S. White, 209-24. London: SPCK, 2009.

———. "Reading the Sermon on the Mount in an Age of Ecological Catastrophe." *Studies in Christian Ethics* 22 (2009): 76-88.

———. "A Story through Women's Eyes (Ruth)," "Women's Perspectives in the Gospels," "Understanding Revelation." In *The Lion Handbook to the Bible*, 4th ed., edited by Pat and David Alexander, 254, 603, 771. Oxford: Lion Hudson, 2009.

———. "The Gospel of John and the Synoptic Problem." In *Studies in the Synoptic Problem: Oxford Conference, April 2008*, edited by Andrew Gregory, Paul Foster, John S. Kloppenborg, and Jos Verheyden, 623-54. Bibliotheca Ephemeridum Theologicarum Lovaniensium 239. Leuven: Peeters, 2010.

———. "Hell in the Latin *Vision of Ezra*." In *Other Worlds and Their Relation to This World: Early Jewish and Ancient Christian Traditions*, edited by Tobias Nicklas, Joseph Verheyden, Erik M. M. Eynikel, and Florentino García Martínez, 323–42. Journal for the Study of Judaism in the Persian, Hellenistic, and Roman Periods Supplement Series 143. Leiden: Brill, 2010.

———. "Is There Patristic Counter-Evidence? A Response to Margaret Mitchell." In *The Audience of the Gospels: The Origin and Function of the Gospels in Early Christianity*, edited by Edward W. Klink III, 68–110. The Library of New Testament Studies 353. London: T&T Clark (Continuum), 2010.

———. "Paradise in the *Biblical Antiquities* of Pseudo-Philo." In *Paradise in Antiquity: Jewish and Christian Views*, edited by Markus Bockmuehl and Guy G. Strousma, 43–56. Cambridge: Cambridge University Press, 2010.

———. "Reading the Synoptic Gospels Ecologically." In *Ecological Hermeneutics: Biblical, Historical and Theological Perspectives*, edited by David G. Horrell, Cherryl Hunt, Christopher Southgate, and Francesca Stavrakopoulou, 70–82. London: T&T Clark (Continuum), 2010.

———. "A Response to Professor Moltmann." *Theology* 93 (2010): 95–96.

———. "Review Article: Seeking the Identity of Jesus." *Journal for the Study of the New Testament* 32 (2010): 337–46.

———. "The Family of Jesus." In *Jesus among Friends and Enemies: A Historical and Literary Introduction to Jesus in the Gospels*, edited by Chris Keith and Larry W. Hurtado, 103–25. Grand Rapids: Baker, 2011.

———. "The First Pioneers: Learning from the Acts of the Apostles." In *Pioneers for Life: Explorations in Theology and Wisdom for Pioneering Leaders*, edited by David Male, 196–210. London: Bible Reading Fellowship, 2011.

———. "Freedom and Belonging." *Christian Reflection* 39 (2011): 11–18.

———. "Jewish Christianity and Rabbinic Judaism: The Case of Simeon ben Clopas." In *Among Jews, Gentiles and Christians in Antiquity and the Middle Ages: Studies in Honour of Professor Oskar Skarsaune on His 65th Birthday*, edited by Reidar Hvalvik and John Kaufman, 31–36. Trondheim: Tapir Academic Press, 2011.

———. "The Language of Warfare in the Book of Revelation." In *Compassionate Eschatology: The Future as Friend*, edited by Ted Grimsrud and Michael Hardin, 28–41. Eugene, OR: Cascade, 2011.

———. "The Story of the Earth according to Paul: Romans 8:18–23." *Review and Expositor* 108, no. 1 (2011): 91–97.

———. "Are the Gospels Reliable?" In John Young, *Lord . . . Help My Unbelief: Considering the Case against Christ*, 159–63. Abingdon, UK: Bible Reading Fellowship, 2012.

———. "The Caiaphas Family." *Journal for the Study of the Historical Jesus* 10 (2012): 3–31.

———. "God's Self-Identification with the Godforsaken: Exegesis and Theology." In *"Godhead Here in Hiding": Incarnation and the History of Human Suffering*, edited by Terrence Merrigan and Frederik Glorieux, 3–17. Bibliotheca Ephemeridum Theologicarum Lovaniensium 234. Leuven: Peeters, 2012.

———. "The Gospel of Mark: Origins and Eyewitnesses." In *Earliest Christian History: Essays from the Tyndale Fellowship in Honor of Martin Hengel*, edited by Michael F. Bird and Jason Maston, 145–69. Tübingen: Mohr Siebeck, 2012.

———. "Humans, Animals, and the Environment in Genesis 1–3." In *Genesis and Chris-*

tian Theology, edited by Nathan MacDonald, Mark W. Elliott, and Grant Macaskill, 175–89. Grand Rapids: Eerdmans, 2012.

———. "Judgment." *Franciscan* 24, no. 3 (2012): 3, 5.

———. "Moses as 'God' in Philo of Alexandria: A Precedent for Christology?" In *The Spirit and Christ in the New Testament and Christian Theology: Essays in Honor of Max Turner*, edited by I. Howard Marshall, Volker Rabens, and Cornelis Bennema, 246–65. Grand Rapids: Eerdmans, 2012.

———. "Robert McLachlan Wilson (1916–2010)." In *Biographical Memoirs of Fellows of the British Academy XI*, 582–98. Oxford: Oxford University Press, 2012.

———. "Saints Before and After Death." In *Theology, Aesthetics, and Culture: Responses to the Work of David Brown*, edited by Robert MacSwain and Taylor Worley, 55–63. Oxford: Oxford University Press, 2012.

———. "Time, Eternity and the Arts." In *Art, Imagination and Christian Hope*, edited by Trevor Hart, Gavin Hopps, and Jeremy Begbie, 7–30. Farnham, UK: Ashgate, 2012.

———. "Are We Still Missing the Elephant? C. S. Lewis's 'Fernseed and Elephants' Half a Century On." *Theology* 116 (2013): 427–34.

———. "The Bible in Mission: The Modern/Postmodern Western Context." In *The Bible in Mission*, edited by Pauline Hoggarth, Fergus Macdonald, Bill Mitchell, and Knud Jørgensen, 43–55. Regnum Edinburgh Centenary Series 18. Oxford: Regnum, 2013.

———. "Christology." In *Dictionary of Jesus and the Gospels*, 2nd ed., edited by Joel B. Green, Jeannine K. Brown, and Nicholas Perrin, 125–34. Downers Grove: IVP; Nottingham: Inter-Varsity, 2013.

———. "James and the Jerusalem Council Decision." In *Introduction to Messianic Judaism: Its Ecclesial Context and Biblical Foundations*, edited by David Rudolph and Joel Willitts, 178–86. Grand Rapids: Zondervan, 2013.

———. "Luke's Infancy Narrative as Oral History in Scriptural Form." In *The Gospels: History and Christology: The Search of Joseph Ratzinger–Benedict XVI*, edited by Bernardo Estrada, Ermenegildo Manicardi, and Armand Puig i Tàrrech, vol. 1, 399–417. Vatican City: Libreria Editrice Vaticana, 2013.

———. "The Power and the Glory: The Rendering of Psalm 110:1 in Mark 14:62." In *From Creation to New Creation: Biblical Theology and Exegesis; Essays in Honor of G. K. Beale*, edited by Daniel M. Gurtner and Benjamin L. Gladd, 83–101. Peabody, MA: Hendrickson, 2013.

———. "2 Corintios 4,6: Visión de Pablo del Rostro de Dios en el Rostro Jesu Cristo." In *Los Rostros de Dios: Imágines y experiencias de lo Divino en la Biblia*, edited by Carmen Bernabé, 231–44. Asociación Bíblica Española 62. Estella, Spain: Editorial Verbo Divino, 2013.

———. "Apocalypses and Prophetic Works in Volume 1 of the New Pseudepigrapha." *Early Christianity* 5 (2014): 127–38.

———. "The Cross and God's Embrace of Suffering." In *Atonement as Gift: Re-Imagining the Cross for the Church and the World*, edited by Katie M. Heffelfinger and Patrick G. McGlinchey, 49–60. Milton Keynes, UK: Paternoster, 2014.

———. "Devotion to Jesus Christ in Earliest Christianity: An Appraisal and Discussion of the Work of Larry Hurtado." In *Mark, Manuscripts, and Monotheism: Essays in Honor of Larry W. Hurtado*, edited by Chris Keith and Dieter T. Roth, 176–200. London: Bloomsbury, 2014.

———. "Did Papias Write History or Exegesis?" *Journal of Theological Studies* 65 (2014): 463–88.

———. "Dualism and Soteriology in Johannine Theology." In *Beyond Bultmann: Reckoning a New Testament Theology*, edited by Bruce W. Longenecker and Mikeal C. Parsons, 133–53. Waco, TX: Baylor University Press, 2014.

———. "Ecological Hope in Crisis?" *Anvil* 30 (2014): 43–54.

———. "Gospel Traditions: Anonymous Community Traditions or Eyewitness Testimony?" In *Jesus Research: New Methodologies and Perceptions*, edited by James H. Charlesworth, 483–99. Grand Rapids: Eerdmans, 2014.

———. "Introduction." In Jürgen Moltmann, *Collected Readings*, translated and edited by Margaret Kohl, 1–6. Minneapolis: Fortress, 2014.

———. "Further Thoughts on the Migdal Synagogue Stone." *Novum Testamentum* 57 (2015): 113–35.

———. "The Gospels as Testimony to Jesus Christ: A Contemporary View of Their Historical Value." In *The Oxford Handbook of Christology*, edited by Francesca Aran Murphy and Troy A. Stefano, 55–71. Oxford: Oxford University Press, 2015.

———. "La Communità della Creazione nella Bibbia e Oggi." *Rivista della Diocesi di Vicenza* 106 (2015): 240–51 (trans. Leopoldo Sandonà).

———. "A Life with the Bible." In *I (Still) Believe: Leading Bible Scholars Share Their Stories of Faith and Scholarship*, edited by John Byron and Joel N. Lohr, 17–28. Grand Rapids: Zondervan, 2015.

———. "Non-canonical Apocalypses and Prophetic Works." In *The Oxford Handbook of Early Christian Apocrypha*, edited by Andrew Gregory and Christopher Tuckett, 115–37. Oxford: Oxford University Press, 2015.

———. "On Systems, Circles and Centers: Christianity as a Christocentric 'System.'" In *A Man of Many Parts: Essays in Honor of John Westerdale Bowker on the Occasion of His Eightieth Birthday*, edited by Eugene E. Lemcio, 79–94. Eugene, OR: Pickwick, 2015.

———. "Sacraments and the Gospel of John." In *The Oxford Handbook of Sacramental Theology*, edited by Hans Boersma and Matthew Levering, 83–96. Oxford: Oxford University Press, 2015.

Coauthored Essays

Bauckham, Richard, and Gordon McConville. "Not All Approaches to the Bible Are Equally Valid." In *Handling Problems of Peace and War: An Evangelical Debate*. Edited by A. Kirk, 55–66. Basingstoke, UK: Marshall Pickering, 1988.

Bauckham, Richard, and Gordon McConville. "Responses to the Dialogue." In *Handling Problems of Peace and War: An Evangelical Debate*. Edited by A. Kirk, 113–20. Basingstoke, UK: Marshall Pickering, 1988.

Bauckham, Richard, and Trevor Hart. "Salvation and Creation: 'All Things New.'" In *The Scope of Salvation: Theatres of God's Drama*, Lincoln Lectures in Theology 1998, 40–54. Lincoln: Lincoln Cathedral Publications, 1999.

Bauckham, Richard, and Trevor Hart. "The Shape of Time." In *The Future as God's Gift: Explorations in Christian Eschatology*, edited by D. Fergusson and M. Sarot, 41–72. Edinburgh: T&T Clark, 2000.

Bauckham, Richard, and Stefano De Luca. "Magdala as We Now Know It." *Early Christianity* 6 (2015): 91–118.

Poetry and Fiction

Bauckham, Richard. "Epithalamion." In *100 Contemporary Christian Poets*, edited by Gordon Bailey. Tring: Lion. Republished in 1995 in *The Lion Christian Poetry Collection*, edited by Mary Batchelor. Oxford: Lion, 1983.

———. "The Dream of the Magi." In *Dreams—Night and Day*, edited by Hugh Hellicar. Brighton: Beyond the Cloister Publications, 1995.

———. *The MacBears of Bearloch*. Inverness: Aultbea, 2006.

———. *The MacBears and the Bishbirds*. Self-published, 2008.

———. "Song of the Shepherds." In *Waiting on the Word: A Poem a Day for Advent, Christmas, and Epiphany*, edited by Malcolm Guite, 104–8. Norwich: Canterbury Press, 2015.

[The MacBears books and assorted poetry may be read at http://richardbauckham.co.uk/.]

General Bibliography

Alexander, Philip. "Reflections on Word versus Image as Ways of Mediating the Divine Presence in Judaism." In *The Image and Its Prohibition in Jewish Antiquity*, edited by Sarah Pearce, 10–27. Journal of Jewish Studies Supplement Series 2. Oxford: Journal of Jewish Studies, 2013.

———. "3 (Hebrew Apocalypse of) Enoch." In *Old Testament Pseudepigrapha*, 2 vols., edited by James H. Charlesworth, 1:223–315. New York: Doubleday, 1983, 1985.

Augstein, Hannah Franziska, ed. *Race: The Origins of an Idea, 1760–1850*. Bristol, UK: Thoemmes, 1996.

Aune, David E. "Charismatic Exegesis in Early Judaism and Early Christianity." In *The Pseudepigrapha and Early Biblical Interpretation*, edited by James H. Charlesworth and Craig A. Evans, 126–50. Sheffield: Sheffield Academic, 1993.

———. *Revelation 1–5*. Word Biblical Commentary 52. Dallas: Word, 1997.

———. *Revelation 6–16*. Word Biblical Commentary 52B. Dallas: Word, 1998.

———. *Revelation 17–22*. Word Biblical Commentary 52C. Dallas: Word, 1998.

Axmacher, Elke. *"Aus Liebe will mein Heyland sterben": Untersuchungen zum Wandel des*

Passionsverständnisses im frühen 18. Jahrhundert. Neuhausen-Stuttgart: Hänssler-Verlag, 1984.

Bailey, D. "Jesus as the Mercy Seat: The Semantics and Theology of Paul's Use of *Hilastērion* in Romans 3:25." PhD dissertation, Cambridge University, 1999.

———. "Jesus as the Mercy Seat: The Semantics and Theology of Paul's Use of *Hilastērion* in Romans 3:25." *Tyndale Bulletin* 51, no. 1 (2000): 155–58.

Balentine, S. E. "Day of Atonement." In *The New Interpreter's Dictionary of the Bible*, vol. 2, edited by K. D. Sakenfeld et al., 42–45. Nashville: Abingdon, 2007.

Balibar, Étienne. "The Nation Form: History and Ideology." In Étienne Balibar and Immanuel Wallerstein, *Race, Nation, Class: Ambiguous Identities*, 86–106. Translated by Chris Turner. London and New York: Verso, 2002.

Barclay, John. *Flavius Josephus: Translation and Commentary*. Volume 10, *Against Apion*. Leiden: Brill, 2006.

Barrett, C. K. *The First Epistle to the Corinthians*. 2nd ed. London: A. & C. Black, 1971.

———. *The Gospel according to Saint John*. 2nd ed. Philadelphia: Westminster, 1978.

Barth, Fredrik. "Introduction." In *Ethnic Groups and Boundaries: The Social Organization of Culture Difference*, edited by Fredrik Barth, 9–38. London: George Allen and Unwin, 1969.

Bauer, W. *A Greek-English Lexicon of the New Testament and Other Early Christian Literature*. 3rd edition of BAGD, revised by F. W. Danker. Chicago: University of Chicago Press, 2000.

Bauman, Zygmunt. *Identity: Conversations with Benedetto Vecchi*. Cambridge: Polity, 2004.

Begbie, Jeremy S. *Resounding Truth: Christian Wisdom in the World of Music*. Grand Rapids: Baker, 2007.

———. *Theology, Music and Time*. Cambridge: Cambridge University Press, 2000.

Benz, E. *Das Buch der heiligen Gesänge der Ostkirche*. Hamburg: Furche-Verlag, 1962.

Berger, Karol. *Bach's Cycle, Mozart's Arrow: An Essay on the Origins of Musical Modernity*. Berkeley: University of California Press, 2007.

Berkman, J. "Towards a Thomistic Theology of Animality." In *Creaturely Theology*, edited by C. Deane-Drummond and D. Clough, 21–40. London: SCM, 2009.

Bird, M. F., and P. M. Sprinkle, eds. *The Faith of Jesus Christ: Exegetical, Biblical and Theological Studies*. Milton Keynes, UK: Paternoster, 2009.

Bousset, Wilhelm. *Kyrios Christos: A History of the Belief in Christ from the Beginnings of Christianity to Irenaeus*. Translated by J. E. Steely. Nashville: Abingdon, 1970.

———. *Kyrios Christos: A History of the Belief in Christ from the Beginnings of Christianity to Irenaeus* (with a new introduction by Larry W. Hurtado). Waco, TX: Baylor University Press, 2014.

Boustan, Ra'anan S. *From Martyr to Mystic: Rabbinic Martyrology and the Making of Merkavah Mysticism*. Texte und Studien zum antiken Judentum 112. Tübingen: Mohr Siebeck, 2005.

———. "Immolating Emperors: Spectacles of Imperial Suffering and the Making of a Jewish Minority Culture in Late Antiquity." *Biblical Interpretation* 17 (2009): 207–38.

Boyarin, Daniel. "Beyond Judaisms: Metatron and the Divine Polymorphy of Ancient Judaism." *Journal for the Study of Judaism in the Persian, Hellenistic, and Roman Periods* 41 (2010): 323–65.

———. "Is Metatron a Converted Christian?" *Judaïsme Ancien—Ancient Judaism* 1 (2013): 323–65.

Bricault, Laurent. *Recueil des Inscriptions concernant les Cultes isiaques.* Paris: De Boccard, 2005.

Brown, David. *Discipleship and Imagination: Christian Tradition and Truth.* Oxford: Oxford University Press, 2000.

———. "Symbol, Community and Vegetarianism." In *Eating and Believing: Interdisciplinary Perspectives on Vegetarianism and Theology*, edited by Rachel Muers and David Grumett, 219–31. Edinburgh: T&T Clark, 2008.

Brown, Raymond. *The Gospel according to John I–XII.* Garden City, NY: Doubleday, 1966.

Buell, Denise Kimber. *Why This New Race: Ethnic Reasoning in Early Christianity.* New York: Columbia University Press, 2005.

Burkert, Walter. *Greek Religion.* Translated by John Raffan. Cambridge, MA: Harvard University Press, 1985.

Butt, John. *Bach's Dialogue with Modernity: Perspectives on the Passions.* Cambridge: Cambridge University Press, 2010.

———. "Bach's Metaphysics of Music." In *The Cambridge Companion to Bach*, edited by John Butt, 46–71. Cambridge: Cambridge University Press, 1997.

Byrne, B. *Romans.* Collegeville, MN: Liturgical, 1996.

Byron, John, and Joel Lohr, eds. *I (Still) Believe: Leading Bible Scholars Share Their Stories of Faith and Scholarship.* Grand Rapids: Zondervan Academic, 2015.

Byron, Reginald. "Identity." In *Encyclopedia of Social and Cultural Anthropology*, edited by Alan Barnard and Jonathan Spencer, 292. London and New York: Routledge, 1996.

Campbell, D. A. *The Rhetoric of Righteousness in Romans 3.21–26.* Sheffield: Sheffield Academic, 1992.

Campbell, Jonathan G. *The Exegetical Texts.* London: T&T Clark, 2004.

Capes, David B. *Old Testament Yahweh Texts in Paul's Christology.* Wissenschaftliche Untersuchungen zum Neuen Testament 2/47. Tübingen: Mohr Siebeck, 1992.

Carson, D. A. *The Gospel according to John.* Grand Rapids: Eerdmans, 1991.

Carsten, Jane, ed. *Cultures of Relatedness: New Approaches to the Study of Kinship.* Cambridge: Cambridge University Press, 2000.

Casey, Maurice. "Monotheism, Worship and Christological Developments in the Pauline Churches." In *The Jewish Roots of Christological Monotheism: Papers from the St. Andrews Conference on the Historical Origins of the Worship of Jesus*, edited by Carey C. Newman, James R. Davila, and Gladys S. Lewis, 214–33. Leiden: Brill, 1999.

Chafe, Eric T. *Analyzing Bach Cantatas.* Oxford: Oxford University Press, 2000.

———. *Tonal Allegory in the Vocal Music of J. S. Bach.* Berkeley: University of California Press, 1991.

Charles, R. H. *A Critical and Exegetical Commentary on the Revelation of St. John.* International Critical Commentary, 2 vols. Edinburgh: T. & T. Clark, 1920.

Chester, Andrew. "High Christology—Whence, When and Why?" *Early Christianity* 2 (2011): 22-50.
Cohen, Martin Samuel. *The Shiʻur Qomah: Texts and Recensions*. Texte und Studien zum antiken Judentum 9. Tübingen: Mohr Siebeck, 1985.
Cornell, Stephen E., and Douglas Hartmann. *Ethnicity and Race: Making Identities in a Changing World*. 2nd ed. Thousand Oaks, CA: Pine Forge, 2007.
Cranfield, C. E. B. *A Critical and Exegetical Commentary on the Epistle to the Romans*. International Critical Commentary. Edinburgh: T. & T. Clark, 1975.
———. *The Gospel according to St Mark*. Cambridge: Cambridge University Press, 1977.
———. "Some Observations on Romans 8.19-21." In *Reconciliation and Hope: New Testament Essays on Atonement and Eschatology*, edited by R. J. Banks, 224-30. Exeter, UK: Paternoster, 1974.
Darwin, C. *The Descent of Man*. New York: Modern Library, n.d.
Davidson, R. M. "The Divine Covenant Lawsuit Motif in Canonical Perspective." *Journal of the Adventist Theological Society* 21, no. 1-2 (2010): 45-84.
Davies, W. D., and D. C. Allison. *A Critical and Exegetical Commentary on the Gospel according to St. Matthew*. Volume 2, *Matthew VII-XVII*. Edinburgh: T&T Clark, 1991.
Davila, James R. "Exploring the Mystical Background of the Dead Sea Scrolls." In *The Oxford Handbook of the Dead Sea Scrolls*, edited by Timothy H. Lim and John J. Collins, 433-54. Oxford: Oxford University Press, 2010.
———. "The Hekhalot Literature and the Ancient Jewish Apocalypses." In *Paradise Now: Essays on Early Jewish and Christian Mysticism*. Society of Biblical Literature Symposium Series 11. Edited by April DeConick, 105-25. Atlanta: SBL, 2006.
———. *Hekhalot Literature in Translation: Major Texts of Merkavah Mysticism*. Supplements to the Journal of Jewish Thought and Philosophy 20. Leiden: Brill, 2013.
———. *Liturgical Works*. Eerdmans Commentaries on the Dead Sea Scrolls 6. Grand Rapids: Eerdmans, 2000.
———. "Melchizedek, the 'Youth,' and Jesus." In *The Dead Sea Scrolls as Background to Postbiblical Judaism and Early Christianity: Papers from a Conference at St. Andrews in 2001*, edited by James R. Davila, 248-74. Studies on the Texts of the Desert of Judah 46. Leiden: Brill, 2003.
———. "Of Methodology, Monotheism, and Metatron: Introductory Reflections on Divine Mediators and the Origins of the Worship of Jesus." In *The Jewish Roots of Christological Monotheism: Papers from the St. Andrews Conference on the Historical Origins of the Worship of Jesus*, edited by James R. Davila, Carey C. Newman, and Gladys S. Lewis, 3-18. Journal for the Study of Judaism in the Persian, Hellenistic, and Roman Periods Supplement Series 63. Leiden: Brill, 1999.
———. "Ritual in the Jewish Pseudepigrapha." In *Anthropology & Biblical Studies: Avenues of Approach*, edited by Louise J. Lawrence and Mario I. Aguilar, 158-83. Leiderdorp: Deo, 2004.
Denzinger, Heinrich, and Adolf Schönmetzer, *Enchiridion Symbolorum*. 36th ed. Freiburg: Herder, 1976.

Dodd, C. H. *Historical Tradition in the Fourth Gospel*. Cambridge: Cambridge University Press, 1963.
Dreyfus, Laurence. *Bach and the Patterns of Invention*. Cambridge, MA: Harvard University Press, 1996.
Duling, Dennis C. "Ethnicity, Ethnocentrism, and the Matthean *Ethnos*." In *A Marginal Scribe: Studies in the Gospel of Matthew in a Social-Scientific Perspective*. Matrix: The Bible in Mediterranean Context, 288–328. Eugene, OR: Cascade, 2012.
Dunn, James D. G. *Christianity in the Making*. Volume 2, *Beginning from Jerusalem*. Grand Rapids: Eerdmans, 2009.
———. *Did the First Christians Worship Jesus? The New Testament Evidence*. London: SPCK; Louisville: Westminster John Knox, 2010.
———. *The Partings of the Ways*. London: SCM, 1991, 2006.
Dürr, Alfred. "'Ich freue mich auf meinen Tod': Sterben und Tod in Bachs Kantaten aus musikwissenschaftlicher Sicht." *Jahrbuch des Staatlichen Instituts fur Musikforschung Preussischer Kulturbesitz* (1996): 41–51.
Eagleton, Terry. *Sweet Violence: The Idea of the Tragic*. Oxford: Blackwell, 2003.
Eckstein, H.-J., and M. Welker. *Die Wirklichkeit der Auferstehung*. Neukirchen-Vluyn: Neukirchener, 2001.
Elon, Menachem. *Jewish Law: History, Sources, Principles*. 2 vols. Philadelphia: Jewish Publication Society, 1995.
Erikson, E. H. *Identity and the Life-Cycle*. New York: W. W. Norton, 1959.
Esler, Philip F. "The Birth of the Maccabean Ethnic State: Ethnic Groups not 'Empire' in the Meaning of 1 Maccabees." Paper presented at the Annual Meeting of the Society of Biblical Literature. Atlanta, November 2015.
———. *Conflict and Identity in Romans: The Social Setting of Paul's Letter*. Minneapolis: Fortress, 2003.
———. *Galatians*. New Testament Readings. London: Routledge, 1998.
———. "Intergroup Conflict and Matthew 23: Towards Responsible Interpretation of a Challenging Text." *Biblical Theology Bulletin* 45 (2015): 38–59.
———. "Judean Ethnic Identity and the Matthean Jesus." In *Jesus—Gestalt und Gestaltungen: Rezeptionen des Galiläers in Wissenschaft, Kirche und Gesellschaft: Festschrift für Gerd Theissen*, edited by P. von Gemünden, D. G. Horrell, and M. Küchler, 193–210. Novum Testamentum et Orbis Antiquus. Göttingen: Vandenhoeck & Ruprecht, 2013.
———. "Judean Ethnic Identity in Josephus' *Against Apion*." In *A Wandering Galilean: Essays in Honour of Sean Freyne*, edited by Zuleika Rodgers, with Margaret Daly-Denton and Anne Fitzpatrick McKinley, 73–91. Leiden: Brill, 2009.
———. "Paul's Contestation of Israel's (Ethnic) Memory of Abraham in Galatians 3." *Biblical Theology Bulletin* 36 (2006): 23–34.
———. "Rival Group Identities in the Matthean Gospel: Evidence from Matthew 1–2 and 23." In *Conception, Reception, and the Spirit: Essays in Honor of Andrew T. Lincoln*, edited by J. Gordon McConville and Lloyd K. Pietersen, 19–35. Eugene, OR: Cascade, 2015.

Bibliography

Feuerbach, Ludwig, *The Essence of Christianity* (*Das Wesen des Christentums*, 3rd ed., 1849). Translated by George Eliot. London: Kegan Paul, Trench, Trübner & Co., 1893.

Fitzmyer, J. A. *Romans*. Anchor Bible 33. New York: Doubleday, 1993.

Ford, J. Massyngberde. *Revelation: Introduction, Translation and Commentary*. Anchor Bible 38. Garden City, NY: Doubleday, 1975.

Foster, Paul. *Community, Law and Mission in Matthew's Gospel*. Wissenschaftliche Untersuchungen zum Neuen Testament 177. Tübingen: Mohr Siebeck, 2004.

France, R. T. "Jesus the Baptist?" In *Jesus of Nazareth: Lord and Christ*, edited by Joel Green and Max Turner, 94–111. Grand Rapids: Eerdmans, 1994.

Fredriksen, Paula. *Jesus of Nazareth, King of the Jews*. New York: Knopf, 2000.

Frey, J., and J. Schröter, eds. *Deutungen des Todes Jesu im Neuen Testament*. 2nd ed. Tübingen: Mohr Siebeck, 2012.

Gieschen, Charles A. *Angelomorphic Christology: Antecedents and Early Evidence*. Arbeiten zur Geschichte des antiken Judentums und des Urchristentums 42. Leiden: Brill, 1998.

Gilhus, I. S. *Animals, Gods and Humans*. London: Routledge, 2006.

Grabiner, Steven. *Revelation's Hymns: Commentary on the Cosmic Conflict*. The Library of New Testament Studies 511. London: T&T Clark, 2015.

Green, Joel. *The Gospel of Luke*. New International Commentary on the New Testament. Grand Rapids: Eerdmans, 1997.

Gunton, Colin E. *The One, the Three and the Many: God, Creation and the Culture of Modernity*. Cambridge: Cambridge University Press, 1993.

Haenchen, Ernst. *John: A Commentary on the Gospel of John*. 2 vols. Translated by R. W. Funk. Philadelphia: Fortress, 1984.

Halperin, David. *The Faces of the Chariot: Early Jewish Responses to Ezekiel's Vision*. Texte und Studien zum antiken Judentum 16. Tübingen: Mohr Siebeck, 1988.

Hart, David Bentley. *The Beauty of the Infinite: The Aesthetics of Christian Truth*. Grand Rapids: Eerdmans, 2003.

Hart, Trevor. *Between the Image and the Word: Theological Engagements with Imagination, Language and Literature*. Farnham, UK: Ashgate, 2013.

———. "Conversation after Pentecost? Theological Musings on the Hermeneutic Motion." *Literature and Theology* 28, no. 2 (2014): 164–78.

Hay, David M. *Glory at the Right Hand: Psalm 110 in Early Christianity*. Nashville: Abingdon, 1973.

Hengel, Martin. "Christologie und neutestamentliche Chronologie: Zu einer Aporie in der Geschichte des Urchristentums." In *Neues Testament und Geschichte: Historisches Geschehen und Deutung im Neuen Testament, Festschrift Oscar Cullmann*, edited by H. Baltensweiler and B. Reicke, 43–67. Zürich: Theologischer Verlag; Tübingen: Mohr-Siebeck, 1972. English translation: "Christology and New Testament Chronology." In *Between Jesus and Paul*, 30–47. London: SCM, 1983.

———. "'Sit at My Right Hand!' The Enthronement of Christ at the Right Hand of God and Psalm 110:1." In *Studies in Early Christology*, 119–225. Edinburgh: T&T Clark, 1995.

———. *The Son of God: The Origin of Christology and the History of Jewish-Hellenistic Religion*. Translated by John Bowden. Philadelphia: Fortress, 1976.
Hick, John. *God and the Universe of Faiths: Essays in the Philosophy of Religion*. London: Macmillan, 1973.
Hick, John, ed. *The Myth of God Incarnate*. London: SCM, 1977.
Hieke, T., and T. Nicklas, eds. *The Day of Atonement: Its Interpretation in Early Jewish and Christian Traditions*. Leiden: Brill, 2013.
Hollenbach, Paul W. "The Conversion of Jesus: From Baptizer to Healer." In *Aufstieg und Niedergang der römischen Welt*, part II, vol. 25, no. 1, edited by W. Haase, 196–219. Berlin: De Gruyter, 1972–.
Horrell, David G. "'Race,' 'Nation,' 'People': Ethnic Identity Construction in 1 Peter 2:9." *New Testament Studies* 58 (2011): 123–43.
Huffmon, H. B. "The Covenant Lawsuit in the Prophets." *Journal of Biblical Literature* 78 (1959): 285–95.
Hurtado, Larry W. *At the Origins of Christian Worship*. Grand Rapids: Eerdmans, 1999.
———. "The Binitarian Shape of Early Christian Worship." In *The Jewish Roots of Christological Monotheism: Papers from the St. Andrews Conference on the Historical Origins of the Worship of Jesus*, edited by Carey C. Newman, James R. Davila, and Gladys S. Lewis, 187–213. Leiden: Brill, 1999.
———. *God in New Testament Theology*. Nashville: Abingdon, 2010.
———. *Lord Jesus Christ: Devotion to Jesus in Earliest Christianity*. Grand Rapids/Cambridge: Eerdmans, 2003.
———. "New Testament Christology: A Critique of Bousset's Influence." *Theological Studies* 40 (1979): 306–17.
———. *One God, One Lord: Early Christian Devotion and Ancient Jewish Monotheism*. Philadelphia: Fortress; London: SCM, 1988; reprint Edinburgh/London: T&T Clark, 1998.
———. "Two Case Studies in Earliest Christological Readings of Biblical Texts." In *All That the Prophets Have Declared: The Appropriation of Scripture in the Emergence of Christianity*, edited by Matthew Malcolm, 3–23. Milton Keynes, UK: Paternoster, 2015.
———. "Wilhelm Bousset's *Kyrios Christos*: An Appreciative and Critical Assessment." *Early Christianity* 6 (2015): 1–13.
Hutchinson, John, and Anthony Smith. "Introduction." In *Ethnicity*, edited by John Hutchinson and Anthony Smith, 3–14. Oxford: Oxford University Press, 1996.
Jewett, R. *Romans: A Commentary*. Minneapolis: Fortress, 2007.
Johnson, E. A. *Ask the Beasts: Darwin and the God of Love*. London: Bloomsbury, 2014.
Käsemann, E. *Commentary on Romans*. London: SCM, 1980.
Keel, O., and C. Uehlinger. *Gods, Goddesses, and Images in Ancient Israel*. Edinburgh: T&T Clark, 1998.
Keener, Craig S. *A Commentary on the Gospel of Matthew*. Grand Rapids: Eerdmans, 1999.
King, Diane E. *Kurdistan on the Global Stage: Kinship, Land and Community in Iraq*. New Brunswick, NJ: Rutgers University Press, 2014.

Bibliography

Klijn, A. F. J., and G. J. Reinink. *Patristic Evidence for Jewish-Christian Sects*. Supplements to Novum Testamentum 36. Leiden: Brill, 1973.
Konradt, Matthias. *Israel, Church, and the Gentiles in the Gospel of Matthew*. Baylor-Mohr Siebeck Studies in Early Christianity. Translated by Kathleen Ess. Waco, TX: Baylor University Press, 2014.
Kugel, James L. "Early Jewish Biblical Interpretation." In *The Eerdmans Dictionary of Early Judaism*, edited by John J. Collins and Daniel C. Harlow, 121–41. Grand Rapids: Eerdmans, 2010.
Landmesser, C., ed. *Theologie und Wirklichkeit. Diskussionen der Bultmann-Schule*. Neukirchen-Vluyn: Neukirchener, 2011.
Leaver, Robin A. "Eschatology, Theology and Music: Death and Beyond in Bach's Vocal Music." In *Bach Studies from Dublin*, edited by Anne Leahy and Yo Tomita, 129–47. Dublin: Four Courts, 2004.
———. *J. S. Bach as Preacher: His Passions and Music in Worship*. St. Louis: Concordia, 1984.
———. *Music as Preaching: Bach, Passions and Music in Worship*. Oxford: Latimer House, 1983.
Lee, Robert E. A. "Bach's Living Music of Death." *Dialog: A Journal of Theology* 24, no. 2 (1985): 102–6.
Liddon, H. *The Divinity of Our Lord and Saviour Jesus Christ*. 8th ed. London: Rivingtons, 1978.
Loader, William R. G. "Christ at the Right Hand—Ps. CX.1 in the New Testament." *New Testament Studies* 24 (1978): 199–217.
Longenecker, Bruce. *The Cross before Constantine: The Early Life of a Christian Symbol*. Minneapolis: Fortress, 2015.
———. *The Crosses of Pompeii: Jesus-Devotion in a Vesuvian Town*. Minneapolis: Fortress, 2016.
Luther, Martin. *D. Martin Luthers Werke*. 120 vols. Weimar: H. Böhlau, 1883–2009.
MacMullen, Ramsay. *The Second Church: Popular Christianity A.D. 200–400*. Atlanta: SBL, 2009.
Maier, F. G., ed. *Fischer Weltgeschichte*, vol. 13, *Byzanz*. Frankfurt: S. Fischer Verlag, 1973.
Malina, Bruce. "Mediterranean Sacrifice: Dimensions of Domestic and Political Religion." *Biblical Theology Bulletin* 26 (1996): 26–44.
———. "Religion in the Imagined New Testament World: More Social Science Lenses." *Scriptura* 51 (1994): 1–26.
Marissen, Michael. *Lutheranism, Anti-Judaism, and Bach's St. John Passion*. New York: Oxford University Press, 1998.
———. "The Theological Character of J. S. Bach's *Musical Offering*." In *Bach Studies 2*, edited by Daniel R. Melamed, 85–106. Cambridge: Cambridge University Press, 1995.
Marshall, I. Howard. *Luke*. New International Greek Testament Commentary. Grand Rapids: Eerdmans, 1978.
Martyn, J. Louis. *History and Theology in the Fourth Gospel*. New York: Harper & Row, 1968.

McGrath, James F. *The Only True God: Early Christian Monotheism in Its Jewish Context*. Urbana: University of Illinois Press, 2009.

Meier, John P. *Law and History in Matthew's Gospel*. Analecta Biblica 71. Rome: Biblical Institute, 1976.

———. *A Marginal Jew: Rethinking the Historical Jesus*, volume 2, *Mentor, Message, and Miracles*. New York: Doubleday, 1994.

———. "Matthew and Ignatius: A Response to William R. Schoedel." In *Social History of the Matthean Community: Cross-Disciplinary Approaches*, edited by David L. Balch, 178–86. Minneapolis: Fortress, 1991.

Mellers, Wilfrid H. *Bach and the Dance of God*. Oxford: Oxford University Press, 1981.

Meyer, Ben F. *The Aims of Jesus*. London: SCM, 1979.

Midgley, M. *Beast and Man: The Roots of Human Nature*. Hassocks, UK: Harvester, 1978.

Milgrom, J. *Leviticus 1–16*. New York: Doubleday, 1991.

Mitchell, Claire. "Behind the Ethnic Marker: Religion and Social Identification in Northern Ireland." *Sociology of Religion* 66 (2005): 1–22.

———. "The Religious Content of Ethnic Identities." *Sociology* 40 (2006): 1135–52.

Moll, Sebastian. *The Arch-Heretic Marcion*. Wissenschaftliche Untersuchungen zum Neuen Testament 250. Tübingen: Mohr Siebeck, 2010.

Moltmann, Jürgen. "Christ's Resurrection—the Resurrection of the Body—the Resurrection of Nature." In *Sun of Righteousness, Arise! God's Future for Humanity and the Earth*, translated by Margaret Kohl, 37–73. London/Minneapolis: Fortress, 2010.

———. *The Coming of God: Christian Eschatology*. Translated by Margaret Kohl. London and Minneapolis: Fortress, 1996.

———. *The Crucified God*. London: SCM, 1974.

———. *Experiences in Theology*. Translated by Margaret Kohl. London/Minneapolis: Fortress, 2000.

———. *God for a Secular Society: The Public Relevance of Theology*. Minneapolis: Fortress, 1999.

———. *God in Creation: An Ecological Doctrine of Creation*. The Gifford Lectures 1984–85. Translated by Margaret Kohl. London/San Francisco: SCM, 1985.

———. *The Spirit of Life: A Universal Affirmation*. Translated by Margaret Kohl. London: Fortress, 1992.

Morris, L. L. "The Meaning of *Hilastērion* in Romans 3:25." *New Testament Studies* 2 (1955–56): 33–43.

Mounce, Robert H. *The Book of Revelation*. New International Commentary on the New Testament. Grand Rapids: Eerdmans, 1977, rev. ed. 1997.

Murdoch, I. *The Sovereignty of Good*. London: Routledge & Kegan Paul, 1970.

Murphy-O'Connor, Jerome. "John the Baptist and Jesus: History and Hypotheses." *New Testament Studies* 36 (1990): 359–74.

Newman, Carey C. *Paul's Glory-Christology: Tradition and Rhetoric*. Supplements to Novum Testamentum 69. Leiden: Brill, 1992.

Newmyer, S. T. *Animals in Greek and Roman Thought*. London: Routledge, 2011.

Osborne, C. *Dumb Beasts and Dead Philosophers*. Oxford: Oxford University Press, 2007.

Bibliography

Pannenberg, W. *Jesus—God and Man*. Translated by L. L. Wilkins and D. A. Priebe. London: SCM, 1968.
Peacock, James L., Patricia M. Thornton, and Patrick B. Inman, eds. *Identity Matters: Ethnic and Sectarian Conflict*. New York/Oxford: Berghahn, 2007.
Pelikan, Jaroslav J. *Bach among the Theologians*. Philadelphia: Fortress, 1986.
Perrin, Norman. *A Modern Pilgrimage in New Testament Christology*. Philadelphia: Fortress, 1974.
Plantinga, Richard J. "The Integration of Music and Theology in the Vocal Compositions of J. S. Bach." In *Resonant Witness: Conversations between Music and Theology*, edited by Jeremy S. Begbie and Steven R. Guthrie, 215–39. Grand Rapids: Eerdmans, 2011.
Reeg, Gottfried, *Die Geschichte von den Zehn Märtyrern: Synoptische Edition mit Übersetzung und Einleitung*. Texte und Studien zum antiken Judentum 10. Tübingen: Mohr Siebeck, 1985.
Ricoeur, Paul. *Oneself as Another*. Chicago: University of Chicago Press, 1992.
Sanday, W., and A. C. Headlam. *Romans*. International Critical Commentary. Edinburgh: T. & T. Clark, 2nd ed., 1896.
Sandbach, F. H. *The Stoics*. London: Chatto & Windus, 1975.
Schäfer, Peter. *Geniza-Fragmente zur Hekhalot-Literatur*. Texte und Studien zum antiken Judentum 6. Tübingen: Mohr Siebeck, 1984.
———. *The Jewish Jesus: How Judaism and Christianity Shaped Each Other*. Princeton: Princeton University Press, 2012.
———. *The Origins of Jewish Mysticism*. Tübingen: Mohr Siebeck, 2009.
Schäfer, Peter, et al. *Synopse zur Hekhalot-Literatur*. Texte und Studien zum antiken Judentum 2. Tübingen: Mohr Siebeck, 1981.
Schleiermacher, F. *Glaubenslehre*. 2nd ed. Berlin: G. Reimer, 1830.
Schnackenburg, R. *The Gospel according to John*. 3 vols. Translated by Kevin Smyth. New York: Seabury, 1980.
Schneider, David M. *A Critique of the Study of Kinship*. Ann Arbor: University of Michigan Press, 1984.
Scott, J. M., ed. *Exile: A Conversation with N. T. Wright*. Downers Grove, IL: IVP, forthcoming.
Segal, Alan F. *Two Powers in Heaven: Early Rabbinic Reports about Christianity and Gnosticism*. Studies in Judaism in Late Antiquity 25. Leiden: Brill, 1977; reprinted Waco, TX: Baylor University Press, 2013.
Segal, E. "Justice, Mercy and a Bird's Nest." *Journal of Jewish Studies* (1991): 176–95.
Shaw, Brent D. "The Myth of the Neronian Persecution." *Journal of Roman Studies* 105 (2015): 73–100.
Sim, David C. *The Gospel of Matthew and Christian Judaism: The History and Social Setting of the Matthean Community*. Edinburgh: T&T Clark, 1998.
Sklar, J. *Sin, Impurity, Sacrifice, Atonement: The Priestly Conceptions*. Sheffield: Sheffield Phoenix, 2005.
Smaill, Peter. "Bach among the Heretics: Inferences from the Cantata Texts." *Understanding Bach* 4 (2009): 101–18.
Smith, D. Moody. *John among the Gospels*. Minneapolis: Fortress, 1992.

Smith, Wilfred Cantwell. *The Meaning and End of Religion*. Minneapolis: Fortress, 1991 (1962).
Sorabji, R. *Animal Minds and Human Morals: The Origin of the Western Debate*. London: Duckworth, 1993.
Stăniloae, D. *Orthodoxe Dogmatik*. Gütersloh: Christian Kaiser Verlag, 1985.
Stanton, Graham N. *A Gospel for a New People: Studies in Matthew*. Edinburgh: T&T Clark, 1992.
Stapert, Calvin. *My Only Comfort: Death, Deliverance, and Discipleship in the Music of Bach*. Grand Rapids: Eerdmans, 2000.
Staudt, Darina. *Der eine und einzige Gott: Monotheistische Formeln im Urchristentum und ihre Vorgeschichte bei Griechen und Juden*. Novum Testamentum et Orbis Antiquus 80. Göttingen: Vandenhoeck & Ruprecht, 2012.
Stökl ben Ezra, D. *The Impact of Yom Kippur on Early Christianity: The Day of Atonement from Second Temple Judaism to the Fifth Century*. Tübingen: Mohr Siebeck, 2003.
Strauss, David. *The Life of Jesus Critically Examined*. Edited by Peter Hodgson. Translated by George Eliot. Philadelphia: Fortress, 1972.
Streeter, B. H. *The Four Gospels*. London: Macmillan, 1930.
Stuckenbruck, Loren T. "'Do Not Worship Me, Worship God': The Problem of Angel Veneration in Early Judaism and Aspects of Angelomorphic Christology in the Apocalypse of John." PhD dissertation, Princeton Seminary, 1993; thereafter published as *Angel Veneration and Christology*. Wissenschaftliche Untersuchungen zum Neuen Testament 2/70. Tübingen: Mohr Siebeck, 1995.
Thiselton, Anthony C. *The Hermeneutics of Doctrine*. Grand Rapids: Eerdmans, 2007.
Toft, Monica Duffy. *The Geography of Ethnic Violence: Identity, Interests, and the Indivisibility of Territory*. Princeton: Princeton University Press, 2005.
Torrance, Thomas F. *God and Rationality*. London: Oxford University Press, 1971.
———. *Theological Science*. London: Oxford University Press, 1969.
———. *Theology in Reconstruction*. London: SCM, 1965.
Toynbee, J. M. C. *Animals in Roman Life and Art*. London: Thames & Hudson, 1973.
Treat, J. R. *The Crucified King: Atonement and Kingdom in Biblical and Systematic Theology*. Grand Rapids: Zondervan, 2014.
Trilling, Wolfgang. *Das Wahre Israel: Studien zur Theologie das Matthäusevangeliums*. Munich: Kösel, 1964.
Turley, Stephen R. *The Ritualized Revelation of the Messianic Age: Washings and Meals in Galatians and 1 Corinthians*. London: Bloomsbury, 2015.
Vanhoozer, K. J. "Does the Trinity Belong to a Theology of Religions? On Angling in the Rubicon and the 'Identity' of God." In *The Trinity in a Pluralistic Age*, edited by K. J. Vanhoozer, 41–71. Grand Rapids: Eerdmans, 1997.
Verbruggen, J. L. "Of Muzzles and Oxen: Deuteronomy 25.4 and I Corinthians 9.9." *Journal of the Evangelical Theological Society* 49 (2006): 699–711.
Verkuyten, Maykel, and Borja Martinovic. "Social Identity Complexity and Immigrants' Attitude toward the Host Nation: The Intersection of Ethnic and Religious Group Identification." *Personality and Social Psychology Bulletin* 38 (2012): 1165–77.

Webb, Robert. "John the Baptist and His Relationship to Jesus." In *Studying the Historical Jesus*, edited by Bruce Chilton and Craig A. Evans, 179–229. Leiden: Brill, 1994.

———. *John the Baptizer and Prophet*. Journal for the Study of the New Testament Supplement Series 62. Sheffield: JSOT Press, 1991.

Webb, Stephen H. *On God and Dogs: A Christian Theology of Compassion for Animals*. New York: Oxford University Press, 1998.

Weiss, Johannes. *Earliest Christianity*. Translated by F. C. Grant. New York: Harper Torchbooks, 1959.

Welker, M. *God the Spirit*. Translated by J. F. Hoffmeyer. Minneapolis: Augsburg Fortress, 1994.

White, Vernon. *Atonement and Incarnation: An Essay in Universalism and Particularity*. Cambridge: Cambridge University Press, 1991.

Williams, Bernard. "The Makropulos Case: Reflections on the Tedium of Immortality." In *Problems of the Self*, edited by Bernard Williams, 82–100. Cambridge: Cambridge University Press, 1976.

Williams, J. J. *Christ Died for Our Sins: Representation and Substitution in Romans and Their Jewish Martyrological Background*. Eugene, OR: Pickwick, 2015.

Williams, Peter F. *Bach: The Goldberg Variations*. Cambridge: Cambridge University Press, 2001.

Wolff, Christoph. *Johann Sebastian Bach: The Learned Musician*. New York: W. W. Norton, 2000.

Wolff, Stefan. *Ethnic Conflict: A Global Perspective*. Oxford: Oxford University Press, 2006.

Wright, G. Ernest. *The God Who Acts: Biblical Theology as Recital*. London: SCM, 1964.

Wright, N. T. *The Climax of the Covenant*. Edinburgh: T&T Clark, 1991; Philadelphia: Fortress, 1992.

———. *Jesus and the Victory of God*. Minneapolis: Fortress, 1996.

———. *Justification: God's Plan and Paul's Vision*. London: SPCK; Downers Grove, IL: IVP, 2009.

———. "Justification by (Covenantal) Faith to the (Covenantal) Doers: Romans 2 within the Argument of the Letter." In *Doing Theology for the Church: Essays in Honor of Klyne Snodgrass*, edited by R. A. Eklund and J. E. Phelan Jr., 95–108. Chicago: Covenant; Eugene, OR: Wipf & Stock, 2014.

———. *The Kingdom New Testament: A Contemporary Translation*. San Francisco: HarperOne, 2011.

———. *The New Testament and the People of God*. Minneapolis: Fortress, 1992.

———. *Paul and His Recent Interpreters*. London: SPCK; Minneapolis: Fortress, 2015.

———. *Paul and the Faithfulness of God*. London: SPCK; Minneapolis: Fortress, 2013.

———. *Pauline Perspectives*. London: SPCK; Minneapolis: Fortress, 2013.

———. *Romans*. New Interpreters Bible 10. Nashville: Abingdon, 2002.

Yamaguchi, Norio. *Sacrifice, Curse and the Covenant in Paul's Soteriology*. PhD dissertation, University of St Andrews, 2015.

Zagefka, Hannah. "The Concept of Ethnicity in Social Psychological Research: Definitional Issues." *International Journal of Intercultural Relations* 33 (2009): 228–41.

BIBLIOGRAPHY

Zander, H. C. *Als die Religion noch nicht langweilig war. Die Geschichte der Wüstenväter.* Gütersloh: Gütersloher Verlagshaus, 2011.

Ziesler, J. *Paul's Letter to the Romans.* London: SCM, 1989.

Contributors

Editors

DANIEL M. GURTNER, Ernest and Mildred Hogan Professor of New Testament, Southern Seminary (USA)

GRANT MACASKILL, Kirby Laing Chair of New Testament Exegesis, University of Aberdeen (Scotland)

JONATHAN T. PENNINGTON, Associate Professor of New Testament, Director of Research Doctoral Studies, Southern Seminary (USA)

Contributors

PHILIP ALEXANDER, Emeritus Professor of Post-Biblical Jewish Literature, University of Manchester (England)

JEREMY BEGBIE, Thomas A. Langford Research Professor of Theology, Duke Divinity School (USA)

DAVID BROWN, Emeritus Professor of Theology, Aesthetics and Culture, University of St Andrews (Scotland)

JAMES R. DAVILA, Professor of Early Jewish Studies, University of St Andrews (Scotland)

CONTRIBUTORS

James D. G. Dunn, Emeritus Lightfoot Professor of Divinity, University of Durham (England)

Philip F. Esler, Portland Chair in New Testament Studies, University of Gloucestershire (England)

Trevor Hart, Rector, Saint Andrew's Episcopal Church, St Andrews, and Honorary Professor of Divinity in the University of St Andrews (Scotland)

Larry W. Hurtado, Emeritus Professor of New Testament Language, Literature, and Theology in the School of Divinity at the University of Edinburgh (Scotland)

Bruce Longenecker, Professor of Religion and W. W. Melton Chair, Baylor University (USA)

Sean McDonough, Professor of New Testament, Gordon-Conwell Theological Seminary (USA)

Jürgen Moltmann, Professor Emeritus of Systematic Theology, University of Tübingen (Germany)

Micheal O'Siadhail, Poet; Distinguished Poet in Residence, Union Theological Seminary, New York (USA); formerly Professor, Dublin Institute for Advanced Studies (Ireland)

N. T. Wright, Professor of New Testament and Early Christianity, University of St Andrews (Scotland)

Index of Authors

Alexander, Philip, 7, 8, 97, 216
Allison, D. C., 189, 195
Aune, David E., 92, 217, 220, 223, 224

Bailey, D. P., 157
Balentine, S. E., 139
Balibar, Étienne, 184
Barclay, John, 185
Barrett, C. K., 73, 169, 170, 173
Barth, Fredrik, 190
Bauckham, Richard, 1, 3, 4, 5, 6, 7, 8, 9, 10, 11, 12, 13, 17, 18, 19, 29, 30, 35, 36, 37, 38, 39, 44, 46, 47, 48, 49, 50, 51, 52, 54, 55, 56, 57, 58, 59, 60, 61, 62, 63, 65, 66, 72, 74, 75, 76, 79, 82, 83, 84, 85, 86, 87, 88, 89, 90, 91, 92, 93, 94, 95, 96, 110, 111, 135, 157, 162, 169, 170, 171, 177, 197, 201, 215, 225
Bauman, Zygmunt, 52
Begbie, Jeremy S., 3, 4, 29, 35, 40, 44
Benz, E., 23
Berger, Karol, 3, 30, 31, 32, 33, 34, 35, 36, 37, 38, 39, 40, 41, 42, 43, 44, 45, 46
Berkman, J., 77
Bird, M. F., 147
Bousset, Wilhelm, 83
Boustan, Ra'anan S., 224, 226, 227
Boyarin, Daniel, 99, 221

Brown, David, 5, 6, 65
Brown, Raymond, 162, 164, 171
Buell, Denise Kimber, 183, 185
Burkert, Walter, 164
Butt, John, 4, 29, 30, 41, 45, 46, 47
Byrne, B., 150
Byron, John, 6
Byron, Reginald, 178

Campbell, D. A., 137
Campbell, Jonathan G., 93
Capes, David B., 91
Carson, D. A., 169
Carsten, Jane, 184
Casey, Maurice, 86
Chafe, Eric T., 30, 40, 42, 44
Charles, R. H., 217, 220, 223, 224
Chester, Andrew, 87
Cohen, Martin Samuel, 215
Cornell, Stephen E., 183, 184
Cranfield, C. E. B., 72, 73, 75, 149, 154

Darwin, C., 77, 78
Davidson, R. M., 141
Davies, W. D., 189, 195
Davila, James R., 13, 85, 86, 93, 215, 216, 218, 220, 221
Denzinger, Heinrich, 76

263

INDEX OF AUTHORS

Dodd, C. H., 162, 170
Dreyfus, Laurence, 31
Duling, D., 187, 189
Dunn, James D. G., 8, 9, 11, 86, 115
Dürr, Alfred, 43

Eagleton, Terry, 57
Eckstein, H.-J., 21
Elon, Menachem, 108
Erikson, E. H., 178
Esler, Philip F., 11, 12, 177, 185, 186, 187, 188, 190, 192, 193, 195

Fitzmyer, J. A., 72
Ford, J. Massyngberde, 217, 220, 223, 224
Foster, Paul, 193
France, R. T., 162, 166, 167, 172
Fredriksen, Paula, 163
Frey, J., 136

Gieschen, Charles A., 220
Gilhus, I. S., 70, 76, 77
Grabiner, Steven, 216
Green, Joel, 162, 174
Gunton, Colin E., 50, 51

Haenchen, Ernst, 169, 172
Halperin, David, 216, 223
Hart, David Bentley, 47
Hart, Trevor, 4, 5, 18, 35, 36, 37, 38, 49, 54, 59, 63
Hartmann, Douglas, 183, 184
Hay, David M., 91
Hays, Richard B., 36
Headlam, A. C., 72
Hengel, Martin, 83, 91, 159
Hick, John, 61, 62
Hieke, T., 138
Hollenbach, Paul W., 162, 165
Horrell, David G., 183, 188, 195
Huffmon, H. B., 141
Hurtado, Larry W., 6, 7, 8, 82, 83, 84, 85, 86, 87, 89, 92, 95, 201
Hutchinson, John, 180, 181, 185, 187

Inman, Patrick B., 179

Jewett, R., 136, 137, 144
Johnson, E. A., 79

Käsemann, E., 137
Keel, O., 101
Keener, Craig S., 191
King, Diane E., 179, 180
Klijn, A. F. J., 128
Konradt, Matthias, 194
Kugel, James L., 93

Landmesser, C., 20
Leaver, Robin A., 32, 40, 41, 44
Lee, Robert E. A., 44
Liddon, H. P., 97
Loader, William R. G., 91
Lohr, Joel, 6
Longenecker, Bruce, 12, 197
Luther, Martin, 19, 22, 43, 80

MacMullen, Ramsay, 12, 197, 198
Maier, F. G., 24
Malina, Bruce, 181, 192
Marissen, Michael, 30, 40
Marshall, I. Howard, 173
Martinovic, Borja, 182
Martyn, J. Louis, 169
McGrath, James F., 86
Meier, John P., 163, 165, 191, 193
Mellers, Wilfrid H., 30
Meyer, Ben F., 165, 166, 167, 173
Midgley, M., 78
Milgrom, J., 139
Mitchell, Claire, 182
Moll, Sebastian, 96
Moltmann, Jürgen, 2, 3, 17, 18, 20, 21, 25, 26, 28, 35, 37, 39, 51, 52, 53, 54, 63, 79, 96
Morris, L. L., 153
Mounce, Robert H., 217, 220, 223, 224
Murdoch, I., 78
Murphy-O'Connor, Jerome, 162, 163, 165, 166, 168

Newman, Carey C., 85, 86, 221
Newmyer, S. T., 70

Index of Authors

Nicklas, T., 138

Osborne, C., 68

Pannenberg, W., 21
Peacock, James L., 179
Pelikan, Jaroslav J., 40
Perrin, Norman, 82
Plantinga, Richard J., 44

Reeg, Gottfried, 224
Reinink, G. J., 128
Ricoeur, Paul, 52

Sanday, W., 72
Sandbach, F. H., 75
Schäfer, Peter, 215, 222
Schleiermacher, F., 22
Schnackenburg, R., 170
Schneider, David M., 184
Schönmetzer, Adolf, 76
Schröter, J., 136
Scott, J. M., 144
Segal, Alan F., 83
Segal, E., 74
Shaw, Brent D., 201
Sim, David C., 193
Sklar, J., 138, 139
Smaill, Peter, 30
Smith, Anthony, 180, 181, 185, 187
Smith, D. Moody, 169
Smith, Wilfrid Cantwell, 181, 192
Sorabji, R., 67
Sprinkle, P. M., 147
Stăniloae, D., 25
Stanton, Graham N., 195
Stapert, Calvin, 42

Staudt, Darina, 87
Stökl ben Ezra, D., 138
Strauss, David, 163
Streeter, B. H., 169

Thiselton, Anthony C., 47
Thornton, Patricia M., 179
Toft, Monica Duffy, 181
Torrance, Thomas F., 59
Trilling, Wolfgang, 195, 196
Turley, Stephen R., 190

Uehlinger, C., 101

Vanhoozer, K. J., 111
Verbruggen, J. L., 74
Verkuyten, Maykel, 182

Webb, Robert, 162, 163, 164, 165, 166, 168
Webb, Stephen H., 78
Weiss, Johannes, 85
Welker, M., 21, 26
White, Vernon, 62
Williams, Bernard, 39
Williams, J. J., 136, 159
Williams, Peter F., 47
Wolff, Christoph, 31
Wolff, Stefan, 181
Wright, G. E., 111
Wright, N. T., 9, 10, 135, 140, 146, 148, 156, 167, 168, 174

Yamaguchi, Norio, 9, 135, 148

Zagefka, Hannah, 182
Zander, H. C., 20
Ziesler, J., 72

Index of Scripture and Other Ancient Texts

OLD TESTAMENT

Genesis
1	102, 103
1:1	102, 112
1:24	25
1:26–28	68, 72
1:27	103
1:29–30	72
2:7	26
2:24	24
3:17–18	72
3:19	25
9:2–3	72
9:9–10	25
15	146, 148, 150
15:13–16	148
24:14	79

Exodus
2:24	150
3:6	95
3:15	95
9:10–11	224
9:12	224
15:13	157
20:3–6	100, 101, 103
20:5	106
23:22	195
23:24	106
24:7–8	158
24:8	151
25:17–22	139
25:22	155
40:35	139

Leviticus
1:9	223
1:13	223
1:17	223
8:6	164
14:8	164
15:1–31	164
16	138
23	138

Numbers
22:21–33	79

Deuteronomy
5:7–10	100
5:9	106
13:3	106
15:12–15	74
22:6–7	74
24:17–18	74
25:4	73, 74
27–32	141

Joshua
24:2	95

2 Samuel
7	174
12:3	79

2 Kings
2:9	217

1 Chronicles
28:12	217

Ezra
9	144

Nehemiah
9	144
9:36	148

Job
2:7	224
19:26	24

Psalms

2	174
18:13–14 [EVV 18:12–13]	219
45	143
48:8 [EVV 47:7]	217
65:2	24
72	143
82:1	93
84:2	19, 24
104:30	26
110	91, 92
110:1	7, 92
110:4	125
145:21	24

Proverbs

8	103, 109
8:22–31	91
11:22	75

Qoheleth

7:9	217
8:8	217

Isaiah

1:2–20	141
3:21	75
4:4	217
5:1–7	194
6	228
6:1–6	222
11:4	217
14:12–20	226
32:15–16	27
40–55	9, 10, 141, 148, 151
40:1–2	151
40:5	25
40:6–7	25
42:1–4	191
45:22–25	92
49	143
49:6	143
51:9	159
52:5	144
52:9	150
52:10	159
52:13–53:12	148
53	10, 148, 150, 151, 153, 158, 160
53:1	159
53:10–12	150
53:12	148
64:4	219
65:4	75
66:3	75, 76
66:17	75

Jeremiah

25:31	25
31:31–34	125

Ezekiel

1	222, 228
1:4	222
1:13	222
1:16	222
1:22	222
1:26	222
1:27	222
1:28	222
3:12	217
10	222, 228
10:1	222
10:2	222
10:6	222
10:9	222
11:24	217
27	225
27:12–24	225
28	226
36:20	144
36:25	164
37:1	217

Daniel

7	228
7:9	220
7:9–10	222
9	141, 144, 148
10:5–6	220

Hosea

4:1–3	141

Joel

2	26, 27

Amos

3:1–15	141

Micah

3:8	217

Zechariah

1:6	217
1:8	223
4:6	217
7:12	217

NEW TESTAMENT

Matthew

1–2	187
1:1–2	191
1:2	189
1:2–17	187
1:18–25	188
1:21	188
1:23	177
2:1	188
2:2	188, 193
2:6	188
3:7b–9	192
3:9	188
4	171
4:15	189, 194
4:17	172
4:23	193
5:4	126
5:17–20	118, 193
5:19	194
5:34	126
5:34–37	126
5:47	189
6:7	189
6:13	199

INDEX OF SCRIPTURE AND OTHER ANCIENT TEXTS

6:20	126	23:12	126	3:7	204
6:32	189, 194	23:28	118	3:8	204
7:6	76	23:30	192	3:10	204
7:7	126	23:31	192	3:11	204, 210, 212
7:23	118	23:33	192	3:15	204
8:5–13	189, 190	23:37	194	3:22	205
8:10–12	189	24:7	189, 190, 194	3:27	205
8:11	190, 191	24:9	189, 190	4	205, 213
8:12	196	24:12	118	4:16–17	212
9:9–13	191	24:14	189, 190, 194	4:35–41	22
9:18–26	22	24:20	118	4:39	205
9:35	193	25	43	5:1–17	75
10:5	189, 194	25:31–46	177, 190	5:1–20	75
10:5–6	118	25:32	189, 190, 191, 194	5:2	217
10:17	193	27:11	193	5:7	210, 212
10:18	189, 190, 194	27:29	193	5:17	206
10:40	177	27:37	193	5:18	206
12:9	193	28:15	193	5:19	206
12:18	189	28:19	119, 189, 191, 194	5:20	206
12:18–21	190	28:19–20	190, 192	5:21–24	206
12:21	189, 191	28:20	119, 177	5:29	206
12:28	217			5:30	206
13:41	118	**Mark**		5:35–43	206
13:54	193	1	171	5:42	206
15:2	164	1:7	202	6:1–4	171
15:11	118	1:8	202	6:3	206
15:21–28	189	1:10	210	6:5	206
15:24	189	1:10–11	202	6:7	206
16	192	1:11	210, 212	6:13	206
18	191, 192	1:13	22, 171	6:14	206
18:15	195	1:14	171, 205	6:16	206
18:17	189, 191	1:14–15	202	6:34	207
18:20	177	1:15	172	6:47–51	207
20:19	189, 194	1:23	217	6:52	207
20:25	189, 194	1:25	205	6:55–56	207
21:33–46	194	1:27	203	7	118
21:41b	194	1:31	203	7:1–15	207
21:43	11, 12, 177, 178, 189, 190, 194, 195, 196	1:39	203	7:3–4	207
		1:42	203	7:15	118
		1:45	203	7:17–23	207
21:44	194	2	204	7:19	118
21:45	194	2:11	203	7:24–30	76
22:43	217	2:12	204	7:28	76
23	192, 193	2:13	204	7:30	207
23:8–9	193	3:5	204	7:37	207
23:8–12	193, 195	3:6	204	8–10	213

Index of Scripture and Other Ancient Texts

Reference	Page(s)
8	208, 213
8:1–10	207
8:2	207
8:11–21	208
8:22–26	208
8:25	208
8:28–29	208
8:34	208
8:35	208
8:38	210
9:1	208
9:2	208
9:3	208
9:7	209, 210, 212
9:14–15	209
9:14–29	209
9:27	209
9:30–32	209
9:35	209
9:37	210
9:38–41	209
9:42	209
9:43–48	209
10:2–12	209
10:17–27	210
10:21–22	210
10:28–31	210
10:32–35	210
10:35–41	210
10:45	150
11:1–6	209
11:7–10	209, 212
11:27–12:27	209
12:1–12	194
12:28–34	209
12:35–40	209
12:36	217
12:41–44	210
13:9–13	210
13:14	211
13:18	118
13:19	211
13:24–27	211
13:31	211
13:32	210, 211, 212
14:1–2	212
14:9	214
14:12–16	209
14:17–52	211
14:21	212
14:36	210
14:61–62	211
14:66–72	211
15:11–14	212
15:21–47	213
15:39	210, 212
16:6	203

Luke

Reference	Page(s)
1:17	217
2:38	150
3:7	167
4	171
4:24	171
6:20b	126
6:21b	126
6:24–25	126
8:2	75
8:26–39	75
11:9	126
12:33b	126
13:28–29	190
14:11	126
15:15–16	75
24:21	150

John

Reference	Page(s)
1–3	172
1:19–4:43	171
1:25	168
1:32–34	170
1:33	217
1:35–51	172
1:35–3:21	170
1:41	122
2:1–11	122
2:1–12	172
2:13–25	172
2:19–22	122
2:23–25	175
3–4	10, 11
3	162, 163, 169, 172
3:1–21	172
3:22	163
3:23	170
3:24	171
3:25–36	173
3:30	171
4	162, 163, 169
4:1–3	174
4:2	171, 172, 173
4:3	170, 171
4:22	123
4:23	122
4:23–24	217
4:25	122
4:44	171
4:45	171
5:13	175
5:16	123
5:18	123
5:22–23	88, 94
6	122
6:15	175
6:41	123
6:52	123
7	175
7:1	123
7:11–12	123
7:13	123
8	122
8:48	123
8:52	123
8:56	122
8:57–59	123
9:22	123
10:19–21	123
10:31–33	123
10:40	175
11:8	123
11:36	123
12:11	123
12:42	123
16:2	123

Acts

Reference	Page(s)
2	26, 186
2:5	186

INDEX OF SCRIPTURE AND OTHER ANCIENT TEXTS

2:9	186	18:18	121	3:1–2	130
2:14–36	119	19:8	121	3:1–5	152
3:2	119	20:3	121	3:1–9	142, 146
3:9–11	119	20:6–15	119	3:2	148
3:12–26	119	20:19	121	3:2–3	152
5:1–10	119	21:1–18	119	3:2–5	146
5:17	122	21:17–26:32	121	3:2b–4a	145
8	120	21:26	121	3:3	149
9:32–43	121	21:39	121	3:4	145, 149
10–11	120	22:3	121	3:5	149
10:1–2	190	24:5	122	3:5a	149
10:1–11:18	120	24:14	122	3:6	149
10:2	121	24:17	130	3:9	145
11:1–3	190	25:8	121	3:19–20	137, 141
12	120	26:5	122	3:20	145, 149
12:17	120	27:1–28:16	119	3:21	140, 147, 149, 154
13–14	120	28:21–22	121	3:21–22	136
13	116	28:22	122	3:21–26	137, 141, 142, 146, 148, 149, 157, 160, 161
13:11	119	28:28	121		
13:12	120	28:30–31	121		
13:13–21	120			3:21–31	148
13:14	121	**Romans**		3:21–4:25	142, 148
13:16–41	119	1–4	142, 150, 159	3:22	149, 150, 152, 157, 158
13:45	121	1:3–4	148		
13:46	121	1:4	21	3:23	137, 145, 152, 155
13:50	121	1:16	130, 143, 200	3:24	150
14:1	121	1:16–17	152	3:24–26	9, 10, 135, 140, 141, 146, 148, 149, 151, 154, 160
14:2	121	1:17	136		
14:8	119	1:18	137, 145		
14:11–13	119	1:18–2:16	145, 147, 149, 154, 158	3:25	136, 138, 140, 149, 151
14:14–17	119				
14:18	119	1:18–3:20	142, 145	3:25–26	137, 146, 153
14:19	121	2:1–16	141, 142	3:26	136, 140, 149, 154
15	120	2:4	155	3:27–31	142, 146
15:5	122	2:5	155	3:29	130
15:7–11	120	2:9–10	130	4	10, 130, 146, 158
15:13–21	127	2:17	142, 144, 146, 155, 157	4:23–25	147
15:19–21	121			4:24–25	148, 152, 153
16:10–17	119	2:17–24	10, 142, 143, 144, 149	4:25	146, 150
17:1–2	121			5–8	142
17:5	121	2:17–3:20	146, 151	5:1–2	155
17:10	121	2:19–20	148, 149	5:1–11	142
17:13	121	2:21–23	143	5:2	152
17:30	156	2:25–29	144, 146, 158	5:6–11	160
18:4	121	2:26	155	5:8–10	9, 140
18:6	121	3	156, 157	5:9	141, 154, 156

Index of Scripture and Other Ancient Texts

5:10b	158	6:14	200	3:5	217
5:20	146	8:6	20, 88	5:22–29	81
7–8	130	9:9–10	73	6:18	217
7:1–8:11	154	9:20	121		
7:7–8:11	146	11	80	**Philippians**	
8	142	11:25	154, 158	2:6–11	21, 84
8:1–4	140	12:13	80	2:9–11	88, 93
8:3	152	14	80	2:19–20	143
8:3–4	154	14:16	217	3:4–6	143
8:9	217	15	80	3:21	200
8:18–25	152	15:20–28	90		
8:20	72	15:24	23	**Colossians**	
8:21–23	73	15:25–26	23	1:20	20
8:31–39	160	15:27	88	2:9	22
8:38–39	200	15:28	24	2:10	24
9–11	130, 142, 152			2:15	24
9:24	130	**2 Corinthians**		3:11	80
10:12	130	4:7	200		
10:13	91	5:17	20	**1 Thessalonians**	
11	80	5:19	20, 90	1:10	140
11:13	115, 121	6:7	200	2:14	127
11:17–18	80	10:4	200	5:9	140
11:25–32	196	11:24	127		
13:10	130	13:4	200	**1 Timothy**	
14:14	118			2	80
15:6	95	**Galatians**		3:16	217
15:8	148	1:13	187		
15:8–9	143, 147	1:14	187	**Hebrews**	
15:9	143	2:1–10	116, 127, 129	1:1–2	124
15:11	143	2:9	116	1:1–4	88
15:13	200	2:11–14	116, 120, 129	1:6	94
15:16	217	2:12	117	2:17	124
15:26	130	2:15–21	117, 120	3:2	124
16	116	2:16	126	3:3–6	124
16:3	116	3	142, 146, 195	3:7–4:11	124
16:6	116	3:13–14	156	7:3	124
16:7	116	3:28	79, 121	7:17	125
16:11	116	5:1	129	7:22	125
16:13	116	5:6	126, 129	8	125
		5:16–23	129	8:8–12	125
1 Corinthians		6:1	217	8:13	125
1:17	200			9	125
1:18	200	**Ephesians**		11	125
2:4	200	1:10	24	11:40	125
4:19	200	1:21	24		
5:4	200	2:22	217		

INDEX OF SCRIPTURE AND OTHER ANCIENT TEXTS

James		4:2–5	222	19:16	219, 220
1:1	126	4:4	223	19:17–18	225
1:5	126	4:6	222	19:20	225
2:1	126	4:6b–8	223	19:21	225
2:2	126	4:8	223	20	219
2:5	126	4:8–11	219	20:1–3	219, 225
2:14–26	126	4:10–11	223	21	43
4:9	126	5:1–13	94	21:3	222
4:10	126	5:1–14	84	21:10	217
5:1	126	5:8	223	22	43
5:2–3a	126	5:9–10	94	22:1	221
5:7	126	6:2–8	223	22:3	221
5:12	126	7:9–12	219	22:8–9	84, 98, 221
5:14	126	7:17	221		
		8:7	223		
1 Peter		8:8	219	**APOCRYPHA**	
1:1	116	9:1–2	219		
2:9	195	9:1–11	225	Tobit	
		11	219	12:18	84
2 Peter		11:19	219, 223		
2:22	75, 76	12:7–9	224	2 Esdras	
3:13	22	12:12	224	19:30	217
		13:1–2	224		
Jude		13:5–8	224	4 Maccabees	
20	217	14:2–3	219	17:22	153, 159
		14:14	220		
Revelation		14:17–20	223	**PSEUDEPIGRAPHA**	
1:1–2	218	15:5	223		
1:5–6	90	16	224	*Apocalypse of Zephaniah*	
1:10	217	16:2	224	6:11–15	221
1:10a	217	16:9	224		
1:10b	217	16:11	224	*Ascension of Isaiah*	
1:11	218	16:17	222	7:18–22	221
1:14	220	17:3	217	8:5	84
1:16	220	17:11	224		
1:17	221	17:16–18	224	*1 Enoch*	
2–3	127, 198, 219	18:1	225	48:1–7	91
2:9	127	18:6	225	48:5	94
2:17	219	18:8	225	62:6	94
3:9	127	18:9–19	225	62:9	94
3:12	219	18:12–13	225		
3:21	220, 221	18:14	225	*3 Enoch*	
4–5	219	18:20	225	1–16/§§1–20	221
4	218, 219, 223	19:5	222	4:9/§6	221
4:1	218	19:10	84, 221	10:1–2/§13	221
4:2	217	19:14	223		

Index of Scripture and Other Ancient Texts

11/§14	221	
12:1–3/§15	221	
12:5/§15	221	
14:5/§18	221	
16/§20	221	
18:1–23/§§23–28	223	

Joseph and Aseneth

14:8–9	90

Psalms of Solomon

17:37	217

DEAD SEA SCROLLS

1QS

2:25–3:9	164
3:15–4:1	90

JOSEPHUS

Antiquities

20.5.1 §97	167

Apion

1.19 §137	185
1.22 §179	186

War

2.3.1 §43	186
2.13.4 §258	167
2.13.4 §259	167
2.13.4 §260	167

RABBINIC LITERATURE

Bavli Qiddushin

41b	108

Bavli Shavucot

47b	108

Genesis Rabbah

16.5	108

Hekhalot Genizah Fragment G8 2b

13b–17	220
43	223

Hekhalot Rabbati

§81	218
§§81–121	216
§99	222
§100	223
§101	223
§102	220
§103	223
§§107–10	218
§108	224
§§108–9	224
§110	224, 225
§111	218, 225
§§112–13	225
§§117–18	224
§119	223, 226
§§119–20	226
§120	224
§§152–73	216
§161	223
§163	223
§169	218
§§170–71	223
§§189–277	216
§190	223
§198	223
§§213–15	223
§216	218
§218	219
§236	223
§245	223
§247	223
§250	223
§251	222, 223
§§268–69	223
§273	223

Hekhalot Zutarti

§338 (//§344//671)–§339 (//§345//672)	222–23
§348	222
§349 (//§361)	219
§356	222
§366 (//§496)	219
§411	223
§420	223
§423	222

Ma'aseh Merkavah

§552	222
§559	223
§590	223
§593	223
§594	223
§595	223

Pesiq. Rabbati

36 (162a)	173

Youth

14	221
23–24	223
30–31	221
39	223
42	221

ANCIENT CHRISTIAN WRITINGS

Acts of Paul

9	217

Athanasius
De inc.

52	19

Augustine
Civ. Dei

1.20	72

Confessions

7.17	72

INDEX OF SCRIPTURE AND OTHER ANCIENT TEXTS

Barnabas		*Tertullian*		Plato	
9:7	217	*Resurrectione Mortuorum*		*Protagoras*	
10:2	217	8.2	27	320C–322D	67
10:9	217	62.1	27	*Republic*	
12:10–11	217			440e–441b	68
13:5	217				
14:2	217	**CLASSICAL SOURCES**		*Symposium*	
				207a–c	68
Didache		Aristotle			
11:7–9	217	*Metaphysics*		Pliny	
11:12	217	II, 4, 1000b	52	*Natural History*	
				8.1	71
Eusebius		*Nicomachean Ethics*		8.7.20–21	70
H.E.		1097b33–1098a4	67	9.24	67
3.27.4	128	*Politics*			
		1332b3–8	67	Plutarch	
Gospel of Philip				*De abstinentia*	
62.35–63.5	77	Cicero		3.11–12	70
Gospel of the Nazarenes		*De natura deorum*		3.18	70
Frag. 15	217	2.154–59	70	*De sollertia animalium*	
		Epistulae ad familiars		962	69
Irenaeus		7.1.3	70	965F–966C	69
Adv. Haer.				972B	69
1.26.2	128	Dio Cassius		987C	69
		68.15.1	70	996E–997A	69
Jerome					
in Matth.		Herodotus		Pythagoras	
12.2	128–29	*Histories*		*Timaeus*	
		1.23–24	67	40–43	68
Origen		3.99–108	67		
Contra Celsum		8.144.2	187	Seneca	
4.5	27			*Epistulae Morales*	
4.74	71	Horace		7.2–4	67
5.66	128	*Epodes*			
		16.33	71	Virgil	
Ps.-Clementine				*Eclogues*	
Recognitions		Martial		4.22	71
1.27–71	129	1.109, lines 6–12	70	8.27–28	71
70.1–8	129				